MIRAGE

MIRAGE

*Why Neither Democrats Nor Republicans
Can Balance the Budget, End the Deficit,
and Satisfy the Public*

GEORGE HAGER

AND

ERIC PIANIN

TIMES 𝕋 BOOKS

RANDOM HOUSE

Library of Congress Cataloging-in-Publication Data

Hager, George.
    Mirage: why neither Democrats nor Republicans can balance the
budget, end the deficit, and satisfy the public / George Hager and Eric
Pianin. —1st ed.
        p.   cm.
    Includes bibliographical references and index.
    ISBN 0-8129-2452-5 (acid-free paper)
    1. Budget deficits—United States.   2. Government spending
policy—United States.   3. Fiscal policy—United States.   I. Pianin, Eric.
II. Title.
HJ2051.H325   1997
336.3'0973—dc20   96-41859
                                                                      CIP

Random House website address: http://www.randomhouse.com/
Printed in the United States of America on acid-free paper
9 8 7 6 5 4 3 2
First Edition

For Monica
and Laurie, Alix, and Stephen

ACKNOWLEDGMENTS

———

Our deep thanks to all those who generously took the time to help us with this task, providing information, insights, materials, editorial advice, and common sense to see us through. The project spanned a considerable period: It was first conceived of during the final months of the Bush administration, launched during the early days of the Clinton administration, and then radically rethought and overhauled after the 1994 election and the Republican takeover of Congress.

In all, more than 160 members of Congress, congressional aides, current and former White House officials, economists, researchers, lobbyists, and journalists contributed to this book. Many were particularly helpful in leading us to a fuller understanding of the complexity, significance, and drama of the budget wars and the political struggles over the deficit. While it is impossible to recognize everyone individually, there are some who deserve special thanks.

We are greatly indebted to Mark Perry, a gifted author, journalist, and editor who worked with us and helped us organize early drafts of the book.

Bill Hoagland, the Republican staff director of the Senate Budget Committee and one of the most knowledgeable men in Washington on budget politics, was indispensable to our research. Bill, with unfailing patience, good humor, and skill, led us through the arcane maze of the budget process and again and again helped us to better understand the political and economic stakes in the budget debate.

Bob Reischauer, both as director of the Congressional Budget Office and, later, as a senior fellow at the Brookings Institution, always made time for our endless questions, strongly disagreed when he thought we were wrong, and gave us an invaluable combination of political and economic guidance.

We also were the beneficiaries of excellent advice and insights from Sheila Burke, former chief of staff for former Senate majority leader Bob Dole; Steve Bell, former Republican chief of staff for the Senate Budget Committee; Stanley Collender, formerly with Price Waterhouse and now managing director of the federal budget-policy group at Burson Marsteller; Bill Dauster, Democratic chief of staff for the Senate Budget Committee; Eileen Baumgartner, former Democratic chief of staff for the House Budget Committee; Larry Stein, a budget expert and adviser to the Senate Democratic leader; Keith Kennedy, former Republican chief of staff for the Senate Appropriations Committee; Texas Republican Senator Phil Gramm; Republican House Budget Committee Chairman John Kasich; Rick May, Republican chief of staff for the House Budget Committee; House Republican Conference Chairman John Boehner; Republican House Appropriations Committee Chairman Bob Livingston; James Dyer and Dennis Kedzior of the House Appropriations Committee staff; former White House Chief of Staff (and ex–House Budget Committee Chairman and ex–White House budget director) Leon Panetta; Barry Toiv, Panetta's longtime spokesman; Texas Democratic Congressman Charles Stenholm; and Joe White, an author and Brookings Institution scholar.

Special thanks to Glenn Kessler, a Washington-based reporter for *Newsday*, who helped us gather some of the material and offered sound advice and encouragement.

The editors of our respective publications were generous in allowing us to undertake the book and to take time away from our day-to-day assignments to work on it. At *The Washington Post*, we would like to thank Leonard Downie, Jr., executive editor; Robert G. Kaiser, managing editor; Karen DeYoung, assistant managing editor for national news; Bill Hamilton, national editor; and Maralee Schwartz and Bob Barnes, political editors. At *Congressional Quarterly Weekly Report*, our thanks to Robert Merry, executive editor; Deborah McGregor, managing editor; and former managing editors Mark Willen and Neil Brown, all of whom were unfailingly generous with their support for this project. To editors Paul Anderson and Jan Austin, who often wondered where their budget reporter had gone, thank you.

Three of the *Post*'s most talented reporters—Dan Balz, the paper's chief political reporter; Ann Devroy, the chief White House correspondent; and Helen Dewar, a congressional correspondent who covers the Senate—were extraordinarily generous in providing us with advice, information, and insights. We are also indebted to the *Post*'s David Maraniss and Michael Weisskopf, whose superb series on Gingrich, Dole, and the Republican revolution (called "Inside the Revolution" and later expanded into the book "*Tell Newt to Shut Up!*") helped illuminate our understanding of what happened in the tumultuous Republican takeover of Congress and the ensuing budget war. Bob Woodward's remarkable book *The Agenda* and his other reporting on the Clinton administration and the congressional Republicans also were crucial to our understanding of the subject matter.

At *Congressional Quarterly*, our efforts were aided immeasurably by health-policy reporter Julie Rovner (now an independent writer), to whom we turned again and again for help on complex health and budget issues; Alissa Rubin, whose wide-ranging expertise in tax, health, and budget policy provided invaluable insights and whose prodigious reporting skills enriched our understanding of what was going on; John Cranford, whose *Budgeting for America* was a wonderfully helpful introduction to the federal budget and whose sharp views constantly helped keep us on track; and Janet Hook (now with the *Los Angeles Times*), who has an uncanny understanding of Congress and was always generous with her time and advice.

Also at *Congressional Quarterly*, thanks to current or former reporters and editors Chuck Alston, David Cloud, Ron Elving, Andy Taylor, Colette Fraley, Dave Rapp, Liz Wehr, Jackie Koszczuk, and Donna Cassata.

Others at *The Washington Post* who deserve special thanks for their help or whose reporting was especially useful to us include David S. Broder, Clay Chandler, Kenneth J. Cooper, Lloyd B. Grove, Guy Gugliotta, Judy Havemann, Kevin Merida, Peter Milius, Dan Morgan, Richard Morin, John E. Yang, Thomas B. Edsall, John F. Harris, John M. Berry, Steven Mufson, Stephen G. Barr, Spencer Rich, James L. Rowe, and Dale Russakoff.

We could not have written this book without the broader under-standing and wider knowledge that came from talking with our com-petitors, reading their stories, and on more than one occasion being pointed to, or graciously allowed to use, particularly good quotes. Thanks to our friends at *The Wall Street Journal*, especially Jackie Calmes, David Wessel, David Rogers, Phil Kuntz, and Chris Georges. And kudos to our budget- and tax-reporting brethren: Alan Fram of the Associated Press, David Baumann and Bud Newman of *Congress Daily*, and David Rosenbaum, Michael Wines, and Adam Clymer of *The New York Times*.

Any project like this requires an enormous amount of research. At *The Washington Post*, Barbara Saffir, Ann O'Hanlon, and Lucy Shackleford (who went on to *Newsweek*) did extremely helpful re-search for the project, as did the *Post*'s talented news-research staff, supervised by Jennifer Belton and including Melody Blake, Richard Ploch, Mary Louise White, Bobbye Pratt, Bob Lyford, and Michael Slevin.

Olwen Price, Ron Wilson, Steve Siegel, and Mary Drake tran-scribed countless hours of taped interviews for us, which proved in-valuable in pulling together the complicated material.

There are few greater favors one can do for an author than to read through the manuscript and bravely offer advice. Those intre-pid souls who read all or part of our drafts and offered invaluable comments include Stanley Collender, Ken Simonson, John Cran-ford, Ron Cogswell, Demetri Coupounas, Helen Dewar, Chuck Al-ston, Bob Reischauer, Julie Rovner, Peter Copeland, Deborah McGregor, Paul Anderson, Dave Rapp, Glenn Kessler, and Rich Cohen.

We are indebted to Gail Ross, our agent, who helped us to see the possibilities of the book and showed patience and support during good times and bad. Thanks, too, to Peter Osnos, the former pub-lisher of Times Books, Steve Wasserman (now books editor with the *Los Angeles Times*), and Paul Golob (now with Basic Books), our edi-tors at Times Books, who saw the importance of the book and helped bring it into being.

This book would have been impossible to undertake without the warm love and unwavering support of our wives, who made huge sacrifices on the home front while their absentee husbands toiled away night after night in the attic. We owe them big time. Eric's wife,

Laurie McGinley, a reporter with *The Wall Street Journal,* also provided sound editing advice and help in pulling together key chapters. Eric's young daughter, Alix, always told him when the chapters were getting too long, and his toddler son, Stephen, loved to jump on stacks of his father's research. Eric also would like to thank his sister, Jill Richards; parents, Larry and Irene Pianin; mother-in-law, Mary McGinley; and aunt Blanche Cullather, who were always there with support, encouragement, and love.

Thanks also to Deborah Howell, Eric's longtime friend and former editor, who could always be counted on for sound advice, good humor, and loyal backing.

George's wife, Monica Healy, a veteran of Capitol Hill and the executive branch, was an invaluable source of political insight, wise commentary, and—true to her calling—positive spin when things seemed especially grim. Writing is a hard business that requires many teachers, most of whom get little recognition at the time; thanks especially to David Griswold, Gardner Defoe, Frederick Tremallo, Geoffrey Wolff, and an extraordinary friend and superb writer who died before this book was done, J. Douglas Murphy.

CONTENTS

———

Introduction   3

1. Getting to Zero   14

2. Old Bulls   46

3. Rosty's Wild Ride   73

4. The Revolution That Wasn't   99

5. Hard, Dirty Work   131

6. "Read My Lips . . . I Lied"   155

7. The Education of Bill Clinton   188

8. Train Wreck   227

9. Endgame   266

Note on Sources   305

Index   315

MIRAGE

INTRODUCTION

———

Tom DeLay screamed at Bill Clinton, fighting the urge to throw something. It was 1:30 A.M. on a winter night in January 1996 in the living room of his high-rise condominium apartment in Alexandria, Virginia. DeLay, the third most powerful man in the House of Representatives, a six-term congressman from Houston, a top enforcer of the Republican revolution, the Republican whip in charge of rounding up the votes that ensured that House Speaker Newt Gingrich could pass his Contract with America legislation, sat raging at his television set.

On the screen, in a replay of the live coverage from earlier that evening, President Clinton was complimenting DeLay and his fellow Republicans, praising the "energy and determination" they had shown in battling for a balanced budget. The president soothingly suggested they should come back to the White House the next morning to resume the budget talks that had broken off a couple of weeks earlier.

There was no chance of that, DeLay knew. They had been whipped. Clinton was twisting the knife, giving the sincere look at who knew how many million viewers, implying that he was reasonable and the Republicans were not, that all it would take to get the budget balanced was a little more talking, and that—Gee, he was ready; were they? DeLay's rage boiled up again, just the way it had

been doing all night. The lying, disingenuous, smarmy *son of a bitch.*
DeLay howled at the TV. It was a good thing the apartment walls
were thick.

Little more than a year earlier, in November 1994, DeLay and Gingrich and 228 other Republicans had staged a stunning upset victory that snatched the House away from the Democrats for the first
time in forty years. Simultaneously, Senate Republican leader Bob
Dole was retaking the Senate he had watched slip into Democratic
hands eight years before. The twin triumphs confirmed the Republicans' belief that theirs was the party of destiny; they were the politicians who had wandered in the desert for more than a generation
before being restored to power with a mandate—they believed—to
end the steady growth of government that the Democrats had engineered since the 1930s.

When they took office in early 1995, the members of the new
GOP majority set out to kill off big pieces of the hated federal bureaucracy and ship other large chunks back to state and local governments. The vehicle for these sweeping changes would be a giant
balanced-budget package whose enormous spending cuts would
force necessary overhauls of Medicare and Medicaid—the twin government health-care programs for the elderly and the poor—plus
overhauls of farm programs, welfare, and government regulation. In
the process, Republicans would slash taxes and finally—fourteen
years after conservative icon Ronald Reagan had promised but
failed to do it—eradicate the deficit. Not a bad year's work.

For months, it had gone astonishingly well as the Republicans'
blitzkriegs led from one legislative victory to another over the ineffectual protests of the humiliated president and the ravaged Democrats. But then, as fall turned to winter and the government shut
down, the Republicans' poll ratings dropped, and whatever mandate they might have had seemed to shrivel like a summer vine;
things had gone terribly wrong.

Clinton had found his voice, the Democrats had restored their
spirits, and the two sides had bogged down in endless, fruitless, and
ultimately maddening budget negotiations. Clinton and Gingrich
had talked and talked and talked until it dawned on the Republicans
that nothing was happening and nothing would happen. The talks
had broken off in early January with no one publicly admitting what

they all knew to be true: It was over. The bright dream the Republicans had dreamed for a generation and worked overtime for a year to realize, the heart of their revolutionary agenda, was dead.

How had it all gone so bad? Just a year earlier Clinton had skated about as close to irrelevance as a chief executive possibly could. Even a month before, at Christmastime, the Republicans had still believed they could bend him to their will. But the president had walked out of every trap they set for him, turned their barbed attacks against them, reversed public opinion, and laid waste to their plans. As he swept his gaze confidently across the deeply unhappy GOP members seated on the left-hand side of the House chamber on the night of January 23, Clinton wore the smile of a victor. He was stealing their lines, appropriating their issues, and somehow—*how the hell had he done this?*—he was recasting himself as a conservative.

DeLay loathed Clinton, thought him a shameless liar. A slight, smooth-faced man with immaculately coiffed hair and a soft Houston drawl that belied a pit-bull conservatism, DeLay was one of the hardest-line leaders in the House, often more in tune with the atavistic freshman class than with Speaker Gingrich, whom he monitored carefully for signs of unacceptable compromise with the White House. For more than a year, DeLay had used his prominent role in the House leadership to drive the GOP agenda rightward, bullying moderates and whipping accommodationists into line. Listening to Clinton reinvent himself and revise the history of the last twelve months had made DeLay writhe in fury in his seat on the floor of the House chamber.

"We know big government does not have all the answers," Clinton said, deftly lifting the central theme of Republican politics. "The era of big government is over." *Talk about brass balls!* DeLay vibrated with anger and amazement. As far as the Republicans were concerned, Clinton was the poster boy for big government, the guy who had written the biggest big-government health-care plan since Lyndon Johnson. Now he had the nerve to stand up there and pretend he was opposed to big government? Did he think anyone would buy this?

DeLay seethed with frustration. Yes, people would buy it. Clinton was remarkably persuasive. DeLay was astounded by his own reaction to the president: He had sat through the speech once on the floor of the House, and now here he was again, like a moth at a light, helplessly watching a rerun in his living room at half past one

in the morning, yelling in helpless frustration at the man who infuriated but somehow also mesmerized him. Part of him wanted to
throw a shoe through the screen, but another part was being hyp-
notized.

Clinton flashed the sincere look again. He and the Republicans
shared many of the same goals, he said, from balancing the budget
and reducing taxes to combating crime and strengthening the family. But he warned he would not agree to spending cuts that would
"undermine our fundamental obligations to our parents, our children, and our future by endangering Medicare, Medicaid, education, or the environment." *Give me a break!* This line particularly
infuriated the Republicans, who had heard it a hundred times by
now and considered it sheer demagoguery. It was the key to Clinton's victory. After months of steady rhetorical effort, Clinton had
gradually reshaped the popular view of the sweeping Republican
proposals. Now what their GOP architects saw as bold efforts to remake the government had become, even to many Republican voters, mindless attacks on children, the elderly, education, and the
environment. Clinton had demonized the GOP agenda in a way that
devastated public support and destroyed the Republicans' political
leverage.

The irony was that just a year earlier, their roles had been completely reversed. Then it was DeLay and the Republicans who were
bashing Clinton and the Democrats for their tax increases (the president's 1993 deficit-reduction bill) and their supposed plan to let
big government run amok (the president's 1994 health-care proposal). The roles might have changed, but the dynamic was the
same, another inning in the tit-for-tat, revenge-seeking game that
had all but paralyzed two decades' efforts to bring the federal budget under control. DeLay's futile, wee-hours rage at the TV was an
apt metaphor for the two parties' larger failure to find productive
ways to do business with each other. In his chair, shouting at Clinton's image, was a hard-edged partisan who viewed compromise as
capitulation. On the screen was an equally hard-edged partisan who
understood the vulnerability that came with governing and disdain
for compromise and who had brutally exploited that weakness.

Clinton saved his best lines for last. "I want to say a special word now
to those who work for our federal government," he began. Federal

workers had been the unfortunate pawns in the budget struggle between the White House and the Republicans; hundreds of thousands of them had been furloughed during two government shutdowns in November and December.

Clinton turned the spotlight on Richard Dean, a forty-nine-year-old Vietnam veteran who had worked for the Social Security Administration for twenty-two years. In April of last year, Clinton said, Dean had been hard at work at the federal building in Oklahoma City when a blast erupted that killed 169 people. Dean freed himself from the rubble and then saved the lives of three women.

As Clinton gestured to Dean, seated high above in the gallery overlooking the House floor, the chamber exploded in bipartisan applause. "But Richard Dean's story doesn't end there," Clinton added before the Republicans fully realized where this story was headed. "This last November, he was forced out of his office when the government shut down. And the second time the government shut down, he continued helping Social Security recipients, but he was working without pay." As he scanned the Republican-dominated chamber with a reproachful gaze, the president declared, "I challenge all of you in this chamber: . . . Never, ever, shut the federal government down again."

It was as if Clinton had reached out and punched the Republicans in the mouth. The Democrats rose to their feet as one and roared their approval. To Republicans, this was the crowning insult. DeLay felt sick to his stomach.

———

It wasn't as if the Republicans had come away with nothing. With a remarkable disregard for their political future and a near religious conviction that their way was the true path, they had moved the budget debate further in a year than it had come in two decades. The question no longer was *whether* to balance the budget but *how*, and even liberal Democrats felt obliged to produce plans to do it, demonstrating just how radically the Republicans had altered the political atmosphere. "Their budgets are phony and everything else," said Republican House Budget Committee Chairman John Kasich, sniffing at some of the Democratic offerings, "but when I look back now, it was a terrific victory." He had won the right to gloat a little. He and the rest of the self-styled GOP revolutionaries had so fundamentally altered budget politics that going back to the old norms would be impossible.

On the other hand, though, no one had more spectacularly mis-played a winning political hand and allowed moral arrogance and political hubris to destroy an opportunity to fix a problem that had nagged the nation for a generation. The last time the United States had had a balanced budget was in 1969, when the effects of former president Lyndon Johnson's 10 percent income tax surcharge helped raise enough revenues to offset temporarily the cost of the Vietnam War. Six presidents and a dozen Congresses had been un-able to repeat Johnson's feat, and once-small and irregular deficits had now become large and chronic. The deficit had grown into the reigning obsession of modern politics, dominating the congressional agenda the way civil rights and Vietnam had in previous decades.

To the uninitiated, Washington's endless annual bickering over the budget seemed like a juvenile brawl that would end as soon as the politicians grew up and got serious. Texas billionaire H. Ross Perot charmed voters by mocking the process and the players and by brag-ging that he could balance the budget without breaking a sweat. But as Perot and anyone else who actually grappled with the details quickly learned, there were compelling reasons why the deficit had humbled and defeated scores of politicians a lot more clever than Perot.

This was no trivial fight over numbers but a grueling battle to the political death over competing concepts of the proper role of gov-ernment and the right to shape the nation's values. The budget is not just some arcane and indigestible collection of dollar figures but a detailed statement of what the nation cares about and what its pri-orities are: this much for education, that much for nuclear weapons, so much for environmental cleanup, child nutrition, aid to the sick, elderly, and disabled, and so on—thousands of decisions that grow out of thousands of battles that in the end define the national char-acter.

Republicans were fighting to radically alter the way the nation governed itself. Democrats were fighting to preserve institutions, programs, and a concept of government they had spent the last sixty years and more building. Did anyone seriously think this was going to be easy?

The deficit has so badly polarized the two political parties that the problem seems, at times, beyond the power of democratic government to fix. The extreme wings of the two parties have always been far apart, but at the end of 1995 the party leaders themselves seemed hopelessly isolated from each other, unable to find common ground. The gulf between DeLay on the right and House Democratic Minority Whip David Bonior on the left, for example, seemed unbridgeable. And as unusually high numbers of centrist Democrats and Republicans bailed out of the increasingly hostile and divided Congress, things seemed likely to get worse, despite hopeful talk about bipartisanship as the 105th Congress convened in January 1997.

The story of how things got this bad is full of heroes and villains who usually turn out to be the same people; this year's responsible politician is next year's heedless demagogue. Part of the reason for this is simply politics, but part of it is also the complex nature of the problem itself, which is both more and less important than it seems.

By world standards, for example, the United States is doing pretty well. Politicians in most other industrial democracies would gladly swap their nations' fiscal problems for those of the United States, whose deficits from 1993 to 1996 either were or were projected to be among the lowest of the Group of Seven nations (Japan, Germany, Great Britain, France, Italy, Canada, and the United States) and comfortably below the average for the world's top twenty-three industrial democracies when measured against the size of their economies.

Even more confounding, there is no obvious, direct link between deficits and all the awful things they are widely believed to cause. When deficits first started to race out of control in the early 1980s, there were dire warnings that they would cause recessions, rampant inflation, or sky-high interest rates. But while deficits stayed high right into the 1990s, recessions turned to good times, inflation virtually vanished, and interest rates fell. It turned out that big deficits were no more a predictor of bad economic times than small ones were guarantors of a healthy economy.

In fact, deficits of the size the United States has experienced since the mid-1970s are less an immediate threat than a subtle, long-term problem, a corrosion that steadily slows the increase in the standard of living for this generation's children and grandchildren. There are some real penalties now, but they tend to be subtle: Thanks to higher interest rates, Americans pay what amounts to a hidden deficit tax on just about everything they borrow money for, from homes and cars to college tuition and vacations. Heavy government borrowing forces up interest rates on every form of credit, elbows aside private borrowers, and slows the growth of the economy. But this is hard to quantify and difficult for most Americans to see.

More visibly, chronic deficits drive up federal spending for interest on the debt, diverting hundreds of billions of dollars a year from more useful spending to simply paying the tab for past borrowing and keeping the nation's credit rating intact. When Jimmy Carter left office in 1981, about ten cents of every federal dollar went for debt interest; eight years later, when Reagan left office after a string of deficits that had almost tripled the national debt, nearly fifteen cents of every federal dollar went to pay interest costs. The number has stuck there since, reducing the useful size of every federal budget dollar to about eighty-five cents.

There is little argument that balancing the budget would have a beneficial effect. Calculations during the political wars of 1995 showed that eradicating the deficit by 2002 would be worth about $1,000 to every American household in the form of lower interest costs, lower federal taxes, and higher wages. The catch is that most of the benefit would go to this generation's children and grandchildren while the cost would be borne now, in the form of cutbacks in federal programs or (depending on who constructs the program) higher taxes.

Given this equation—the reward is years away, and the cost and political risk are immediate—the question is why the deficit is such an obsession *right now.* The good-government reason is that every year of delay means larger spending cuts and/or tax increases when the job is eventually done. But there is more to it.

The deficit has always been a much more potent moral issue than a fiscal one. Although Americans are willing to run up enormous personal debt with credit cards, mortgages, and charge accounts, they exhibit a strong puritanical streak when it comes to their government, which most voters feel should live strictly within its means. While the economic arguments over a balanced budget can be murky and ambiguous, the moral case is shiningly clear—which is why congressional debate over the constitutional balanced-budget amendment often focuses much more on ethical purity than on fiscal prudence.

What's more, the deficit is also a proxy for general distrust of government and a symbol for the incompetence of politicians, who fail year after year to do what seems to be the government's most fundamental job: make the federal checkbook balance. And for conservatives of both parties, fighting the deficit has always been a good reason for shrinking the federal government, which interests them much more than simply balancing the budget.

All these factors combine to force the issue to the top of the congressional agenda, where politicians alternately exploit it and are victimized by it. Promising to balance the budget is irresistible. There is hardly a president in this century who has not gotten to office in part on a promise to do it. But the end result is virtually always abject failure. Once in office, presidents and members of Congress confront deep public ambivalence: Voters want a balanced budget, but since they *benefit* from big deficits (which keep taxes lower and spending on popular programs higher), they consistently reject most of the realistic ways to get to balance, resisting spending cuts and saying no to tax increases. That leaves politicians with no popular way to do the job, and it raises the reward for attacking deficit reduction rather than backing it.

Hard-won budget deals have kept the deficit from going out of control, but the real problem is not what happens this year or next year but what happens about a decade from now, when the huge baby boom generation begins to retire. Deficits that have been subdued in the late 1990s—ducking below $110 billion in 1996 for the first time since Jimmy Carter left office—are projected to head for the stratosphere early in the next century. Even the sober and cautious Congressional Budget Office (CBO), the independent agency that analyzes budget proposals for Congress, projects potential catastrophe. While economists are ambivalent about the effects of deficits the size of the ones common today, few economists would disagree with the CBO's disaster scenario for a decade or two from now.

Retirement of the baby boomers, beginning in 2008, will quickly double the elderly population eligible for benefits at the same time the number of working-age Americans will rise just 25 percent, worsening an already troubling mismatch between the people who collect Social Security, Medicare, and other "entitlements" and the people who actually pay the bills. Unless Congress and the president reduce benefits, raise the taxes that pay for them, or find an alternative way to run the system, the result will be deficits unlike anything the nation has ever experienced.

The CBO forecasts deficits and a national debt that as soon as 2020 will be bigger than any recorded since the Second World War and by 2030 will grow much larger than the worst wartime deficits and debt. The national debt held by the public today is about $4 trillion; the CBO forecasts its soaring to more than $21 trillion by 2020 and to a staggering $81 trillion by 2030, almost three times the size of the nation's entire economy. A national debt that size would require huge, all-consuming annual interest payments, which would set off a vicious cycle that could quickly push the United States into the company of Third World countries whose fiscal policies have touched off firestorms of hyperinflation and economic chaos. The usually staid CBO paints a horrifying picture of a future not so far away in which rising debt and deficits provoke foreign investors to dump U.S. securities, the dollar plunges in value, interest rates shoot up, the stock market collapses, and the economy plunges into a severe recession. The projection reads more like a potboiler than an economic report; the fact that it comes from the CBO makes it scarier than fiction.

"Policymakers would surely take action before the economy was driven into such dire straits," the CBO says reassuringly. And they probably will, eventually. But the lesson of 1995—and of all the budget fights that went before—is that it is all but irresistible for policymakers to score political points rather than work toward a bipartisan plan to balance the budget. The politics of deficit reduction have always been more politics than deficit reduction, a game of advantage seeking whose goal is to win back control of Congress or the White House by following a simple rule: When you're in power, vilify the deficit; when you're out of power, vilify the other guy's solutions. Cynical and irresponsible? Of course. But it works.

No one was more shrill in attacking Clinton's 1993 deficit-reduction plan or more adamant in refusing to help craft a compromise than then House Republican Whip Newt Gingrich or Senate Republican leader Bob Dole. Gingrich and Dole persistently condemned Clinton's plan, made sure no Republican in the House or Senate ever voted for it, grossly misrepresented it as nothing but tax increases (it was far from a perfect plan, but it did include some real spending cuts), and then predicted disaster for the nation when

Clinton barely got it passed with Democratic votes alone. The next year, Gingrich and Dole leveled the same sort of fire at Clinton's health-care plan and demolished it. Then they used the tax increases and the health-care plan to help bash the Democrats and take over Congress in the 1994 elections.

It is hard to argue with success. But by the same token, it was little wonder that Clinton and the wounded Democrats turned around and played the same game in 1995, focusing on short-term political gain, bashing the Republicans' plans to cut projected spending on Medicare, Medicaid, and other programs, and surging in the polls as the Republicans plummeted. The following November, Clinton crushed Dole in the presidential election, becoming only the third Democrat in this century to be elected to two terms. Republicans gained two seats in the Senate but lost precious ground in the House.

The same revenge cycle has been going on for the better part of two decades. The 1995 débâcle did not emerge from a vacuum; everything both sides did and said resonated back down the years, and every step they took had a long chain of history behind it. Republican veterans in the Senate who had lived through the earlier battles had learned to be wary and cautious; those who did not know what had happened—mostly gung-ho House members new to Washington—repeated classic mistakes and suffered for it.

It was the predictable repetition of a pattern that has become familiar since the deficit first spun out of control in the mid-1970s. The Republicans' all-or-nothing, holy war attitude in 1995 sowed the seeds of their defeat, unifying and invigorating a tired and defeated Democratic minority that rose up, attacked, and bled them to death over the course of the year. To get the problem solved, both parties have to find a way to work together. But the likelihood that obstructionism will eventually leverage them back into power means they almost never do.

Mirage is the story of how the nation slid into the deficit mess, why it has been impossible to get out, and how wave after wave of confident and able politicians has come to Washington with surefire plans for fixing the problem only to give up in humiliated defeat. All that was supposed to change in 1995, when Republicans seized control of Congress and vowed to live up to promises to eradicate the deficit at last. Instead, events merely confirmed past patterns and added to the growing sense of hopelessness.

Chapter 1

GETTING TO ZERO

On a late-winter day in February 1995, the senior Republican leaders of the House of Representatives assembled in a windowless conference room deep inside the Capitol for a two-hour meeting that would—almost as an afterthought—produce the most important decision Republicans would make all year.

For almost two weeks, an increasingly pointed disagreement had been building between House Speaker Newt Gingrich and House Budget Committee Chairman John Kasich. Until lately, this had been closed-door business that no one outside this room knew much about. But now the press had begun to sense the split between the Speaker and the Budget chairman over whether or not the Republicans ought to commit themselves to balancing the budget in seven years. Gingrich said yes; Kasich said no.

Every time the issue came up in the private leadership meetings they were holding virtually every day, the voluble, hyperkinetic Kasich threw out a cloud of objections. "Guys," he would say—Kasich called everybody "guys"—"you have no idea how much trouble you're in for." *He* was the budget expert, *he* knew the numbers, *he* had been doing the grunt work of assembling alternative budgets for the last six years, and *he* could tell them from experience that the numbers they were talking about were huge beyond their imagination. Frequently, Kasich got so passionate that he waved his arms to emphasize his point and even jumped up out of his seat and stalked around the room, unable to sit still. No one wanted to balance the budget more than he did, but it was a question of practical politics: Cuts big enough to eradicate the deficit in seven years would be an excruciatingly tough sell, even among Republicans. "Guys," Kasich would say, "I know we want to do this, but I'm not sure that we can develop a plan that people will vote for."

Gingrich, for his part, was a great listener; this was something he prided himself on, that he heard out his colleagues, genuinely absorbed what they had to say. But on this point, he had heard Kasich enough. He believed that balancing the budget was the core of what the GOP was about, no matter how difficult it might be. In their Contract with America of the previous fall, Republicans had promised voters that they would pass a balanced-budget amendment to the Constitution; what voter would not read that as a promise to go ahead and balance the budget? Wasn't keeping their promises what made them different from Democrats? Gingrich dreamed of sweeping change that would radically restructure the federal government, making it much smaller and less powerful than the behemoth that Democrats (and many Republicans, for that matter) had built since the advent of the New Deal. Ground zero for all this change was the budget, where vast social-spending programs would be slimmed down, killed off, or shipped back to the states.

"You only get the moral authority to truly change things if you're offering something that is as definitive as balance," Gingrich explained later. Just producing another big deficit-reduction bill would not be enough. "There is a deep historic commitment to balancing the budget, and it's a goal that gives people a hard yardstick against which to measure their behavior."

In strategy sessions during the months following the election, Frank Luntz, an influential Republican pollster and one of Gingrich's political consultants, had pushed hard for a balanced budget. Luntz saw the Republicans' assault on the deficit in epic terms. The GOP could secure its place as the majority party for a generation to come by defying the conventional wisdom that the deficit was now a fact of life, annoying but essentially ineradicable. Luntz imagined the scene: On New Year's Eve at the end of 2002, two glowing balls would be lowered in Times Square, one ushering in the new year and the other signaling the end of the deficit. Who would have done that? The Republicans.

The only question in Gingrich's mind was not whether but when. Hotheads might say they'd balance the budget in a year or two or three, but privately just about everyone at the Republican leadership level agreed that even five years—the length of the usual congressional budget plan—was just too risky. The cuts would have to be gargantuan, far too big to attract a majority, even in the GOP-controlled House. Some also feared that if they pulled that much federal spending out of the economy that quickly, they might invite a slowdown or make a recession more likely. On the other hand, a ten-year budget plan was too drawn out to be credible. Forecasters were shaky enough with five-year projections; even their forecasts of what the economy and the budget would do one or two years from now were often wildly off the mark. Some joked that numbers ten years hence fell into the WAG category—wild-assed guess. Gingrich had been quietly checking GOP budget strategy with Washington's old hands. Former Federal Reserve Board chairman Paul A. Volcker and others had advised Gingrich that seven years was about as long as Republicans could stretch a plan and still lay any claim to credibility. Gingrich made up his mind: a balanced budget in seven years.

Kasich, on the other hand, had been pushing for weeks for a formula that would leave them wiggle room. A detailed, full-blown plan to balance the budget could generate spending cuts so big that the numbers themselves might overwhelm the debate. Instead of spelling out all the cuts necessary to get to balance, Kasich suggested, they would put the budget on a *path* to balance. "I was saying we should be on the glide path because I wanted to make sure we didn't overpromise," Kasich said later. "I was trying to protect the credibility of the whole party. You don't want to go out and say 'I'm going to bat .400 this year' unless you've got a reasonable chance of doing that."

The glide-path idea also seemed like a plausible compromise to Kasich's colleague in the Senate. Senate Budget Committee Chairman Pete Domenici had urged making a "down payment" on a balanced budget. He was worried that if he laid out a realistic plan to balance the budget over five or seven years, Republicans would flinch. They always had—even Ronald Reagan had flinched in 1981 when he found out how big the cuts would have had to have been to redeem his 1980 campaign promise to bring the deficit down to zero.

In early January, House Majority Leader Dick Armey had let slip during an appearance on NBC's *Meet the Press* what the inner leadership councils really thought of the spending cuts they were about to ask rank-and-file Republicans to support. "Once members know exactly, chapter and verse, the pain that the government must live with in order to get to a balanced government, their knees will buckle," he said. No matter—now leaders had decided it was worse to shy away than to charge the machine guns, and it was up to Kasich to give them the plan.

Kasich knew all about knees buckling: For a long time, he had kept propped up in front of him on the desk in his private office a 1993 note from a fellow Republican insisting that two highway projects in the congressman's district be spared when Kasich put together an alternative to President Clinton's new budget. The note was an important reminder that Republicans were just as likely as Democrats to run from tough spending cuts and just as willing to embrace gimmicks instead. When serious deficit-reduction efforts collapsed in 1985, for example, Republicans led the successful effort to adopt the Gramm-Rudman-Hollings mechanism, which promised to balance the budget in five years with automatic spending cuts. As the years went by, however, Congress found ways to evade most of Gramm-Rudman-Hollings's automatic cuts, and the budget remained stubbornly unbalanced. The experience taught that no robotic mechanism could guarantee a balanced budget; in the end, there was no substitute for the gritty process of cutting spending.

Kasich was also deeply worried that the job of expanding the normal five-year budget plan to seven years would force him to leave the numbers in the critical last two years too blurry, producing a document that hardheaded budget analysts (and the media) would quickly deride as dishonest. Credibility was everything to Kasich. For all his brash, can-do aggressiveness and the disdain he showed critics and doubters, he was deeply sensitive to charges that his numbers were phony or his budgets built on flimflam. It would have been insupportable to him to work all year to produce nothing but another Gramm-Rudman-Hollings. But he knew, too, from years of jawboning, how hard it was to get votes for real cuts. Kasich would smile and roll his eyes and sigh in exasperation as he described trying to sell a real deficit-cutting plan, particularly to some of his Republican allies. "Oh, man!" he would say. "Oh, man!"

But as Kasich and Gingrich argued in the GOP's inner councils, other leaders began to worry that the disagreement over balancing the budget was drifting out of control, that it had better get resolved before the press started writing stories about splits in the Republican ranks. Ohio Republican John Boehner, the chain-smoking head of the Republican Conference, the group that included all House Republicans, decided to force the issue. Toward the end of this lengthy leadership meeting in mid-February, he brought the matter up. Kasich was already collecting his papers, ready to leave. Boehner asked Gingrich, Would there be a concrete, seven-year plan to balance the budget or not?

Gingrich said flatly, "We're going to zero in seven years."

But Kasich immediately started in again with his objections. Where was it "engraved in stone" that they had to do it in seven years? "I don't think we should go out and say that until we can credibly show we can do it," Kasich said. "I don't know whether we can get the numbers together to make it credible."

Gingrich usually wore his indulgent, sharklike smile during these discussions. He and Kasich had become unusually close over the last few years. Gingrich admired Kasich's enormous energy and commitment, his willingness to push his colleagues to stand for something instead of merely throwing brickbats. Kasich, nine years Gingrich's junior, had become something between a son and a younger brother to the Speaker, who patiently tutored him in the difficult art of leadership, cleaned him up and encouraged him when he got his nose bloodied in the endless internecine Republican wars, and knocked him around a little when he needed to be straightened out. The darkening in Gingrich's face signaled that today, right now, there was going to be some knocking around. His smile vanished, and his voice cut through the suddenly silent room like a crack of thunder. "All those in favor of going to zero, raise your hands," he said, looking pointedly around the table.

Everyone but Kasich raised his or her hand: Gingrich; Boehner; Dick Armey, the hulking, slow-eyed Texas majority leader; Bill Paxon, chairman of the National Republican Congressional Committee; Susan Molinari, the Staten Island moderate brought in to leaven the otherwise hard-right leadership; Nevada Congresswoman Barbara Vucanovich, a devout conservative and secretary of the House Republican Conference. Putting a final exclamation point on Gingrich's message were three of Kasich's fellow committee chairmen, leaders of the most powerful panels in the House: Ways and Means Chairman Bill Archer, Appropriations Chairman Bob Livingston, and Rules Chairman Jerry Solomon. Their hands all went up. Kasich smiled weakly.

Gingrich turned to him and snapped, "Motion carries. You're outvoted, John. We're going to zero."

———

That breezy, seemingly offhand decision to lash themselves to a promise to balance the budget would have enormous consequences. For Republicans had now promised nothing less than ripping up and rewriting the social contract that had governed the relationship between voters and the federal government for the sixty years since the New Deal. To make good on this promise, Republicans would have to take on the huge social-benefit programs that had become some of the most popular—and most expensive—things the government did.

Politically, this was a death wish. For the first time in history, a political party had staked virtually everything on its ability to eliminate the deficit, a Sisyphean challenge that had caused almost every politician who had tried it over the last twenty years to walk away in humiliated frustration, frequently thrown out of office by the very voters who had commanded him or her to try in the first place. Although voters wanted a balanced budget, they hated all the tax increases and spending cuts involved in getting one.

To Gingrich and many of his comrades, though, this most recent avowal seemed no more than a formal restatement of a promise they had made the previous fall, when they had run for office under the banner of the Contract with America, with its implicit pledge to eradicate the deficit. Gingrich had invited voters to tape the ten-point Contract to their refrigerators (Republicans bought advertising space in *TV Guide* in order to publish the Contract) and then to throw the Republicans out of office if they failed to live up to their

promises. Once they were elected and put in charge of both houses
of Congress for the first time in forty years, there could be no question about forging ahead. "There was never any doubt that balancing the budget was going to be item number one," said Bob
Livingston. "We were on board for it totally and unequivocally."

Yet none of them had really ever looked at the numbers the way
Kasich had. If they had, they might have been as scared as he was.
Ever since he'd gotten his seat on the Budget Committee in 1989,
Kasich had been painstakingly drawing up alternative budgets, doing the mind-numbing grunt work necessary to deconstruct and re-
configure the trillion and a half dollars the federal government
spent every year. Kasich took the work far more seriously than most
of his colleagues did.

During the long years when they were out of power, no one expected the Republicans' opposition budgets to do anything more
than make a rhetorical statement, and they were often laughably
sloppy collections of poorly thought out ideas that failed to meet
even a minimal credibility test. In 1993, for example, Jerry Solomon
produced an alternative plan that he claimed would balance the
budget in five years. It was a draconian, politically toxic cut-and-
paste assemblage of every budget-cutting idea he could put his
hands on, including a plan to end all agricultural subsidies. All agricultural subsidies except one, that is, and here was the detail that
told all anyone needed to know about Solomon's proposal: The plan
would eliminate every subsidy except the one enjoyed by dairy farmers, who just happened to be a critical constituency in Solomon's
central New York district.

Privately, Kasich remained deeply concerned that balancing the
budget could not be done, regardless of what the others said. "None
of them knew whether it was possible or not. They didn't know what
they were voting on. But I was the one having to put it all together," he
later said. "And you know, when things work out, it's everybody's idea.
If it didn't work out, it would have been 'this idiot Kasich,' you know?"

No matter. Gingrich announced the commitment to the press,
and the word went out that it was okay to say it: They would get to
zero in seven years—period. From the Speaker on down the line,
House Republicans repeated the promise so often and so explicitly
that there now could be no pulling back without major embarrassment.

The idea, according to Connecticut Republican Congressman Chris Shays, a key Kasich lieutenant on the Budget Committee, was to do to rank-and-file Republicans what Spanish explorer Hernán Cortés did to the troops he had brought with him to conquer Mexico in 1519. When the soldiers saw the wild Yucatán jungle, took full measure of the peril ahead, and realized that many of them would likely die, some clamored to go back to Spain. Cortés had a cure for that: He burned their ships. Going back was not an option. Same with Gingrich. By so publicly and so adamantly promising they would get to zero, the Speaker had presented his party with two choices: Find a way to do what no Republicans and no Democrats had managed to do since 1969, or perform the congressional equivalent of dying in the jungle. "Sometimes us foot soldiers need to be told by the generals, 'You know, that hill may look insurmountable, but by God you're going to get there,' " said Rick May, the Budget Committee's chief of staff, the man on whom most of the burden of drawing up the plan fell. "You get so wrapped up in why you can't do something. Gingrich, to his credit, pointed the way."

The decision was made, but that didn't make the job any easier. For one thing, the House Republicans had committed themselves to a maddeningly unreachable goal. Whether or not the deficit goes up or down usually has as much to do with economic cycles and other unpredictable events as it does with the actions Congress and the White House take; a recession, a war, or an unforeseen fiscal disaster like the savings-and-loan débâcle of the late 1980s can create monstrous deficits that are utterly beyond Congress's immediate control. Promising a balanced budget seven years down the road—or even significant deficit reduction over two or three years—is a crapshoot. It works as long as no unforeseen circumstances intervene, but unforeseen circumstances always seem to intervene. It is as if a farmer were to guarantee an unbroken string of bumper crops, serene in the belief that there would never be droughts, floods, or bugs.

Republicans were also making a promise that had been made over and over again to absolutely no effect, a pledge that had caused enormous grief and embarrassment for those who had repeatedly tied themselves to it over the last two decades. Jimmy Carter promised to balance the budget when he ran against Gerald Ford in 1976, and after Carter's abject failure, Ronald Reagan won office in 1980 in part on the claim that he could do what Carter had not. Reagan failed even more spectacularly, presiding over record postwar deficits. Republicans tore themselves up throughout Reagan's first term trying to undo the damage and get the budget back on track.

Moreover, Gingrich and company were committing themselves to spending their hard-won political capital on something excruciatingly hard to accomplish. Political fallout aside, the promise to balance the budget would be very tough to redeem. In the course of making their pledge, they had put more than half of federal spending off the table (defense, Social Security, interest on the debt) and then gone ahead and made things even tougher by insisting on cutting taxes as well, giving up revenue they desperately needed. It was Houdiniesque—defiantly piling one obstacle on top of another until what they planned to do seemed plainly impossible. Most people who understood how the budget worked thought they were nuts. Reagan had confronted virtually the same math and found the job impossible. Something would have to give.

The defeat of the balanced-budget amendment in the Senate in early March—after Gingrich and the House leaders had decided to go to zero—gave GOP leaders a perfect opening to say, Sorry, all bets are off; we can't eliminate the deficit after all. Kasich had been counting heavily on the Constitution to make his job not just easier but possible. "The most important vote will be the vote on that balanced-budget amendment," he had said just days after Republicans routed Democrats in the 1994 elections, making him chairman-elect of the Budget Committee. "Once that's done, guys can't say, Why are we doing this? What's the reason here?" In those heady days after the election, the balanced-budget amendment (whose effect Texas Republican Senator Phil Gramm liked to compare to "a stone wall at your back in a gunfight") seemed a sure thing. Kasich savored the prospect of doing his job with such a mighty tool in his back pocket. "The ultimate hammer," he mused, "the ultimate budget hammer." Now they had no hammer, but they would press on anyway.

Paradoxically, going all the way to zero made the job easier, not harder. "What Newt realized was that when you put the zero on the board, it changes the dynamics," said Ed Gillespie, a senior aide to

House Majority Leader Dick Armey. If the goal hadn't been zero but just reducing the deficit, the reaction from members was likely to have been "Well, screw you. Go cut somebody else's program," said Gillespie. Zero, on the other hand, made everyone vulnerable.

Zero was also critical for selling the program to the public—and to the members of Congress who would have to vote for it. The alternative was to reduce the deficit by, say, half or—what was even more abstract—to stabilize the deficit as a percentage of the size of the economy (as measured by the gross domestic product, or GDP), as some economists preached and President Clinton had tried to do. But voters and politicians understood "zero" and were unmoved by "half" or some formula that allowed deficits to continue as long as they grew no faster than the GDP. Who could explain that at a Rotary meeting?

As a rookie president in 1993, Clinton was told by Congress's then Democratic leaders that his first order of business had to be a serious deficit-reduction plan. But as he put the plan together, the overwhelming advice from economists and politicians was that it not be too tough. Balance was out of the question. Democrats failed to grasp the potency of zero. As a result, Clinton wound up leading his party through the worst sort of political torment for next to no reward. Yes, Clinton and the Democrats passed a real plan that actually reduced the deficit (a better record than Ronald Reagan or George Bush, for that matter). But for what? Polls showed most voters believed the Democrats had done nothing or had *raised* the deficit—a big ingredient in the evil soup of disappointments that led voters to throw Democrats out of office in 1994 in record numbers.

That bitter lesson had not gone unread by Republicans—their relentless attacks, after all, were what had turned public opinion against the Clinton plan. Doing another "big" deficit-reduction plan and making Clinton's mistake all over again would be a waste of time. "There was some desperation at work," said Gillespie. "If we don't do it, if we don't act boldly, they'll throw us out of here as fast as they did the Democrats." The ambitious plan to go to zero was entirely characteristic of Gingrich. What the Speaker understood was that deficit politics had always been hobbled by the lack of a genuine crisis. Deficits almost never threatened immediate danger; they were more of a long-term threat to the nation's standard of living, termites in the basement instead of a wolf at the door, in economist

Charles L. Schultze's famous phrase. Over and over again leaders drifted because there was no real emergency, reacted frantically on those rare occasions when there was one (the emergence of huge new deficit numbers in the fall of 1981, for example, or the stock market crash of October 1987), and tried, mostly in vain, to invent artificial crises that would regularly force action (the Gramm-Rudman-Hollings anti-deficit law, which would slash spending automatically if Congress did not act).

Gingrich fixed the equation. If there was no reliable crisis to force action, he would be a crisis all by himself. No compelling reason to go to zero? He would command it. No political will to see the fight through to the end? He would burn their boats. A president with a veto? Gingrich would shut the government down. Washington had rarely seen anything as bold—or as reckless—as this man Gingrich.

From the moment he finally arrived in Congress in 1979 after two unsuccessful attempts at getting elected, Newt Gingrich ignored the things that consumed most new congressmen—which committees and subcommittees can I get on? what should my first bill be about?—and focused instead on the only thing that truly interested him: how to blast Republicans out of their seemingly permanent minority status and into control of the House.

Members of both parties regarded him at first as a monomaniacal kook, an irritant, a loudmouthed bomb thrower who made many senior Republicans just as uncomfortable as he made the Democrats. In fact, such a posture was part of his plan; in Gingrich's view, those moderate, go-along, get-along Republicans were just as much an obstacle to the revolution as Democrats. There was no point in negotiating with the enemy for bits and pieces here and there, as accommodationists like House Minority Leader Bob Michel did. The point was to destroy the Democrats and take over. Gingrich had the ability to look years ahead, to imagine a world that did not yet exist, to concoct a plan for getting there, and to stick to it, slowly winning converts along the way. Many of his skeptical colleagues, however, could not see where he was going, and his tactics sometimes made them intensely uncomfortable.

In mid-1987, for example, Gingrich decided to take on powerful

Democratic House Speaker Jim Wright, the flamboyant Texas Democrat who had succeeded Speaker Tip O'Neill and had come under
fire for the way he was peddling a ghostwritten book. One of the tactics in Gingrich's strategy for wresting power from the Democrats
was to portray the majority party as decayed and corrupted by its
decades-long hold on power. The case against Wright was a reach,
perhaps, but it offered the highest possible profile; if Gingrich could
show that the nation's most senior Democrat was tainted, he would
blacken the entire party. Gingrich's closest friends and advisers were
nearly unanimous in advising him not to try it. Wright was too powerful. The case—that the Speaker had crossed an ethical line in
marketing thousands of copies of his ghostwritten book to lobbyists—seemed thin, hard to make. Gingrich would seem petulant,
mean-spirited, excessively partisan.

But Gingrich turned out to be right. Brilliantly intuitive, he had
seen what no one else saw—that Wright was vulnerable, that he
could not only be attacked but he could also be brought down. In a
remarkable victory, Gingrich's campaign attracted help from Common Cause, gathered momentum, sparked an official internal
House investigation, put Wright on the defensive, and finally led to
his humiliating resignation two years later, in 1989. Wright's defeat
propelled Gingrich nearly as high as the Speaker had fallen; he
could no longer be dismissed as inconsequential and slightly
strange; he had aimed at the king and killed him.

The victory over Wright sealed Gingrich's position as leader-in-
waiting of a party tired of its long winter out of power. Even party
moderates repelled by his positions on many issues admired his
chutzpah and hoped he could somehow lead them out of the wilder-
ness; it was moderates who gave Gingrich a narrow two-vote edge in
the 1989 election that made him minority whip. That made Gingrich the number-two House Republican, right behind the back-
slapping, golf-playing Peorian Bob Michel, who had cut a mostly
go-along, get-along course for the GOP minority for the last decade.
When Republicans finally took over the House five years later, there
was no question whom they would elect to become the first Republican Speaker of the House in forty years.

Now, at fifty-one, Gingrich looked like the intense, small-college
academic that he was before he came to Congress, with an unkempt
shock of gray-white hair, a pronounced paunch, rumpled, off-the-

rack sport jackets occasionally set off by tartan ties that seemed jarringly out of place in the House's forest of lawyerly stripes. He spoke
in an edgy, mile-a-minute tenor and took extraordinary care with his
language, choosing words and phrases for their power to change
perceptions and shift the terms of debate. It was Gingrich who insisted Republicans use the phrase "liberal welfare state" to describe
what two generations of Democratic congressional hegemony had
built. When he set Republicans on the path to balancing the budget
in 1995, he insisted that they abandon ordinary budget jargon and
give up phrases such as "spending cuts"—Republicans were not *cutting* spending, they were merely *reducing the rate of growth.* Gingrich
carried the edict so far that House Budget Committee technicians
were forbidden to send marching orders to other committees in the
form of cuts; instead, they had to publish spending levels, which
confused committee aides and threatened to bog down the budget
process. Secretly, Budget aides circulated a list of orders translated
into the old, forbidden style that everyone understood.

If all Republicans began to sound like Newt in 1995, there was a
reason: For years, his voice had been emanating from the car cas-
sette players of hundreds of would-be Republican representatives as
they drove to work every morning and from one political function
to another at night. Gingrich taped inspirational lectures and
mailed them to candidates around the country; more than any
other figure, he was the living, breathing embodiment of the radical
Republican revolution, the voice the faithful heard day after day, en-
couraging them, educating them, inspiring them, giving them talking points, cheering them on.

Gingrich was utterly ruthless when it came to getting what he
wanted, and what he wanted was a party that did not blur its ideology
or needlessly give its enemies weaknesses to shoot at. Hence his astonishing willingness in 1990 to oppose the sitting president of his
own party for the sin of bargaining with Democrats to give up the one
core tenet that Gingrich believed should define the difference between Republicans and their enemies: that Republicans did not raise
taxes. "You are killing us," President George Bush told him in a private meeting in 1990 to try to get Gingrich to back off; "you are just
killing us." Gingrich heard Bush out but refused to change his course.

Gingrich won a striking victory by defeating the first budget deal
in 1990, but in the process he dealt the president a mortal political

blow that helped cost Bush the White House in 1992. It seemed at the time a remarkably destructive thing to do: Democrats went on to rewrite the budget deal in a form more to their liking, and Republicans finished the year in humiliating disarray. But as usual, Gingrich was looking far down the road. Deficit reduction and the fate of an ideologically suspect Republican president were not as important as party definition and political positioning. Republicans could always balance the budget—*after* they took power. In the meantime, this was war, and there would be casualties. It was better that there be no doubt about where the party stood on its defining issue.

In the House and in Republican circles, Gingrich was a cult figure: His rhetoric and his ceaseless will carried others along in his thrall; it was he who had delivered them from the bondage of minority status, like some latter-day Moses leading the Israelites out of Egypt. There was little question that when he decided that the best strategy was to go for a zero deficit, everyone, including Budget Committee Chairman Kasich, would follow him, despite his or her doubts.

———

If all they had to do was balance the budget, it would have been work enough for a year or two. But Republicans wanted much more than just to save money; they wanted to shrink and defang a federal government they thought had gotten too big, too powerful, too paternalistic. Programs born in Franklin Roosevelt's New Deal or in Lyndon Johnson's Great Society—welfare, Medicare, Medicaid, food stamps, school lunches—would be radically remade, most of them handed over to the states. Republicans would end the basic guarantee the poor now had to minimum food, shelter, and health care; who got what would be left up to the states.

The GOP plans reopened a debate unresolved since the founding of the country, when anti-Federalists deeply suspicious of a powerful central government squared off against Federalists, who believed that the only way the nation could lever itself into prosperity and world status was with such a unifying force. State governments, wrote anti-Federalist leader Thomas Jefferson in 1798, were "the very best in the world," whereas the federal government was an "arbitrary" power that had "swallowed more of the public liberty than

even that of England." Delete the reference to England, and Jefferson's words could have fit into any generic Republican speech from
the floor of Congress in 1995.

Despite vague claims that the states could serve the same people
for less money, there was every expectation that many who now had
their basic needs met by federal programs would instead be forced
to fend for themselves. It was no exaggeration to call that change a
revolution. Budget fights usually boiled down to splitting the difference between numbers, but this was shaping up as a policy Ar-
mageddon, a showdown between two entirely different visions of
what the government was and how it ought to work.

All this would surely take a long time to resolve in any ordinary
Congress—perhaps a year or two just to overhaul the mammoth
federal health-care programs and still more time for welfare. But by
choosing to shoehorn all these sweeping policy changes into the
budget, Gingrich had drastically reduced the time in which to
make it all come together. It was now March, and just seven months
were left before the only real deadline in the congressional budget
process, the October 1 start of the new fiscal year. Without new
spending bills in place by then, big pieces of the government would
have to shut down. In the heady early days of 1995, Republicans
could ignore Democrats and President Clinton, but Clinton could
ultimately veto any bill the Republicans sent him, and if the weakened president wanted to retain any allegiance from what remained of his devastated party, he would have to use that veto.

October 1 was still a long way off. But Congress's unwieldy budget
process had fifteen separate, interlocking parts that took vast
amounts of time to work through. First, Congress had to pass a budget resolution, which set the broad outlines of the cuts they would
make to balance the budget over the following seven years. Then
they had to pass thirteen one-year appropriations bills to fund the vis-
ible part of the federal government—the vast bureaucracy and just
about everything it underwrote except social benefits and interest
on the national debt (national defense, space exploration, highway
construction, law enforcement, child nutrition, education, and so
forth). Then, in the year's main event, they had to pass the huge,
budget-balancing reconciliation bill, so named because it would rec-
oncile taxes and social-benefit programs with balanced-budget goals.

Before they got to any of that, however, House Republicans were determined to spend the first hundred days of the new Congress working their way through the ten planks of their Contract with America. Most of these had little or nothing to do with the budget (term limits, regulatory reform, applying the laws Congress wrote to Congress itself, and so on). There would be some budget work done on a huge package of tax cuts and the spending cuts to pay for them, but the Senate, which traditionally went second on budget matters and evinced mostly disdain for the Contract, had already signaled that it would wait until the House produced its real, non-Contract budget and would ignore anything else.

The House Republicans' fixation with the Contract might have been great politics, but it would wreak havoc with the budget schedule. A budget and appropriations process that ordinarily got started in February or March would now not get under way in earnest until the hundred days had gone by, in April. Instead of seven months in which to handle their immense agenda, Republicans would now have only six months or perhaps just five. Events would show that it wouldn't be enough time.

In the meantime, behind the scenes, Kasich, his chief of staff, Shays, and other Budget Committee members began meeting in groups to explore just how they would balance the budget. They confronted a bleak reality. Most federal spending was off the table, and they had promised to cut taxes, not increase them. Where were they going to find the money to pay for tax cuts and balance the budget with what was left?

As they sat down to work in early 1995, the list of the five biggest programs in the federal budget looked like this:

Program	1996 Spending (in billions)	Percentage of Budget
Social Security	$351	22
Defense	$262	16
Debt interest	$257	16
Medicare	$178	11
Medicaid	$96	6

The top three couldn't be touched. First, they had pledged not to cut Social Security. Republicans had been clobbered over the years by Democrats for real and imagined attempts to cut back benefits or otherwise make more rational a program that both sides admitted— privately—was out of control. Gingrich left no doubt that Social Security would eventually be overhauled, but not now. "The current political system is incapable of dealing with it, and we would simply destroy our majority trying," he explained. Second, Republicans had criticized Clinton during the campaign for cutting defense spending, and now they had to either increase it or, at the very least, leave it where it was. Ever since the collapse of the Soviet Union, defense had been a major source of spending cuts for Congress's deficit-reduction efforts. No more. Third, they could not directly cut interest payments on the debt without risking the nation's first-ever default on its Treasury obligations, which was unthinkable.

This made 54 percent of the budget untouchable, and it left Republicans no practical alternative but to go after big savings in the next biggest programs—Medicare and Medicaid, two of the most popular programs ever created by the federal government.

Medicare had begun thirty years earlier as one of LBJ's Great Society programs. In exchange for a tiny payroll tax during their working years, retirees got heavily subsidized hospital care for as long as they lived; seniors also paid modest monthly premiums for doctor care. Taxpayers held these premiums down by picking up more than two thirds of the cost. Polls showed not only that Medicare was enormously popular but that the elderly thought of it as part of Social Security and therefore immunized by Republicans' solemn vow not to go after Social Security to balance the budget.

Past attempts to cut the alarmingly steep rate at which Medicare spending was growing (more than four times the rate of inflation from 1995 to 1996 alone) had sometimes proved extremely difficult. Beneficiaries hardly peeped when Congress steadily cut back payments to doctors and hospitals, but they resisted and even raged at attempts to force them to pick up a bigger share of program costs. Nonetheless, Kasich had no choice. In the short run, there was nowhere else to find the money. And in the long run, if Republicans could not restrain the growth of federal health programs, both Medicare and Medicaid, the joint federal-state health-care program for the poor, would simply eat the budget alive. The two health entitlements were among the largest and fastest growing of all federal programs.

By mid-March, plans were firming up for unprecedented cuts in Medicare. Balancing the budget by 2002 would cost roughly $900 billion to $1 trillion, and the Medicare proposals would supply almost a third of that, slashing projected spending for the big program by $250 billion to $300 billion over the next seven years. The largest previous cut in Medicare had been the $56 billion over five years in Clinton's 1993 deficit-reduction package; measured on that same five-year scale, the Republicans' proposed cut of some $140 billion was fully two and a half times as much. When seniors groups got wind of this, they signaled ominous displeasure. The $56-billion cut in 1993 "was pushing the envelope," said John Rother, legislative director of the powerful American Association of Retired Persons (AARP). These new cuts would be "too much, too fast, too destructive." The cuts were far too big to load entirely onto doctors and hospitals, as Congress had done in the past. Beneficiaries would get hit hard, and the entire system would be at risk. "The American people will let a lot of things go before they're willing to see Medicare taken apart," Rother warned.

Behind the scenes, Republicans were worried and divided. Some GOP strategists were eager to go ahead, certain they could sell the changes as necessary ones. But GOP National Committee Chairman Haley Barbour, the deceptively folksy Mississippi lawyer who was emerging as a key go-between for the House and Senate Republican leaders, feared that a war over Medicare risked badly wounding the party, and he argued for a two-year delay. Leaders argued back that the numbers left them no other way out; without savings from Medicare, they could not hope to balance the budget. If they did not act, the problem would only get worse and more politically radioactive. They had to go ahead now.

What to do? One day in late March, Barbour got a call from Deborah Steelman, an attorney, insurance company lobbyist, and former senior health care adviser to President Bush. The Medicare trustees were going to claim, in their latest report, that the Medicare problem really wasn't all that bad, Steelman warned him. Their latest report? Barbour had never heard of the Medicare trustees' report. Sure, Steelman told him, it came out every year. The officials in charge of monitoring the health of the trust fund that collected the Medicare payroll tax and paid for Part A hospital costs had to report every year on the fund's fiscal soundness. Barbour was intrigued.

The Medicare trustees' report had come out every year since 1970 and was usually widely ignored. It routinely showed Medicare going broke in about a decade or less, and Congress periodically made changes that pushed the day of reckoning off another few years. But when the 1995 report was issued on April 3, Barbour could hardly believe what he read: "The Federal Hospital Insurance (HI) Trust Fund, which pays inpatient hospital expenses, will be able to pay benefits for only about 7 years and is severely out of balance in the long range. . . ." The report went on to urge Congress to take action to control costs and fix the financial imbalance. It concluded, "The Trustees believe that prompt, effective and decisive action is necessary." It got even better. Three of the six trustees were Clinton Cabinet officials: Treasury Secretary Robert Rubin, Labor Secretary Robert Reich, and Health and Human Services Secretary Donna Shalala. They had signed the report, publicly and unequivocally endorsing both the seven-year drop-dead date and the urgent warning to Congress to do something.

Barbour could not believe his good luck. "I said, 'This is manna from heaven. We have been providentially given the answer to our problem.' " Barbour called Gingrich. Now they had a perfectly good reason to go ahead with their Medicare plans and a superb way to completely reorient the debate. How could Democrats attack them when three of the highest-ranking officials in the Clinton administration were on record practically begging Congress to act? Republicans would no longer have to defend plans to cut Medicare to balance the budget; instead, they would be overhauling Medicare to save it from certain bankruptcy.

The trustees' report had given Republicans an argument that would take time to develop. For the moment, nobody knew Medicare was in danger of going belly-up in seven years, and getting the message out would take months of endless repetition. In the meantime, the Democratic attacks were drawing blood. Democrats were linking the Republicans' big package of tax cuts to the Medicare cuts, charging the GOP with cutting seniors' health benefits to finance tax breaks for fat cats. The attacks were simple and straightforward, and Democrats repeated them over and over again, exhibiting uncharacteristic discipline. It was working. Republicans realized they had to find a way to change the public's perception of what they were doing. They understood that changing perceptions began with changing language, and they set about doing that.

The word *cut* was forbidden. Republicans aggressively argued that even after they pulled nearly $300 billion out of spending for Medicare over the next seven years, Medicare spending would still go up over that period, not down. From Gingrich and rank-and-file members of Congress to GOP press secretaries and conservatives cruising electronic bulletin boards in places such as America On-line, Republicans began enforcing this new budget-speak with surprising tenacity. Reporters who talked about GOP plans to "cut" Medicare could count on being confronted in Capitol hallways, called at home, or even e-mailed on the Internet. The correct phrase, reporters were instructed, was "reducing the rate of growth." The pressure paid off. According to one account, an elated Kasich burst into a private meeting of Republican leaders with a copy of a *Washington Post* story on Medicare that nowhere talked about cuts. "Look at it! Look at it!" shouted the Budget Committee chairman. "They finally got it right!"

In fact, though, Republicans *were* cutting spending deeply, and they wanted to have it both ways. For years, they had savaged Democrats for cutting defense spending, but the defense budget in 1994 was the same—$284 billion—as it had been in 1987. Judged by the new GOP budget rules, that was not a cut at all, just a reduction in the rate of growth. But would anyone seriously argue that defense spending had not in fact been *cut?* In those seven years, troop strength shrank from 2.2 million to 1.6 million, Army divisions contracted from 28 to 20, the Navy's fighting fleet was downsized from 568 ships to 387, and Air Force fighter wings dropped from 36 to 22.

This was how things worked in the real world: Inflation eroded the value of money every year, and the population grew every year. The budget's opening bid simply showed what staying even would take. Was it a cut if the number was less than that? Republicans pointed out that spending for the average Medicare beneficiary would rise from $4,700 in 1995 to $6,200 in 2002. "Only in Washington would that be considered a cut," Republicans said indignantly. But the cost of providing the *same* services that beneficiaries enjoyed under the current Medicare system would rise to $8,000 by

2002. Democrats argued that Republicans were cutting Medicare by $1,200 per beneficiary. Republicans countered that beneficiaries would continue to get just what they were getting now, but market-place efficiencies would drive the government's cost down—no cut, just a slowing of the rate of spending growth.

The biggest "cuts" would come from payments to doctors and hospitals, the same targets Congress had aimed Medicare cuts at for years. All beneficiaries would pay slightly higher premiums, and better-off beneficiaries would pay even more. But that would not produce enough savings. To make up the difference, the GOP would try to encourage seniors to give up traditional and expensive fee-for-service medicine (go to any doctor, go as often as you like, and bill Medicare for the fee) for managed care (go to health-maintenance-type organizations, which receive a flat fee up front and hold down costs in part by strictly limiting access to doctors and specialists). The promise was that health maintenance organization (HMO)–style efficiencies would offer seniors the same medical care or better but at less cost to the government. This was a grand gamble. Some HMOs were beloved by their members; others cut costs by making it tough to get to a doctor at all. The joke was that fee-for-service had been replaced by plea-for-service. Would enough seniors migrate to HMOs to reduce costs radically? Maybe; maybe not.

Gingrich and the others knew they had to be extraordinarily careful about the way they talked about this, and they turned to pollsters to help them refine their language. Key GOP pollster Linda DiVall convened focus groups to test which words would help Republicans soothe the elderly into accepting the GOP Medicare proposals. She strongly advised Republicans against saying they were "changing" Medicare, since that made seniors understandably anxious. Ditto for mentioning "freeze" and "cap." DiVall and fellow GOP pollster Bill McInturff used careful focus-group tests to evolve the phrase "protect, improve, and preserve Medicare." Gingrich changed the order of the three verbs to "preserve, protect, and improve." Then pollster Frank Luntz learned from his own focus groups that "improve" seemed to raise seniors' expectations too high. He suggested "strengthen" instead, and the final phrase was born: Republicans would "preserve, protect, and strengthen Medicare." Almost instantly, it was on the lips of virtually every Republican who said anything about Medicare. This followed Haley Barbour's down-home formula for rhetorical success: "Repeat it until you vomit."

———

Although they were still getting over their stunning loss of Congress and were clearly still awkward in the unfamiliar role of a political minority, Democrats had begun to find their voice on budget matters. Long practiced in the art of class warfare from battling the Reagan and Bush administrations, Democrats now turned their fire on the newly target-rich environment on Capitol Hill. Every day seemed to offer another example of GOP attempts to eliminate or cut back some program for the poor or the middle class; Democrats repeatedly hammered away at the idea that while this was going on, Republicans were pressing ahead with a broad package of tax cuts whose chief benefits would go to the wealthy.

Democrats scored a dramatic early success when they scotched Republican plans to kill the two-decades-old federal program that guaranteed poor children a free school lunch. The GOP had proposed cutting back projected spending on the program and shipping it back to the states on a block-grant basis with little federal oversight. "We trust the states," explained one GOP House aide. Vermont Democratic Governor Howard Dean called this "the most despicable, mean-spirited legislative proposal I have seen in all my years of public service." Children marched on the Capitol to protest. Republicans pressed ahead anyway, but they had clearly been wounded, an ominous sign for the higher-stakes battle over Medicare.

In 1981, attacks like this one had jarred the new Republican White House, and the Reagan administration had quickly backed away from plans to sharply cut some of the big social-spending programs, a reversal that helped doom Republicans' chances of balancing the budget. Gingrich was determined not to repeat Reagan's failure. Republicans' ratings in the polls were dropping sharply as Democrats kept up their attacks, but these wounds were an acceptable short-term cost, Gingrich thought. If they stuck to their promise and produced a balanced budget, he believed, voters would not just forgive them, they would lionize them.

Gingrich's hopes rested on other factors as well. One was an utterly changed Congress, not just different from the one Reagan had had to work with but unlike any in modern memory. A House that had long been top-heavy with veteran members was now filled with newcomers; more than half of the restless new GOP majority were freshman and sophomore members, many of them legislators who had won office on radical promises to turn government upside down. Some were so extreme in their anti-government zealotry that they frightened even their leaders. With their raw contempt for the very institution they had been elected to and their passionate, collective determination to change things, they offered Gingrich the political equivalent of a Doberman pinscher: He intended to use them to great effect and was confident he could control them.

Gingrich also set about consolidating his own power. He knew from watching his predecessor, Democratic Speaker Tom Foley, how powerful committee chairmen weakened a Speaker. Foley had been a prisoner of Democratic power barons who had been chairmen of their committees for a decade or more, men Foley had little inclination or latitude to push around. Early on, Gingrich sent out an unmistakable message that this would not happen to him by staging a stunning coup at the powerful Appropriations Committee. He knew that Appropriations would be critical to any successful attempt to balance the budget and radically shrink the government. The panel had almost complete control over one third of federal spending; the entire federal bureaucracy fed at the committee's broad hand. A few lines buried in an appropriations bill could kill a program or starve an entire agency. Moreover, appropriations bills usually moved like express trains through the legislative process, which meant they could carry legislative directives (the agency shall not do this and that) that might languish if attached to slower-moving authorizing bills.

Gingrich needed control over the committee, but there was a problem: In line to take charge of the seniority-bound panel were four moderate Republicans, all in their sixties or seventies, each of whom had been immersed in the back-scratching appropriations culture for years. None could be counted on to carry out Gingrich's radical agenda unquestioningly. Like a general who shoots an insubordinate officer as an object lesson to the rest, Gingrich bypassed the top four members of Appropriations and picked the younger, more gung-ho Bob Livingston as the committee's new leader. Livingston, fifty-one, had also been drawn into the go-along, get-along appropriations lifestyle over the years, but Gingrich sensed in him an energetic conservatism that was clearly missing in the others. Gingrich's instinct was correct; at his first appearance as chairman, Livingston, a tall martial-arts buff with an affable manner but a hair-trigger temper, pulled out a huge bowie knife and displayed it to the committee as a sign of what was to come. When Democrats began complaining that the Republicans' spending cuts were eviscerating programs for the poor, Livingston exploded, "We can play this compassion game all day, but it won't cut it!"

With strong personalities in all the top spots, there was bound to be friction as Gingrich's team began the difficult work of making good on the GOP budget promises, and one of the first blowups came almost immediately. With his hands at last on the levers that controlled federal spending, Kasich was determined to turn his Budget Committee into an all-powerful policy directorate for the rest of the House committees. After all, he was the one who had been studying the big picture and cranking out detailed GOP budget alternatives all these years; now that they had to do it for real, his giving the orders only made sense.

But just because there was a revolution on did not mean that the House's many authorizing committees (which created programs and wrote their funding guidelines) or the Appropriations Committee (which jealously guarded its absolute authority to decide how much money those programs did or did not get) would roll over like obedient puppies. Who the hell did Kasich think he was? There had always been tension between the Budget Committee and everyone else, but suddenly Kasich was taking it to new heights. Livingston in particular did not take to Kasich's new bossiness, but Livingston was not winning any congeniality awards, either. The Louisianan had big plans for cutting and killing off programs and felt he did not need the authorizers second-guessing him; the authorizers felt just as strongly that they should have a hand in the process, and clashes erupted. Soon there was low-grade warfare on multiple fronts. Armey and Gingrich had to step in.

Armey had a Texan's knack for expressing himself in stories and modern-day parables, which he frequently borrowed from pop culture. At an early February leadership lunch, Livingston was trying to back Kasich off, telling him to quit ordering appropriators around, when Armey decided to try to broker a peace agreement. He said he had been listening to the two men go back and forth and was surprised that they did not realize that they pretty much agreed with each other. They both wanted to cut spending. "John," Armey said, "you remind me of Bruce Willis in the movie *Die Hard,* when he's standing in all this chaos and he gets a phone call and somebody asks him how he's doing and he says, 'To tell you the truth, I'm feeling damned unappreciated.' " Armey said he sympathized. Kasich was raring to go, but what he had to realize was that everyone else was raring to go, too, including Livingston.

Then Armey directed himself to Livingston: "Bob, I watch you and Kasich talk, and you remind me of Paul Newman in *Cool Hand Luke.* I think what we've got here is a failure to communicate," he said, mimicking that movie's signature line. "You've got the same problem with the authorizers that Kasich has with you," Armey told him. "What you've got to do is realize everyone has a role to play."

Essential to the effort but high maintenance, Kasich sometimes seemed like a powerful missile whose guidance system was ignoring signals from ground control. Ultimately, Gingrich brokered a deal. The Budget Committee would work out overall numbers in consultation with the appropriators and the authorizers, who would then be bound to produce cuts that met those targets. Only if the committees failed to meet their targets could Kasich come back and impose specific policies.

Kasich was crestfallen when he dragged himself back to meet with some of his top Budget colleagues. Shays tried to cheer him up: "John, do you realize what just happened? They bought into the numbers!" The authorizers might have resisted Kasich's attempt to impose specific policies, but his tough numbers, the grim numbers that would make a balanced-budget package work—everyone had swallowed them. Didn't Kasich get it? This was a huge victory, and Kasich was moping as though he'd lost his best friend. Shays recalled, "I said, 'John, you won!' "

For all his occasional problems, there was probably no one better suited for the budget job than Kasich. Boyish, strong willed, and brash to the point of almost juvenile disrespect, Kasich had an "oh, yeah?" attitude toward the budget that made him temperamentally ideal for the Gingrich revolution. In his early days in the Ohio State Senate, when senior Republicans told him it would be irresponsible to vote against the tax increases they said they needed to square accounts, Kasich's "oh, yeah?" response was to write his own budget, to prove it could be done without more taxes. He did the same when he got to Congress, proposing alternative budgets that were equally dismissive of what House Democrats and Republican presidents proposed. He got only a handful of Republican votes for his first proposal in 1989, but in 1991 the Kasich alternative beat President Bush's budget in a showdown on the floor—to the vast annoyance of White House Budget Director Dick Darman.

The grudging respect he slowly built among his colleagues on budget issues was sometimes at odds with their personal feelings about him. Many in the House and Senate found his hyperactivity grating. Kasich was so maniacally energetic that his Ohio colleagues hated to get caught sitting next to him on the flight home from Washington; sometimes they pretended to be asleep if they saw him coming down the aisle. Reporters distracted by his jumpiness once counted his furious eye blinks and found that in the same amount of time it took the slow-talking, almost reptilian Majority Leader Dick Armey to blink twice, Kasich shuttered his eyelids up and down thirty-six times.

Kasich was irreverent, candid, outspoken, and informal: As Budget Committee chairman, he delighted in calling the distinguished economists he summoned before the panel "pal" as he joked with them during public hearings. He once created an incident when he tried to bully his way onstage at a Grateful Dead concert at Washington's RFK Memorial Stadium (he said later he'd been trying to see his friend, country singer Dwight Yoakam). He once killed time waiting for a press conference to start by raving to reporters about the new Neil Young–Pearl Jam album and urging them to go out and buy it. He stood out among the lawyers who populated Congress as a proudly blue-collar politician, the son of a mailman from a small town in Pennsylvania, a fact he mentioned repeatedly whenever he was trying to establish his credentials as a populist budget cutter. What he hardly ever mentioned publicly was how his Christian faith had deepened after a drunken driver blindsided and killed his mother and father as they pulled their car out of a Dairy Queen parking lot in 1987; Kasich now attended regular Bible classes and quietly proselytized among his colleagues.

When Republicans were asked to choose between Kasich and a more middle-of-the-road colleague to be the senior Republican on the Democrat-controlled House Budget Committee in 1992, they opted for Kasich, just as they had chosen Gingrich over a more moderate rival in 1989. Kasich returned the favor by pushing his colleagues to change their act; when an overwhelming majority of House Republicans wanted to do no more than sit back and criticize President Clinton's budget plan in 1993, Kasich insisted they support a credible alternative plan, to show that Republicans stood *for* something, not just against what the Democrats proposed. In a fiery private meeting of all House Republicans, member after member stood to say that Kasich was wrong, that his plan would only muddle their criticism of Clinton. Only one man sat next to Kasich and told him what he was doing was exactly right: Newt Gingrich.

When Republicans took over Congress two years later, Gingrich did not hesitate to turn over to Kasich the new majority's most difficult challenge. The job was more than just finding a way to balance the budget; Kasich was taking a crash course in leadership, growing publicly as he responded to Gingrich's tutoring. Characteristically, Kasich explained Gingrich's advice in sports metaphors: "When you walk in the clubhouse, you are somebody that people look to. So, you know, get to practice early. Don't let the tail of your uniform hang out. If you get hit by a pitch, don't whine about it. If you have a nagging injury, suck it up—because you're a leader."

———

Three months after the Republicans' February powwow, it was time to regroup and rethink their strategy. In early May, GOP leaders isolated the party's congressional members at the Xerox Document University, a low-slung collection of buildings in the outlying Virginia suburb of Leesburg, a place one GOP aide said had all the charm he expected of Stalinist concrete architecture. XDU's singular virtue was its isolation; reporters could get no closer than the main gate.

Until now, the budget task forces had been working like the cells of a terrorist organization, assembling the pieces of the budget the

House was scheduled to vote on by the end of the month. That vote would be their critical first step, the first time Republicans had publicly revealed a specific plan that would eradicate the deficit. Gingrich, Kasich, and other leaders were concerned: Was everybody still on board?

At the initial meeting at XDU, some 230 Republicans there were seated in one big room and given handheld devices that allowed them to answer yes or no to a series of carefully chosen questions, some broad, some quite specific: "Are you committed to a balanced budget?" "Are you committed to a balanced budget in seven years?" "Should farm subsidies be lower?" "Should funding for the National Endowment for the Arts be abolished?" In front of them was a giant screen, where results of the informal polling were instantly displayed: unanimous support for balancing the budget in seven years, for instance, and a remarkable 85 percent approval for lowering farm subsidies. "It was rock solid," said GOP Conference Chairman John Boehner, who helped organize the event and was hoping the results would show that bedrock support. "Everybody understood that we had to do this, and we were going to do this—no ifs, ands, or buts about it. The question was, How do we get there?"

At the same time Boehner was trying to gauge where the rank and file were, he was also building in a little automatic discipline. When budget details were eventually unveiled, members could be counted on to protest individual cuts. But when farm-state members argued that the agriculture cuts were too deep, for example, leaders could remind them of these poll results and pressure them to go along.

Members also heard a sharp warning about the external public-opinion polls they would see over the next several months. Michigan Governor John Engler told them to brace themselves for a staggering drop in their popularity as they took the steps necessary to balance the budget. He recounted his own story: how he had imposed deep, across-the-board spending cuts upon taking office in 1991, killing off an entire state department, throwing some six thousand employees off the state payroll, and—to great controversy—ending general welfare assistance to eighty thousand able-bodied adults without children. Engler's poll ratings plunged to below 20 percent, and he was publicly blamed for the suicide of a former welfare recipient. "Try picking that up in your morning paper," he told the House Republicans.

But Engler, who had become a key outside adviser to Gingrich, said that things turned around in his second year in office, once Michigan citizens realized that the awful predictions about the effects of the cuts were not coming true. He won respect for having taken a tough but necessary course, and he was reelected in 1994 with more than 60 percent of the vote. What the House Republicans were doing now was "almost a carbon copy" of what he had done, he told them. They should stay tough, weather the bad polls, and trust that voters would thank them when it was all over.

True, said Republican pollster Robert Teeter later, but with one important caveat: When it was all over, voters had to see clear results. When it was all over, voters had to be able to say of the House Republicans, "They balanced the budget."

When it finally came time to lay out the balanced-budget plan, Gingrich and the others hung back. Kasich wanted to keep talking about the big picture, to make sure everyone was signed on for the crusade. That was not working. "One thing you learn about members in large groups is that dealing with two hundred thirty of them in a room about esoteric things that they can't quite sink their teeth into—they're just not real interested," said Boehner. "John didn't want to lay all his specifics out too soon because frankly you don't need this group, that group, every group in America marching on the [Budget Committee] members before they mark up the bill. All John would talk about was the big, broad issues. Well, they wanted specifics and they wanted them now."

Members would not be denied. For six hours, they pushed Kasich to lay out the details and argue them. As Boehner described it, "We debated a lot of programs, a lot of ideas. John was playing Phil Donahue—honest to God. He looked like Phil Donahue; he had a cordless mike—walking around. It got to be a real show, but I'll tell you, the members just—that's exactly what they wanted to do. Thank God we stumbled into it."

Everything did not go smoothly. Agriculture Committee Chairman Pat Roberts—a Kansan so intimately tied to the farm economy that he kept a tote board in his office to record the day-to-day fluctuations of commodity prices—was rebelling against the size of the cuts in farm subsidies. A deep split in the party pitted radical reformers, who wanted to do away with farm price supports altogether, against traditional farm-state Republicans, who wanted to retain some sort of a safety net for farmers. For the moment, Roberts's concern was that Kasich's cuts—nearly $12 billion over seven years—were much too big. Roberts wanted half that, and he confronted Kasich privately in XDU's communications room.

Roberts argued that cuts as deep as those Kasich was proposing would rock the farm economy; he also warned that they would hand Democrats a wonderful opportunity to come into farm states during the 1996 campaign, criticize Republicans, and promise to save the subsidies. If Republicans lost heavily in the farm belt, their grip on the House could slip. Kasich took the point. When the two men emerged, they had an informal agreement to lower the cuts from $12 billion to $9 billion.

Not all Kasich's encounters went as easily. Summoned to a private meeting with Dick Armey, Ways and Means Committee Chairman Bill Archer, and Commerce Committee Chairman Tom Bliley, Kasich was summarily informed that the budget resolution's Medicare section—the heart of the plan, Kasich felt—was to be a single vague paragraph promising savings. Orders were to downplay any suggestion of Medicare "cuts," which meant that little or none of the specific money-saving strategies Kasich and his Medicare team had worked for weeks to develop would be included. Budget resolutions often lack detail, but Kasich knew that it would be critical to spell out ideas for translating into reality the huge cuts in projected Medicare spending they had in mind. Otherwise, critics could accuse them—justifiably, Kasich thought—of pulling numbers out of thin air.

Kasich was furious. Armey informed him that Gingrich had authorized the change. Kasich said that didn't matter; he wasn't going to accept it. "It was really bad news," he recalled, "absolutely outrageous." He stalked out of the room and convened the Budget Committee Republicans. They decided to dig in their heels. Shays and others had worked hard for weeks on real plans for overhauling Medicare in ways they thought seniors would accept. The bottom line for Kasich was credibility. He could not do the hard work of persuading his colleagues and the public to buy a budget whose very heart was a "nebulous" paragraph, he said. "I can't go and sell something I don't feel good about."

Confronted by Kasich and the united Budget Committee Republicans, Armey backed down. From that point on, Kasich fought mostly smaller actions at Leesburg. "I had to use humor; sometimes I had to joke; sometimes I had to plead." In the end, a "magic thing occurred," and the conference coalesced. To mark the occasion, leaders presented Kasich with a gift that was part good-spirited dig, part heartfelt tribute. It was a piece of stone into which were cut the words BALANCED BUDGET 2002. They had come a long way from the moment when Kasich wondered where it was "engraved in stone" that they had to balance the budget in seven years.

———

The House Republicans left Xerox Document University in an energized state, and their leaders moved quickly to take advantage. Five days later Kasich rammed the budget through a fifteen-hour session of the Budget Committee, passing it shortly after 1:00 A.M. on May 11. The vote was 24–17. Not only did the Republicans hold every member, but they picked up conservative Mississippi Democrat Mike Parker, a former funeral director who later in the year would switch parties to become a Republican.

On the House floor a week later, the outcome was similarly foreordained. Democrats complained bitterly about the spending cuts, but they were decidedly outvoted. The simple political fact of life in the House is that a cohesive majority can crush the minority. Democrats had done that to Republicans for years, passing budgets that Republicans could only warn would come back to haunt them. Now Democrats were warning that they would savage the GOP budget every bit as badly as Republicans had mauled the Clinton budget in 1993. This was all-out partisan war, and some Republicans were already a little nervous about the stakes. "I think there are a number of members on both sides who don't yet really understand how tough some of these spending cuts are going to be," said Michigan moderate Republican Fred Upton.

For now, though, most Republicans were delighted with their victory. Budget Committee chief of staff Rick May, who had compared Gingrich to a general who ordered his troops to take a seemingly insurmountable hill, looked down from the heights and said, "You get to the top, and you say, 'Gee, that wasn't so hard.' " Everything had fallen into place. Spending cuts so ferocious that Kasich had worried his colleagues would flinch had shot through virtually unanimously (the only Republican to vote no was a congressman who had unexpectedly toppled the incumbent in a heavily Democratic Chicago district and was now fighting for his political life). The tough new bunch of freshman and sophomore Republicans had stood together and backed the plan.

Even more gratifying, the GOP had so utterly transformed the political dynamic that significant numbers of Democrats were voting for balanced-budget proposals. Though only 8 of the House's 199 Democrats crossed party lines to vote for the GOP plan, many more voted for a Democratic balanced-budget alternative. By the time the House voted, 238–193, to pass the Republican budget, more than 80 percent of the House—360 of its 435 members—had backed some plan to balance the budget. In the seven months since the November 1994 elections, what had been little more than a widely derided Republican campaign promise had turned into the reigning political imperative of 1995.

In a little-noticed comment on NBC's *Meet the Press* a few weeks later, House Minority Whip David Bonior, a Michigan liberal who defined the Democrats' combative, progressive core, signaled just how much things had changed. A year earlier, liberal Democrats would have scoffed at the notion that the budget should be balanced. They had shed blood in 1993 to pass Clinton's big deficit-reduction package, and they had little interest in doing more. But the world had changed around them. "The question isn't about a balanced budget," he said. "I think we've had a general debate in this country, and people want us to balance the budget. We all agree with that. The question is, Who is going to make the sacrifices to do that?"

Chapter 2

OLD BULLS

———

While Gingrich was busy consolidating his gains in the House of Representatives, the Senate was spending weeks bickering over the balanced-budget amendment. To underscore the political stakes, Majority Leader Bob Dole issued an unusual order: All senators were to be present on the Senate floor on March 2 and seated at their tiny, well-polished mahogany desks before the clerk began calling the roll for the final vote. Usually, senators drifted in and out of the chamber during votes, clogging the narrow aisles and creating a din as they chattered among themselves.

But Dole, nearing seventy-two and exhausted and testy after a long, frustrating struggle to try to pass the amendment, wanted none of that now. Like a stern schoolmaster who had grown impatient with his unruly pupils, the majority leader had ordered his ninety-nine colleagues to sit in silence until their names were called and then to stand and announce their votes in the stillness of the historic chamber. Tall, still darkly handsome, his withered right hand perpetually grasping a pen so no one would try to shake it, Dole was at last beginning to show his age, as if the ceaseless grind of his third of a century in Congress had at last begun to wear down his mighty will.

The balanced-budget amendment was a key plank in the House Republicans' Contract with America, and Gingrich had passed it quickly at the end of January by winning the votes of scores of Democrats and virtually all the House Republicans. Now it was Dole's turn to produce, and he was under enormous pressure, not just because this was the first real test of how the Republican revolution would play in the Senate or because the balanced-budget amendment was critical to what Republicans were trying to do this year. Dole was making one last run for the presidency, and his candidacy was founded on the claim that he could get things done. By that criterion, on this issue he was in deep trouble.

Dole needed sixty-seven votes, or two thirds of the entire Senate, to pass the constitutional amendment and send it to the states to be ratified. But he was still one vote short, and he had decided to cast a spotlight on the opponents in a final, desperate effort to make one of them uncomfortable enough to switch his or her vote. Furious that he was on the verge of failing where Gingrich had just succeeded so brilliantly, Dole lashed out at his opponents, especially six Democrats who had previously voted for the amendment but were now voting no, lest they give him and the Republicans such an important victory. "Promises that were made are in the ash can," he growled. Dole complained that it was the free-spending Democrats who stood in the way of the amendment, which enjoyed more than 80 percent popularity in public-opinion polls. In fact, though, about a dozen Democrats, including the two Illinois liberals, Senators Paul Simon and Carol Moseley-Braun, had announced they would support it, and Simon was a leader of the pro-amendment campaign.

The real challenge for Dole was to hold all fifty-four of the Senate's Republicans together, and there he was failing. Blocking the amendment was liberal, anti-war, pro-spending Mark Hatfield of Oregon, the Republican chairman of the Senate Appropriations Committee and the embodiment of everything the angry young House revolutionaries hated about the Senate and its aging leaders. During his nearly three decades in Washington, the patrician, silver-haired Hatfield, now seventy-two, had displayed an independent streak that often infuriated his Republican colleagues. The former Oregon governor, once talked up as a possible presidential candidate, often sided with Democrats on key issues. In a vote that struck some colleagues as particularly egregious, he had backed President Clinton's national service program, a plan that allowed young people to work their way through college by performing community service but was denounced by many Republicans as a boondoggle. Nevertheless, Hatfield was an old friend of Dole's, and the majority leader was reluctant to pressure him, particularly because Hatfield, a strict constitutional constructionist, was standing on deeply held principle. But if Hatfield stayed a no, Dole risked losing the amendment, which would bring him the wrath of the GOP right wing, the derision of the House, and trouble on the campaign trail.

Faced with a similar threat in the House, Gingrich would have resorted to intimidation, political bribery, or public humiliation to get his way. As House Budget Committee Chairman John Kasich discovered when he tried to stand in the way of the Speaker's plans to balance the budget in seven years, Gingrich could be ferocious with those who tried to thwart him.

Dole's power paled by comparison. While Gingrich had passed over senior members early in the year to pick more malleable committee chairmen, Dole couldn't get away with such a tactic in the Senate, where seniority was still deeply rooted. Senators had much more power in their chamber's day-to-day affairs than House members did; each could stall and even stop the entire body, not just with filibusters but with little-known traditions, such as the one that allowed senators to put "holds" on bills to block them from floor debate. As he glared around the Senate floor the morning of the balanced-budget vote, Dole saw nothing but free agents, senators virtually impervious to any pressure he might try to bring. The fact that he had managed to make all of them sit obediently in their chairs only gave the illusion that he had them under control.

Dole had been through this maddening experience before. Unlike Gingrich, who had spent his political career until now as a gadfly in the minority, Dole had led the Senate once before and understood all the constraints and difficulties that came with power; the prospect of taking on that responsibility again was a decidedly mixed blessing. From 1981 through 1986, when Republicans controlled the Senate for the first six years of the Reagan presidency, Dole served as chairman of the Senate Finance Committee and then as majority leader. Back then, he had been a key lieutenant in the Reagan revolution. In 1981, he helped Reagan cut taxes deeply, only to unleash huge deficits; when he tried to stanch the red ink, first with tax increases and finally with cuts in Social Security and other key programs in 1985, what he got for his trouble was a voter backlash that turned the Senate back to the Democrats and put Dole in the minority again. He still bore the scars of that débâcle. Now he had his majority-leadership job back again, but with a twist: He would be thrust into another revolution, this one led by younger, more ideologically hard-line conservatives who thoroughly distrusted pragmatic deal makers like Dole. There had long been tension between Dole and Gingrich over policy and tactics; it was Gingrich who had long ago tagged Dole with the nasty sobriquet that had followed him ever since: "tax collector for the welfare state." Now, for the good of the party, the two men had to pretend to like each other.

Gingrich's rise confronted Dole with an almost impossible balancing act. Dole's own middle-of-the-road instincts put him right in the philosophical mainstream of the Senate's old bulls, mostly moderate Republicans who had been through the experience of governing once before and who had little patience with the brash new House members' self-righteous zealotry. But with their remarkable legislative output in the first hundred days of the new Congress, those impatient House revolutionaries were pushing Dole hard to the right. Moreover, the firebrands had established a beachhead in the Senate chamber, where six of the eleven Republican freshmen and nearly a third of the fifty-four Republicans were veterans of the House, where they had learned a brand of politics far more freewheeling and confrontational than that practiced in the Senate.

In the House, it was only mildly shocking to see a young conservative, Iowa Republican Jim Nussle, come to the floor to speak with a grocery bag over his head to symbolize Republicans' shame for the institution and disgust at the Democrats; in the Senate, such a thing would be unthinkable. In the House, members shouted at one another on the floor, routinely impugned one another's motives and integrity, and played tough, street-fighting politics that was all but unknown in the far more polite and formal Senate. When first-term Pennsylvania Democrat Marjorie Margolies-Mezvinsky voted for President Clinton's budget proposal in 1993 at great risk to her career, Republicans across the aisle jeered and hooted at her, shouting "Good-bye, Marjorie!" as she fled the floor in tears. The House chamber in the midst of a tough debate sometimes took on the edgy air of a frat house well into a Saturday-night beer party, full of sullen, hostile energy, frequently seeming on the verge of spinning out of control.

By contrast, an elaborate, ultra-civil decorum was critical in the Senate. Senators almost without exception referred to one another as "my good friend" or "my distinguished colleague," and voices rarely rose. The determined gentility was vital to the way the Senate did business; with just 100 members to the House's 435, each senator's vote was four times more important than a House member's, and it was at least that many times more important not to offend, not to make enemies, not to burn bridges the way House members frequently did. The Senate has always been the more contemplative body, the saucer into which the hot coffee from the House would be poured to cool it, as George Washington explained to Thomas Jefferson two centuries ago. So it was no surprise that the revolutionary flame burned much hotter in the House. The Senate's staggered six-year terms meant that only a third of the body had been chosen in the last election. By contrast, the entire House must stand for election every two years; right now more than half the Republican members were newcomers who had been elected in the last two elections and felt more allegiance to the passions of the angry voters who had elected them than to the institution or its traditions. House GOP leaders adroitly harnessed that energy with a sophisticated whip and party-message system and engineered unprecedented change, racing through a legislative agenda in the first few months of 1995 that would have been an entire year's business under the Democrats.

———

If Dole was uncomfortable about putting heavy pressure on his old friend Hatfield, others were not. A steady stream of Republicans, from Alfonse D'Amato of New York and John Ashcroft of Missouri to Orrin Hatch of Utah, the chief sponsor of the amendment, visited Hatfield's office, delivering the same message: Dole and the party needed this victory to preserve momentum and keep up with the House. Hatch, a party loyalist and a domineering chairman of the Judiciary Committee not used to being told no by his colleagues, reminded Hatfield that the stakes in this battle were "huge" for the Republicans and for the country. Hatch even sent

TV evangelist Reverend Robert Schuller to see him; Schuller argued for the amendment, showing the senator a picture of his famous Crystal Cathedral in California, which Schuller noted had been built without incurring a single dollar of debt. Schuller said the federal government ought to operate that same way. After Schuller left, Hatfield went to the Senate floor and found Hatch and told him, "It didn't work." Hatch laughed and said, "I've got Billy Graham lined up." Even former president George Bush called to work on Hatfield, to ask him to reconsider. But to all of them, Hatfield's response was the same: He shared the Republicans' determination to balance the budget, but he couldn't bring himself to support the amendment.

Hatfield had assumed the Appropriations chairmanship from Democrat Robert C. Byrd of West Virginia, the Senate's leading opponent of the balanced-budget amendment. Both men shared the increasingly unfashionable belief that government was fundamentally an engine for good and that by shaping spending bills in an enlightened manner, the legislative branch could make major strides in education, health care, and job opportunities. The two men also shared an almost mystical faith in the Constitution. To both, the balanced-budget amendment was a threat to the delicate, constitutionally ordained balance of power in Washington and to the primacy of Congress in matters of spending. They also felt that the amendment was nothing more than a procedural gimmick advocated by those who lacked the political will to balance the budget the old-fashioned way, through leadership and compromise.

To be sure, the amendment traded on the seductive notion that the budget could be balanced by decree instead of through the grinding hard work of cutting back programs and raising taxes. Members who had little stomach for slashing spending could vote comfortably for the balanced-budget amendment and pretend they had solved the deficit problem when in fact all they had done was take a largely symbolic first step. And the amendment's effectiveness was hardly a sure thing; Congress had a long history of wriggling out of restrictions and mandates it placed on itself. The sorry history of the 1985 Gramm-Rudman-Hollings anti-deficit law, which mandated a balanced budget in five years and never worked, was a case in point.

Congress had been arguing over the amendment off and on since the founding of the nation. The debate's modern history went back to the 1930s, when a Minnesota Republican congressman introduced a version in the depths of the Depression on the theory—widely held then but considered lunacy today—that forcing the government to cut spending and raise taxes would somehow pull the economy out of its awful slump (just the reverse proved to be true when the extraordinary borrowing and spending during the Second World War finally ended the Depression). Proponents still ascribed vast, almost magical fiscal properties to the amendment, but its primary virtue in the late twentieth century was political. President Reagan turned to the amendment as political cover when his own policies began to create enormous deficits in the early 1980s, and Republicans and conservative Democrats had clamored for it even as they proposed and supported wildly unbalanced budgets. In the last decade, the House had passed it every few years, and so had the Senate, but never in the same year.

Adoption of the amendment would be a huge political victory for Republicans, so Democrats who had supported it in the past began to drop their support. Senate Minority Leader Tom Daschle was only the most prominent example of a Democrat who had backed the amendment in previous years but now found a convenient excuse to vote no. Daschle complained that the Republicans would not disclose in advance how they planned to actually balance the budget; others worried about what would happen to Social Security when it came time to do the balancing or whether the federal courts would assume control of the budget if Congress refused to comply. All valid complaints, perhaps, but ones that had not seemed nearly so worrisome to Daschle and others in previous years.

Despite the defections, Dole's brightest prospects were still with the Democrats, and for one brief moment he thought he might be able to pull off a victory. Senator Sam Nunn, a conservative Democrat from Georgia who had been wavering for weeks, finally threw his support to the amendment a couple of days before the final vote, after he secured language that would block the courts from interfering in budget matters. Nunn was an influential figure, and Hatch and others assumed that if they could turn him, other Democrats would follow. But they overestimated the Georgian's effect on his colleagues; Nunn pulled no one with him, and Dole remained one vote short.

Since the November 1994 election, the Democrats had flailed about ineffectually, incapable of finding their bearings or settling on a legislative agenda. Now, however, they had found something that could unite them: Not only could they beat Dole and the Republicans on a major vote, but they could also show their core constituency that they were warding off a mindless mechanism that would slash Social Security and other programs that had helped poor and vulnerable Americans for two generations. Labor organizations, social-welfare advocates, and national seniors groups, fearing the worst, demanded that the Democrats oppose the amendment. The White House opposed the amendment as well, despite its popularity among the vast majority of voters. Clinton worried that its passage would give Republican budget cutters more leverage than they already had to eviscerate long-held Democratic priorities.

Dole had first scheduled the vote for late February. The night before, Keith Kennedy, Hatfield's staff director, was summoned to Dole's office for an important meeting. When Kennedy got there, however, Dole wasn't in. Instead, the staff director was greeted by Hatch and Idaho Republican Senator Larry Craig, a floor manager of the amendment. The two senators were excited; they said they had come up with a way out: Hatfield simply would not vote when the final roll was called. Instead, he would find an excuse to be away from the floor.

It was a remarkable request. Hatfield would just walk away while the Senate was casting one of the most important votes of the year. "We were willing to suggest anything to pass the amendment," Hatch admitted later. "We were clutching for straws in the dark." With Hatfield absent, the magic number would drop from sixty-seven votes to sixty-six—two thirds of the ninety-nine senators who would be voting. That meant that all Dole had to do was hold the votes he already had: the fifty-three Republicans and the thirteen Democrats willing to vote yes. "What do you think?" Hatch asked Kennedy. Hatfield's aide replied warily, "I'll take your offer back to him, but I've got to tell you I don't think this will work." Kennedy had served Hatfield for twenty-three years and knew his boss well. When he went back and explained the idea to him, Hatfield shook his head. He didn't want to disappoint his colleagues, but he couldn't weasel out of the vote, either. Hatfield was worried by what the suggestion said about Dole's mounting anxiety; Hatch and Craig never would have floated the idea if they had not cleared it with Dole first. The majority leader must be terribly concerned to make such a request.

For Dole, his friendship with Hatfield was one thing, but his own political survival was another. Connie Mack of Florida and Rick Santorum of Pennsylvania, both former House members who had little patience with the Senate's seniority system, were leading a band of conservatives who were pressing Dole to force Hatfield into line or punish him. With the vote approaching, Hatch went to Dole and insisted he make one more try to get Hatfield on board. There was nothing to lose, Hatch advised the leader.

About an hour before the vote, Dole arranged to visit Hatfield in the ornate offices of the Senate Appropriations Committee on the first floor of the Capitol. Until now, through all the years the two had worked together in the Senate, Dole had never leaned on the maverick Hatfield to stick with the party when Hatfield's instincts led him astray. Sure, Dole would needle him before a tough vote, passing him in the hall and grunting "aye" and giving him a thumbs-up sign and a grin. It was done "with all light touches, with this marvelous humor that he has," said Hatfield. This was different, though. In the privacy of Hatfield's office deep in the elaborate Appropriations suite, Dole now openly pleaded with his friend to change his mind. "Mark," Dole said, "this is going to be a reflection on your leader." Dole told him how important it was to him in his run for the presidential nomination. Losing this vote could be crushing to his campaign, which was built on the notion that he was a leader who could get things done. "Isn't there any way you could do this?" Dole begged him.

The ordinarily private and self-contained Dole had never before appealed to Hatfield on such personal grounds, had never made himself so vulnerable. It was the most personal conversation the two men had had in the quarter century they had been in the Senate together, and Hatfield felt terrible anguish at having to say no. They talked through the options, such as Hatfield's simply ducking the vote, but the Oregon senator said he could not do that, either. Dole seemed more and more distressed. Then Hatfield stunned him.

"There is an option," Hatfield said. "That is, I'll write up my resignation from the Senate. You'll have ninety-nine votes, two-thirds majority."

At first Dole reacted as if he didn't understand. It was an extraordinary sacrifice. Hatfield was willing to walk away from the office he had held for twenty-eight years, give up the chairmanship of one of the most powerful committees in Congress, go into retirement just as Republicans were on the verge of remaking government—all to bail out his friend and spare the party the embarrassment of losing the vote. When Dole gathered his wits, he said firmly, "Of course not—I wouldn't consider that. That's not an option."

There was now no doubt where Hatfield stood. Characteristically, Dole sought to lighten things as he stood to go. "Well, we're still a half hour away from the vote," he said wryly; "maybe you'll change your mind."

Hatfield felt deeply moved. "We wear masks around here so much," he said later. "For someone literally to take off their mask and say, Here I am in a vulnerable position, I think is probably the highest tribute one human being can extend to another human being. When some other human being says, 'I need you; I desperately rely upon you at this point,' [it] is of such vital importance to me. It was a moment of anguish that I treasured. . . . Here was this man, really so open, so real, so sincere. I had a reaction for days after, like someone hit in the stomach."

Dole left Hatfield's office and went on a desperate search for the final vote, looking to find one Democrat who had voted for the amendment before and might somehow be persuaded to do it again. Sensing that Kent Conrad of North Dakota might be wavering, Dole drew him into the Republican cloakroom for a last-minute bargaining session. It almost worked. Conrad's opposition revolved around the treatment of the Social Security trust fund, and Dole offered a compromise that would have maintained the trust fund's sanctity. But with a deal seemingly within reach, Minority Leader Daschle raced into the cloakroom, yanked Conrad out of the meeting, and brought him back to his office for a heart-to-heart chat. A chastened Conrad began making additional demands, and Dole's overtures came to nothing.

Now facing certain defeat, Dole returned to the Senate floor and announced that he was delaying the vote for at least another day or two, to buy time to try to recruit another Democrat. By doing that, however, Dole broke a time agreement he had made with Daschle, a deal worked out by both sides to bring the debate to a close and hold the showdown vote at a specific time. Dole felt he had no choice, but the delay enraged the starchy Byrd, an ardent opponent of the balanced budget and a stickler for Senate rules and decorum. Byrd, a former majority leader himself, fumed that Dole was using "sleazy, tawdry" tactics in an unseemly effort to win at any cost. Dole bristled: He wasn't doing anything that Byrd and the Democrats hadn't done when they ran the place.

The delay did no good. Daschle had shored up his ranks, and no other Democrats even hinted that they might switch. With nowhere else to turn, Dole called up the amendment for a final vote on the morning of March 2. Looking morose and dejected, he sat in his leader's chair in the first row, staring vacantly down at his shoes as the clerk began to call the roll: "Mr. Abraham . . . Mr. Akaka . . . Mr. Ashcroft." Seated directly behind Dole was Hatfield, who also appeared grim faced and miserable. As he waited for the clerk to call his name, Hatfield leaned way back, his hands tightly grasping the arms of the chair and his jaw set, looking, by turns, like somebody about to be catapulted into space or electrocuted. Hatch, a Mormon who believes in the power of prayer, held his breath and prayed silently that Hatfield would change his mind. When the clerk finally called out "Mr. Hatfield," the Oregonian slowly rose to his feet and, in a whisper almost inaudible to the crowded gallery, said simply, "No." The amendment was defeated—and Dole was devastated.

As the vote came to a close, Dole tried to make the best of the bad situation. He switched his own vote from yes to no, a parliamentary trick that would allow him to move to reconsider the amendment at any time. That would keep the issue open indefinitely, giving him more time to find the single vote he needed. This would not be the last word on the balanced-budget amendment, he vowed in a packed, postmortem press conference immediately after the defeat. The amendment could be brought up for another vote next year, possibly timed for maximum impact during the campaign.

Reporters asked Dole whether Republicans were still committed to balancing the budget by the year 2002, the target date contained in the amendment. "Yes," Dole shot back without hesitation, and within seconds all the other GOP leaders clustered around him on the podium—Lott, Hatch, Craig, and others—spontaneously shouted out "Yes!" as well. Dole hadn't bothered to poll the other leaders in advance. Their response was just as impulsive as the response of the House Republicans when Gingrich, without warning, asked them to raise their hands if they agreed with him that the budget had to be balanced within seven years. Dole described his setback on the Senate floor as little more than a bump in the road, an unfortunate disappointment that would have little significance in the long-run battle to conquer the deficit. "We'll find out where all these [Democrats] are when we get to the tough votes," he said, trying to change the subject and get the focus off Hatfield. "They'll be hiding behind the couches and everything else in there."

But the newscasts that night and the newspaper headlines the next morning told a different story. Dole and the Senate Republicans had laid an egg, and the repercussions were serious. An analysis on the front page of *The Washington Post* summed up the fiasco and offered a worst-case assessment. The headline read, IN DEFEAT FOR GOP, DIFFICULTIES FOR DOLE; IMPACT MAY BE FELT IN SENATE, CAMPAIGN.

————

Mark Hatfield wasn't the only Republican prepared to buck the conservative tide. The House might be brimming with newcomers bent on religiously passing every provision of the Contract with America and dismantling big government, but the Senate was still largely under the control of veteran Republicans who had spent much of their careers helping to build up programs that were now under assault. For the past two decades, the Republican leadership in the Senate had been dominated by moderates such as Hatfield; Bob Packwood of Oregon, the Finance Committee chairman and chief author of the 1986 tax reform; John Chafee of Rhode Island, a former Navy secretary and the most liberal Republican voice on the Finance Committee; and Pete V. Domenici of New Mexico, the chairman of the Budget Committee and a pivotal player in the unfolding budget drama. During the Reagan era, these men fought battle after battle with supply-siders like Gingrich and Jack Kemp, who favored a full-speed-ahead agenda of tax cuts while the moderates carefully preached attention to keeping deficits in check.

In his memoir, *The Triumph of Politics,* Reagan Budget Director
David Stockman disparaged Domenici and other GOP moderates as
Hooverites whose thinking was stuck in the GOP dark ages (President Herbert Hoover had insisted on trying to balance the budget
right through the early days of the Great Depression—madness,
Stockman thought). He was exasperated by Domenici's stubborn refusal to surrender to the transforming effect of supply-side tax cuts.
All Domenici wanted to do was cut spending and balance the budget, Stockman fumed.

Now Domenici and the rest of the same Senate moderates who
had so annoyed Stockman were at intraparty war again, this time
with a new generation of House Republicans obsessed with a large
tax cut that the senators feared could jeopardize the GOP's first legitimate opportunity in fifteen years to eradicate the deficit. The
moderates argued repeatedly with Dole that he should put aside
consideration of a tax cut until Congress delivered on the necessary
spending cuts.

Even without the tax cuts, Domenici was worried that support for
balancing the budget would evaporate when senators saw the size of
the spending cuts that would be necessary. During a closed-door,
post-election meeting of Senate Republican leaders in December
1994, Domenici argued strongly for a go-slow approach, suggesting
they make a substantial down payment on deficit reduction by the
end of the decade but avoid promising to go all the way to zero. Privately, Domenici and his Budget Committee staff director, Bill
Hoagland, had worked through the preliminary math and realized
that to balance the budget by 2002, Congress would have to cut
nearly $1 trillion of projected spending, making wholesale reduc-
tions in such politically popular programs as Medicare, Medicaid,
farm subsidies, veterans' benefits, and highway construction. Nothing of this magnitude had ever been attempted before. When his
colleagues saw these numbers, Domenici believed, they would be
horrified.

Compact and stocky, with a weathered, owlish face and a gravelly
voice that was a telltale sign of his long years of chain-smoking (he
had quit with great difficulty), the sixty-three-year-old Domenici carried himself with Western directness. He was often blunt, quick to
laugh, but just as quick to anger; for a politician, his skin was very
thin, and reporters often got sharp, one-word answers when they

pushed him on tough subjects. Early in 1995, balancing the budget was a very tough subject. The son of an Italian-immigrant grocer, Domenici grew up in Albuquerque in a large, strict Catholic family that placed a premium on obedience and loyalty to family and church. From his hardworking father, he absorbed the notion that things were only as good as you made them by worrying and planning, working and saving. "My dad always believed there was a direct relationship between working hard and growth," Domenici said. "He felt he had to be worried about next week and next year, had to put money in the bank, that it was important to settle down and not be indecisive, to stay at something." His father's guiding principle was attention to duty, and Domenici grew up with the same mindset.

The young Domenici's all-conference performance as a pitcher on his college team earned him a coveted contract with a Brooklyn Dodgers farm team in 1954. But once he arrived in the bigs, his nerves got the better of him; he lost his control and quickly washed out. For all his brusqueness, Domenici was a deeply anxious man, a habitual worrier who could spend hours vacillating over a problem and seeking reassurances from his top aides. "Pete has a tendency to want to avoid the final, hard commitment as long as he can, until he has an opportunity to visit with everyone and anyone with an opinion on the issue," said a longtime associate. Democrats called him Poutin' Pete behind his back because he whined so much. Dole once jokingly threatened to commit suicide if he had to keep listening to Domenici's gloomy fiscal projections.

As a young Albuquerque lawyer with eight children and a thriving practice, Domenici had no plans to be a politician; only when friends tired of his endless complaints about government and pushed him to do something about it did he agree to run for office. He turned out to be a natural, winning election as an Albuquerque city commissioner and then mayor. He displayed a deft touch at squeezing the federal government for urban-renewal and job-training grants and other federal aid. In 1972, he parlayed his popularity in the state's largest city into a seat in the Senate. The Budget Committee was just a luck-of-the-draw assignment; happenstance quickly elevated him to the committee's senior Republican position. In 1980, lightning struck when the Republicans swept into control of the Senate for the first time in twenty-eight years, riding to victory on the coattails of Ronald Reagan's landslide presidential victory. Domenici woke up the day after the election a committee chairman.

Suddenly, Domenici was in deep water. As Budget chairman in the GOP-controlled Senate, he was one of a handful of men (Finance Committee Chairman Dole, Appropriations Committee Chairman Hatfield, and Majority Leader Howard Baker were the others) who would be critical to Reagan's ambitious plans to cut taxes, build up defense, and somehow still balance the budget. The New Mexico grocer's son had grown up believing there was no free lunch, and Reagan's new religion of supply-side economics, which suggested that tax cuts would practically pay for themselves by supercharging the economy, made him uneasy. When candidate George Bush dubbed Reagan's policies "voodoo economics" early in the campaign, he was speaking for skeptics like Domenici. This was the start of a terrible, ongoing internal conflict. Instinctively, Domenici knew what he should do, but the political imperatives and his own colleagues continually told him to shut up, go along, wink at the numbers, and be a team player.

His first big test came almost immediately. Reagan had promised to balance the budget within four years, but early in 1981 the CBO and Domenici's own staff were projecting that instead of getting to a balanced budget by 1984, Reagan's proposals were more likely to leave a deficit of $70 billion or more at the end of the four years. Stockman desperately needed an economic forecast that was optimistic enough to legitimize Reagan's proposals. That put Domenici in a tough spot: He would have to vouch for any projections before the rest of his Senate colleagues, and to do that with any conviction, he had to be comfortable with the numbers.

Stockman went ahead with an optimistic economic forecast that was immediately and widely denounced as a "rosy scenario" that bent reality to fit Reagan's political needs. Domenici was so worried about being an accomplice to deceit that he warned Howard Baker he would resign as Budget chairman unless the numbers were changed before Reagan unveiled his budget in Congress in mid-February. But the majority leader would not solve the problem for him; if Domenici wanted better numbers, Baker told him, he would have to confront Stockman directly. Domenici blinked. Unsure of his own command of the numbers and unwilling to take on Stockman directly, he instead arranged a fight between surrogates: his own chief economist versus Stockman's. The economists fought to a draw, but Domenici lost. Stockman tweaked the forecast only slightly in Domenici's direction, leaving most of it intact; Domenici swallowed hard and went along.

Later that spring, Domenici was tested again. As the budget numbers predictably began to unravel, Stockman resorted to a desperate tactic to disguise $44 billion in deficits with what came to be called the "magic asterisk," a footnote to the budget that promised unspecified future savings. Domenici balked at first, protesting that the tactic was obvious flimflam. In a private meeting at the White House, the argument boiled down to whether to display the $44 billion "below the line" as a deficit or "above the line" as an asterisk denoting savings to come, as Stockman insisted. Domenici argued for honest budgeting: below the line. He had been braced by Steve Bell, his top aide, who told him that unless he held fast, "You'll go down in history as the only Budget Committee chairman who didn't know how to count." But at a key moment, Dole stepped in. "Put it above the line, Pete," he ordered. Domenici gave in again. He knew when the administration's policies were going astray, but in the clinches, when he had to choose between standing his ground or caving, he usually caved.

Gail Fosler, a top Domenici budget aide in the early 1980s, said those painful, draining fights with Stockman and Reagan profoundly affected Domenici. In the years that followed, she said, the Budget Committee chairman hardened his stance on the deficit and worked to make up for his early mistakes and displays of weakness. For example, he battled Reagan on defense spending and eventually helped force reductions that blunted and then reversed Reagan's extraordinary peacetime buildup. "In a way," said Fosler, who went on to become chief economist for the Conference Board, a business group, "the power of Domenici's opposition to Reagan on the deficit was born in his complicity with the Reagan policy early on. He had been a loyal—a reasonably loyal—supporter and a reasonably loyal instrument in enacting the president's program. But from then on, there were major confrontations."

———

Hardly anyone outside congressional budget circles remembered the details of the bitter 1981 budget wars anymore, but anyone who had lived through them the way Domenici had could never forget. When he saw the happy-face supply-side economics embodied in the House Republicans' Contract with America, it was déjà vu. The Contract promised to balance the budget while cutting taxes and increasing defense spending. Had no one learned anything? He had been swept along once already in a conservative economic movement with promises too good to be true; he wasn't about to repeat those mistakes. But still he could not help viewing the political revolution that Gingrich and the other House Republicans had engineered with a mixture of awe and jealousy. They had brilliantly channeled the public's disgust and frustration with Clinton and the Democratic Congress into a historic victory. Now Republicans believed they had a mandate to carry out their pledges to create a smaller, less intrusive government, to overhaul the welfare system, and to rein in Medicare and other entitlement programs that were fueling the deficit. Domenici didn't disagree.

But the House Republicans also wanted huge tax cuts: roughly $350 billion over seven years, including a $500-per-child family tax credit (to be available to families making as much as $200,000 a year), a 50 percent reduction in the capital gains tax, and a raft of generous business write-offs and depreciation schedules. Budget cutters like Domenici knew they were looking at a $1-trillion mountain of spending cuts to balance the budget; now House Republicans wanted to increase the size of the mountain by a third. Insanity, Domenici thought. "I believe the first responsibility to the future is to get a balanced budget," Domenici said in early 1995, laying down a marker. While he might eventually support modest tax relief for the middle class, he said, deficit reduction had to come first. "There is no commitment to any size tax-reduction plan in the Senate. We're clearly interested in what the House says and does, but everybody knows the senators are very concerned about the deficit." The hard-line tax cutters on the House side (and among his own Senate colleagues) might fume at him, but the Senate Budget chairman had just laid down the law.

But tax cuts had a logic and a momentum of their own. Polls repeatedly showed that Americans preferred deficit reduction to tax cuts, but House GOP leaders said the pollsters were asking the wrong questions. It wasn't, Would you prefer tax cuts or a balanced budget? It was, Would you prefer tax cuts *and* a balanced budget? They could have both.

There were, in fact, several compelling reasons to cut taxes, some political, some economic. The spending cuts would be painful, and tax cuts would help lessen the pain—an old budget trick. Carefully targeted tax cuts might help stimulate economic growth and job creation, but even sympathetic economists said the Republicans' $500-per-child tax credit (the single most expensive part of the tax package) would have no effect on growth. Privately, some Republican strategists were straightforward about why they were pushing the tax cuts so hard. Reason number one: The Christian right had helped make the Republican revolution, and the Christian right wanted family tax cuts; they would get them. Reason number two: Republicans had to do things that would define their party and differentiate them from Democrats. Republicans cut taxes, Democrats did not; if Democrats cut taxes a little, then Republicans would cut them a lot. Reason number three: House Republicans had promised tax cuts in the Contract with America.

Texas Republican Bill Archer, the radical tax cutter who had just taken over as brand-new chairman of the House's tax-writing Ways and Means Committee, warned his fellow Republicans that breaking their tax-cut pledge would be as self-destructive as President Bush's ill-fated decision to break his no-new-taxes pledge in 1990. "We ran on it, we signed it, and we'll do what we said we're going to do," Archer pronounced flatly.

In the Senate, though, Domenici's worries about tax cuts were shared by other moderates who were more concerned about balancing the budget than about making good on a House GOP campaign pledge. Packwood estimated that a dozen or more Senate Republicans, including a number of other committee chairmen, would vote against any GOP budget plan that was thrown out of balance by a large tax cut.

Even with so many Republican senators opposing the tax cuts, however, there was still a powerful countervailing conservative force in the Senate that had caught tax-cut fever from the House. Many of these senators were transplanted House members who shared in Gingrich's revolutionary fervor. The Senate's leading tax-cut proponent was Majority Whip Trent Lott of Mississippi, a media-savvy former House member who had won his leadership post by elbowing aside Alan Simpson of Wyoming, a more moderate Republican who had been Dole's right-hand man for years. And of course there was Phil Gramm, Dole's chief rival for the Republican presidential nomination and a persistent counterweight to Dole, who constantly pulled the majority leader to the right.

Taxes loomed as a central issue in the upcoming presidential primaries, and Gramm planned to use his uncompromising support of tax cuts as a crucial way of setting himself apart from his rival. Gramm, maneuvering to put the knife in Dole, told reporters that if the tax cuts failed in the Senate, Dole would be to blame.

Dole, like Domenici and Packwood, initially had doubts about the tax cuts. He, too, had spent years in the trenches trying to undo the deficit crisis wrought by Reagan's supply-side tax cuts, and he shared Domenici's suspicion of the House Republicans' promises of lower taxes and lower deficits. Early in the year, he told reporters there were no guarantees the Senate would follow suit in passing the heart of the House Contract, including the tax cuts. "We're going to let the coffee cool," he cracked. "In fact, we're going to let it get cold." Dole's rich disdain for the House upstarts and their frenetic agenda was often only thinly disguised. But as his presidential prospects brightened in the spring of 1995, he felt mounting pressure to appease his party's powerful right wing, and tax cuts were item number one on the conservatives' agenda. Dole had been badly outflanked on the tax-cut issue once before, losing the critical 1988 primary in taxphobic New Hampshire to George Bush when Bush painted him as someone who had fought to raise taxes before and would surely do so again.

Now he carefully recalibrated his image, signing the no-new-taxes pledge he had pointedly refused to agree to in 1988. Then, Dole had privately disparaged Bush for locking himself into such an inflexible position, but Bush had gone on to bury Dole and win the nomination. Dole would not make the same mistake again. If he had to sign the pledge he had once thought so unwise, he would do it. It was his last chance at the nomination; there was no clearer indication of how desperate he was to get it.

Now, with the loss of the balanced-budget amendment, it became imperative for Dole to get out in front of a large tax cut. In informal conversations with Domenici, Dole left little doubt about what he wanted. "He said more times than once, 'There's going to be room for tax cuts, isn't there?' " Domenici recalled. "'You're going to make room for it, aren't you?' "

———

By late March, Domenici had abandoned his earlier plan to make just a down payment on a balanced budget and opted to go all the way. Although he claimed he'd changed his mind on his own, convinced he'd take just as much heat for a package of cuts big enough to make a down payment as for a package big enough to get to zero, the decision was really never his to make. Once Gingrich ordered Kasich to go to zero in the House, the Senate had no choice but to go along as well. How could Domenici say balancing the budget was not possible if the House went ahead and did it? But he could still try to set the parameters of the package, and he announced that while he would propose a seven-year plan to balance the budget, his plan would not include a tax cut. "I believe that I can see daylight getting to a balanced budget," he said. "Anyone who wants to do more to pay for tax cuts can do that, but it may make it impossible to get to balance."

Domenici's warning did not make the Senate conservatives back off, however; they began drafting tax-cutting legislation of their own along the lines of the House plan. "Most Senate Republicans, like Republicans in the House, are committed to tax cuts," Trent Lott told reporters after a weekly Senate GOP policy luncheon at the Capitol. "I've never met a tax cut I didn't love." Under heavy pressure to say where he stood, Dole began to sign on with the tax cutters. "We're going to cut taxes," he said. "We're going to look at the capital gains area of reduction. We're going to look at tax credits. We're not backing away from the tax cut."

With this kind of pressure, it was beginning to seem unthinkable that Domenici could bring a budget resolution to the floor without at least some tax cuts attached. Domenici's dilemma was how to placate the conservative tax-cut zealots without compromising his own principles and alienating the moderates.

His solution was brilliant in its simplicity: He decided to hold out the promise of a future tax cut but make it contingent on the Republicans' fulfilling their promise to balance the budget. He would dangle a tax cut of unspecified dimensions, to be the reward for Congress's taking on the entitlement programs, cutting more deeply than before into spending for the day-to-day operations of government, shutting down hundreds of government programs and agencies, and doing all the other unpleasant chores necessary to achieve a balanced budget. "We wanted them to focus on the spending cuts before they got into the dessert," said Bill Hoagland, the Budget Committee's staff director.

It was Hoagland, a soft-spoken, Nordic-looking budget whiz, who first came up with the idea in January, while he and Domenici were sitting through the farewell testimony of Robert Reischauer, the outgoing director of the CBO. Reischauer, a Democrat who was nonetheless regarded as one of the most straightforward budget experts in Washington, was telling the Budget Committee members of the prospects of huge spin-off savings that would come if Congress made good on its pledge to balance the budget. The windfall would materialize in the form of reduced interest payments on the national debt and higher revenues that would come from a surge in economic growth triggered by lower deficits. An astounded Hoagland leaned over and whispered to Domenici, "Hey, boss, will you look at that number?" The CBO initially pegged this potential "fiscal dividend" at $140 billion through 2002. Later, in April, the agency raised its estimate to $170 billion. This was precisely half the size of the House Republicans' tax cut. As far as Domenici and Hoagland were concerned, that would be more than enough.

The idea had its shortcomings. Even under the best of circumstances, the vast majority of the fiscal dividend would not materialize until well after the 1996 election, too late to be claimed for tax cuts now, tax cuts that would do the Republicans some political good before the elections. Also, it was unlikely that Gingrich and the House Republicans would be satisfied with such a small package. But those were details to be worried about later, when House and Senate leaders finally sat down to iron out differences between their two budget plans. On February 15, Domenici took the idea to Dole, who liked the sound of it and encouraged him to keep working.

Domenici wanted to be careful about how he played his new fiscal-dividend card. Rather than parading the idea before the full committee, where conservatives as well as Democrats could take potshots at it, he quietly shopped it around, member to member, until, as Hoagland described it, "it took on a life of its own."

With the tax-cut problem solved for the moment, Domenici turned his full attention to hammering out the budget resolution. Balancing the budget on paper is a relatively simple thing to do. Congressional offices are littered with plans for eliminating the deficit, developed by groups ranging from the moderate Concord Coalition to the libertarian Cato Institute and the archconservative Heritage Foundation. Sometimes intriguing and innovative, the plans are for the most part politically implausible. Detailing $1 trillion or more in spending cuts is one thing; almost anyone with a list of federal programs can do that. Getting a majority of Congress to vote for them is quite another.

Domenici's real-world challenge was to forge a coalition of the eleven other Budget Committee Republicans—each with his own agenda—around a plan that would squeeze about $800 billion out of some of the most popular programs in the country (the balance would come from lower interest payments on the national debt, the happy by-product of lower deficits). The members of the Budget Committee represented the full range of interests in Congress, from big cities to rural communities, from the huge defense and aerospace industry to small businesses, from the nation's poor to the nation's wealthiest businesspeople and investors, from seniors anxious to protect their programs to young people clamoring for "generational equity" in entitlement programs.

Cutting spending alone would not be enough. To make good on the Republicans' promise, Domenici would also have to outline dramatic structural changes in government programs. Programs dating back to the 1930s New Deal and the 1960s Great Society would have to be given a complete overhaul. Whole Cabinet departments would be reorganized, scaled back, and in at least one or two cases, eliminated.

Working out the details was grueling. Domenici held about forty private meetings with committee members and Senate leaders, often huddling late into the night. Throughout, senators constantly pressed Domenici for major concessions on such hot-button issues as agriculture, defense, Medicare, student loans, and the earned-income tax credit for the working poor. In some cases, such as the deep cuts originally proposed for farm subsidies, he compromised to soften the blow for key senators.

He was far less accommodating with the defense hawks, however. The resolution he drafted closely paralleled Clinton's own defense budget and would drop defense spending from $270 billion in the current year to $263 billion in 1996 before allowing it to inch back up to $269 billion in 2002. Protectors of the defense establishment, men like Majority Whip Trent Lott, Armed Services Committee Chairman Strom Thurmond of South Carolina, and Arizona Senator John McCain, a former Navy pilot and Vietnam prisoner of war, objected to the spending dip in the middle years, which they derisively dubbed "the bathtub." But Domenici thought it preposterous to provide more money for defense than even the Pentagon and the Joint Chiefs of Staff were requesting—as the House was doing and as the Senate hawks wanted.

On April 5, the House overwhelmingly approved the GOP tax cuts, sparking renewed calls in the Senate for a comparable package. Gramm summoned reporters the next day to say that now that the House had taken the plunge, the Senate would be under immense pressure "to get with the program." But Packwood, the Finance Committee chairman, returned Gramm's salvo: "I've been down this road too often: tax cuts now, spending cuts later."

Packwood, a sixty-two-year-old veteran of a quarter century in the Senate, was perhaps the most adamant opponent of a tax cut. He had teamed up in 1986 with then House Ways and Means Committee chairman Dan Rostenkowski of Illinois to rewrite the federal tax code, lowering income tax rates and eliminating many costly tax loopholes. The House Republican plan would reopen some of these loopholes and also provide tax credits that would do little, if anything, to stimulate the economy.

Packwood's words still carried weight in Washington; after all, he chaired the committee that would have to write any new tax legislation. But his influence had waned considerably because of the Senate Ethics Committee's investigation of him on devastating charges of sexual and official misconduct. The Ethics Committee had spent two years probing allegations that, on at least eighteen occasions, Packwood had made unwelcome sexual advances toward women, including his own Senate employees. Once a commanding presence in the Senate, he had been reduced to pariah status, dodging reporters, working to head off public hearings on the sexual-advance charges, and generally hanging on by a thread.

The Budget Committee voted May 11 along party lines to send Domenici's budget plan to the floor. The resolution would freeze or reduce spending for most domestic programs except crime, dramatically scale back spending for welfare and nutrition programs, produce major savings and structural changes in Medicare and Medicaid, slash foreign aid by a quarter, and eliminate more than one hundred federal programs and agencies. Just as in the House GOP plan, more than 65 percent of the total cuts in Domenici's proposal were made in social-welfare programs for the poor, the young, and the elderly. The plan hit the target for balancing the budget by 2002, and as Domenici noted with pride, it did so without gimmicks. There were no magic asterisks or phony economic assumptions built into the Senate budget. Unlike the House version, which built the $170-billion fiscal dividend right into its calculations and took credit for the savings before they materialized, Domenici prudently kept the fiscal dividend in reserve. If the savings eventually appeared, they could be used for tax cuts. But he wasn't counting on them now to make his numbers add up.

Democrats were not as impressed with Domenici's handiwork. California Senator Barbara Boxer, a liberal Democrat, attacked the budget plan as a scandalous retreat from the government's traditional jobs of preserving the environment and helping the poor. "When I see it in writing, it's uglier than it sounded," she said. South Carolina Senator Ernest "Fritz" Hollings was suspicious of Domenici's tax strategy, arguing that it was nothing more than a placeholder for a much larger tax cut that Dole would insert later in the process. "We've got Gramm and his cabal after Dole, who is saying to his best of friends Domenici, 'You've got to save me, you've got to do this, you've got to do that,' " Hollings said in his deep Southern baritone.

In fact, once the budget resolution got to the Senate floor, Dole assumed control and began to give form to Hollings's prophecy. About two weeks before the floor vote on the budget resolution, Dole went on the CBS News program *Face the Nation* to declare that "we're going to have tax cuts. We're going to deal with capital gains rate reduction, some child-care credit," and so on. Dole was no longer talking about some vague, conditional, future tax cut but about a big tax cut *this year.*

The Senate rejected a move by Gramm to incorporate the full, $350 billion House tax cut, as twenty-three of the Senate's fifty-four Republicans sided with all the Democrats to say no. After that stinging rejection of the Senate's most ardent tax-cutters, Republicans grudgingly coalesced around an alternative blessed by Dole that would specifically earmark the $170-billion fiscal dividend for tax cuts. The difference between the wording of the amendment and Domenici's original plan was so slight that many reporters wrote it off as insignificant, but in fact the change was critical. Domenici's language—the dividend *may* be used for a tax cut—would have created only the possibility of cuts. Dole's compromise essentially changed just one word—*may* became *shall,* making tax cuts a certainty in the Senate and opening the way for him to negotiate larger cuts with Gingrich. The Senate gave final passage to the budget resolution, 57–42.

By the week of June 19, following more than three weeks of behind-the-scenes haggling by House and Senate Republican leaders, it was clear that whatever deal the conferees came up with would include an unconditional tax cut. The only question was how big. Domenici's months-long resistance began to collapse. It was as if the Budget chairman felt that he had done his duty in committee: Once the resolution reached the Senate floor, it was Dole's show. New Hampshire Republican Judd Gregg recalled that from the day the Budget Committee completed its work, the members generally assumed that a large tax cut would be part of the final House-Senate deal. No one seriously talked about trying to hold the line at $170 billion. Hollings had been right: In the crunch, Domenici, ever the loyalist, would back his leader.

One day during a chance encounter between Domenici and a reporter in the Capitol's subway, Domenici mused about the difficulties of resisting a tax cut in the current political climate. Asked whether he intended to continue fighting for a more modest tax cut, he paused and thought for a moment and then replied, "Look, you know that at some point I'm going to have to compromise on this."

Packwood's opposition also faded; he was battling for his political life amid the growing demand for hearings on his ethics problems, and Dole was a sympathetic ally. It was hard for Packwood to say no to Dole on a tax cut after the majority leader had gone to bat for him with the Christian Coalition, which along with other conservative groups had joined in the call for the Ethics Committee to hold public hearings. During a meeting with Christian Coalition leaders, Dole urged its executive director, Ralph Reed, to tone down the group's rhetoric, suggesting that in exchange he would guarantee eventual approval of the $500-per-child tax credit. "I think you're going to be happy with the tax plan, but if Packwood is bounced out of his chairmanship because of the ethics charges, we kind of go back to square one," Dole told Reed.

By now, the Senate was holding out for $230 billion in tax cuts while Gingrich and the House were insisting on $250 billion. With members anxious to get out of town for the July 4 recess, the House and Senate were stuck, a deceptively small $20 billion apart. House negotiators knew from their talks with hard-core House freshmen that the conservatives' comfort level was not much lower than $250 billion. On the other hand, Senate tax-cut opponents already thought they had moved an enormous distance by coming to $230 billion; they felt they had started not at $170 billion but at zero— technically, they had begun with no tax cuts at all, since all the cuts had been conditional.

In the end, negotiators knew that when the crunch came, the unpredictable House freshmen were more likely to rebel than were their more moderate brethren in the Senate. House leaders were willing to give ground to the Senate on spending—a little more on agriculture and education and a split of the House-Senate difference on defense. But Gingrich warned Dole in a private June 22 meeting that House leaders had to have a big tax-cut number or risk revolt among the freshmen.

Dole returned to his office and had Domenici and other Senate negotiators summoned to a meeting. Dole was hosting an ice-cream-social open house in his main office, so the meeting was moved to the back office of Sheila Burke, Dole's chief of staff and a key player in the deliberations. Dole was late for the meeting, so Burke asked where Domenici and the others stood. "We're still insisting on no more than $230 billion," Domenici told her. Burke, clearly exasperated, snapped, "That's not enough. We're going to have to have more." Soon Dole wandered in from the ice-cream party and asked for an update. He was anxious to wrap up the talks that afternoon, and he wanted the tax issue resolved now. When Domenici said they were still holding out for $230 billion, Dole seemed more agitated than Burke. "That will never pass," he said. "Even I wouldn't vote for that." With that, all remaining resistance faded, and Domenici and the others concurred with Dole on the need to move to at least $240 billion to close the deal. The members filed out of Burke's office with the understanding that the final number would be left to Dole.

Domenici told reporters on his way out that it might take another day to work out all the wrinkles, but Dole followed him out the door and contradicted his Budget Committee chairman, saying he wanted things wrapped up before the sun went down. Around 5:00 P.M., Dole marched into Gingrich's office and closed the door; fifteen minutes later he came out and muttered to reporters waiting outside that "I need my calculator," meaning Domenici and Hoagland. Gingrich needed his calculator, too, but Kasich was already at National Airport, waiting to board a plane home to Ohio. Fortunately, Kasich made one final call to the Capitol shortly before boarding his flight and was frantically ordered back. He returned just in time for the final deal.

When Domenici and Hoagland arrived at Gingrich's office, the Speaker handed them a piece of paper outlining the agreement. It showed a $245-billion tax cut, $5 billion more than Dole had offered. Domenici gazed at the paper for a moment, then looked up and said, "Okay, let's do it." Moments later Gingrich was out the door, gleefully joking with reporters and cameramen crowded outside. "You're gonna love the tax cut," the Speaker said to the well-paid journalists. The deal was done.

Chapter 3

ROSTY'S WILD RIDE

Could it be that balancing the budget wasn't so hard after all? At every step so far, the skeptics and the doubters had been wrong. The skeptics had said Republicans' willpower would wither once the balanced-budget amendment was defeated. Wrong: The loss of the amendment made the Republicans only more determined. Skeptics had said the House and Senate leaders would never be able to pass gimmick-free House and Senate budgets that got to zero. Wrong: They had done it with amazing ease, losing just a single GOP vote. Well, the skeptics had said, they may have done that, but they'll never get the House radicals and the Senate's old bulls to work out their deep differences over tax cuts. And now the Republicans had done that as well.

John Kasich and Pete Domenici were actually making this look easy. They had put together a huge but extraordinarily risky budget that broke a cardinal rule that most political experts thought had long ago been written in blood: Stay away from Medicare if possible; if you have to cut it, whack the doctors, hospitals, and other providers who deliver Medicare services; don't antagonize beneficiaries by raising their premiums or their copayments or cutting their services. The big GOP budget did hit providers hard, but to get all the savings they needed, Republicans had to go after beneficiaries as well, raising premiums and copayments and effectively cap-

ping the amount Medicare would provide, exposing seniors to the
uncertain mercies of the marketplace in ways government health
care had never done before.

But so far the seniors' groups had gone along. The backlash Democrats were hoping for had not materialized. The further Republicans got in the budget process, the more momentum they
developed. Things seemed to be taking on such an air of inevitabil-
ity that some began to wonder, What exactly was the big deal? Why
had the budget wars gone on for so long, taken so much energy,
sapped so much political goodwill, eaten up so many incumbents?
This didn't seem to be so tough.

To understand why all of this was in fact such a big deal—why it
took a transforming election, gritted teeth, and enormous political
willpower even to think about balancing the budget (and why the
Republicans still had plenty of hard work ahead and a great deal to
worry about)—it is important to remember that this has never been
easy, from the time when Alexander Hamilton and Thomas Jefferson sparred over the deficit in the days after the American Revolution to House and Senate floor fights over entitlements two hundred
years later. But to get a real sense of the dangerous passions the budget can stir up, it helps to go back to a sunny day in August 1989.
George Bush had been elected president the previous fall. The in-
famous budget summit that would engulf Washington and help end
Bush's presidency was still almost a year away. Congress was in the
midst of its traditional summer recess, and members were back
home, taking the pulse of their constituents. The House and Senate
were both still in Democratic hands, and the Democratic chairman
of the mighty House Ways and Means Committee, source of all Congress's tax bills and much of its health legislation, had gone back to
his Chicago district to try to put down a growing rebellion by an unlikely guerrilla group. What happened to Chairman Dan Rostenkowski that afternoon offered a harrowing lesson in the volatility
and danger of deficit politics.

The meeting at the Copernicus Senior Citizens Center on
Chicago's North Side had gone badly, and all Dan Rostenkowski
wanted now was to get out. The broad-shouldered sixteen-term con-

gressman had been locked in a room for nearly an hour with five senior citizen activists who had nothing for him but complaints, and the building's cooling system was no longer enough to dispel the combined effects of the warm August day outside and the relentless criticism inside. Rostenkowski chafed in his blue suit and ran his finger impatiently around the inside of his starched shirt collar.

The seniors, all of them members of Chicago elderly-rights groups, had been handpicked to meet with the Illinois Democrat as part of an arrangement to spare Rostenkowski a shouting match with the scores of elderly protesters waiting for him outside. The seniors were in a simmering rage over the new catastrophic-coverage program Congress had added to Medicare in 1988, a little over a year earlier. The new plan insured elderly citizens against the prolonged, wasting illnesses that commonly bankrupted them and their spouses before killing them. But to pay for it, Congress had added a new Medicare surtax that got bigger the more income a beneficiary had. And there was the problem.

Rostenkowski talked about increased benefits and dignity and old-age security, but all most of the seniors could see was the tax. Admittedly, this was a new wrinkle in the relationship between elderly citizens and the federal government, the notion that the wealthiest elderly should pay much of the cost of additional Medicare benefits. Seniors across the country had rebelled. Did farmers alone bear the cost of agriculture subsidies? No, they didn't; so why should retirees have to pay for their subsidies by themselves? Social-insurance benefits should be paid for by everybody, the activists at the Copernicus Center told the congressman sharply.

For anyone familiar with the near regal obeisance Rostenkowski received in Washington, this was an odd scene. As the immensely influential chairman of the House Ways and Means Committee, Rostenkowski customarily operated at the highest levels of Washington's power elite; he was a man who made deals with presidents and senators (this was five years before he would be indicted for misusing his office and would subsequently lose his bid for reelection). Colleagues sought his favor, lobbyists courted him, and staffers jumped to his commands, all with a deference that frequently veered into obsequiousness.

But not here, not today. Today Rostenkowski was smack in the middle of his gritty home turf, in the heart of the heavily Polish

American Eighth Congressional District he had represented for thirty-one years. To these people, he was no king, no committee chairman. He was just Danny, their longtime congressman, the guy who ran interference for them if the federal bureaucracy screwed up their benefits, the reliable pol they could count on to show up at the Pulaski Day Parade.

For Rostenkowski, this was a critical test. If he couldn't talk sense to people who had known him as their congressman for three decades, where could he make headway? At first, he tried gentle humor: As a sixty-one-year-old himself, he reminded them, he would soon be covered by Medicare, and he wanted as generous a program as possible. Then, as the meeting wore on, he tried to level with them. They were overreacting, he told them bluntly. The new law was a good thing, something that would provide them with far more insulation than they had now against the catastrophic financial costs of the chronic, wasting illnesses that so often were the fate of the elderly. Typically, the astronomical expense of care and treatment would ravage the elderly's savings and resources, forcing them to empty their bank accounts, sell their furniture, their cars, their homes, and the rest of a lifetime's accumulated possessions until they were sufficiently impoverished to qualify for Medicaid, the medical welfare program that would pay their hospital and nursing-home bills until they died. Is that what they wanted?

What seniors wanted, they had been telling Rostenkowski and other members of Congress for months, was what they had paid for with a lifetime of contributions to the Social Security and Medicare trust funds. They wanted their benefits, and they didn't want to have to pay more for them. Wasn't that the deal? Wasn't that what they had worked all their lives for?

Rostenkowski and other backers of the new law had a more fundamental concern, one that seniors usually shut their minds to. These were troubled times for the country, Rostenkowski believed. Year after year the federal government was running dangerously high deficits, as much as $300 billion a year, and programs like Medicare and Medicaid, those giant, self-perpetuating engines of deficit spending, had to be restrained, or the crisis would only get worse. It was time for better-off beneficiaries to stop treating the program like welfare for the rich. Medicare was a terrific deal for senior citizens. The elderly got hospital care in exchange for having paid a small payroll tax when they were working; for doctor visits, they paid a modest monthly premium equal to about one quarter of the actual cost of the insurance, with the balance picked up by taxpayers. Even with the new surtax, it was still a great deal. The wealthiest beneficiaries, who would pay the highest tax rate, still stood to get far more in benefits than they ever paid into the program in payroll taxes, just as they did with Social Security.

But just as with their Social Security benefits, few of Rostenkowski's critics understood the math. Though both programs were in fact huge transfers of money from working Americans to retirees and from the better off to the less well off, politicians almost never dared explain the issue that way. The elderly had long ago come to the unshakable belief that everything they got came from the contributions they made during their working lives, and the idea that they should be forced to pay again for what they had already "bought" with their contributions struck them as pure theft. No wonder they were mad: Lobbying groups had fanned their anger with a shrill direct-mail campaign that played on the fear that their tenuous fixed incomes would be shrunk. In some cases, the letters deliberately led low-income beneficiaries, who would actually pay no tax, to believe they would pay the same high tax expected of coupon-clipping Medicare recipients. Not true—but dislodging that idea once it had become fixed in the seniors' minds was proving impossible.

Rostenkowski, who had helped write the law himself, tried to explain to the activists that no one at the Copernicus Center made enough money to require him or her to pay anything approaching the maximum $800 a year the richest elderly person would have to pay in additional taxes. But Jerry Prete, sixty-nine, a retired Catholic Charities social worker, insisted that was not true. "It wasn't the richest people—people making ten thousand dollars would pay the eight hundred dollars," he said later. "We were talking about— retired union workers, retired shopkeepers, retired clerks would be paying for that program." Prete and the others had brought along their own CPA to back their claims with numbers. Rostenkowski could not convince them they were wrong. Around and around they went, making no progress.

When the meeting at last broke up, nothing had been resolved. Rostenkowski and the two aides who had accompanied him walked

out of the stuffy room and into the Copernicus Center's large dining hall, working their way through a thickening crowd toward the
front door. The first TV cameras caught Rostenkowski here, and on
the news that evening they showed a man clearly uncomfortable and
anxious to be gone. The congressman was hoping somehow to avoid
getting stuck in a crowd of about 150 seniors, some carrying signs
that said ROTTENKOWSKI, who had been waiting impatiently for him
throughout the private meeting.

But what had begun as a bad day was about to get much worse.
Just as the congressman was trying to get out, another group of one
hundred or so retirees was pushing into the center for a free lunch
of hot dogs and baked beans provided by the city. The dining area
was now taking on a confused, unsettled air. Some of the old-timers
recognized Rostenkowski and began to applaud him. "That's
Danny," one said. "He's one of us." But the applause changed to
boos when their representative brushed past them, refusing to stop
and answer questions. "Talk to us! Talk to us! You work for us!"
somebody shouted. Then the crowd's simmering anger hit the boil-
ing point. Angry, insulting shouts erupted. People screamed boos at
him. "Liar!" "Chicken!" In the congressman's wake, TV cameras
found raging faces. "We think that this man is inhuman!" sputtered
an elderly man, his face red with hatred. As Rostenkowski and his
aides pushed through the exit, a knot of furious men and women
surged outside behind him.

By now, Rostenkowski had begun to sense that something was
wrong, and it was beginning to dawn on his aides that the congressman's troubles had not been spontaneous. In fact, a rough script was
unfolding. Two days before the meeting, network correspondents in
Washington had been tipped off that something would happen at
the Copernicus Center, and they had their Chicago affiliates there
to cover the congressman's appearance. As Rostenkowski looked
anxiously up and down North Milwaukee Avenue for the car that
had brought him, aides felt instinctively that their boss had been
lured into a trap. As it turned out, this *was* a setup, devised by the seniors' groups and abetted by the media, and Rostenkowski's tough-
looking, deeply lined—and now heavily perspiring—face would be
flashed across TV screens across the country that night to illustrate
the story of an arrogant, powerful member of Congress who had

brushed off aggrieved senior citizens' concerns about their Medicare benefits.

Rostenkowski began to move forward again, heading for the Chevy Caprice an aide had waiting for him, engine running. But he had several yards to go and a gauntlet of TV reporters to run. "Is this the first time you've ever been chased out of a meeting?" one of them asked, poking a microphone at him.

Disgust and anger were bright on Rostenkowski's face, and his voice failed to conceal his contempt for the question. "You think I was chased out of that meeting?" he said.

"It sure looks like it," said the reporter.

"These people are nuts," the congressman muttered as he pried open the door to the car, got in, and told his driver to get the hell out of there. The driver blew the horn and began inching away from the curb, but the furious knot of sign-wielding protesters encircled the car and blocked the way, forcing the driver to lurch to a stop. Rostenkowski was trapped.

When the driver tried to inch the car forward again, a tiny, white-haired woman leaned forward over the hood. "You hurt her!" screamed a man. "You're trying to hit her! You're trying to run her down!" Panic and fury swept through the crowd, redoubling their rage. Screaming, the protesters bashed the car with their fists and their placards.

The woman leaning over the car was Leona Kozien, and she would later become a minor celebrity, Rostenkowski's chief tormentor of the day. With her rose-colored, heart-shaped sunglasses and a placard that said SENIORS FOR REPEAL OF THE CATASTROPHIC ACT, she hardly looked like a match for the beefy congressman inside his heavy sedan. But she was not to be denied. On an impulse, she began slowly climbing up the hood. Kozien, a woman who had never before gotten involved in any kind of demonstration, now was spread-eagled on the hood of the Caprice. She continued to inch her way forward until her face was pressed up against the windshield. Peering through the glass, she was eyeball to eyeball with the by now badly shaken Rostenkowski. "I was a little nervous," Kozien later told reporters who clamored to interview her. "But I could see through the car window that he looked more afraid than I was."

With no other way out, Rostenkowski sprang from the car and

started half-running, half-walking up North Milwaukee Avenue. "There he goes!" somebody in the crowd shouted. "Coward! Coward!" shouted others. "Recall!" "Impeach him!" It was a breathtaking scene: Dan Rostenkowski, son of a prominent Chicago alderman, a onetime protégé of the late and beatified mayor Richard J. Daley, a thirty-one-year veteran of the House of Representatives who had served under eight presidents going back to Dwight D. Eisenhower, the chairman of a committee that wrote the tax laws of the land, and a political comer once touted as the next Speaker of the House— now he was just a frightened man being chased down a street in his own city by a gang of enraged septuagenarians.

The TV crews hustled to keep up. With the cameras on him, Rostenkowski strove for a measure of dignity and damage control. "I don't think they understand what the government's trying to do for them," he puffed; "I don't think they understand what's going on." Then he cut through a gasoline station, broke into a sprint, and joined up again with his driver, who had somehow managed to extricate the car from the crowd and drive it around the block. The driver had opened all four doors, to give the congressman as many ways as possible of getting into the car. "Let's get the hell outta here," Rostenkowski gasped as the driver gunned the engine. Tires screeching, the car shot away as the elderly protesters jeered in rage and triumph.

———

Barely three months after Rostenkowski's hellish ride, Congress reacted as if it, too, had been humiliated, jeered, and chased down the street. In November 1989, in abject retreat, the House and Senate voted overwhelmingly to repeal all but a few vestiges of the catastrophic-coverage legislation they had passed with great fanfare just a year and a half earlier. Members who thought they'd been doing the right thing—providing critical benefits for the elderly in a fiscally responsible way—were shocked and bitter. "There's a very sour feeling among many congressmen," said California Democratic Congressman Henry Waxman, an author of the plan. On Capitol Hill, the specter of Rostenkowski running down the street, chased by angry elderly protesters, was etched as an indelible object lesson in the minds of his colleagues: Tamper with entitlement programs such as Medicare or Social Security, and you risked constituent fury, interest-group rage, even public humiliation.

On the other hand, though, what choice did they have? Members of Congress were in a bind, whipsawed between the nation's conflicting convictions about what its government ought to do. The nation's bighearted impulses to help its sick, its elderly, and its poor and underprivileged had led to the creation of Medicare, Social Security, child welfare, and other entitlements in the first place. Just microscopic pieces of the budget when they were begun, they had mushroomed until they now accounted for half of every dollar the federal government spent. Despite that large and growing cost, however, recipients had become convinced they were *entitled* to benefits no matter what their need and no matter what the strain on the budget. Middle-class Americans who traditionally had gotten little or no direct aid from the federal government had gradually become some of its biggest and most insistent claim holders. "Rights" to increasingly expensive retirement and health-care benefits that had not existed until relatively recently in the nation's history had quickly calcified into the most unshakable features of the American social compact.

Now the federal government was stuck with generous programs that increasingly outran the means to pay for them. Social Security and Medicare recipients could typically expect to receive far more benefits during their retirement than they paid for during their employment. For a married worker who retired in 1995 and his or her nonworking spouse, benefits amounted to a quarter of a million dollars more than the worker and his or her employer contributed in taxes, with interest. Social Security alone would pay that worker as much as three times the value of a lifetime's payroll taxes and interest; Medicare benefits would amount to as much as four times taxes, premiums, and interest.

To pay out benefits like these and still keep Social Security and Medicare in the black, Congress had to keep raising the payroll tax, the once-tiny levy that paid for Social Security and Medicare. The payroll tax gradually got so big that it wiped out the Reagan-era income tax cuts for middle-income Americans, whose total tax burden actually grew during Reagan's first term in office despite the celebrated cuts in income tax rates. By the end of the 1980s, the payroll tax had grown so big that two thirds of American families were paying more payroll taxes than income taxes.

But because Americans balked at paying ever higher federal taxes, Congress gradually shrank other taxes proportionately and began to starve the rest of the budget. From the administration of John F. Kennedy to the present day, the payroll tax has shot up from 17 percent of the federal tax burden to almost 40 percent of it. Meanwhile, corporate taxes dropped to half the share they had accounted for a generation earlier.

All that squeezing has kept the federal tax burden roughly constant, at about 18 or 19 percent of the size of the nation's economy (described in economic jargon as the gross domestic product, or GDP). But spending has not sat still; voters have demanded more entitlements, more aid to education, more highways, more federal prisons, and more of everything else the federal government provides. In Kennedy's day, the government spent about 19 percent of GDP, but by the mid-1970s, entitlements and other federal spending increased the share to 22 percent of GDP, and it has generally fluctuated between 22 and 23 percent ever since. Measured against taxes of 18 to 19 percent of GDP, that leaves a gap of roughly 3 to 5 percent—the annual deficit. Gradually, as the problem persisted despite repeated attempts to fix it, the deficit grew to dominate the national political debate.

Why not simply cut spending until it equals taxes? The last time the government consistently spent about 19 percent of GDP was in the early 1960s, before the advent of Medicare and Medicaid, before automatic cost-of-living adjustments (COLAs) for Social Security, before food stamps, before aid for higher education, and before the government did a lot of the things voters take for granted today.

On the other hand, it would be just as difficult to raise taxes until they equaled spending. Jimmy Carter let taxes drift up to about 20 percent of GDP and gave Ronald Reagan a critical opening to challenge and unseat him. Voter pressure has helped keep the total federal tax burden at 19 percent of GDP or less for most of the last generation.

Critics constantly denounce Congress for spending money on this or that boondoggle, but members are usually responding to constituent demands. A farmer surely thinks urban mass transit is a waste of money, just as city dwellers wonder why they should be taxed to pay for farm subsidies. In the best tradition of logrolling, the cost of agriculture subsidies is food stamps and bus and subway subsidies, and vice versa. "There is nothing in the federal budget that got there by accident, nothing that parachuted in from Mars," said Massachusetts Democratic Congressman Barney Frank one April day in 1992 when House and Senate members were gnashing their teeth over how to compromise on yet another budget-cutting plan. "Everything in the budget represents a substantial constituency."

That would help explain why getting anything out once it's in is so hard to do and why members of Congress and presidents tie themselves in knots year after year, wrestling with a seemingly endless succession of budget plans. There have been seven such plans over the last fifteen years alone, and while the vagaries of long-term spending projections make it impossible to estimate accurately how much those packages have shaved off intervening deficits, a conservative guess is that they have combined to make the national debt as much as $2 trillion smaller than it would have been had Congress done nothing. But economic downturns, the defense boom of the 1980s, entitlements that grew like weeds, and the refusal of American voters to wean themselves from middle-class benefits or tax themselves enough to pay for them had all combined to eat up all that deficit reduction, with a dismal result: chronic deficits of $100 billion to $200 billion or more—as former White House budget director David Stockman used to say, "as far as the eye can see." But things would have been unimaginably worse had those successive budget deals not been made, and the struggle has certainly been a compelling one, with moments of nobility and stupidity, violence and compassion, greed and selflessness, honor, betrayal, courage, and sacrifice—the indispensable themes of great novels and real life. Who would have thought all this drama could be found in the deficit?

The fight has been going on now with increasing intensity for the last two decades, bringing presidents and parties into office with great plans and promises and driving them out humbled, failed, and rejected. The notion that there is some easy fix to this intractable national problem is demonstrably wrongheaded, but politicians prosper by offering such snake oil anyway. How else to explain the national thrill when Texas billionaire Ross Perot assured national TV audiences in 1992 that he could slash the deficit down to zero by getting tough with tax cheats, foreign allies, and rich people who got Social Security benefits they didn't need. A balanced budget, he bragged, "and you haven't even broken a sweat."

If only it were that easy. In fact, though, Americans and their fore- bears have been wrestling with debt and deficits for more than three centuries, with no easy resolution in all that time. Just in the two hundred plus years since the United States formally became a na- tion, it has run yearly deficits an average of about half the time (more in the twentieth century, less in the nineteenth), building up and only occasionally whittling down a substantial national debt. In its entire history, the United States has been debt free for exactly two years—1834 and 1835—and the Herculean effort it took to do that helped trigger a nasty recession that pushed the country right back into debt again.

How did a nation with such a profoundly Calvinist regard for the evils of debt become such a wanton debtor and get itself so deeply in hock? And why have the prodigious efforts of the last twenty years failed to get the country out? A satisfactory answer begins not with Gingrich or Clinton or Bush or even Ronald Reagan but with the first unnamed government official who, in a moment of absolute desperation, ran a deficit. In 1690, the provincial government of the American colony of Massachusetts had rounded up troops, sent them off to fight the French for the king of England, and now had no ready funds with which to pay their salaries. The government could not possibly raise enough taxes on short notice from property owners to pay the tab. But the troops were armed, angry, and on the verge of mutiny. What to do?

Thus began the first recorded instance of deficit spending. The provincial government issued paper money, redeemable for gold at a later date, in effect borrowing against the taxes its citizens would eventually pay. The scheme worked, and the mutiny was defused, but a dilemma that would vex Massachusetts and the rest of the na- tion for the next three centuries was born. Colonial Massachusetts and, eventually, every other colonial government found they could meet their obligations in difficult times by spending more than they raised in revenues. That gap between taxes and spending—filled for the moment with paper money—was the deficit. From colonial times to the present, Americans have viewed these deficits with deep ambivalence: profligate, irresponsible, and dangerous—yes; but also a useful tool and a necessary evil in times of crisis.

Even the profoundly moral Founding Fathers who fought for independence in the 1770s ran the war on credit. Deficit spending took off during the Revolutionary War, when the Continental Congress issued $200 million or more in paper currency called continentals and the newly formed states floated a like amount of paper. "Congress stuffed the maw of the Revolution with paper money," wrote one historian, and when it was over, the new nation was left with combined federal and state debts of about $77 million, a laughable sum today but stupendous enough at the time to touch off a bitter debate about what to do. The ensuing argument revealed a deep split in American beliefs about the right way to handle the nation's finances, a fundamental rift that persists to this day.

Then as now politicians argued bitterly over how to divide economic authority between the federal government and the states, whether to allow the federal government to run deficits or force it to stick strictly to balanced budgets, and whether to spend federal money on "investments" to benefit the common good. The debate was shaped by two of the most dominating of the nation's founders, Alexander Hamilton and Thomas Jefferson.

Hamilton was a remarkable figure—brilliant, aristocratic, charming—who arrived in New York City an unknown, out-of-wedlock alien from the West Indies and made his way to the upper reaches of American politics by the time he was twenty-five. Despite the deep anti-British sentiment that guided the Revolution, Hamilton did not disguise his unabashed admiration for the way the British had built themselves into a world power with the leverage of public debt. He thought a strong central government made much more sense than a loose-knit group of fractious and semi-autonomous states, and he believed that well-managed borrowing could lift the nation from economic insignificance to real economic power.

Jefferson couldn't have disagreed more. An agrarian where Hamilton was an aristocrat, at ease with farmers, frontiersmen, and laborers when Hamilton preferred the company of bankers and businessmen, Jefferson was viscerally suspicious of a powerful federal government and fiercely opposed to the borrowing that could make it thrive. He didn't like moneylenders and middlemen, and unlike Hamilton he shared the populist view that a national debt only enriched wealthy speculators while making life tougher for working Americans. At the heart of Jefferson's opposition to a large national debt was his conviction that it would foster a voracious and "corrupt" central government, prey to all the moral decay that infected debt-ridden European governments in general and the British government in particular. In a letter to a friend in 1798, in which he argued for the addition of a balanced-budget amendment to the Constitution, Jefferson declared (in a passage echoed in speeches often made by House and Senate Republicans in 1995 and 1996) that state governments were "the very best in the world" whereas the federal government had become "arbitrary" and had "swallowed more of the public liberty than even that of England."

For Jefferson and the Jeffersonian Democrats who embraced his views for the next two centuries, the idea that the federal government should balance its budget was just as important a philosophical ideal as a fiscal policy—probably more so. A balanced budget symbolized natural harmony, Calvinist thrift, and the avoidance of corruption, giving it a powerful moral aura that has resonated throughout American history and continues to do so just as powerfully today. At its core, the balanced-budget ideal has much less to do with economics than with moral rectitude, which is what makes it such a potent political force.

Government policies and national attitudes toward annual deficits and national debt were ambivalent from the start and have remained so ever since. Hamilton, the nation's first Treasury secretary, borrowed more money after the Revolution. When Jefferson was elected president in 1800 and took control of fiscal policy, he reversed course, balancing the budget and paying down the national debt during all eight years he held office. Despite his earlier rhetoric, though, Jefferson did not press Congress for a balanced-budget amendment. And while he lowered the debt (from about $81 million to $57 million), he did not eradicate it. In fact, it was Jefferson who added to the national mortgage with the $15-million Louisiana Purchase, a textbook example of the value of wise deficit financing—and at about four cents an acre, a deal too good to pass up.

Frugality governed the federal budget right up until the War of 1812, when deficits suddenly shot out of control for the same reason they would do so again and again for much of the next two centuries. From the Revolution onward, wars were always an acceptable reason to abandon any attempt to balance the budget. Each new conflict forced the country to at least double or triple previous federal spending, quickly outrunning the nation's ability or willingness to raise taxes high enough to conduct the fighting on a pay-as-you-go basis. When the conflicts were over, the nation would be left with astronomical, once undreamed of debt.

The Civil War was orders of magnitude worse. Deficits, never bigger than $31 million before the war, catapulted into the hundreds of millions and rose to nearly $1 billion in 1865.

But in the same pattern that governed the aftermath of almost every war the nation has fought, fiscal policy returned to frugality again as soon as the conflict was over. When Ulysses S. Grant rode away after signing the peace treaty at Appomattox Court House in 1865, one thing was foremost on his mind: What now? his aide asked. Now, Grant said, we must muster out these soldiers in order to bring down the government's expenditures.

Government spending had risen by a factor of twenty by the last year of the war; now it dropped sharply, to less than half, then to a third, and finally to less than a quarter of what it had been in 1865. A limited government that offered no entitlements but veterans' benefits kept a lid on spending for most of the next fifty years. Throughout, deficits were rare, and in 1916, on the eve of the First World War, the nation's accumulated debt was insignificant—just 3 percent of the size of the nation's economy.

This way of measuring the size of debt and deficits—comparing them to the size of the overall economy (or GDP)—is crucial. Dollar amounts get thrown around all the time, but without context they are meaningless. The national debt is like a homeowner's mortgage: What's affordable depends on how much the homeowner makes. A $100,000 mortgage might be a crushing burden for a young person just a few years out of college, but it could be a light load for that same person thirty years later, after his or her income has grown. The important thing to know when talking about the size of the debt or the deficit is *compared to what?* The GDP percentage answers that question instantly.

Policymakers argue endlessly about the right amount of debt for the nation to carry, but there is no simple answer. The national debt on the eve of the Great Depression, in 1929, was a comparatively small 17 percent of GDP, seemingly no problem. In 1946, at the end of the Second World War and the beginning of the greatest economic boom of the twentieth century, it was 114 percent of GDP, a staggering amount. Amid the fairly healthy economy of 1996, the nation was carrying a debt of about 50 percent of GDP. The size of the debt is clearly no guarantee of economic performance, but debate fixates on it nonetheless. Some politicians even advocate paying it all off, though this is little more than a dream. As hard as it is to balance the budget, it verges on absurdity to imagine that we could do that *and* run enough budget surpluses to pay off everything we have borrowed—or even a substantial chunk of it.

The United States paid off its debt once, more than 160 years ago, when Andrew Jackson became the only president ever to make the United States debt free. The nation's fiscal policy has never been so influenced by the personal financial disasters of one man. As a young lawyer and businessman, Jackson had sold some property to another businessman on credit. When the buyer could not keep up with the payments, he was sent to debtor's prison, where he died. Jackson himself was nearly ruined when the buyer could not pay him, and he carried with him forever after a loathing of debt and credit, public or private. When he ran for president, Jackson declared the debt a "national curse" and promised he would eradicate it if elected.

When he took office in 1829, he was as good as his word. The nation had already been running surpluses in the aftermath of the War of 1812, and Jackson made those surpluses even bigger, by forcing the states to take over payment for "internal improvements," such as roads, canals, bridges, ports, and so on (shifting spending to the states has always been a popular way to shrink the federal deficit). From 1829 to 1834, Old Hickory drove down the national debt from some $49 million to virtual zero. For two glorious years—1834 and 1835—the nation was rid of all the interest-bearing debt it had run up during its two wars and fifty-eight years of existence, leaving less than $38,000 in miscellaneous obligations. This remains the only time in all of U.S. history that the nation was effectively debt free.

Meanwhile, though, the state governments that Jefferson had declared such engines of perfection were doing what the federal government was not: borrowing, often at reckless levels, to finance the highways, bridges, and other internal improvements that Jackson had forced them to pay for (an early example of what 1990s' politicians would criticize as "unfunded mandates"). An economy wobbling on a precarious structure of state-bank credit finally collapsed in the Panic of 1837, which ushered in a bleak, seven-year depression that sobered state governments and led virtually all of them to rewrite their constitutions in the 1840s to impose balanced-budget requirements on themselves.

Some economists argue that the fiscal privations required to pay off the debt—or even just to balance the budget—can be dangerous to the economy. Indeed, the years leading up to the Great Depression were marked by the same sort of fiscal Calvinism that Jackson had insisted on almost a century earlier. Immediately after the First World War, the United States tightened its budget, ran eleven back-to-back surpluses, and lowered the debt from $25 billion to less than $17 billion. But the payoff for all this righteousness was not the sustained economic boom that budget balancers always expect. Instead, on an October day in 1929, the bottom dropped out of the stock market and out of the American economy. Almost overnight the nation descended into an economic and social nightmare, the worst crisis in its history. The last surplus the nation would see for the next sixteen years came and went in 1930. The economy was sliced almost in half. More than a million families had their mortgages foreclosed and lost their homes. Nine million savings accounts simply vanished in bank failures. A quarter of the workforce was laid off. Farms were destroyed. Men, women, and children lived in the streets. For a time, the nation seemed to be on the brink of revolution.

Today even rabid deficit hawks accept the idea that trying to eliminate the deficit during an economic downturn is exactly the wrong thing to do. It is widely agreed that government spending should expand to help lessen the impact of bad times. But that was a lesson the nation learned during the Depression, and then only after years of futilely and destructively struggling to balance the budget—widely believed at the time to be the proper cure. President Herbert Hoover increased public-works spending in the early stages of the crisis, but he backed off when the deficit reappeared in 1931 and 1932. Democratic presidential candidate Franklin Delano Roosevelt attacked Hoover as a spendthrift and campaigned in 1932 on promises to slash government spending and balance the budget. Although FDR is popularly thought of now as a free-spending president, he did not start out that way, and he never fully embraced the extraordinary fiscal pump priming advocated by English economist John Maynard Keynes.

Until Keynes, the commonly accepted economic wisdom was that recessions would eventually correct themselves when pent-up demand finally built up enough to burst forth and reignite the economy. That theory failed spectacularly during the Great Depression, when demand died and simply failed to revive. Traditional economists were at a loss as to what to do. Keynes's medicine was simple: massive federal spending, as much as it took for as long as it took to artificially stimulate demand and get the economy going again. Keynes couldn't have cared less about what form the spending took; he only half jokingly recommended burying jars full of money and paying people to dig them up. The point was to overcome the terrible inertia, whether that took, in his words, "pyramid-building, earthquakes, even wars."

Keynes's prescription required letting go of any hope of balancing the budget, but FDR could not do that. He took less ambitious steps and pulled back too soon: When the economy began to poke its head up in 1933, Roosevelt tried to reduce spending by cutting veterans' benefits and federal salaries. He warned Congress that "too often in recent history, liberal governments have been wrecked on the rocks of loose fiscal policy." FDR's advisers put enormous pressure on him to stay true to his balanced-budget pledge: His own budget director resigned in 1934 to protest the deficit, insisting that the "immediate fate of Western civilization" hung on FDR's willingness to balance the budget.

When the economy seemed to be recovering in 1937, Roosevelt grew more concerned about inflation than unemployment and laid out new plans to cut federal spending. "I have said fifty times that the budget will be balanced for the fiscal year 1938," he said. "If you want me to say it again, I will say it either once or fifty times more." But the economy collapsed yet again, and Roosevelt finally yielded to a limited form of Keynesianism, pushing spending higher in 1939 and 1940 than it had been since its wartime peak in 1919.

The crucial legacy of this era was not FDR's public-works spending or relief projects, however, but the first big wave of entitlement programs. Reacting to bank failures, massive unemployment, and a shocking rise in poverty among the nation's children and elderly, FDR persuaded Congress to enact the first strands of the national safety net. Deposit insurance for banks and savings institutions came first in 1933, followed in 1935 by unemployment insurance and Social Security, which was aimed primarily at retirees but also included a small program to protect needy, fatherless children (this subsequently became Aid to Families with Dependent Children [AFDC], long the keystone of the modern welfare system).

In the meantime, though, the nation was preoccupied with struggling out of the Depression, which did not happen for good until the onset of the Second World War. Keynes was right: The gigantic, deficit-financed spending boom that came with worldwide war healed the U.S. economy. It also produced the largest deficits in modern history.

In the two decades before the war, the federal budget hovered between $3 billion and $9 billion a year; within four years, the nation was spending ten times as much: more than $90 billion a year in 1944 and 1945. There was no way to tax Americans enough to pay for this all at once, and the deficits were staggering. Measured against the economy, no deficit from the end of the Civil War to today comes anywhere close to those the nation ran to fight and defeat fascism. When the war was finally over, the nation's publicly held debt had shot up from $43 billion to $242 billion. For the first and only time in modern history, the national debt was larger than the entire national economy: 114 percent of GDP. If all that borrowing was going to have an evil effect, it would surely have happened then.

But what happened next was extraordinary. A feared postwar depression never materialized. Instead, the economy boomed as consumer demand, constrained by years of economic depression and war, finally found an outlet. And for the first time in its history, the nation gave up trying to run budget surpluses and abandoned the idea of paying off the debt.

While there were fewer and fewer budget surpluses (three in the 1940s, three in the 1950s, two in the 1960s, and none after that), the deficits that did occur in the first quarter century after the war were almost all small ones, which kept new borrowing to a minimum. The booming growth in the economy easily raced ahead of the tiny growth in the national debt, and as the economy got larger, the debt became comparatively smaller even though it was still growing when measured in dollars. By 1962, the debt was down from its wartime high of 114 percent of GDP to about 45 percent, the same as it had been before the war, in 1940. In effect, a growing economy had allowed the nation to "pay off" the entire war debt in the sixteen years from 1946 to 1962. By 1974, the national debt had come all the way down to 24.5 percent of GDP, the lowest it had been since the early years of the Depression.

The twenty-nine years from the end of the war to 1974 were a critical period in U.S. economic history and convincing proof that balanced budgets are not a prerequisite for a strong economy or a reduction of the nation's debt. Despite the succession of small but persistent budget deficits, the nation's debt load steadily fell—*when measured against the growing economy.* Meanwhile, by virtually all classic economic indicators, economic growth from 1947 to 1974 was spectacular. The size of the economy nearly quintupled, and worker productivity grew so strongly that the U.S. standard of living doubled in twenty-seven years. To get a sense of just how stunning that was, consider that doubling our standard of living now takes almost 270 years.

John F. Kennedy ran for president in 1960 as a fiscal hawk and a budget balancer. But the new president, in the words of biographer Richard Reeves, "had come to office in the great tradition of American presidents, more or less blissfully ignorant about economics." JFK's economic advisers quickly convinced him that deficits were not so awful; economist Walter Heller taught Kennedy the concept of the "full-employment deficit," the idea that the government should deficit-spend in times of less than full employment as a way of giving the economy enough gas to get it back to full speed.

That sounded good to Kennedy, who wanted to strengthen the soft economy he had inherited from President Eisenhower. "Everybody talks about our deficit," he said to a friend. "Everyone wants us to cut spending. They don't seem to understand that it's the deficit, the spending, that's keeping the economy pumped up. I love that deficit." Under pressure from Heller, Kennedy took a further stimulative step, pressing Congress for large tax cuts, something both Presidents Harry Truman and Dwight Eisenhower had consistently resisted. Passed by Congress and signed by President Lyndon Johnson three months after Kennedy's November 1963 assassination, those tax cuts were then the largest in history. Kennedy and his advisers had sold them based on the notion that they would so stimulate the economy that they would ultimately produce more revenue than they lost, in effect paying for themselves. This was precisely the argument that Ronald Reagan and the supply-siders would use to justify their own huge tax-cut proposals almost twenty years later.

This is a murky area, where the truth is much more a matter of faith than it is subject to irrefutable proof. Most economists scoff at the supply-siders' argument. Yes, the Kennedy-Johnson tax cuts were followed by a surge in economic growth and a commensurate increase in tax revenues. Most mainstream economists insist this had more to do with the steady growth in the money supply or the increased consumer demand and heated-up economy that resulted from the tax cuts—classic Keynesian "demand-side" stimulus. Supply-siders say no; it was because business got big tax cuts that increased investment incentives, and wealthy individuals got their top tax rates cut from 90 percent to 71 percent, increasing their incentive to invest the money that would no longer be taxed away. Who's right? "Economists do not surely know the answer to this question," wrote economist Herbert Stein, chairman of President Nixon's Council of Economic Advisers, who personally declared that he found the supply-side claim "weak."

This spat might seem largely irrelevant to national fiscal policy, but it was a dispute that would eventually prove enormously important. A seductive idea was now loose—that tax cuts (something that politicians love to make but that their fiscal consciences are forever warning them they cannot afford) were now somehow magically okay since they could pay for themselves. The great supply-side debate was still a decade away, however. For now, the immediate effect of the Kennedy-Johnson tax cuts was to give policymakers the dangerous delusion that they had at last found the magic key to reliably managing the economy, which made anything seem possible. The nation could have both "guns and butter," in President Johnson's memorable phrase: It could begin ambitious Great Society programs while fighting a war halfway around the world, in Vietnam.

By now, the nation had run deficits almost constantly since the end of the Second World War, but they were so small (an average of less than 1 percent of GDP) that they seem almost inconsequential in comparison with what was to come. Nonetheless, debate raged over keeping them in check, especially in 1968, at the peak of the Vietnam War, when expenses outran revenues by more than $25 billion, or 3 percent of GDP, the largest deficit since 1946. Anti-deficit sentiment was so strong that President Johnson persuaded Congress to levy a temporary 10 percent surcharge on income taxes, and the result was a modest $3.2-billion surplus the next year. It would be the last such surplus for the rest of the century.

The critical fiscal legacies of the 1960s were two huge health entitlements, only one of which (Medicaid) was directed at the poor; the other, Medicare, went, somewhat like Social Security, to virtually everyone over age sixty-five in exchange for a modest payroll tax (or, in the case of Medicare outpatient coverage, in exchange for a monthly premium that covered only about one quarter of the actual cost). Like Social Security, Medicare and Medicaid started small but grew prodigiously; Medicare spending alone would literally double on average every five years for the next twenty-five years. By 1995, the two health entitlements had become the fourth and fifth largest programs in the federal budget. From little more than a quarter of federal spending in Kennedy's day, all the nation's entitlements had grown to almost half the budget just two decades later.

None of this looked as if it were going to be a problem in the mid-1960s, in those guns-and-butter days when the economy was growing at the heady rate of more than 4 percent a year. But when that go-go growth cooled to about 3 percent in the 1970s and then fell below 3 percent in the 1980s, the means to pay for these generous entitlements vanished. Instead, the costs were met by rising inflation (which kicked taxpayers into higher and higher tax brackets), by slashing the defense budget after Vietnam, and by larger deficits, which began to surge in the mid-1970s.

Besides fast-growing entitlements, Johnson's bequest to President Richard Nixon was a troubling inflation rate, born largely of overheated spending for the Vietnam War and LBJ's reluctance to apply the brakes for fear of worsening unemployment. Barely 2.4 percent a year on average throughout the 1960s, inflation nearly tripled, to 7.1 percent, in the 1970s. This surge had all sorts of baleful effects on the budget during the Nixon administration, but one stands out. In a hugely destructive bidding war, politicians practically knocked one another over to provide higher and higher benefit increases to protect Social Security recipients from rising prices.

When Nixon sought a 10 percent increase in 1969, Democrats—chiefly House Ways and Means Committee Chairman Wilbur Mills—raised it to 15 percent. Ditto for Nixon's proposed 6 percent increase the following year, which was raised to 10 percent. Determined to rein in this rampant generosity, Nixon tried to get Congress to "index" benefits directly to inflation, reasoning that automatic increases to keep up with inflation were better than letting Congress raise benefits whenever—and by however much—it felt like.

But Mills fought on, and Nixon got indexing enacted only in 1972, when Mills tied it to a whopping 20 percent increase in benefits that the Arkansan hoped would boost his presidential candidacy (it did not). Indexing did not take effect for another two and a half years, and in the meantime, Congress jacked up benefits another 21 percent, more than offsetting the inflation unleashed by the 1973–74 Arab oil embargo.

Benefit increases were out of control. After rising by tiny increments from 1952 to 1965, benefits rocketed up by more than twice the rate at which prices rose from 1967 through 1972, propelled by a Congress that was overcompensating for inflation. By the time indexing finally took hold, inflation had soared as well, and benefits climbed another 40 percent from 1979 through 1981.

When Nixon resigned under the cloud of Watergate in August 1974, the nation was a little more than halfway through the deepest recession since the end of the Second World War, a downturn provoked by the Organization of Petroleum Exporting Countries (OPEC)–organized oil embargo and made worse by the Federal Reserve's campaign to choke off the inflation that was being fed by higher oil prices. Although not apparent at the time, this was a turning point. The recession marked a sudden and unexpected end to the era of small deficits, remarkable economic growth, and steady shrinkage in the relative size of the national debt. Up to this point, the United States had never gone more than sixteen years without balancing its budget, and then only during the extraordinarily bad times of the Depression and world war. Now the nation would go at least thirty years or more without a single budget surplus, from 1970 through at least the end of the century.

Just as FDR had done when he ran against Hoover in 1932, Democratic presidential candidate Jimmy Carter attacked the incumbent Republican president in 1976 for running "the largest deficit in our history"—never mind that Gerald Ford's red ink was created mostly by the recession. Woe unto candidates who get to office on a promise to balance the budget; Carter, like FDR, would soon have to eat his words.

Once elected, Carter promised to balance the budget by 1981. But soon he was wrestling, just as Ford had, with unemployment and inflation, blaming the deficit on "inadequate revenues that come in from a sluggish economy." By December 1977, when Carter wanted to stimulate the economy with tax cuts, he dropped his balanced-budget pledge altogether: "I just can't give a firm commitment on how we will balance tax cuts versus a balanced budget by 1981," he said.

Carter's deficits were actually either equal to or smaller than Ford's when measured as a percentage of GDP. But in dollars—the benchmark understood by most journalists, politicians, and voters—Carter's deficits looked bigger: Ford's biggest was $74 billion; Carter ran one that big and followed with one even bigger, $79 billion, the biggest in dollars since the Second World War, enough to give Ronald Reagan an opening to denounce the "runaway deficit of nearly $80 billion" as proof of Carter's incompetence.

Worse yet, a strange new problem seemed to be afflicting the economy. Economic orthodoxy until now had held that high unemployment and high inflation could not coexist; high inflation was supposed to be the sign of a superheated economy in which almost everyone had a job. But inflation rose ominously through Carter's term, and by the time it hit 11 percent in 1979 and 13.5 percent in 1980, unemployment had started back up again, too, to 7.1 percent in 1980. Together the inflation and unemployment rates added up to the "misery index," a tool Carter had used to devastating effect against Ford in 1976. Unfortunately for Carter, the 16.5 percent misery index he had beaten up Ford with in 1976 had climbed to 20.6 percent in 1980, thanks to sharply higher inflation. "Are you better off now than you were four years ago?" Reagan asked voters. The answer was a landslide that elected him, turned the Senate over to the Republicans for the first time in twenty-six years, and filled the House with so many new Republicans and conservative Democrats that even though the House remained in Democratic hands, Reagan for a time had effective control of all of Congress.

————

On the eve of Ronald Reagan's presidency in 1980, the principles the nation had worked out over the last two hundred years still seemed deeply embedded in the national psyche: Avoid borrowing if possible, but run a deficit in times of war and during serious economic crises; as soon as the crisis is past, do whatever it takes to get the budget under control again, and begin paying off the debt. That had worked right up until the end of the Second World War, when circumstances forced an adjustment. The enormous costs of the Cold War, the rise of entitlements, and the growth of the idea of full-employment budgeting combined to generate persistent deficits. But for almost thirty years, those deficits stayed small enough that the national debt steadily shrank as the economy grew. By 1980, however, three factors were combining to push deficits out of control.

The most important was the startling growth of entitlements. Once LBJ and Congress added Medicare and other mid-1960s programs to Depression-era benefits such as Social Security, entitlements simply exploded. In 1975, this mandatory spending (mandatory because the laws that created entitlements require the government to provide the money no matter what) overtook the discretionary spending that had long made up most of the budget. Congress had to appropriate discretionary spending every year, or it would die; mandatory spending could remain on budgetary autopilot year after year unless Congress forced itself to go back into the budget and tamper with it, something lawmakers were loath to do. In 1962, the discretionary-mandatory split was 70:30: Nearly three quarters of the budget was easily controlled, year-to-year appropriated spending, and less than a third was autopilot money. But by 1980, a growing population of retirees and other beneficiaries had combined with new programs to push entitlements up from 30 percent of the budget to almost 50 percent of it. Alarmingly, half the budget was now autopilot money.

The second problem was inflation, which began rumbling in the 1960s and then took off in the 1970s, fed by oil-price shocks in 1974 and 1979. The effect on the deficit was devastating. Entitlements were indexed to inflation, and the resulting automatic COLAs were enormous; inflation plus high interest rates also helped drive up the cost of paying interest on the national debt.

The third problem was the coming recession, which was the price the nation was about to pay for wiping out inflation. Federal Reserve Board Chairman Paul Volcker's tight-money policy raised interest rates until the prime rate for short-term borrowing hit an astonishing 20 percent in 1980. When the economy finally succumbed to Volcker's relentless campaign in 1981, the resulting recession was brutal, the worst downturn since the Great Depression. As it almost always had throughout history, the deficit soared as the economy plummeted.

Whoever was to be president in 1981 would have severe problems with a rising deficit. The question was whether that president would make things better or worse. Ronald Reagan campaigned on an economic platform that economist Herbert Stein summed up caustically as "the economics of joy." Gone were the Calvinist, Goldwater-era notions that the nation had to suffer through root-canal spending cuts to rid itself of the deficit. The new economics taught that there was a painless way to balance the budget and reinvigorate the economy, chiefly through lowering taxes.

A decade later politicians like Rostenkowski would preach tough choices and the virtue of paying for new entitlement benefits. But for a magical time at the beginning of the 1980s, those dreary rules were set aside. Reagan felt no need to anguish over voters' contradictory demands the way Rostenkowski and other cash-strapped politicians would at the end of the decade. As Reagan entered office, Americans were, as always, thoroughly ambivalent: They wanted fiscal prudence and a balanced budget after the nation's economic roller-coaster ride under Jimmy Carter, but they also felt entitled to a broad array of social services and benefits and did not care to pay more for them. Americans wanted it all, and as far as Reagan was concerned, they should have it. This constituted a grand experiment. The only question was whether it would work.

Chapter 4

THE REVOLUTION
THAT WASN'T

———

In early February 1981, eight days before President Ronald Reagan was to unveil his historic budget and tax-reduction plan to Congress and the nation, the president, his Cabinet, and his senior staff gathered to ponder the darker side of Reaganomics. The Republican president's aggressive young budget director, David Stockman, had called the urgent meeting to lay out a series of painful cuts in domestic spending that would be essential if Reagan was to make good on his seemingly contradictory campaign promises to cut taxes, rebuild the nation's defenses, and balance the budget. With little more than a week to go before Reagan was scheduled to unveil his budget before a joint meeting of Congress, Stockman and his number crunchers had come up with only about half the cuts that would be needed to balance the budget in three years. "We can make it add up," Stockman told Reagan and the senior officials, "but what remains to be cut is nearly as big as what we've already cut. The additional cuts will be far tougher than anything we've already agreed upon."

Reagan did not hesitate. He said his administration would do "whatever it takes" to make the necessary cuts, using a phrase Stockman later called Reagan's mantra. It turned out to be meaningless. Before the meeting was over, Stockman would be confronted with a surprising and unpleasant reality: Reagan's commitment to a balanced budget was little more than a rhetorical flourish. He and his closest advisers hadn't the stomach for the gut-wrenching spending cuts that were necessary to reduce the deficit substantially, let alone wipe it out. For all his glib campaign promises to eliminate the deficit, something no president had managed to do since Lyndon Johnson did it with his last budget in 1969, Reagan was not going to deliver. The revolution, hardly begun, was doomed to fail from this moment forward. Before the meeting was over, Reagan and his top advisers would make decisions that would make balancing the budget impossible.

It was an eerie harbinger of what was to come fourteen years later, when Gingrich and the other Republicans took over Congress with virtually the same promises. Democrats thought they could kill the 1994 GOP revolt in its crib by attacking Republicans for replaying the same voodoo policies Reagan had tried and failed to implement, leaving record peacetime deficits and a budget crisis that would linger for the rest of the century. But the 1995 Republicans happily embraced Reaganomics: Reagan's policies might have failed to reduce the deficit, but they had helped usher in the longest peacetime economic expansion since the end of the Second World War, a nearly eight-year boom that made many people rich and left a pleasant "morning in America" memory in the minds of millions of voters. If the choice was between Bill Clinton's tax increases and Ronald Reagan's tax cuts, Gingrich said, voters would choose tax cuts in a heartbeat. Privately, however, Gingrich and other GOP strategists vowed not to repeat the devastating mistakes Reagan had made. For all his enormous popularity, his remarkable communications skills, and a Congress that—at least for the critical first eight months of his presidency—virtually bowed down before him, Reagan had not been able to make it work.

What Reagan and his aides did on this day in February 1981— and for the next eight years—would define budget politics for the rest of the century. An extraordinarily popular president with both the mandate and the necessary political tools to do the job confronted a deficit problem that had not yet spun out of control. Instead of fixing it, he not only made it worse, but he also made it infinitely more difficult for all his successors to fix it as well. This day and repeatedly thereafter, Reagan made sacred cows of programs that should have been cut, targeted programs that even his Republican allies refused to trim, and tried to fill the gap with vague efforts to slash "fraud, waste, and abuse." By continually reassuring voters that there were easy fixes, he cheapened the discourse and undermined support for politicians—his own budget director among them—who knew how painful the real cuts had to be and desperately needed public support to get them enacted.

Even before Reagan took office, the deficit was festering, thanks in large part to rampant inflation, a looming recession, and the relentless growth of entitlement spending. Reagan made it worse by fulfilling only two of his three campaign promises. He said he would increase defense spending, and he did. When Stockman protested the huge size of the buildup, the president dismissed the objections. "Defense is not a budget issue," he declared. Reagan was also true to his pledge to cut taxes. In doing so, he took what was already a troubling gap between tax revenue and spending and dramatically widened it. Seduced by an almost magical theory that made a virtue of what Republicans liked to do anyway—cut taxes—Reagan kept his promise to push through enormous tax cuts but then flinched when Stockman tried to present the bill to pay for them fully. The third promise was to balance the budget. That was the one he broke.

Ever since the Great Depression, Keynesian economics had taught that government could manage the economy's periodic slowdowns by treating the demand side of the economy, chiefly by making the federal government the megaconsumer of last resort, spending vast amounts of federal money on public-works projects and government contracts to kick-start moribund demand. Increased demand would pump money into the economy, give consumers more to spend, reopen closed stores and factories, and put people back to work.

Supply-siders said that was wrongheaded. Instead of feeding demand-side consumer spending, the trick was to stimulate the supply side of the economy—investors, entrepreneurs, business, and industry—by busting the shackles formed by high tax rates, which discouraged work, investment, and growth.

In its basic form, this was nothing new or controversial. Even liberal Democrats agreed that taxes were now so high that in some cases they discouraged work or investment. But in its more radical form, the supply-side prescription was as extreme as pure Keynesianism: Where Keynes advocated spending as much government money as it took to jump-start a stalled economy, hard-core supply-siders demanded tax cuts as big and as broad as possible to unleash investment and productivity. Just like the Keynesians, the supply-siders were unconcerned about what their prescription might do to the deficit.

What appealed to Reagan and many others was supply side's simplicity, at least as described by economist Arthur Laffer, who could sketch it on a piece of paper in seconds. The Laffer curve, as it came to be called, showed the relationship between tax rates and tax revenue. At first, the line headed upward as tax rates rose—higher rates meant more dollars for the Treasury. But as rates got higher and higher, tax collections began to fall off, and the curve started to flatten out and then finally descended, describing a bell-shaped arc. Laffer's point was simple: When tax rates got too high, taxpayers began to hide their income or work less; the net result was that they paid less taxes. By lowering rates, government could collect the same amount of revenue or even more, since there would be greater incentive to work, invest, and earn. The president loved the idea, since it reminded him of his movie-actor days. After just four pictures in a single year, Reagan the actor had risen into the 90 percent tax bracket, where the rate was so high it made little sense to keep working.

Some of the most ardent supply-siders preached that this formula was so potentially magical that tax cuts would pay for themselves. This delightful outcome meant that the GOP's traditional Calvinist equation, which demanded spending cuts to pay for tax cuts, was suddenly obsolete. This was the theory, anyway. In the bitter aftermath, when deficits had gone from merely bad to truly awful, many supply-siders denied that anyone had ever said such a thing. But Jack Kemp, the GOP congressman and former Buffalo Bills quarterback who was a key supply-side leader, said exactly that in a 1979 book describing the supply-side revolution. "Instead of high tax rates with low production, government can raise the same amount through low tax rates," he wrote.

When Reagan's election made it begin to look as if supply-siders might actually get their way with huge tax cuts, traditional, deficit-minded Republicans sent up warnings. Shortly after the election, Senator Bob Dole, about to become the new Republican chairman of the tax-writing Senate Finance Committee, suggested putting tax cuts off altogether until Congress had taken care of the deficit. Skepticism and worry were so common that even the Senate's new majority leader, Tennessee Republican Howard Baker, openly called Reagan's plan a "riverboat gamble."

"I mean, it was hard to find anybody in power who didn't see it was a problem," said Richard Darman, a senior Reagan White House adviser. "But the society was very much in an anti-Carter, anti-malaise, anti-misery-index frame of mind, and Ronald Reagan was exceedingly popular, and people were willing to take a risk with a new program that promised growth—and it so happened he promised it painlessly."

David Stockman considered himself a supply-sider, but a hard-nosed one. He had done the math. Even with the rosiest of economic scenarios the new administration could whip up, the truth was that there would be heavy revenue losses in the early years. To help offset the impact of those big tax cuts, Stockman was insisting on domestic spending cuts of $130 billion. That was a huge number. Stockman's cuts dwarfed anything that had gone before: The biggest spending-cut plan until then had been a $50-billion package pushed by congressional Democrats in 1980. And Stockman's numbers were huge even by the supposedly stringent standards of 1995, when Newt Gingrich and congressional Republicans were pushing nearly $1 trillion in spending cuts over seven years. If the total spending cuts over the first three years of the 1981 plan are adjusted for inflation to permit a direct comparison with the spending cuts in the first three years of the 1995 plan, Stockman's $220 billion in cuts beat Gingrich's $185 billion.

This was strong stuff, and Stockman knew it would run into resistance among Democrats. Sure enough, even before Reagan submitted his first budget plan to Congress, news reports about the administration's draconian cuts in education, welfare, food stamps, and school lunches touched off an uproar among special interest groups, seniors, and welfare advocates. What Stockman did not anticipate was how much resistance his plans would run into in the Reagan Cabinet, where some officials were soon grumbling that all this talk of insensitive cuts was giving them political problems.

The budget director had little sympathy for his fainthearted colleagues. Many top Reagan administration officials were aging, complacent, well-to-do businessmen and government leaders who lacked the revolutionary fire that animated the thirty-four-year-old Stockman. Tall and slender, with a helmet of prematurely graying hair, he was brilliant, driven, and remarkably hardworking, even by Washington standards. During his two terms as a congressman from Michigan, he had immersed himself in the intricacies of the budget until he had mastered it, accruing a knowledge that gave him immense power in the body's ceaseless budget debates. He seemed to have little life outside the thick budget books he lugged everywhere. "He was a very ascetic person," recalled a senior White House aide who worked closely with him. "He had one and a half suits, one pair of shoes, no frills in his life whatsoever. Very spartan."

Stockman took Reagan literally when the president said he wanted to cut taxes and balance the budget simultaneously, the seemingly contradictory policies candidate George Bush had derided as "voodoo economics." But to do so, Stockman knew he would have to orchestrate a historic retrenchment of government, turning the clock back on many of the New Deal and Great Society programs that were now growing faster than almost any other category of federal spending, relentlessly driving up the deficit. This was not a bad thing at all in Stockman's view; he wanted to remake government—return it to core functions, curb its relentless growth, dismantle the welfare state that Democrats had spent two generations building up—just as much as he wanted to balance the budget. Each goal fed the other. But doing it would require mercilessly slashing federal spending programs in a way that would cause pain and dislocation to millions of Americans.

In the cool, rational world of budget numbers, this made perfect sense. Programs that had begun as thin safety nets had grown fat and generous over the years, far too expensive for a badly stretched federal government to maintain unchanged. Stockman turned his accountant's eye on Social Security and dozens of other subsidies and privately determined that everything would have to go on the chopping block: price supports for farmers, tax incentives for businesses, and welfare for the able-bodied poor. "They were getting more than they deserved, needed or were owed. For the Reagan Revolution to add up, they had to be cut off," Stockman wrote later. "It required the ruthless dispensation of short-run pain in the name of long-run gain."

In the world of politics, however, this was crazy. As the fateful Reagan Cabinet meeting heated up, Stockman tried to allay some of the officials' jitters about the deep spending cuts that would be laid out in the president's address to Congress on February 18. For one thing, he noted, everybody would be affected: Barge operators, dairy farmers, general aviation, big oil, and other moneyed interests would take a hit along with the poor and the middle class. The pain was to be equally apportioned among the prosperous and the struggling, he insisted. And besides, there were a number of social programs that hadn't been cut a dime—or at least hadn't been yet. Stockman casually ticked off programs that so far had been spared: Social Security, Medicare, the Head Start preschool program for poor kids, Supplemental Security Income for the poor, disabled, and elderly, and summer jobs for inner-city youth.

Stockman never should have rattled off that list; presidential counselor Ed Meese and others at the meeting pounced on it as great public relations: This would show that the administration wasn't out to hurt the vulnerable. The amiable Meese, unschooled in Washington budget matters, was more concerned about protecting Reagan's political interests than about advancing Stockman's fiscal agenda. Meese told Stockman he should get together with the White House communications people and put out a press release highlighting all the social programs that were *not* being cut.

Aghast, Stockman balked. Meese and the others gathered around the conference table were completely missing the point: The purpose of the meeting was to settle on more cuts, not to take programs off the table. But it was too late. Meese could not be dissuaded. The senior presidential adviser declared a compromise on the spot: A "sacred cows" list would be issued that included the five programs Stockman had mentioned plus two more—school lunches for low-income children and veterans' disabilities. The next morning a front-page story in *The New York Times* announced Reagan's decision "sparing seven basic social programs from budget cuts." Stockman's heart sank. Declaring these programs sacrosanct would make balancing the budget virtually impossible, and now that the decision to spare them was public, Reagan could not back away from it.

With one ill-considered stroke, Meese had fenced off seven programs that accounted for $240 billion a year in spending—then about one third of the entire federal budget. Add defense (which was in for big increases) and interest on the national debt (untouchable, as always), and Meese's breezy policymaking had just ruled off limits a breathtaking 68 percent of all federal spending. Now they would have to find a way to get rid of the deficit by cutting only from the rest. Before Reagan had even made the trek up Capitol Hill to announce the details of his plan, his top advisers had raised the white flag in the coming budget wars.

———

The incident was emblematic of why the Reagan revolution never really got off the ground and why, instead of balancing the budget, Reagan fueled the largest deficits in peacetime history. The president had no stomach for making over the government from the ground up, and no plans to try. He was softhearted, easily swayed by hard-luck stories, and liable to shift policy on the basis of an appeal to his emotions. Stockman's strategy would have required ignoring the wrenching dislocations that would inevitably come from remaking the role of the federal government. "Only an iron chancellor would have tried to make it stick," Stockman wrote. "Ronald Reagan wasn't that by a long shot." A onetime Democrat, Reagan was still a great admirer of Roosevelt (he had voted for FDR and the New Deal four times) and had no desire to undo the social-welfare and economic-security programs Roosevelt had set in motion nearly half a century before.

Reagan would go after some programs on ideological grounds—legal services for the poor, for example—and he gave Stockman free rein to trim some popular programs, such as job training and daycare subsidies. But he believed in the fundamental concept of a social safety net to protect the elderly and the poor from plunging into the abyss. The basic structure of government—the welfare state Stockman hated—would remain. Reagan failed to balance the budget not because Democrats blocked him, though they certainly fought to hold on to programs they had nurtured for years and made an explicit trade to give Reagan defense increases if he would lay off social programs. The chief reason Reagan failed to eradicate the deficit was because Republicans from the White House on down refused to cut spending as deeply as they had to. That was no surprise, since Republicans had worked shoulder to shoulder with

Democrats for decades to build these spending programs in the first place. They might rant about shutting down the Education Department, for example, but two Republican secretaries of Education later the department had not only survived, it was bigger than it had been when Reagan took office.

During all eight years of Reagan's presidency, just one significant spending program was completely abolished: general revenue sharing grants to local governments, killed off in 1986 by mutual consent of Reagan, the GOP Senate, and the Democratic House. The much-maligned Comprehensive Employment and Training Act (CETA) was also repealed—but quickly replaced by the Job Training Partnership Act, which had almost the same objective.

While Reagan was the inspiration for the 1995 revolutionaries, the bitterly regretted failures of what he did in 1981 were what helped shape the way Republicans fought the second revolution. Reagan's legislative blitzkrieg acknowledged a reality of Washington politics: There is no better time to change the world than the moment you get into office. Reagan pushed the heart of his economic program through Congress in his first six months in the White House, passing an unprecedented package of spending cuts and then coming right back to pass an extraordinary package of tax cuts more than twice as big—all before Congress broke for the 1981 August recess.

But then trouble set in, and analyzing all this fourteen years later, the latter-day revolutionaries recognized three chief mistakes they were determined not to repeat.

First, there was a wide recognition that the tax cuts had gotten out of hand in 1981, and those who bore the worst scars—in particular, senators such as Pete Domenici, Bob Dole, and other old bulls who had lived through both eras—worked hard to keep the tax cuts under control this time.

Second, Republicans admitted that while they had overachieved on the tax cuts in 1981, they had spectacularly underachieved on spending cuts. Not in 1995. Cuts matched and even exceeded the rhetoric. And there would be virtually no shrinking from cuts to politically sensitive programs. Almost everything went on the block: Medicare, Medicaid, school lunches, food stamps, and on and on, all of Meese's sacred cows except Social Security, which had burned Republicans so badly over the years that Gingrich and Dole decided not to mess with it lest they derail their effort before they even started it.

Third, they would not repeat Reagan's hugely expensive defense buildup. Reagan had campaigned on a pledge to boost defense spending by 5 percent (on top of inflation), but by the time he got to the White House, Carter had already done that. Reagan went ahead anyway, layering another 5 percent hike on top of Carter's and driving defense spending up higher than Presidents Kennedy and Johnson had raised it to fight the Vietnam War. More than $2 trillion later, the United States had stared down the Soviet Union, but with a hideous increase in its annual deficits and national debt.

Runaway defense spending wouldn't be tolerated by the Republican leaders in 1995. The Republicans' Contract with America had promised to beef up defense after several years of decline under Clinton. But John Kasich, the House Budget Committee chairman, fought bitter internal battles with GOP defense hawks demanding higher defense spending, and he won. Defense in his proposed budget would "grow," but only by $9 billion from 1995 to 2002, from $270 billion to $279 billion. In real, inflation-adjusted terms, this was no growth at all but a cut of almost 16 percent. Just to keep up with inflation, the Pentagon would have to get $332 billion in 2002, not $279 billion. Though they were loath to talk about it, the stark truth was that after taking inflation into account, the Republicans were cutting defense even more deeply than they were cutting social spending.

The Republicans' goal in 1995 was so seemingly bland as to be unobjectionable: just limit the growth of federal spending to roughly the rate of inflation or a little more. Given the natural acceleration of revenues in a growing economy, this was all it would take to balance the budget; Reagan had simply failed to do it. Author David Frum pointed out in his book *Dead Right* that if federal spending had risen no faster than inflation between 1979 and 1989, the nation could have spent every dollar it did on defense, enjoyed all the Reagan tax cuts, and still run a substantial budget surplus. "There was no arithmetic reason that the Reagan program could not have succeeded," Frum wrote. "Reagan's budgets were wrecked by the inability and unwillingness of the most conservative administration since Coolidge's to resist the rise of social welfare spending."

Reducing the vast complications of two generations' worth of social-welfare programs to simple arithmetic made the job sound easy and nonthreatening, which was exactly how the 1995 Republicans wanted to frame the debate. When the Democrats talked fear and change and wholesale program dismantling, Republicans like John Kasich spoke soothingly of glide paths and reductions in the rate of growth. Programs would still get more money over time, Kasich said, just a little less than the Democrats wanted. President Clinton's 1996 budget projected that spending would grow by a little more than 5 percent a year through 2000. Under the GOP budget plan, spending would grow by just under 3 percent a year all the way to 2002, only slightly faster than the projected inflation rate. That sounded painless.

But in fact it was grueling work. To get growth down from 5 percent to 3 percent, Republicans had to radically recast the programs Reagan had refused even to touch. The 1995 Republicans might not be the "iron chancellors" Stockman had dreamed of, but they were much bolder than Reagan was. The changes they voted for were breathtaking. This meant far more than just "reforming" welfare, for example. It meant ending the guarantee that poor children and their mothers could turn to the government for some minimum level of assistance, a social contract that went all the way back to the darkest days of the Great Depression, when poor children literally starved to death. The same transformation would occur in Medicaid; the absolute guarantee of minimum medical care for the poor would end. From now on, fifty state governments would decide who got help and how.

There was surely room in these programs for big, even radical changes, for the new efficiencies and the drive and intelligence that some state governments would bring to programs until now rigidly controlled by the federal bureaucracy. But the 1995 Republicans' bold plan to prod Medicare beneficiaries toward the uncertain mercies of HMOs and devolve welfare and Medicaid to fifty state governments, sending it on with block grants and best wishes, seemed in its own way every bit as much a riverboat gamble as Reagan's risky bet on supply-side economics.

———

Charlie Stenholm's first brush with supply-side economics came in 1978, when he first ran for Congress in his sprawling West Texas

prairie district. A forty-year-old cotton farmer and Democrat, Stenholm hailed from Stamford, Texas, a tiny dot on the map midway between Fort Worth and the New Mexico border, a place where
ice-cream socials are still common and the cotton gin is the local
hangout. As executive vice president of the Rolling Plains Cotton
Growers Association, Stenholm had traveled to Washington to fight
a ruling unfavorable to Texas cotton growers and in the process had
developed a passion for politics. Now he was aiming to go back to
the capital full-time.

Stenholm's Republican opponent, a young Abilene businessman,
preached a new political gospel that was gathering momentum back
East: the supply-side promise of a painless route to roaring economic expansion and reduced deficits, all by simply cutting tax
rates. Tall and gangling, with a quick, toothy grin and Jimmy Stew-
art good looks, Stenholm argued that the Republicans' economic
theories had a something-for-nothing quality that ran counter to his
hardheaded Swedish American notions of fiscal conservatism. "I just
don't believe you can cut taxes and continue to increase spending
for defense and everything else and still balance the budget," Stenholm said. "It just doesn't make any sense."

Raised in a strict Lutheran farm community where church elders
preached the virtue of frugality and the evils of debt, Stenholm, like
other conservative Southern Democrats, supported defense but advocated cuts in practically everything else—social-welfare spending,
highway construction, Medicare, and even farm subsidies—to bring
down the deficit. That November, Stenholm won the argument over
supply-side economics. Residents of his conservative, predominantly
Democratic congressional district voted overwhelmingly to send
him to Washington. Two years later he was reelected, but the political ground was shifting beneath him. Reagan and conservative Republicans had swept into power, and the supply-side doctrine
Stenholm had so strenuously opposed was now very much in vogue.

In the weeks following his 1980 reelection, Stenholm went from
saying "absolutely no" to supply-side economics to saying "maybe."
Like a lot of other members with deep misgivings about this untried
new theory, he was feeling pressure from his constituents to adjust
to the new reality. "Folks told me, 'Look, Charlie, we tried it the
other way for years, and it didn't work,' " he said. " 'Maybe we ought
to give the president a chance.' "

An otherwise marginalized conservative in a liberal party, Stenholm was about to rise to undreamed-of influence and prominence. But he was also about to make a decision that he would spend most of the rest of his congressional career trying to undo. Like Woody Allen's character Zelig, who improbably appeared at major historical events, Stenholm would pop up at virtually every big fiscal battle for the next decade and a half. Democrats like Stenholm are important because budget fights are almost always agonizingly close, and the swing group of Democratic conservatives can shift the balance of power by defecting to the Republicans or providing their own party a thin margin of victory. In 1981, Stenholm's willingness to say "maybe" was critically important to Stockman and the Reagan forces. With the Senate back in Republican hands for the first time in twenty-eight years, the House loomed as the critical battleground on which the success or failure of Reagan's agenda would be determined.

Despite the Reagan sweep, Democrats still held a fifty-one-seat advantage in the House. The arithmetic left Reagan with two alternatives. He could strike some middle-ground deal with House Speaker Tip O'Neill and the House's dominant liberal Democrats, but this would require him to trim his plans, a course with virtually no appeal to the triumphant new president. Or he could make an end run, bypassing the liberal Democrats and forging an entirely different coalition. To succeed at this, GOP leaders would have to hold all the House Republicans together (including independent-minded moderates and liberals from the Northeast and Midwest) while the administration picked off enough conservative Democrats to build a new House majority. This was much more to the new president's liking, and it seemed within reach: A swing of just twenty-six Democrats would give Reagan and the Republicans working control of the House.

Though still a relative newcomer to Congress, Stenholm emerged after the 1980 election as the leader of Reagan's target group: the House's fifty or so conservative, mostly Southern Democrats. Unlike some of his more nakedly ambitious colleagues, Stenholm struck those who knew him as a straight shooter: determined but utterly trustworthy, not the sort of member who said different things to different people. He seemed a natural leader of the Boll Weevils, as these Southerners came to call themselves—a slightly self-deprecating reference to the highly destructive agriculture pest. Cotton farmers might hate boll weevils, but they feared and paid attention to them, just the way the congressional Weevils now expected party leaders to begin to feel about them.

The Weevils had reacted to Reagan's victory with a mix of alarm and excitement. On the one hand, they feared that it was only a matter of time before they, too, would lose their seats in the conservative Republican tide. After all, whatever their philosophy, they were still Democrats. On the other hand, though, they found much to like in Reagan's free-market economic ideas. While many were determined to remain loyal to their battered party, their ties to the party leadership were badly frayed. Democratic liberals had long treated them as second-class citizens. Suddenly, Republicans were courting them, and much of the new GOP doctrine seemed to make sense. Cut spending and cut taxes—wasn't that, within limits, what conservative Democrats had long been advocating? And what better way to inoculate themselves against GOP challengers back home than to find a way to agree with the popular new GOP president?

Even before Reagan's inauguration, Kenneth Duberstein, a congressional lobbyist for the new administration who grew up in a Jewish neighborhood of Brooklyn, donned a pair of cowboy boots and made the trek to Stenholm's Capitol Hill office to seek his support for the president-elect's program. "I thought we could work together," Duberstein recalled. "Stenholm clearly wanted to go heavily on spending cuts. He thought there were enough conservative Democrats there who would be willing to work with Reagan." In return, Duberstein made an offer that Stenholm and the rest of the Boll Weevils eagerly accepted: an open door at the White House and frequent meetings with the president and his top aides to discuss their concerns about taxes and budget policy.

Stenholm liked Reagan's determination to slash federal spending; if anything, he thought the new president was going too easy. The night of Reagan's February 18 speech to Congress, Stenholm told Duberstein he thought the president was a "piker" for not seeking even deeper spending cuts. Stenholm was a deficit hawk, a politician who tended to put more emphasis on cutting the deficit than on any other priority. Nonetheless, his continuing worries about the president's tax-cut proposal left it unclear whether he would cross party lines in the end to vote with the GOP all the way down the line.

The White House needed allies whose defection on both the budget votes and the tax votes was certain.

To get them, the administration eventually aligned itself with two of the most calculatingly ambitious Texans in the House: Phil Gramm, a member of the Budget Committee, and Kent Hance, who sat on the Ways and Means Committee. Hance, a garrulous, good-natured lawyer from Lubbock, envisioned a larger role for himself than his junior status in the House provided, and he took delight in being courted by White House Chief of Staff James Baker and Treasury Secretary Donald Regan. Much more than Gramm, he was candid with the Democratic leadership about his inclination to throw his support to Reagan. "Kent Hance at least had a sense of humor about his bald-faced defections," said then House Speaker Jim Wright, a fellow Texas Democrat.

Wright and Dan Rostenkowski, chairman of the House Ways and Means Committee, did not think Hance's betrayal amusing, though, and they did what they could to make his life miserable, punishing him with a series of petty indignities. When Ways and Means Committee members went on a retreat to Baltimore, Hance was seated at the back of the bus, next to the toilet. Rostenkowski even stooped to ordering an aide to remove the rollers from Hance's chair in the committee room. The strain of his turncoat role wore visibly on him: Repeatedly during the year, his face broke out in a nervous rash.

The steely Gramm, on the other hand, had none of Hance's compunctions, and while leaders were inclined to forgive the good-natured Hance, they came to loathe Gramm. "Kent is weak," one House Democratic leader told *The Washington Post*. "Gramm is venal." Gramm, a former Texas A&M economics professor and a committed supply-sider, had arrived in Washington in 1979 on fire to do big things. Gifted with a razor-sharp intellect and the ability to over-power antagonists in head-to-head debate, the deeply conservative free-market economist immediately sought center stage in the House. The other Boll Weevils joked not a little snidely that the most dangerous place to stand was between Gramm and a TV camera. Sonny Montgomery, a senior Boll Weevil from Mississippi, grumped that Gramm had "brass balls" and was impervious to criticism.

Max Friedersdorf, Reagan's chief congressional lobbyist, said Gramm soon began calling him daily, sometimes hourly, to offer inside information from the Democratic camp and to suggest appro-

priate strategies. Initially, the White House had only modest hopes
of picking up Southern Democratic support, according to Friedersdorf. It was Gramm who pointed the way to an evolving core of Boll
Weevils who were sympathetic to Reagan and ready to defect. "It was
almost like he created this thing out of whole cloth, and before long
we were working hand in glove with him," Friedersdorf said.

While Hance worked on a tax-cut deal that would lure Democratic support, Gramm focused on federal spending. Early in 1981,
Gramm secretly plotted with new Budget Director Stockman, his
onetime House colleague, to draft the Reagan alternative to the
House Democrats' budget resolution. He gave no warning to Wright
(who had helped him get his prized seat on the Budget Committee)
or to House Budget Committee Chairman Jim Jones, a conservative
Oklahoma Democrat who harbored some sympathy for the Reagan
revolution and naïvely thought he could work out a compromise
with Stockman. Jones had no idea at the time that Stockman's strategy was not to negotiate but to crush him.

The showdown was set for early May, and it was a critical roll of
the dice for Reagan: To win, he would have to hold all the House Republicans in line—not a sure thing, with Gypsy Moth liberals making noises about defecting to the Democratic budget—while luring
a critical mass of Democrats. In the ten days leading up to the
House's critical May 7 budget vote, Reagan met personally with a
dozen Republicans and sixty Democrats while a grass-roots lobbying
effort and advertising campaign waged by White House political operatives were hitting those same members back in their home districts.

The Boll Weevils were the key to the GOP strategy, and the White
House used all the considerable resources of the presidency to woo
them, showering them with invitations to White House dinners, tick-
ets to the Kennedy Center, presidential cuff links, and autographed
pictures of the president. A privileged few were flown to Camp David
in the presidential helicopter one weekend for a day of presidential
stroking. Some members held out for serious concessions, and Budget Committee Chairman Jones complained bitterly (and to absolutely no effect) that the Democratic cloakroom "had all the
earmarks of a tobacco auction." Members openly bragged about the
favors they had gotten from the White House. John Breaux, who
wheedled higher price supports for sugar, a key crop in his south-

west Louisiana district, was asked by a reporter whether that showed his vote could be bought. No, Breaux replied with a huge grin, but "it can be rented."

Yet with the showdown on the House floor looming, many of the Boll Weevils were torn. They hadn't decided whether to break with the leadership and help pass the president's alternative or stick with their party and back Budget Committee Chairman Jones's resolution, which would have given Reagan most but not all of the spending cuts he wanted. The turning point was a tense meeting in Sonny Montgomery's "war room," the spacious congressional office Montgomery had decorated with his Army memorabilia from the Second World War and the Korean War. Gramm had dominated meetings of the Southerners from the start, but this time he held back for dramatic effect, allowing the conversation to run for a while without putting in a word. When he finally rose, he chided his colleagues for their lack of political nerve. "You guys are going to have to show some balls," he snapped.

Congressman Jack Hightower, another Texas Democrat who frequently clashed with Gramm, quipped that since the political beating he'd been taking from Democratic leaders, "mine are the size of mustard seeds."

"That's obvious," Gramm replied.

Evoking the memory of the Alamo for the benefit of the other Texans in the room, Gramm declared that it was "time to draw the line in the sand" and see who really was committed to rebuilding the economy, restoring the nation's defenses, and balancing the budget. "I'm going with the Reagan program—even if I'm the only Democrat who votes for it," he said.

Hightower reminded him that everyone who crossed Colonel William Travis's famous line in the sand at the Alamo—thereby voting to stay and fight instead of surrender to the Mexicans—had been killed. Gramm replied, "Yes, but the ones who didn't cross the line died, too. Only no one remembers their names."

When the vote was over on the House floor, fully sixty-three Democrats, including forty-five Southerners, had crossed party lines to join a united Republican front to approve the Gramm-Latta budget substitute, as it was called (after Phil Gramm and Republican Del Latta of Ohio), the blueprint for the administration's economic plan. The vote stunned and embarrassed Democratic leaders, who had lost control of the House they nominally dominated. It was a re-markable triumph for Reagan, and it clearly showed the way for him to get his program through Congress. But this budget battle was merely the preliminary round for the larger fight over the tax cut.

Just as Gingrich would make tax cuts the "crowning jewel" of the Contract with America in 1995, Reagan had made the tax cut the single most important element of his plan. The Democrats had seri-ously underestimated the president's single-mindedness on this is-sue. Rostenkowski, the Chicago pol who had recently taken over the chairmanship of the Ways and Means Committee, mistakenly thought he was clever enough to finesse Reagan's strategy, forcing the president to settle for a less ambitious tax-cut plan. He ignored Tip O'Neill's advice, which was to let Reagan have his way rather than risk incurring the voters' wrath by challenging the popular new president.

Reagan's original tax cut was expensive: three years of 10 percent cuts for individual taxpayers—the so-called 10-10-10 plan—along with generous write-offs for businesses. Bowing to some of the Boll Weevils' concerns about the deficit, the president modified his plan to reduce the first-year cut to just 5 percent (5-10-10). To beat Rea-gan, Rostenkowski crafted a cheaper alternative: two years of tax cuts with a third-year cut that would go into effect only if the econ-omy and the deficit were doing well enough to justify it. Reagan rejected that and threatened to veto anything short of an uncondi-tional three-year cut.

Now it was a matter of political dominance, and not a little pride. Reagan had badly bloodied the Democrats in their own House on the spending cuts. Did he think he could do that on the tax cuts as well? Determined to hold Democrats together against the Republi-can White House, Rostenkowski and Wright abandoned their earlier plans for a more modest tax cut targeting the middle class. Instead, they entered an all-out bidding war for the allegiance of the Boll Weevils and other swing votes. The war quickly went nuclear.

Business interests and orthodox Republicans who had little if any interest in supply-side economics pushed for the inclusion of a vari-ety of tax breaks for business. The White House quickly acquiesced. Democrats bargained just as furiously. The Southerners demanded and received an increase in the exemption on the estate tax as a fi-nancial boon for farmers and small businessmen. To satisfy Stenholm and other Texas Democrats, the White House agreed to tax exemptions on windfall profits for tiny oil producers and for royalty owners who leased their land to drillers. And so on.

By constantly one-upping each other over a two-month period, the White House and the Democrats managed to increase the overall long-term cost of their original proposals by nearly a third. In their mad rush for votes, the Democrats had abandoned any pretense of promoting responsible tax legislation, and in fact their bill would have cost more than Reagan's over a two-year period. By challenging Reagan, Rostenkowski had unleashed an orgy of vote buying that turned a bad bill into a truly awful bill. Congressman David Obey, a liberal Democrat from Wisconsin who was dismayed by the bidding, said, "It would probably be cheaper if we gave everybody in the country three wishes."

Part of the problem was that Rostenkowski was inexperienced as a committee chairman and outclassed as a vote buyer. Just hours before several key Boll Weevils publicly threw their support to the president and tipped the scales in the administration's favor, Rostenkowski had met with them in his office and was convinced the Southerners would stand by him. Instead, a critical bloc of Georgia Democrats left his office and traded their support for promises to protect the peanut subsidy.

Stenholm was a tougher sell; although he had become a crucial player in the administration's Southern Democratic strategy, he continued to hold out against the tax cut. He had studied the numbers closely enough to see there was no way to accommodate a hefty tax cut and still reach a balanced budget. Moreover, Stenholm at heart was a Democrat. Others, like Gramm and Hance, were Democrats in name only (and would later bolt their party to join forces with the Republicans).

Hance had tried everything, including crawling on his hands and knees into Stenholm's office one evening and begging him to support Reagan's tax cut. "Now do I have your vote?" he asked hopefully. Stenholm grinned slyly and replied, "Almost."

It would take one more meeting before Stenholm would decide. This one, arranged by James Baker, another Texan and one of Stenholm's political idols, was a private session in the Oval Office with Reagan himself. Now seated with the president and Baker, Stenholm felt the ground giving way beneath him. Reagan wasn't about to beg for his vote, as Hance had done. Rather, he appealed to Stenholm's patriotism and sense of fair play. The president believed his economic programs deserved a fair chance. He turned his famous, disarming smile on the Texas congressman. Was Stenholm so certain he was right and Reagan was wrong? So sure that he would stand in the way of the legislation's passage? It was an argument Stenholm had been hearing with increasing frequency. The calls from his district were overwhelmingly in favor of Reagan's tax cut. Now the president of the United States was telling this young, second-term Democratic congressman in a one-on-one lobbying session that he held the fate of the president's policies in his hands. Stenholm realized he really had no choice. Squirming a little in his chair, he smiled and told Reagan, yes, the president could count on him. The passage of Reagan's tax cut was assured.

Stenholm would come to regret that decision deeply. Inadvertently, he and other conservatives who genuinely cared about balancing the budget had touched off a tax-cut bidding war that only made the problem worse. Years later, reflecting on his fateful yes to Reagan, Stenholm mused that the president had used exactly the right argument that day. Who knew whether supply side would work or not? "I guess if there was one rationale that was appealing, it was having to admit that you really didn't know the answer," he said.

Part of the reason the deficit went haywire in the 1980s was Reagan's disastrous bet on supply side and the failure of will on the part of the president and congressional Republicans when it came to cutting spending. But not all of it. Caught up in post-election euphoria, Reagan and his advisers were all but oblivious to the economic forces that would help destroy their balanced-budget goals.

Federal Reserve Board Chairman Paul Volcker's relentless two-year campaign to wring inflation out of the economy by tightening the growth of the money supply was working extremely well. But for the moment, at least, the cure was almost as devastating as the disease. Volcker's policies sent interest rates soaring and helped trigger a recession; that led to surging unemployment and higher payments for unemployment insurance, food stamps, and other costly social programs. All that meant a much bigger deficit.

Paradoxically, the end of inflation, while very healthy for the overall economy, was a disaster for the federal budget. High inflation had reliably increased tax revenues year after year, giving Congress and the White House an ever-growing supply of funds with which to pay for federal programs and keep the deficit at bay. Suddenly, inflation that had averaged more than 7 percent a year in the 1970s and peaked in the low double digits in 1979–81 plummeted to less than 4 percent a year. The effect on tax revenues was disastrous: Even though the economy began to surge, tax revenues dropped, from $618 billion in 1982 to $601 billion in 1983. Revenues recovered thereafter, but they would never again rise as quickly as they had during their inflation-propelled ride in the 1960s and 1970s.

The deficit had rumbled along largely under control for most of the thirty-five years since the end of the Second World War, but now it would accelerate spectacularly out of control. Reagan had inherited from Carter a deficit of $79 billion. A year later Reagan's first deficit was $127 billion; in 1983, it was up to $207 billion. By 1986, it had crested at $221.2 billion, and then it began to decline, in part because Congress was finally putting its foot down on defense spending.

Deficits make debt, and Reagan's deficits took the $700-billion debt the nation had accumulated in its 204-year history and nearly tripled it, bringing it to more than $2 trillion by the time Reagan left office eight years later. The sharply bigger debt came with a nasty price: cripplingly higher interest costs for servicing all that borrowing. From roughly nine cents of every dollar the government spent when Reagan came into office, the carrying cost of the national debt rose to almost fifteen cents of every federal dollar by the time he left, an onerous surcharge that displaced other, more useful spending and bought nothing but the continued ability to keep borrowing.

The reason the Reagan-era deficits were so poisonous to budget politics for the remainder of the century was that they left a terrible hangover, even after the deficits themselves began to recede in the early 1990s. William Niskanen, a member of Reagan's Council of Economic Advisers, said the compounding effect of these skyrocketing interest costs—paying interest on top of interest on top of interest—did more than any other piece of the budget to create today's chronic, "structural" deficits, which stay high whether the economy is in a boom or a bust. The arcane math of budget analysts makes Niskanen's point startling clear: Measured as a percentage of the economy from 1981 through 1989, defense spending dropped 4 percent and entitlements grew by 4 percent. Over the same period, debt interest ballooned by 48 percent.

Looking back on this fiscal wreckage as he drew up plans for his own revolution in 1995, Gingrich was of at least two minds about Reagan. On the one hand, Reagan had failed. There was no getting around it. In the early 1980s, Gingrich had been just a noisy backbencher with no real influence in Congress, out of step with most of his own party, relegated to the sidelines. But even from the sidelines, he could see Reagan's revolution unravel almost from the start. "The high-water mark of Reaganism was the summer of eighty-one," Gingrich said. Reagan refused to face up fully to the government's spending crisis, and after that it was mostly downhill, a long, slow slide that would culminate with Gingrich's taking on Reagan's nominal Republican heir, George Bush, in a battle to the political death in 1990 for the soul of the party.

On the other hand, Gingrich also viewed Reagan as the vanguard of the revolution, the first wave that made possible the attempt the Georgian and his followers would make a decade and a half later. According to Gingrich, in 1985, Reagan had told him, "Look, it took us over thirty years to get into this mess. I'm the first wave of change. We're going to get as far as we get, and then it's your problem." Gingrich felt the same admiration for Reagan that a New Dealer would have felt for President Woodrow Wilson, who almost single-handedly created the modern-era progressive movement—but left the bulk of the Democratic transformation to FDR. "The fact that he didn't get it all done doesn't diminish the fact that all of the New Dealers looked back on Wilson as a giant," Gingrich observed. "I think Reagan was a giant. But when I look at the gap between where we wanted to go and where we went, you have to feel that this was a thoroughly unimplemented revolution."

———

What is so surprising in hindsight is how quickly the revolution went bust. One moment, Reagan was the undisputed conqueror of

Congress. The next moment his program looked like a disaster, and alarmed Republicans were bickering among themselves about the deficit and a fast deteriorating economy.

Congress had barely finished work on Reagan's budget and tax cut and departed for the August 1981 recess when the stock market, responding to worries about a mounting deficit, abruptly nose-dived. Investors large and small took a severe beating, and panic gripped the financial community. The gloominess was compounded by the first telltale signs of an oncoming recession: long unemployment lines and a sudden surge in bankruptcies and foreclosures. Inflation was declining, but so was the economy. Reagan's once soaring poll ratings were beginning to slip as well, but the president seemed unfazed. He spent the entire month vacationing on his ranch high in the mountains overlooking Santa Barbara.

Reagan's advisers were deeply worried. Throughout that fall and into the winter, Stockman and James Baker tried to persuade the president to mount a major effort to deal with the deficit crisis, thus reassuring the financial markets that the situation was not as far out of control as it seemed. Stockman wanted to rally the weary Congress to approve still another round of spending cuts and to consider raising taxes as well. To get Reagan's attention, he circulated figures showing that the deficit might top $100 billion for the first time in history. How embarrassing—the terrible Jimmy Carter deficits Reagan had ridiculed on his way to the White House had topped out at a mere $79 billion.

The way Reagan reacted to this set the course he followed for the rest of his presidency. The president refused to be alarmed by the deficit projections. He stuck to his core beliefs, downgraded the goal of a balanced budget from a must-do to a nice-to-have, and concentrated on holding on to his tax cuts and his defense buildup. By November, he had publicly abandoned his campaign pledge to balance the budget by 1984. "I did not come here to balance the budget—not at the expense of my tax-cutting program and my defense program," he said.

The rest of his presidency can hardly be called a failure, but judged on the narrow criterion of his budget battles, the rest of his rule was downhill: a series of nasty economic-policy fights, rearguard actions, dead-on-arrival budgets, and despite his repeated public insistence that he would not accept them, tax increases that would have been humiliating if anyone other than the popular president had signed them. In public, the president vigorously defended his supply-side convictions and resisted entreaties from his own party to do what was necessary to fix the deficit. Privately, however, Reagan often gave relatively free rein to administration pragmatists to pursue accommodations with congressional leaders that ran counter to his professed philosophy.

If there were any lingering doubts about where he stood, Reagan meant to dispel them in his January 1982 State of the Union Address. A confident and jaunty president rode to Capitol Hill to serve notice that he would not suffer the fate of other presidents who had allowed events to force them away from their original agenda. The nation was experiencing some tough economic times, he acknowledged, but he insisted his economic policies were not to blame. Rather, he said, the problems stemmed from decades of reckless Democratic tax-and-spend policies. In words that would galvanize the right wing of his party and frame the budget debate for the next fourteen years, Reagan declared: "Raising taxes won't balance the budget. It will encourage more government spending and less private investment." Then the president added, "I will not ask you to try to balance the budget on the backs of the American taxpayers. I will seek no tax increases this year and I have no intention of retreating from our basic program of tax relief."

At a moment when his own budget director and key members of Congress were advising that tax increases were vital to avoiding a crisis, this was an extraordinary message. In fact, Reagan would raise taxes that year and repeatedly over the next several years; the president's own intransigence on spending cuts made that inevitable. But the image of a party and a president dedicated to cutting taxes—even if doing so was often at odds with what reality indicated they should do—would remain one of Reagan's most remarkable political sleights-of-hand.

Reagan's assertion that government could not reduce deficits by raising taxes was bogus, as many of those in the House chamber that night well knew. Mayors, county executives, governors, and presidents had resorted to tax increases throughout the century to control or eliminate deficits. As a rule, politicians do not continue to do unpopular things that don't work. The president and his supply-side allies argued that raising taxes would invariably stifle productivity and economic growth, but they had little if any data to bolster their theory. On the contrary, in the 1970s and 1980s, Japan and industrialized European countries with larger or faster-rising tax burdens than that of the United States also had considerably higher productivity growth than the United States—at least in part because they devoted more of their tax resources to modernizing their infrastructure and educating their labor force. But Reagan was pointing to a larger truth about raising taxes, which is that when times are good, politicians create new programs to take advantage of increased tax revenues, and when times go bad, the temptation is to raise taxes even more to preserve those new programs.

As the roar and cheers went up in the packed House chamber, Bob Dole strained to keep from scowling. Dole had heard Reagan's arguments before, during GOP strategy sessions, and had grown impatient with the president's inflexibility. It didn't take a political savant to see that the administration and the Republican Party were in deep trouble over the economy and the deficit. Everywhere he went back home, people asked Dole the same question: "Why don't you reduce the deficit, Bob?" When reporters sought his response to the president's speech, Dole was characteristically blunt: "I don't want to raise taxes," he said, "but I do want to reduce the deficit."

A brooding figure with a sardonic wit, Dole had a reputation as a mean-spirited hatchet man, a leftover from his early days in the House and from his high-profile role as Gerald Ford's vice-presidential running mate in 1976, when Dole did the street fighting so Ford could take the high road. For many, Dole was little more than the vice-presidential candidate who had called both this century's world wars "Democrat wars" during the vice-presidential debate, a comment so odiously partisan that even his backers winced. Those who knew him insisted he was a far more complex man than that dig suggested.

Though he was nominally a hard-edged conservative Republican, his own hardscrabble upbringing had left him with an empathy for the poor and downtrodden that didn't fit the image of an arch conservative. He had grown up poor in Kansas during the Depression, and he was haunted throughout his life by the painful memory of the time his family had moved into the basement of their home in Russell, Kansas, so they could make ends meet by renting out the upstairs. His experience as a young soldier in the Second World War would be even more indelible. Just three weeks before the end of the war, Dole took a German high-explosive shell fragment in the right shoulder, a horrible wound that damaged his spinal column and came very close to killing him. The strapping, 194-pound athlete who went off to fight came home to Kansas a 122-pound physical wreck. With characteristic tenacity, he worked agonizingly to rehabilitate himself. One day, when he was shuffling painfully around his hometown, trying to walk a little farther than he had managed the day before, a man came up to him and said, "Well, don't you think it'd been better if you'd just died?" Dole lost the use of his right hand for the rest of his life. Decades later he still did not look in mirrors except to tie his tie.

As a young conservative in the House at the height of Lyndon Johnson's Great Society, Dole voted against Medicare (a vote the Democrats would use against him in 1995) and the first of the big anti-poverty programs. He also had a mixed record on civil rights. But his profile began to change after he won a seat in the Senate in 1968 and moved into a larger political arena. He began serving with Senator George McGovern, the prominent South Dakota liberal Democrat, on the Select Committee on Nutrition and Human Needs, a panel McGovern chaired. The conservative Dole and the liberal McGovern became a high-profile political odd couple. Together they began pushing the government deeper and deeper into the nutrition business. "I mean, until there's a better way, there's some people who just have to rely on those kinds of programs," Dole said once in explaining why he backed programs that his more conservative colleagues opposed. "They're not bad people. They're not lazy people. They're not, but because of circumstances or birth or whatever, they don't have any options."

As chairman of the Finance Committee, Dole was critical to the Senate's passage of Reagan's economic program. Throughout the first several months of 1981, he was a loyal team player for the Republican president. But by the fall he had become deeply frustrated with Reagan's unwillingness to adjust to the changing economic situation. When GOP strategists began to target safety-net programs for a second round of spending cuts, he balked. He had helped trim welfare and food stamps during the first round, but enough was enough. "We've about tapped out the big dollars," he told Reagan. "Somebody is going to have to start taking a hit besides welfare recipients." Corporations and middle- and upper-income Americans would have to shoulder a larger share of the burden if the White House and Congress intended to wage war on the deficit. And that could mean only one thing: Reagan would have to raise taxes.

From here on, Dole's pragmatic approach to tax policy would define him more than any other single issue. First as the Finance Committee chairman and later as the Senate Republican leader, Dole demonstrated a steely willingness to raise taxes to control a rampant deficit. "Dole has his fingerprints on everything that is bad and good on taxes," said David Keene, a Republican political consultant during that period and a longtime Dole crony. Long before Reagan delivered his no-new-taxes pledge, Dole had quietly assigned Bob Lighthizer, his top aide, to begin drawing up proposals for raising additional tax revenue. What followed were three major tax increases in as many years, all with Dole playing a central role—and all of them signed by Reagan. Party hard-liners like Gingrich look back on this and see unforgivable treachery. Pragmatists see a vital, incremental effort to keep deficits under control and the financial markets calm.

Accompanied by modest spending cuts, the three tax increases helped dampen deficits, which soared at first but gradually came back under control. The markets quieted. Barely a year after the cometlike rise of tax cutting as the reigning idea behind U.S. fiscal policy, the nation abruptly reversed course. In 1982, Dole pushed through the largest tax increase in postwar history—a $98.5-billion, three-year hike that the public-relations-conscious Dole dubbed the Tax Equity and Fiscal Responsibility Act (which quickly got slimmed down to the meaningless acronym TEFRA). It did not touch income tax rates, and it was sold to Reagan as loophole closing for businesses not paying their fair share (though its dozens of provisions also included hikes in the excise taxes on cigarettes, telephone service, and airline tickets, and so on). When they saw this coming, some of the administration's leading supply-siders resigned, and it was TEFRA that caused an angry young Congressman, Newt Gingrich, to hang on Dole the label that would forever define him to party right-wingers: "tax collector for the welfare state."

In the controversial 1983 effort to bail out the wobbling Social Security trust fund, Dole and other leaders agreed to speed up a planned increase in the Social Security payroll tax, levy the first-ever taxes on Social Security benefits for better-off beneficiaries, and increase the tax on self-employed people: altogether, roughly another $100 billion in tax increases over seven years. Then, in 1984, a presidential-election year, Congress approved the Deficit Reduction Act (DEFRA), a $50-billion package of tax-code fiddling whose provisions were mostly too obscure (restrictions on industrial-development bonds, a repeal of the net-interest exclusion, a change in the rules on income averaging, and so on) to get the public excited.

Dole's willingness to raise taxes made him a traitorous pariah to the supply-siders and the neoconservative Republicans who populated the House. "Dole's sin in their eyes was he did not believe cutting taxes was the answer to everything," said Keene. Kemp and Gingrich vilified Dole and his moderate Republican allies in the Senate as a reactionary force bent on manufacturing a deficit crisis to justify raising taxes. Committed supply-siders continued to believe that the deficit would take care of itself if the government stuck to the new policy of lower taxes. Kemp repeatedly preached that "all deficits are not created equal" and that deficits caused by tax cuts were not only defensible but desirable. In the long run, Kemp assured, the economy would take off, and the deficits would vanish.

Dole made no secret of his contempt for this kind of thinking and the people who pushed it. He told a joke about a bus going over a cliff: The good news was that the bus was carrying a group of supply-siders; the bad news was that there were two empty seats. The decorated war veteran had climbed the political ladder one rung at a time. He was disdainful of what he saw as a bunch of know-nothing Republican upstarts who stood on the sidelines in the House, where their minority status allowed them to avoid the tough business of governing, and took potshots at their GOP colleagues in the Senate, who had to find a way to make things work. "My view was that we had to govern," said Dole a decade later. "We had a majority in the Senate. And if you're in the minority and you don't have to be responsible for passing anything or moving anything, you've got a lot more flexibility."

The supply-siders' attacks on Dole glossed over one important distinction. Though he repeatedly pressed for more revenue to complement spending cuts, Dole never tampered with income tax rates. Reagan's great achievement had been in reducing the top marginal tax rates from 70 percent to 50 percent, and Dole had little interest in trying to undo that. Given the president's obstinacy on this subject, it would have been a hopeless mission. Instead, the senator focused on eliminating excessive tax breaks, finding ways to broaden the tax base by making the tax system more inclusive, and improving methods of tax collection to maximize the government's revenues. "He was essentially a loophole closer," explained Robert McIntyre of Citizens for Tax Justice, who followed Dole's career for a quarter century. As Dole frequently pointed out, raising taxes was much harder work than cutting taxes. His principal challenge was to convince Reagan that none of this threatened the core tax cuts or the party's image.

In 1982, Dole reassured Reagan that TEFRA was not really a package of tax increases at all, at least not in any way that counted. "Reagan would never abandon his philosophy on anything if he believed it was right," said Marlin Fitzwater, Reagan's press spokesman. "But he could be convinced that a pig was a sow's ear when it really wasn't. And I think that's how they did it. They told him it was loophole closing." Dole also reminded Reagan that Republicans were taking hits for being the party of the rich. Dole sold TEFRA to Reagan as a populist package that eliminated the worst excesses of the 1981 tax-cut bidding war, primarily hitting corporations that had avoided paying any taxes because of an overly generous federal tax code. TEFRA's minimum tax would force wealthy individuals and corporations with enormous deductions to pay at least something. It also eliminated the tax "leasing" provision of the 1981 bill, which allowed corporate giants like General Electric and General Dynamics to buy tax breaks from, or sell them to, other corporations. Dole was taking on the business establishment, one of the Republican Party's most devoted constituencies. "Somebody said, 'Well, you're increasing taxes,' " Dole recalled. "I said, 'My God, we're closing a mammoth sinkhole.' "

Reagan not only bought Dole's arguments, but he pushed hard to get the package past skeptical Republicans. He took to TV to insist this was not the largest tax increase in history but the largest tax *reform*. The president was brilliant at publicly posturing as a foe of tax increases while privately giving his top aides the latitude they needed to negotiate the terms of those increases. In the eight years of his presidency, Reagan signed eighteen separate tax bills, fourteen of which raised taxes.

Gingrich forgave Reagan many things, but he had a dim view of the president's position on tax increases. "Reagan's technique was to be against taxes, against taxes, against taxes—sign the bill—against taxes, against taxes, against taxes," Gingrich said.

The best example of Reagan's remarkable knack for approving tax increases while decrying them came the day after he signed TEFRA. He traveled to Foxboro, Massachusetts, to participate in a televised business round table. Warning in his self-deprecating way that he might have to "kick himself" later, he said that what he would really like to do next was to get rid of the corporate income tax altogether. "This was after signing TEFRA, which was almost all on the corporate side," said a senior aide amazed at the president's ability to manipulate reality. "The whole country thinks, 'Here he goes again; he's going to cut taxes even more.' He just signed the largest tax increase in the history of the country, and all the press play is on how he's going to eliminate the corporate income tax."

Dole either lacked Reagan's finesse or didn't care. Yeah, he had raised taxes—what of it? Pragmatists in both parties admired him; ideologues, predictably, loathed him. Gingrich and Dole would be at each other's throats for years over this supposed apostasy, one of the higher-profile battles in what would be a long-running war for the party's soul on the issue of taxes.

By the mid-1980s, the Republican Party was in turmoil. The tenacious Gingrich and members of his Conservative Opportunity Society were dedicated to "breaking the minority Republican mind-set of the past." And that meant challenging men like Dole, Howard Baker, and House Minority Leader Bob Michel of Illinois, who were all part of the old guard, impediments to the radicals. In 1984, Gingrich told *The Washington Post:* "There is clearly a welfare-state wing of the Republican party that sees itself as running essentially a cheaper and narrower version of the Democratic welfare state. If they spent as much energy on trying to rethink and reform the welfare state, it would be a vastly healthier party." This acid was aimed squarely at Dole, whose stubborn fidelity to safety-net programs angered revolutionaries who wanted to radically remake them. It would take them another eleven years, but Gingrich would finally get a chance to pull the party together behind his "replacement model" for the Democratic (and Dole-Republican) welfare state—in

1995, when Republicans proposed to ship Medicaid, AFDC, and other programs back to the states. In 1995, after more than a decade of failed battles to get the deficit under control and in the middle of his last try for the White House, Dole would go along.

But in 1984, he dismissed Gingrich as a minor annoyance, the way a horse might flick away a fly with his tail. "He's making a lot of noise," Dole said of Gingrich, "but I haven't seen any impact." Dole won many of the skirmishes, but Gingrich and his band of conservatives were slowly winning the larger war of redefining the Republican Party, wresting it away from the pragmatic deal makers and putting it in the hands of the hard-liners.

Tensions broke into the open during a platform fight that split the 1984 Republican National Convention in Dallas. Gingrich, Mississippi GOP Congressman Trent Lott, and other young conservatives seized control of the party's Platform Committee and inserted a no-tax-increase plank over Dole's strong objections. Democratic presidential nominee Walter Mondale had charged a month earlier at the Democratic convention that Reagan secretly planned to raise taxes after the election, and the GOP conservatives were determined to kill such speculation.

Gingrich not only demanded and obtained an "ironclad" pledge against tax increases, but he also put the party on record as supporting a vast new array of tax cuts that, if approved, would have added another $160 billion to the deficit. An agitated Dole warned against "boxing the president in" with the tax pledge. The deficit by then had climbed from Jimmy Carter's $79 billion to more than $200 billion, all on the Republicans' watch. Dole rejected as fantasy supply-siders' claims that the deficits would start to melt away once the economy began responding to Reagan's tax cuts. "Here, we're sitting with a great deficit and they're running around cutting taxes," Dole complained to reporters at the convention. "I think we've lost our way a little bit on fiscal policy."

Escalating the nastily personal sniping that would continue for years between the two men, Gingrich retorted that Dole was "the Walter Mondale of the Republican Party." The glorious Reagan revolution of 1981 had now degenerated into squabbling between the dominant wings of the party: root-canal realists versus morning-in-America tax cutters, one side convinced the lesson of 1981 was that there was no magic, the other side equally sure that the GOP had not gone far enough, cut taxes deeply enough, or stuck to its convictions with enough tenacity.

Reagan's victory over Mondale that fall set up an internal struggle over which wing would define the party's direction during Reagan's last term and beyond. Gingrich, Kemp, and Lott might wield ideological clout at the GOP convention, but their underclass status in the Democrat-controlled House meant they had little real power with which to set the party's course. The fact that Dole and like-minded Republican pragmatists controlled the Senate gave them the authority to steer a presidency that had essentially run out of ideas. In Dole's view, the revolution had begun to go off the rails when Reagan abandoned his core promise to radically reduce the deficit. Instead of cutting back bloated defense and social spending, the president had gone the other way. Now Dole would drive.

Chapter 5

HARD, DIRTY WORK

S hortly after 1:00 A.M. on May 10, 1985, the Senate entered its sev-
enteenth straight hour of debate on the 1986 budget. Senate
Majority Leader Bob Dole, who had staked his leadership on this
moment, stood to talk to his colleagues one more time. He walked
them all briefly through the painful spending cuts they were about
to vote on, admitted they were tough but insisted they were fair, un-
characteristically paused to recite a few lines from a Robert Frost
poem ("Two roads diverged in a yellow wood," et cetera), told his
colleagues it was "the moment of truth," and then sat down, prepared to roll the dice.

Dole had no idea whether he had the votes. With his blessing, a
group of moderates from both parties had been working on a fallback budget package in case his failed. That the Republicans expected a close vote was evident from the fact that Vice President
George Bush was sitting in the presiding officer's chair at the front
of the chamber. Bush had jetted back from Phoenix earlier that long
day, cutting short a Western speaking tour to play one of the vice
president's rarest but most important roles, waiting to exercise his
right to cast a Senate vote in the event of a tie.

The budget that Dole had put together with the help of Budget
Committee Chairman Pete Domenici was immense and daring:
$300 billion in spending cuts over three years, more than twice as

big as the cuts in the Gramm-Latta budget Reagan had rammed through Congress in 1981, and big enough, they hoped, to cut the deficit in half by 1988, as Reagan and Dole had both promised. It remains the largest serious deficit-reduction proposal ever to come to a vote in Congress; it dwarfs even the big budget proposals that would follow it in the 1990s. The cuts behind which Dole and Domenici had so painstakingly assembled what they hoped was a majority were breathtaking, even for Republicans who jawed ceaselessly about the need to slash government programs.

Defense hawks would have to grit their teeth and vote for the first major reversal in the Reagan defense buildup. Supporters of the government's vast array of domestic spending programs—a group that included most Republicans, no matter their rhetoric—would have to hold their noses and vote for sharp cutbacks across the board and for the outright death of thirteen popular programs. And in their single most audacious act, Republican senators were about to touch the untouchable third rail of American politics by freezing Social Security COLAs for a year. There were few votes more difficult; of the fifty-three Republicans in the Senate, nineteen were up for reelection the next year. Dole was gambling not just with individual senators' political careers but with the Republicans' hard-won control of the Senate.

A package like this would have been a tough sell under any circumstances, but Dole's job was made even harder by a curious fiscal reality. The strange paradox of the mid-1980s was that despite frighteningly large deficits—the biggest by far since the Second World War—nothing very bad had happened to the economy. By the time of the vote, the longest peacetime expansion since the war had been under way for two and half years. At the same time, though, the deficit had gone wild. In the thirty-six years between the end of the war and Reagan's first inauguration, the deficit had exceeded 3 percent of the GDP just three times as modest borrowing kept the red ink under control; now it would stay above 3 percent of the GDP for seven years straight—the worst peacetime record in the nation's history, exceeded only by the succession of huge deficits during the war. Nonetheless, interest rates fell, inflation came under control, unemployment went down, and the economy boomed. What, exactly, was the big deal?

Dole's difficulty in 1985 was the same one that he and other Republicans would have a decade later in trying to convince the public that it was essential to take stern measures against a deficit that was not obviously making anything worse. By the mid-1980s, it was gradually becoming clear that the popular doomsday arguments against deficits—that they would cause recessions, depressions, runaway interest, and soaring inflation—were wrong. Most economists would eventually concede there was little direct connection between deficits, even big ones, and short-term economic disaster. Yes, economists said, deficits were bad for the economy, particularly the big, chronic deficits that plagued the nation during the 1980s. But the problems deficits caused—less private investment, lower long-term standards of living, lower productivity growth—were subtle, slow to develop, and hard to see, not the sort of immediate crises that reliably forced action in a democracy.

This was Dole's problem in the pivotal years of 1985 and 1995, the only two times the GOP mounted an all-out assault against the deficit. In both years, there was a lingering fear that more delay might eventually cause economic problems, but there was no fiscal crisis that required action right away. Nonetheless, Republicans went boldly, almost recklessly, forward both times. Why?

Of course they had promised to do it in both years, and in both years the chairman of the Federal Reserve (Paul Volcker in 1985 and Alan Greenspan in 1995) jawboned them and held out the likelihood of lower interest rates if they did their duty. In both years, Republicans were convinced they would never have another chance quite so good (Stockman called it their "last, best chance" in 1985, reasoning that Reagan's second and last honeymoon gave them a window that would soon close; House Budget Committee Chairman John Kasich said over and over in 1995 that he would never again be able to assemble enough votes to get such big cuts). In both years, they were also driven by a desire to machete the federal government down to size, and in both years they worried they would look incompetent if they did nothing to balance the nation's checkbook. By 1985, Republicans had held the White House and the Senate for four years, and they could hardly keep blaming the deficit on Jimmy Carter or drift into yet another election with the problem unfixed. "Obviously we jeopardize the [Senate] majority if we don't act on the deficit," said Dole—haunting words given what followed.

In the end, though, all these other reasons were beside the point.

Republicans risked their political lives in 1985 and again ten years later because one man grabbed center stage, demanded they do it, and persuaded his colleagues to go along. In 1985, it was Bob Dole; in 1995, it was Newt Gingrich who forced everyone else to follow him into the maelstrom.

Dole, like Gingrich a decade later, was a brand-new leader in 1985, elected by his colleagues to pull together a Senate majority that former majority leader Howard Baker had proved increasingly incapable of disciplining. As Senate Finance Committee chairman for the last four years, Dole had proved himself a brilliant legislator, stepping into the vacuum Reagan left when he abdicated his leadership role on the deficit. Now it was Dole's chance to walk upon a much larger stage, and with his eye on the 1988 GOP presidential nomination, he was eager to prove himself. He immediately and publicly took on the hardest single job he could find: He would lead the Senate to the passage of a credible deficit-reduction package, one that would make good on Reagan's airy promise to cut the deficit in half over the next three years.

To do that, though, Dole needed help from a friend, Budget Committee Chairman Pete Domenici. Dole was the big-picture guy and the political arm twister. Domenici was, as Dole would later call him, his "calculator," the man who knew the numbers and the intricacies of the budget as well as any other senator. Though the two were close, Domenici had challenged Dole the year before in the race to succeed Howard Baker as Senate leader. Characteristically, however, Domenici did it timidly and too late, virtually guaranteeing he would lose. By the time the ambitious, hard-charging Dole had sought the support of twenty-five or thirty of his colleagues, Domenici would only say that he was "seriously interested" in the leader's job but had not yet gone to his colleagues to ask for their votes. Domenici finished third in a four-man race.

The majority-leader contest was a stark example of the differences between the two men. Dole was aggressive, quick to calculate the politics of any situation, quick—often too quick—to speak and act, and very self-contained. People said both admiringly and critically of Dole that he kept his own counsel to a degree unusual for a leader: He consulted few people, virtually never shared his private feelings, and operated largely on his own.

Domenici was all Dole was not: terminally cautious, agonizingly slow to act, a deep worrier who asked everyone for his or her opinion and let himself be buffeted by his own staffers, who were often tougher and more aggressive than their boss. Domenici had a crippling inferiority complex that could slow or completely stop him. To an interviewer, Domenici once confessed a "natural inclination to worry a great deal about myself, to worry about and second-guess my abilities and argue with myself about my basic capabilities."

Despite their different natures, Domenici and Dole were as close as any two senators, and they frequently backed each other in major initiatives. There was a clear distinction between the two, however: Dole had always been the senior partner. From the time in 1981 when Dole ordered Domenici to forget his objections and go along with Stockman's "magic asterisk" budget gimmick, Domenici had willingly knuckled under to Dole's leadership.

Friends, rivals, friends again—after Dole won the leadership race, the two men set out together to accomplish what Reagan had so stubbornly refused to do. But now Dole assumed the primary role on the budget that Domenici had had all to himself when the hands-off Baker was leader. Through the grueling months it took to assemble the Republican budget, the two men worked as allies—most of the time. Domenici was much more the prisoner of the budget process than Dole was, and when the situation looked hopeless, Dole could stand back and make jokes that the Budget Committee chairman could not. "It's all sort of a game anyway," Dole would say, or "It's all going to be decided in conference, so we just ought to put a zero in there." Despite that occasional needling, the two men worked well together, a one-two team that often simply overwhelmed their colleagues. In the endless backroom sessions with Republican senators, Dole applied pressure, and Domenici supplied the budget arguments. "A formidable combination," admitted one senator who had been squeezed in the Dole-Domenici vise. Dole's secret was relentless persistence and extraordinary stamina; he simply wore down reluctant senators with endless tenacity. He held scores of meetings and took attendance. When one senator said he couldn't vote for the budget because Dole had not consulted him, Dole shot back that the senator had been invited to fifteen meetings and had attended only four—now what was this about not being consulted?

Just as Clinton would in 1993 and Gingrich would in 1995, Dole gambled his leadership from the start on a terribly dangerous vote on deficit reduction. Had Dole lost that critical Senate vote on May 10, it would have been a disaster for him. "I could see the epitaph," he said later; "here lies the leader who only lasted three months." He was only half-joking.

Stockman admitted all but publicly early in 1985 that Reagan could not deliver a real budget proposal. Indeed, Reagan's February budget was, as usual, more an ideological tantrum than a practical political blueprint for getting the deficit down. It demanded deep cuts in many of the same domestic spending programs the president had repeatedly tried to gut or kill over the previous four years, only to have members of Congress—including Republicans—tell him they weren't interested. When the GOP-controlled Senate Budget Committee brought it up for a vote later that year to give the White House a reality check, only four of the committee's twenty-one members voted for it. Even a majority of the panel's Republicans rejected it.

In the House, meanwhile, the Democratic majority looked on with bemused detachment. Reagan had clobbered Mondale in the election, disparaging the Democrat's insistence that fixing the deficit required sacrifice; now let Reagan figure a way out of the mess. House Budget Committee Chairman Bill Gray spoke for many of his colleagues: "I've always said, from day one, that the Republicans won the national election last November, they control the Senate, and they control the White House. They are always bragging about the president's forty-nine-state mandate. So we are the loyal opposition; we expect them to govern."

Stockman found himself "impaled on an awful dilemma": The White House had to have big deficit reduction, but getting that meant a deal with the House Democrats, and the price would be some sort of a tax increase. "The final play *had* to yield a tax increase," Stockman declared. "It was vital." Stockman found Dole, Domenici, and the rest of the Senate GOP bulls "more than willing to get the disagreeable business of raising taxes over with." What other choice did they have? "Look," said Domenici budget aide Steve Bell, "if you're going to get a body that's controlled by Democrats and a body that's controlled by Republicans and you're going to ask the Democrats to vote for Social Security restraint and real spending cuts, you're going to have to give them something."

They would run a con, then. Publicly, Stockman, Dole, and Domenici would obey Reagan's no-tax edict and assemble a spending-cuts-only package. To be credible, it would have to go where the money was—to defense and Social Security. In the end, they would have to have some savings from both, but when Reagan saw how deep the cuts had to be, he would agree to some tax increases in order to lighten up on the defense and Social Security reductions. That was the theory, anyway.

Reagan had been elected in part on his pledge to increase defense spending, but the six-year buildup that Carter began and he accelerated stands out from all the other boom-bust cycles in twentieth-century defense spending. Reagan drove up peacetime military spending faster, higher, and longer than Presidents Kennedy and Johnson raised it to fight in Vietnam. Before Reagan's buildup, defense spending since the Second World War had never risen for more than three years in a row; but once Reagan took office, it shot up for six years straight. By the time it was over, the Pentagon was astonishingly flush: It had fully half again as much money to spend every year as it had when the buildup began.

The spending was so excessive that even loyal Republicans began to balk. By early 1985, Congress was openly skeptical of any increase in defense dollars, and when Reagan was preparing his new budget, Dole bluntly warned him not to ask for another big defense increase. When the president ignored the warning and insisted on inflation plus a handsome 6 percent more in new defense outlays, his stubbornness triggered rebellion. Dole and Domenici said no.

Meanwhile, on the domestic side of the budget, the Senate leaders confronted a problem just as big as the Pentagon. Driven by COLAs tied to the inflation rate, Social Security was draining more and more resources from the rest of the budget. Congress had raised the payroll tax to keep Social Security solvent, but over time that raise simply displaced taxes that paid for everything else.

The mushrooming cost of the retirement program also had a debilitating social effect. Retirees were keeping up with inflation, but the working men and women whose payroll taxes kept the hand-to-

mouth system going were not. Social Security was badly in need of a
budget fix to bring it in line with fiscal reality. Republican senators
had wanted to begin to scale back Social Security in 1981, but Reagan had stopped them dead. "Fellas," he said at a critical March
1981 strategy meeting, "I promised I wouldn't touch Social Security.
We just can't get suckered into it. The other side's waiting to
pounce." Just two months later, however, desperate for spending
cuts to make Reagan's first budget work, Stockman floated the idea
of cutting back Social Security's early retirement benefits, which
gave partial monthly payments to workers retiring at age sixty-two.
But in a disastrous political miscue, cuts that were supposed to be
phased in over time were mistakenly described as immediate reductions, and the plan exploded in political catastrophe. The Senate
ran from the idea even before any formal proposal had been made,
voting 96–0 against anything that would "unfairly penalize early retirees." This feckless, on-again, off-again bumbling had the worst
possible effect. Eventually, Social Security would have to be part of
any deficit fix; its sheer size simply made that inevitable. But these
blunders were making the program politically inviolable.

"From the beginning, Republicans stumbled around this issue
like public drunks," said Domenici aide Bell, who remembered his
frustrated disbelief when Reagan decreed the program untouchable
at the March 1981 meeting, just after having taken office. Had Republicans acted to curb the program modestly when Reagan was at
the height of his power, the nation could have saved billions of dollars over the ensuing years and, more important, would have set the
precedent that no part of the budget was above review. But the Republicans, with Reagan at the helm, missed their chance. Years later
Bell still seethed over the missed opportunity, calling it "that immense, inconceivable fuckup, that terrible political error."

Reagan proved right about the Democrats, however. They were
waiting to pounce, and they pounded the issue remorselessly in the
runup to the 1982 midterm elections. House Republicans had
never supported the Stockman plan, had never even had a proposed
bill from the White House to consider. But the Republican administration had momentarily floated such a plan, and Democrats had
hammered away to great effect. House Republicans lost a staggering
twenty-six seats, stripping Reagan of working control of the House
for the rest of his presidency. Republicans who survived were left

with the acrid taste of grabbing a live wire and barely living through it. They vowed never to make that mistake again.

Two years later, however, Senate Republican leaders were thinking the unthinkable again. In December 1984, Republican governors came out in favor of a budget-wide spending freeze that would include defense and Social Security. In January 1985, Dole orchestrated a hearing in which the former chief economic advisers to three presidents all warned that Congress had better find a way to redeem Reagan's pledge to cut the deficit, a feat they said would be difficult or impossible without hitting Social Security. Former Ford adviser Alan Greenspan said he saw no way of making a "really frontal assault on the deficit" without cutting entitlements, particularly entitlement COLAs.

Gradually, the COLA freeze became the linchpin of the Dole-Domenici budget. It was big money—$22 billion in deficit reduction by itself over three years and more than $33 billion when wrapped in with similar COLA freezes in other federal pension programs. But it was much more than just money. Social Security had grown and grown as successive Congresses and presidents had layered on benefits never contemplated when the program was begun in the dark days of the 1930s. Republicans saw the one-year COLA freeze as a modest effort to trim the growth of benefits, not the benefits themselves. Most important, though, was the symbolic impact.

"If we could get Social Security cuts—restrained, slow down the rate of growth, whatever you want to say—the most sacred of sacred cows, then we could take on anything else," explained Bell. "Because we could always say, Well, now, wait a minute, if your Aunt Millie out there in Dubuque, Iowa, retired and living on Social Security, is willing to forgo her increase, you sons of bitches, you can forgo yours. You could have told the farmers, you could have told all the discretionary programs, you could have told defense, you could have told everybody. Symbolically, it was the most important thing because it was supposedly the untouchable. That's why we had to do it. Crack that, and you crack the budget problem."

But of course it was political poison. In the House, both Democrats and Republicans refused to back it. Democrats delighted in pointing out how unequivocally Reagan had promised not to touch the COLA. "I have to say my pledge during the campaign carried with it the clear implication that present Social Security beneficiaries would get their cost-of-living increases as well," Reagan had told the conservative journal *Human Events* earlier in the year. "I made that pledge and so, therefore, I feel bound by it."

It wasn't just the specter of elderly revenge over COLAs that had senators spooked; the Dole-Domenici budget was so full of spending cuts that it was an excruciatingly tough yes vote, even for those Republicans who thundered about how much they wanted to cut spending. Many were pulled on board at the last minute only when leaders agreed to spare favorite programs. Dole and Domenici had had to woo conservative, anti-spending Republicans by promising to—well, to spend money. This was good old-fashioned logrolling: Utah's Orrin Hatch received restoration of 70 percent of the funding for the Job Corps; South Dakotan Jim Abdnor won a promise not to phase out the cut-rate loans offered by the Rural Electrification Administration, and North Carolina's Jesse Helms and other farm-state senators got generous restorations of planned cuts in a variety of farm-subsidy programs.

Putting together a serious deficit-reduction package and getting it passed is hard, dirty work, even tougher when that package consists of nothing but spending cuts. In the twenty years since the deficit went out of control, Republicans have tried this just three times—in 1981, in 1985, and again in 1995. Each time they learned the same lesson all over again: If the cuts are meager enough to pass, as they were in 1981, they will not fix the problem; if they are big enough to fix the problem, as they were in 1985 and 1995, they will turn out to be politically intolerable.

There are few better illustrations of this than the hellish five months it took Dole and Domenici to construct the budget they offered in May 1985. Everyone wanted to reduce the deficit, but everyone had a different way to do it. By May 10, Dole and Domenici had made five separate attempts to put together a package that Reagan and a majority of the Senate could support. When the two leaders finally came to the Senate floor in the early morning hours of May 10, there was only a tentative assurance that this try, their sixth, would finally succeed.

By now, Dole and Domenici had threatened, cajoled, and bribed their colleagues and appealed to their better nature and sense of duty in more than one hundred meetings throughout the late winter and early spring. They had spent more than seventy-one hours on the Senate floor, debating the budget and holding forty-two roll-call votes. They had put cuts in, taken them out, and then put them back in again as everyone agonized and worried about his or her constituents' wrath and calculated whether he or she could really vote to cut defense and tell Social Security recipients to forget about an inflation adjustment next year.

Reagan seemed to be on their side. There was a sense of collective responsibility and a collective fear of doing nothing. In the end, there was also a little head knocking, a little senator-to-senator hardball with the handful of Republicans the leaders needed to put the plan over the top. "There were forty-five or forty-seven of us willing to buckle up our guts and take the heat together," said Senate Majority Whip Al Simpson of Wyoming. "And so people say to the others, 'Well, how about it, pal?' "

Around the time Dole started his last speech before the vote, an ambulance had pulled up outside the Capitol, bringing a vote Dole had to have. California Republican Senator Pete Wilson, who had undergone emergency surgery to remove a ruptured appendix less than forty-eight hours earlier, was brought from Bethesda Naval Hospital to the building's second floor and gently shifted from his hospital gurney to a wheelchair, still attached to a sustaining bottle of intravenous solution. Weak and exhausted, looking shockingly pale, Wilson had insisted on making the wee-hours trip in from the Washington suburbs to give Dole what turned out to be a crucial vote. "I just want to know one thing," Dole asked Wilson's doctor, "Can he say yes?"

With Wilson's help, Dole was winning by just one vote, 49–48, when Hawaii Democrat Spark Matsunaga rushed into the chamber and knotted it up at 49–49. All eyes in the packed Senate chamber turned to Bush. "The vice president votes aye," Bush said, and it was done. The largest deficit-reduction package in history had squeaked through the Senate 50–49. In the end, it had all come together in a rare moment of sheer courage. Back in his office, Dole uncorked a bottle of champagne to celebrate. The party, however, was premature.

———

The big package unraveled almost as soon as it was passed. Quickly, House Republicans who bitterly opposed what the Senate had done were whispering in Reagan's ear. On the sly, without warning their Senate brethren about what they were doing, Republican Congressmen Jack Kemp and Trent Lott went around to the White House to warn the president that the COLA freeze just wouldn't fly in the House. Couldn't Reagan see that this would be a repeat of the 1982 election débâcle all over again?

Lott became—his words—the "Grand Pooh-Bah" of leaving Social Security alone. "I don't know how many times Republicans have to be burned on the Social Security issue," he said later. "The Democrats have demagogued it, they have pounded us on that issue for years, and Republicans kept insisting we've got to do the right thing. That's baloney. . . . You can say Republicans are irresponsible on certain issues, but there's no question that when it comes to demagoguing on Social Security, Democrats are totally irresponsible. . . . They made that issue, as Tip O'Neill once said, the 'third rail of politics.' They scared the fool out of people. And particularly in the South, that issue is dangerous." A little more than a month after the Senate vote, Lott went public with a letter to Senate leaders signed by sixty-seven House Republicans urging the senators to drop the COLA freeze. "We speak for a very large majority in the House," Lott warned. Senate Republicans had expected to have to fight House Democrats, but now they had a two-front war that included their House GOP colleagues as well.

As expected, House Democrats passed a budget that matched the Senate's savings, but they ostentatiously left out the COLA freeze. Instead, they cut back Reagan's defense buildup even more deeply than the Senate had.

As far as Senate Republicans were concerned, House members from both parties were acting as if they had no stake in a realistic budget, but it was the House Republicans' what-the-hell attitude that particularly inflamed the Senate's GOP leaders. Senators who had put their political lives on the line by voting for Dole and Domenici's tough budget plan now found themselves alone at the end of a very long limb. Then, with no warning, Reagan sawed it off.

At an early-July cocktails–at–the–White House private meeting with top congressional leaders, Reagan walked off alone for a moment with House Speaker O'Neill. The Speaker had gotten Reagan's attention with the House budget's deep cuts in defense, and Reagan had been brooding about the Senate's Social Security freeze. The president offered Tip a deal: Reagan would drop his support for the Social Security freeze if Democrats would give up their deep defense cuts and come up to the Senate defense number, giving the Pentagon at least an inflation increase. The quiet little agreement between Reagan and O'Neill rocked that year's budget politics and has resonated ever since. Dole and Domenici had been sure of Reagan's support, even if that meant backing him off from strongly held positions on defense and Social Security. But with no warning and no apologies, the president cut the Senate leaders off at the knees. Dole and Domenici were mortified. They had hung the deadly COLA-freeze vote on almost all their Republican colleagues and now had nothing to show for it.

The big deficit-reduction package evaporated. The Senate's COLA freeze was gone. The House's big defense cuts were also gone. To make up for that, Reagan demanded and got a vague "understanding" that there would be more cuts in domestic programs, but everyone knew that was polite fiction: There was no hope for enough cuts to make up for all the savings they had now lost. The cocktail-party agreement became known as the Oak Tree Deal, because Reagan and O'Neill supposedly confected it while sipping their drinks under an oak tree. Dole found bitter humor in the tree metaphor. "They made a little agreement under a tree," he said. "It was Bob Dole's limb that got sawed off."

Reagan appeared either not to understand or not to care how badly he had wounded the Senate Republicans. Senators, usually exquisitely deferential, were enraged. "If the president can't support us, he ought to keep his mouth shut," growled Iowa Republican Charles Grassley. The ordinarily self-contained Dole accused Reagan of "surrendering to the deficit," a blast of near intemperance from a man whose internal rage was certainly far worse. Even in this moment of political despair, Dole retained enough self-discipline to avoid saying what Republicans really thought: that Reagan had utterly betrayed them, not just killing any chance of real deficit reduction but imperiling them in the coming election. The mood? "Anger. Anger. Despair," said New Hampshire Republican Warren Rudman.

Talks went on for weeks to salvage a respectable deficit-reduction package, but the effort was doomed from the start. Domenici demanded that Reagan's vague "understanding" be converted into real spending cuts, but House Democrats were hardly eager to help the

Senate Republicans. When Domenici complained that the House's proffered spending cuts were too small, House Budget Committee Chairman Bill Gray called Domenici's remarks "sanctimonious."

House Majority Leader Jim Wright urged negotiators to "exorcise the devils of bad feeling" and said none of them should "preach . . . any more than we have to."

"Don't preach to us!" shot back Domenici, who finally gave up in exasperation. "Everywhere I turn, it seems there is nowhere to go," he said.

The White House was no help in smoothing things over. In a July 18 speech that conveniently ignored Reagan's catalytic role in the mess, Chief of Staff Don Regan condemned Democrats and Republicans alike for the "ridiculous" and "disgraceful" budget impasse and accused them of flinching from the deficit crisis. "They are afraid to come to grips with it," he said. Regan later tried to make up to a furious Dole by presenting him with a Chaska Indian peace pipe. "I just wanted Senate Republicans to know I'm at peace with them," said the chief of staff. Dole put his ear to the pipe and asked, "Is it ticking?"

By late July, things were going nowhere. Since the previous December, Senate Republicans had considered no fewer than thirty-five different budget plans. All were dead. On August 1, the House and the Senate approved a compromise budget that proponents publicly declared would cut spending almost enough to cut the deficit in half by 1988—but when the Congressional Budget Office drained the proposal of fakery and cooked numbers, the cuts were nowhere near that deep. When Congress finally filled in the budget details with actual spending cuts the next year, the bill saved a pathetic $18 billion over three years. This was all that was left of Stockman, Dole, and Domenici's ambitious plans of more than a year earlier to craft a package that would save almost $300 billion.

In a fitting ending to this sad story, Stockman gave up in despair and frustration and resigned as Reagan's budget director that August. Looking back later on this final débâcle, he declared that the Senate Republicans had been "heroes that night when they walked the plank and passed the Dole-Domenici budget. They had put a cap on the COLAs of 40 million voters. They had cut, nicked, and squeezed wherever their collective politics permitted. It was utterly the best that could be done. But it was all for naught." Reagan had blocked them at every turn. "There was not a rational possibility left to deal with the irrationality that had descended on the nation."

But where Stockman saw hopelessness and despair, Texas Republican Senator Phil Gramm saw opportunity. Shortly before the August 1985 recess, just as Dole and Domenici gave up all hope for a serious budget package, Gramm called on the Budget Committee chairman in Domenici's Dirksen Building office. Gramm, forty-three, had been a senator for barely seven months, but he had arrived from the House earlier that year with a reputation that made moderate Republicans like Domenici wary. Aggressively conservative and abrasively self-promotional, Gramm was not the kind of politician who deferred to senior members, waited patiently for a chance to make his mark, or particularly cared whose toes he stepped on.

Domenici, meanwhile, like Stockman, was deeply frustrated at having worked for months only to produce a political fiasco. "He was very, very despondent and very depressed that he had put his colleagues through a tough vote [only] to have that mean nothing," said a close associate. "He, I think, didn't care. There was a period of time when he [thought], Oh, what the hell. I try my best, I work my tail off around here, and I get shafted."

Gramm had voted with Domenici for the failed May budget package, but he had a plan for getting the same thing done a different way. If they couldn't make Congress and Reagan swallow a big deficit-reduction package under the normal rules, he said, why not change the rules?

Right now there were no explicit targets for the deficit. Gramm proposed to set them. The targets would start high but drop sharply each year, down to a little more than $100 billion by 1988, just what Dole and Domenici had aimed for in their budget proposal, and then to zero, a balanced budget, by 1991. To make those targets hold, Gramm said, they would put in place a radical new fallback system of automatic spending cuts. If Congress and the White House failed to use the regular budget process to cut spending or raise taxes enough to meet the deficit target, a doomsday machine of automatic cuts would lop off enough spending to do the job, scything indiscriminately through programs good and bad (and thus motivating politicians to avoid it by doing their jobs). The normal budget process had failed in part because the deficit, as bad as it was, was a long-term problem, almost never the kind of immediate crisis that could reliably galvanize Congress into action. Gramm's plan would fix that by creating an artificial crisis every year. The new mechanism would not say how to get the deficit down—which taxes to raise, which programs to cut, which of the tough decisions they had long been unable to make should now be made. It would simply say: Do it.

Gramm and other conservatives had floated similar ideas in the past with no success, but now the Texan cannily sensed an unusual opportunity. Not only was Congress reeling from its failure to produce serious deficit reduction, but members were about to have to cast one of the most politically odious votes of their careers—to raise the debt ceiling, the limit on the amount of money the federal government can borrow to pay its bills. There was no getting around this evil chore; all the deficit spending they had permitted up to this point had to be paid for somehow, and the alternative to raising the debt ceiling was forcing the federal government into default, an unthinkable scenario.

This time around, though, the increase the Treasury Department said was necessary to keep the nation solvent would bump the nation's accumulated debt up from $1.8 trillion to $2.1 trillion, more than double what it had been when Reagan took office and for the first time above the symbolic $2-trillion mark. Gramm understood that if he could offer members an attractive deficit-reduction proposal to tack on to such a painful debt-limit vote, he would have a real chance for success.

Gramm's idea was a gimmicky way of getting the deficit monkey off Congress's back and walking away from this failed year with something to brag about. Members of Congress might not have cut much of anything, but this robotic mechanism promised cuts in the future. Domenici wasn't sure it would work and wasn't sure it was a good idea, but he was weary and beaten. He gave Gramm his blessing. Said an aide, "What did we have to lose?"

Gramm was junior in the Senate and not well regarded; all his head-butting determination might not be enough to get his proposal passed without help. To fix that, he allied himself with two more senior members who could broaden his reach. New Hampshire Republican Warren Rudman had an ego at least as big as Gramm's, and the gruff former state attorney general could be almost as abrasive. But he had five years in the Senate to Gramm's one, and he had won the respect of his colleagues for his hard work. Rudman had been working on a similar idea, and the two naturally fell in step. Rudman believed in the plan and fought hard to pass it, but he always seemed a little apologetic about the implicit admission that Congress simply could not do its work without a gimmick. "A bad idea whose time has come," he called it.

The two Republicans in turn needed a Democrat to give the plan a bipartisan gloss, so they signed on South Carolina Democrat Ernest "Fritz" Hollings, a mercurial senator and former chairman of the Budget Committee. Hollings was a fiscal conservative who had run for the presidential nomination in 1984 on a pledge to freeze spending.

Gramm-Rudman-Hollings struck many in Congress as a dangerously nutty combination of gimmickry and bad governance. Among other things, critics worried that it would transfer too much power from Congress to the White House, which would have the power to trigger the automatic spending cuts. In the White House, the first reaction was delight. Senior aides even tried to convince reporters that Reagan had dreamed all this up himself, during long walks on his California ranch. On the advice of Chief of Staff Regan, President Reagan publicly announced his enthusiastic support for Gramm-Rudman-Hollings on October 4. Too late the White House realized that an automatic spending mechanism might cut everything, including things the administration didn't want cut at all, such as defense. Belatedly, the White House switched sides and began to try to kill the plan.

Ultimately, however, Gramm-Rudman-Hollings proved irresistible, since it seemed to promise something to everybody. Republicans saw it as a mechanism that would grind down wasteful domestic spending programs. Democrats believed it would finally force Reagan to lower defense spending and raise taxes. Conservatives saw a tool that would institutionalize the Reagan revolution by forcing a reduction in the size of government. Liberals saw a weapon that would require Reagan to squeeze his own priorities to make room for theirs. What helped clinch the deal was that it would allow everyone to go home at the end of an otherwise awful year and tell voters that he or she had passed something that would actually balance the budget.

In reality, Gramm-Rudman-Hollings was critically flawed from the start, since negotiations over its innards put so much spending off-limits to the budget ax. Social Security, veterans' benefits, Medicaid, food stamps, and a few other low-income programs were completely exempt from automatic cuts while reductions for Medicare and other health programs were sharply limited. Designing Gramm-Rudman-Hollings turned out to be no different from any other deficit-reduction exercise: It was all about shifting the pain elsewhere. When it was done, 60 percent of the federal budget was almost entirely off-limits. Cuts would come only from the remaining 40 percent, half from domestic spending and half from defense. By loading all the cuts onto less than half the budget, the drafters guaranteed that it would fail if it ever came to a serious test.

In the meantime, though, making defense vulnerable went a long way toward evening up the balance of budgetary terror between Reagan and congressional Democrats. Number-two House Democrat Tom Foley, the majority whip, said putting defense at risk was like "kidnapping the only child of the president's official family that he loves and holding it in a dark basement and sending the president its ear."

On December 11, a remarkably brief two and a half months after the proposal was first publicly presented, Congress cleared it, and Reagan signed it into law the next day. On its face, it was a failure from the start, since it never brought the budget anywhere close to balance. In 1986, the first year the new law was in effect, the deficit set a new record ($221.2 billion) and exceeded the first Gramm-Rudman-Hollings target by $50 billion. By mutual agreement, Republicans and Democrats had limited maximum cuts in the first year to a bearable $11.7 billion no matter how bad the deficit got. This was a small enough sum that simply letting the cuts go into effect rather than trying to work the regular budget process to meet the deficit target made sense. So the first year Gramm-Rudman-Hollings was active, the doomsday machine actually took effect. It wasn't much of a doomsday.

If Senate Republicans were hoping Gramm-Rudman-Hollings would be a political life raft for them, they were bitterly disappointed. They were devastated at the polls in November 1986, losing a net eight seats as the Democrats easily won back control of the

Senate. There were numerous elements at work in the disaster, but as far as Dole, Domenici, and many of the losing candidates were concerned, the factor that turned the tide in several close races was a ruthlessly demagogic, last-minute campaign by Democrats to beat up GOP Senate candidates for having tried to cut Social Security.

Lott and Kemp seemed to have been right. "I give them credit for showing courage and taking a stand and being united," said Lott of his Senate Republican colleagues and their 1985 budget. "I thought it was a courageous act on their part. But it was politically insane, and guess what happened? They lost the majority in the next year. So my political advice on this has been vindicated."

It was the Senate leaders' worst nightmare come true, and the scars would stay with Dole and Domenici for years. No wonder they were far warier and more cautious than Gingrich and the hard-charging House Republicans in 1995. The lessons of 1985 were simple: Republicans who had made the hard choices laid themselves open to attack and defeat. Serious efforts to reduce the deficit seemed to bring only woe.

One of the paradoxes of Reagan's presidency is that despite everything he did to frustrate efforts by Dole, Domenici, Stockman, and others who tried to bring the deficit down, the deficit wound up dropping sharply during the last three years Reagan controlled the budget. After racing up from 1982 to 1986, the deficit suddenly fell almost as fast. From a record $221.2 billion in 1986, it plummeted to less than $150 billion in 1987 and barely budged for the next two years, inching up to just $155 billion in 1988 and then down to $153 billion in 1989. Meanwhile, the economy continued to grow, shrinking the deficit even more in real terms, from a troubling 5.2 percent of GDP in 1986 to 2.9 percent of GDP in 1989. What was going on?

Defenders of Reaganomics take this as proof that Reagan's core supply-side policies actually had begun to work—an analysis that collapses under scrutiny. The drop in the deficit came about largely in spite of anything Reagan did and often due to policy changes he fought. But the argument will never be fully resolved, and it came roaring back in 1993, when Republican Christine Todd Whitman was elected governor of New Jersey on a Reagan-like platform of supply-side tax cuts, and again in 1994, when the GOP takeover of Congress brought supply-siders out of the congressional woodwork, demanding an encore.

Supply-siders will forever claim it was their medicine that created the 1980s economic boom and ultimately helped bring the deficit down, crediting the "seven fat years" of growth that *Wall Street Journal* editorial page editor and influential supply-sider Robert Bartley insisted were the direct result of Reagan's policies. Even former Reagan chief of staff and Treasury secretary Jim Baker, never a supply-sider when he served in the Reagan administration, saw those last three deficits as a vindication of Reaganomics—deficit reduction through growth. "We got it down to 3 percent [of GDP] in 1989, and we did it through supply-side economics," he said. "We did it through stimulating growth, putting some restraints for the first time—some serious and substantial restraint—on federal spending. We had caps, we had Gramm-Rudman, and they couldn't spend. And so we got it right back down to where it was in 1980, the last year of the Carter administration." This is a remarkable statement: one of the chief architects of Reagan's fiscal policies taking pride in having returned the deficit to where Reagan had found it eight years earlier. Baker's declaration neatly elides the fact that it was Reagan who helped take the deficit to such dizzying heights in the first place.

Defenders insist Reaganomics ignited huge growth in the 1980s, an acceptable tradeoff for the equally enormous deficits. Asked whether he felt "guilty" for his role in helping to cause the biggest deficits since the Second World War, supply-side evangelist Jack Kemp was dismissive: "Guilty? If I'm going to take any blame for the deficit, then somebody is going to have to give me some credit for launching the most powerful economic recovery in this century."

The economy clearly did well during most of the 1980s, but there is broad debate about whether growth was as exceptional as Kemp claimed or only about par for an expansion that followed four years of economic stagnation and two recessions between 1979 and 1982. Supply-side critics such as MIT economist Paul Krugman argue that the 1980s growth was actually a little less robust than the growth during the "golden years" of the 1960s and early 1970s and in any case nothing special.

There is no dispute that growth played some part in bringing the deficit down, but there were clearly other factors at play. The biggest surge of growth during the Reagan administration came right after the 1982 recession, when deficits were highest; by 1987, when the deficit finally began to fall, growth had cooled off. Jim Baker and other Reaganites insist that the other big factor was the Gramm-Rudman-Hollings spending restraint. But the evidence contradicts them. After that first $11.7-billion cut in early 1986, Gramm-Rudman-Hollings's doomsday mechanism was never again allowed to go into effect. Instead, Congress and the White House conspired to ignore the deficit targets. To avoid big spending cuts in the election year of 1988, they simply changed the deficit targets to give themselves a two-year extension, pushing the date for a balanced budget to 1993.

Not only did Gramm-Rudman-Hollings dismally fail to balance the budget, but its inflexible targets often led not to real deficit reduction but to perversely creative avoidance behavior by congressional budgeteers, who turned out to be much better at getting around the law than complying with it. Since Gramm-Rudman-Hollings counted only on-budget spending, for example, billions of dollars in spending were deliberately placed "off budget." The deficit didn't change, just the accounting. It was just this sort of fakery that eventually so disillusioned Hollings that he declared himself "divorced" from the law, which has since been called simply Gramm-Rudman.

For these reasons it is popular to deride Gramm-Rudman as an utter failure. But the truth is more complicated: In some important ways, the law changed budgeting for the better. Gramm-Rudman's most valuable effect was to replace good intentions, always thoroughly unreliable, with a shaky new discipline. The law erected obscure but critical procedural barriers to spending that, if nothing else, gave members a new argument with which to begin to resist ("I'd love to back that proposal, but my hands are tied by Gramm-Rudman").

The new law created the expectation, if not always the reality, that the federal government would henceforth run on a pay-as-you-go basis. In the past, new programs had always been additive: We'll continue to fund existing programs, *and* we'll do these new things.

Gramm-Rudman created a zero-sum game that slowly began to require that new initiatives be paid for, either by finding new revenues
or by cutting existing spending.

The most compelling example of this was the 1986 struggle over
tax reform. Just five years earlier both sides had indulged in a ru-
inous bidding war to expand Reagan's 1981 tax cuts. But in 1986,
even though much of Gramm-Rudman had been temporarily sus-
pended by the courts early in the year, its ethic dominated the proceedings. Leaders decreed that the tax-reform bill would be revenue
neutral, which meant that any tax cuts would have to be paid for
with tax increases. Investors rushing to avoid the law's hike in capital gains taxes helped produce a nearly $22-billion revenue windfall
in 1987.

This helps explain why the deficit dropped the way it did in the
late 1980s: It was not one or two big things but a lot of smaller factors, some planned and some accidental, that came together where
politics alone had failed.

The unexpected bonus from tax reform was one factor, the first-
year Gramm-Rudman spending cuts another. Sustained economic
growth helped, especially when it was joined by an unexpectedly low
1.1 percent inflation rate in 1986 that dramatically lowered COLAs
(and therefore federal spending) for a wide variety of federal benefit programs. Most important of all was Congress's finally putting a
stop to the Reagan defense buildup in the otherwise doomed 1985
budget wars. After shooting up for six years straight, defense spending dropped—at least in inflation-adjusted terms—for the next five.
Alone, no single item would have been enough to knock the deficit
down to less than 3 percent of GDP for the first time in Reagan's
presidency, but together these factors did it.

———

Reagan may have driven deficit hawks crazy, but his political skills—
and his sheer chutzpah—were remarkable. He got into office in part
by ridiculing Jimmy Carter's deficits—and then nearly tripled them.
He ran up more debt in eight years, adjusted for inflation, than Roosevelt and Truman had borrowed to fight the Second World War,
but somehow he emerged with a reputation as the nation's premier
battler for a balanced budget. He raised taxes over and over again

and signed the largest tax increase in modern U.S. history, but somehow he never damaged his anti-tax reputation. Reagan was the embodiment of economist Herb Stein's cynical advice. "For the politician it is important to be regarded as on the side of reducing deficits," said Richard Nixon's former chief economist, but "it is not important for him to do anything about it."

Dole took the opposite view, calculating early on that the most important thing he could do for his party and his own political ambitions was to make right what had gone so badly wrong in 1981. He spent the next five years working as hard as anyone else in Washington to drive deficits down, repeatedly taking enormous political risks that finally blew up in his face.

Supply-siders like Reagan never really cared much about the size of the deficit, reasoning that the growth their big tax cuts would unleash would eventually take care of the red ink. "I would take a temporary deficit if it would lead to a growing and expanding economy," said supply-sider Jack Kemp. The trouble was that the deficits, once unleashed, seemed endless. Dole took the unvarnished view of a Kansas wheat farmer: There was no magical way to solve the problem by "growing" out of it. Painful work would be required, either cutting spending or raising taxes.

He did both, but where Reagan and Kemp and others could weave morning-in-America rhetoric around their growth theories, Dole was virtually tongue-tied when it came to explaining why all this pain was necessary. Even the fundamental issue—why the deficit was so important—left him all but inarticulate. "Well, I guess that's what I've been told all my life by my constituents—how can the government—why don't you do something? Why don't you reduce the deficits? Somebody has to pay. My kids are going to have to pay. Someday they're going to call in the credit card. I mean, everything you can think of," Dole said in an interview. "I mean, it just seemed to me that all the talk about balanced budgets and how bad the deficit was—I'd listened to all this stuff—and you only owe it to yourselves, duh-duh duh-duh—and I could even understand there might be times when some conflict or somewhere you had to borrow money and run a deficit and all this stuff. So I guess just basic philosophy for me, maybe it wasn't Republican, maybe it was just basic Midwest philosophy."

For all his brilliance in assembling the votes to pass that huge

package of spending cuts in 1985, Dole was virtually incapable of explaining why anyone should care. Reagan—who did little but make
Dole's job harder—ran rhetorical circles around the well-inten-
tioned Senate leader, got reelected triumphantly, and rode off into
the sunset with most Americans believing that he—not Dole—was
the one who really wanted to make the budget work.

What did Dole get? When it came time to parlay all his hard work
into the presidential nomination he believed he deserved in 1988,
Vice President George Bush hung Dole's tax increases all over him
in notoriously tax-averse New Hampshire, reducing the senator to
sputtering fury. "Stop lying about my record" was all an enraged
Dole could say. All his hard work in 1981, 1982, 1983, 1984, and
1985 had only given George Bush a chance to beat him up.

Dole would get his revenge soon enough, though. George Bush
was left with a deficit that seemed finally to be under control but was
not, and Reagan's luckless understudy fell heir to all the bitterness
of an eight-year history of intransigence, posturing, phony solutions,
misleading rhetoric, and partisan mistrust and hostility. Into that
buzz saw walked a more callow man, unsure of his own convictions
and publicly pledged, but privately unfaithful, to Reagan's.

Chapter 6

"READ MY LIPS . . . I LIED"

The defiant six-word declaration that would ultimately unravel his presidency came a little more than halfway through the speech George Bush made when he accepted the Republican presidential nomination in New Orleans in August 1988.

"The Congress will push me to raise taxes, and I'll say no," he began, setting up the line, deftly linking two of the things the Superdome full of Republicans most loathed: taxes and the Democrat-run Congress. "And they'll push and I'll say no," he continued, building momentum. He was working hard to get out from under the shadow of Ronald Reagan, the man to whom the vice president had been such a self-effacing understudy for the last eight years that he seemed devoid of any firm convictions of his own. "And they'll push again and I'll say to them"—and here he paused for dramatic effect—*"Read my lips: no new taxes!"*

By the end of the campaign, two and half months later, the phrase would be so familiar that crowds would shout it out in thunderous unison with the candidate. Even in Bush's quavery imitation of Clint Eastwood, the line had punch. A candidate with no edges suddenly had one, and the buoyant, giddy throng in New Orleans's mammoth sports arena exploded with surprised delight. In one clear stroke, Bush had made himself sound tough and gone a long way toward placating those on the right wing suspicious of his moderate Republicanism. His public pledge was more than just a catchy message to voters, however; it was a blood oath to the right wing. Bush was one of them.

Some aides cheered, some listened with concern. Once Bush got elected, he would be doing business with a Democratic Congress that saw taxes as an essential part of any serious deficit-reduction plan. The pledge had turned any future budget talks into a test of manhood. If it ever came down to a tough negotiation, one side was going to have to back down.

Most new presidents charge in and try to remake the world in their first one hundred days in office, but Bush came to the White House with no such plans. He had been vice president for eight years, and he viewed himself in some respects as a caretaker for Reagan's legacy, a preserver of the status quo. "We don't need radical new directions," he said at the outset of the 1988 campaign. Whether it was the deficit or any of a dozen other issues he eventually wanted to address, there was no rush. "The agenda, in terms of issues and timing, is a four-year agenda," Bush Chief of Staff John Sununu said. In the inner councils of the White House, Bush often counseled ambitious aides to go slow. "You don't get extra credit for doing things early," he said.

Compared with Reagan, Bush was far better equipped to understand the complexities of the budget—he had been a Phi Beta Kappa economics major at Yale; but unlike Reagan, he seemed bored by the budget debate and held no strong views on it. As a rival candidate for the Republican presidential nomination in 1980, he derided Reagan's implausible fiscal strategy as "voodoo economics," but he eagerly signed on as a voodoo priest once he got the vice-presidential spot. The famous no-new-taxes pledge was more the sentiment of Peggy Noonan, the speechwriter who crafted it, than something Bush believed; as soon as he was elected, he began to strategize with top aides about how to wiggle out.

Bush had the best résumé in America: naval pilot, war hero, successful businessman, congressman, envoy to China and ambassador to the United Nations, CIA director, and vice president. The obvious next step was the presidency, a job he felt entitled to not because he had bold new ideas to implement, as Reagan had, but because he had waited in line, distinguished himself, and was now next. Bush rode the remaining Reagan tide to victory over hopelessly ineffectual Democratic Massachusetts Governor Michael Dukakis in a campaign of irrelevancies (the flag, prison furloughs, Dukakis's tank ride) that left him in an impossible spot (no new taxes) from which to make the deal he eventually would have to make with the Democratic Congress.

The rule of deficit politics is that big deficit deals usually get done in one of two ways: Either a crisis occurs, such as the October 1987 stock market crash that shocked President Reagan into agreeing to a budget summit and a modest budget deal with Congress. Or the president takes the initiative, exercises leadership, pulls together the ever-fissioning factions in Congress, and forges a majority that holds its collective nose and adopts a plan. Congress cannot do this on its own if the president will not acquiesce. Dole had tried in 1985, only to fail when Reagan withdrew his support; Gingrich would try again in 1995, defying Clinton to stop him. In 1990, there was no serious effort by any congressional leader to deal with the budget. It was up to Bush.

As soon as he was elected, senior aides began to argue over whether the new president should quickly find some face-saving way to abandon the tax pledge and compromise with the Democratic Congress on a serious deficit-reduction package. Some deal with the Democratic-controlled House and Senate would be inevitable before the end of Bush's first term, if only because the Gramm-Rudman law required that the president balance the budget by 1993. After all, some aides noted, Reagan had been elected California governor on a promise of no new taxes but had broken that pledge his first year in office, signing the state's largest-ever tax increase and explaining it away by insisting he'd had no idea how bad the state deficit really was until he'd gotten into office. A senior Bush adviser admired Reagan's chutzpah but pointed out that Bush could hardly have gotten away with the same trick. "It would have been awkward for him to explain where he had been for eight years if we did that," said the adviser. "And beyond that, it would have been difficult in terms of the personal relations with President Reagan and Reagan Republicans. So that plus the credibility issue itself led to the notion among those of us who felt there had to be a deal that there had to be a reasonable interval."

At a private, post-election meeting of Bush's top staff to discuss strategy for 1989, campaign manager (and soon to be Secretary of State) James Baker flatly ruled out abandoning the tax pledge—for now. "We're not going to do it this year," he said. Privately, though, White House pragmatists like Dick Darman believed it was just a matter of time, and they sent out a message to Democrats to be patient. "Darman had always hinted to me, you know, Give us some room from the campaign so that we feel we can have a little more flexibility to try to do something on the revenue side," said California Democrat Leon Panetta, then chairman of the House Budget Committee.

It may have seemed to Bush and his advisers that the president had plenty of time, but he did not. The economy and the budget rules were working inexorably against him. The booming economy he had inherited from Reagan was headed for trouble, cooled by the Federal Reserve Board's steady efforts, beginning in March 1988, to raise interest rates to ward off a new round of inflation. By the time Bush took office in early 1989, the Fed had pushed key short-term interest rates higher than they had been in at least three years. Banks followed suit, and the prime rate jumped to 11.5 percent. Mortgage lending dropped, home sales went down, and very early on, Bush's economic advisers were telling him that the longest peacetime expansion in U.S. history was going to slow and quite possibly end. That was grim news for the deficit, since any economic slowdown would mean shrinking tax revenues and higher spending. That in turn would exacerbate Bush's other big problem, the ever-tightening Gramm-Rudman deficit targets, which were due to get steadily smaller and harder to meet in each year of his presidency.

All this looks quite ominous in hindsight, but in the heady days after Bush took office it was not nearly so clear. The economy was still okay, and the first Gramm-Rudman target could be met with the usual combination of modest deficit reduction and artful flimflam. So Bush drifted through his honeymoon year bound tightly to his tax pledge, and he frittered away his enormous political capital on an embarrassing slide-by budget deal that reflected the stalemate between no-new-taxes Republicans and no-entitlement-cuts Democrats. A transparently phony year-end package technically met Gramm-Rudman's $110-billion target, but only with billions in trickery, such as kicking nearly $2 billion in Postal Service spending off budget and making almost $1 billion in Medicare cuts that existed on paper but were unlikely to save nearly that much in the real world.

As 1990 began, official Washington expected more of the same. In a forecast widely denounced as preposterously optimistic, the White House projected a deficit of just slightly more than $100 billion. Getting down to the new Gramm-Rudman target of $74 billion could be done with a largely pain-free package that would combine the real and the unreal: modest defense cuts, Medicare adjustments, spending speedups (to move spending out of the target year), user fees, and a small package of revenue raisers that both sides could pretend were not really taxes. In late January 1990, Bush told *The Wall Street Journal* he saw no need for any big budget compromise with Congress. "You've got a disciplinary guideline out there in Gramm-Rudman. And what I want to do is meet those targets," he said. Then the roof fell in.

At about the same time Bush unveiled his sunny $100-billion deficit forecast, the CBO was projecting a much gloomier number: $138 billion. The economy, the CBO said, was much softer than the White House was assuming. If the CBO projection was right, the gap between the Gramm-Rudman target and the likely deficit was suddenly a very serious problem, too big to finesse with the usual gimmickry.

Things quickly got worse. By March, the CBO's deficit forecast had jumped again, to $161 billion. The bailout costs for the nation's savings and loans were mushrooming as the size of the disaster was becoming more apparent. All by itself, the projected S&L rescue cost would swell from an annoying but minor $7 billion in January to a staggering $97 billion by September. Even worse, a steadily deteriorating economy would add a breathtaking $103 billion to the January deficit estimate by the end of the year.

It was becoming clear that there was no hope of meeting the Gramm-Rudman target, not with finesse and budget tricks and not even with real deficit reduction. The gap between the target and the deficit was now $90 billion or more; abruptly pulling that much government spending out of the economy in a single year (or mixing spending cuts with tax increases to get the same amount) would kick another prop out from under the steadily weakening expansion. Now Bush was in a box. He could not meet the Gramm-Rudman target, but he could not ignore it, either. This was an election year, and members of Congress would have a hard time facing voters in the fall if they once again finessed the deficit targets the way Reagan and Congress had before the 1988 elections, when they had voted themselves a two-year extension rather than make tough cuts.

In the space of just a couple of months, Bush had gone from complacency to the verge of desperation. Some conservative Republicans were insisting that he hang tough with the budget he had submitted in January and let Congress worry about the Gramm-Rudman target. But the logical conclusion to that strategy was a train wreck right around the time of the fall elections, when huge Gramm-Rudman cuts would go into effect. The resulting chaos— widespread federal-employee furloughs and a drastic cutback in mundane but critical federal services, such as air-traffic control and poultry inspection—would make all of them look incompetent and irresponsible. "He was in an impossible position," said CBO Director Robert Reischauer later. "And the way you get yourself out of an impossible position is to invite others in."

On a cool evening in early May, Bush summoned the top leaders of Congress down to the White House and asked them to convene a budget summit with the administration. Democrats smelled a trap, but they could not say no to a president asking them to help save the economy. "They wanted to find a way of getting us into a clinch so we were all a little bit pregnant from the result," said a senior Democratic aide. For the first time, Bush seemed to be signaling that his no-new-taxes pledge might be reversible after all; he promised the negotiations would be conducted "with no preconditions." Although the phrase was deliberately ambiguous and committed the White House to nothing but talk, hard-rock Republicans immediately interpreted it as a sign of backsliding on the tax pledge.

Bush had no choice, however: He simply had to have some kind of a deal. Republican hard-liners in Congress viewed huge and disruptive Gramm-Rudman spending cuts as a preferable alternative to any budget agreement with taxes in it, but the party's moderate wing was bailing out. Middle-of-the-road Republicans such as Massachusetts Congressman Silvio Conte regarded the looming automatic spending cuts as "devastating" and believed the White House would have to find some way to avoid them even if that meant dealing with the Democrats on taxes. If Bush played hardball and stuck to his pledge, he would lose not only Congress's Democratic majority but a significant faction of his own party in the House and the Senate as well.

The GOP fault lines extended right into the White House, where Chief of Staff Sununu began to fight furiously to keep Bush from breaking his pledge. Sununu and Budget Director Darman ostensibly worked together closely and agreed on major policy initiatives, but it was Sununu's job to protect Bush's ties to the party's right wing, and that often appeared to put him and Darman at cross-purposes. Both were brilliant men, but neither was humble about it, and their arrogance and insistence on control could be intensely grating, both on Capitol Hill and especially inside the White House. "Sununu and Darman considered themselves Jupiter and Saturn while treating the rest of as Uranus," complained a member of the White House economic team.

Sununu, an engineer who had turned to politics as a second career and became governor of New Hampshire, had found he could get his way with New Hampshire's huge state legislature by intimidation. He was a bully, ill disposed to bother with the finesse and charm Darman was capable of deploying when he needed to. Sununu believed in politics by brute force. When the budget talks progressed too slowly, he repeatedly threatened to blow up the summit and walk away. "Sununu always had his hand on the plunger," said a Democratic participant. "Darman was always trying to seek an accommodation. A lot of it could have been good cop, bad cop by design, but I think a lot of it was Sununu really taking the hardball, hard-line, harsh-politics line, probably more protective of Bush in not just a political sense but a definitional sense."

Congressional Republicans who had to find a way to make a deal quickly grew to dislike Sununu. Frequently, when Treasury Secretary Nick Brady, Budget Director Dick Darman, and Sununu entered the Capitol together to confer with the summit negotiators, the wise-cracking Senate Minority Leader Bob Dole would mutter to those waiting around the table, "Here come Nick, Dick—and Prick." (Dole almost got caught one day when the administration officials walked into the room just as he was delivering his by-now familiar line. "Here come Nick, Dick—and Paul!" he improvised as Sununu entered, looking mystified.)

Sununu's bridge building to the GOP right wing left Darman free to pursue a pragmatist's course, which was exactly what the much

more moderate budget director preferred to do. A long and frequently unhappy history of run-ins with the party's right wing had
left the wealthy, Harvard-educated Darman thoroughly mistrusted
by GOP conservatives, who saw him as a dangerous deal maker with
no allegiance to Reaganism or supply-side economics. They were
right. Darman was contemptuous of the extreme supply-siders,
whom he regarded as intellectual cranks, and he had a pragmatist's
abiding faith in compromise. He was convinced there was a deal on
a grand scale to be had on the budget, and he felt he was one of only
a few with the intellectual and political skills and the knowledge of
the budget to put it together. "Being as arrogant as they say I am,"
he said later, "I did think that I knew more about the combination
of the programs and what to do about them all and how you might
get it done and the processes of pulling together coalitions to get
these things done."

Darman was driven in no small measure by the conviction that a
real budget agreement would finally fix the huge deficit problem he
himself had helped create when, as deputy assistant to the president,
he worked with Budget Director David Stockman to pass the Reagan
program in 1981. Back then Darman had had a moment of doubt
when the cost of Reagan's tax-cut bill began to get out of hand. "I
don't know which is worse," he had worried to Stockman, "winning
now and fixing up the budget mess later or losing now and facing a
political mess immediately." But he took only a moment to decide.
"We win it now, we fix it later," he said. Now, in 1990, later had finally
arrived. "The thought never crossed my mind, and I don't think it
ever crossed Stockman's mind, that we would wait a decade," he
would say that October.

Darman styled himself as the only one who could broker a deal
this volatile, simultaneously bringing factions within each party together and helping the two parties find common ground. He spent
a lot of time with the House Democrats, often working out of Majority Leader Dick Gephardt's spacious ground-floor office complex
in the Capitol. Democrats appreciated the attention, but there was
always a nagging sense that all his brilliance was being put to some
nefarious end. "We always mistrusted him," said a senior House Democratic aide. "He was too cute by half. Dick Darman is a brilliant
individual; none of us assumed that we were as brilliant as Dick Darman was. I'm being somewhat facetious but also truthful. Therefore,

when he does something, you always say, 'What does this mean?' You can't take anything he says on face value."

From the start, Democrats were split. They all wanted Bush to run up the white flag on taxes, but Senate Majority Leader George Mitchell and the other Senate Democrats were much more willing to drag their feet and drive Bush crazy until he finally, unequivocally caved in. House Speaker Tom Foley and the other House Democrats, whom Darman was patiently wooing day after day, were much more eager to get the process going. For the first several weeks, both factions hung together in a deliberate stall, convening an eye-glazing series of informational sessions at which a parade of Democratic committee chairmen came in to testify about how important their programs were. The point was to convey to the White House that they could not hope for a deal based on spending cuts alone. The White House wanted a deal by midsummer, and administration officials repeatedly asked when the exercise would be over. The Democrats were in no hurry. "We were always of the view that we should just continue to walk through the fields, day by day, grinding them down," explained a senior House Democratic aide.

The split on the Democratic side became more obvious when the administration floated a slightly modified version of Bush's January budget in an attempt to get negotiations going. Senate Democrats Mitchell and Budget Committee Chairman Jim Sasser just laughed it off. "Simply putting a new suit on that old corpse isn't going to revive it," cracked Sasser. But House Democrats thought it was time to engage, and they worried that the Republicans would paint them as obstructionists if all they did was say no. Panetta and Foley in particular wanted to lay down a Democratic offer to get things moving, but Mitchell and Sasser, who were far more partisan, were adamant: no deals until Bush made an explicit move toward taxes. Senate Democrats were irritated with, even contemptuous of, their House colleagues, who they thought misunderstood the strategic importance of forcing Bush to abandon his tax pledge. "Foley operated from a tremendous position of fright," said a senior Democratic aide. "He believed that we would be—and he gave this speech numerous times—publicly castigated in the most brutal way, that the president would use the bully pulpit to say that the Congress couldn't function."

One of the hardest strategies to follow in war or politics is simply to wait. Behind the scenes, House and Senate Democrats fought angrily over the senators' insistence on sitting on their hands. "We'd reached a point where we needed to move on something and get it done," said Panetta. But Mitchell and Sasser simply said no. "We stood stock-still, against the great pressure of Leon and Foley desperately wanting to make their first bid," said a Senate participant. Despite the internal rancor, the Democrats presented a united front, giving no indication that they couldn't simply wait all summer and into the fall. Bush himself had waited and temporized and stuck to his no-new-taxes pledge through 1989 and had built no foundation for a compromise with the Democrats. He was now in deep trouble.

There had been no warning before Senate Majority Leader Mitchell, House Speaker Foley, and House Majority Leader Gephardt were summoned to the White House early on the morning of June 26 to an urgent meeting with the president. The imperious Sununu, who put out the calls, had strongly resisted Democratic overtures to Bush to soften his tax stand. But with budget talks going nowhere and the deficit projections and the economy only getting worse, Bush suddenly, unexpectedly, gave in. Early in the meeting, it was clear to Mitchell that Bush had already made up his mind. Foley gave a passionate speech about the need for a balanced-budget package that included both spending cuts and tax increases. It was the same old Democratic line that Republicans had been rejecting for months. But this time, Bush shocked the Democrats by agreeing with Foley. "Well, I think you're right," the president said; "let's go ahead and do it."

Bush asked Sununu and Darman to draft a statement to that effect, but when it was handed around the room ten minutes later, Mitchell frowned and asked for a few minutes to huddle in a side room with Foley and Gephardt. Sununu and Darman had written the statement in the third person, so that all the negotiators—including the Democrats—would appear to share the responsibility for putting taxes on the table. That wasn't the way it was going to be, Mitchell insisted. He took out a pen and quickly edited the statement, crossing out the third-person references and substituting the first-person "me," to make it clear that it was *Bush* who was calling for tax increases. Back at the table, the president agreed to the rewording. In accordance with Mitchell's editing, Bush would say explicitly that it was "clear to me" that among the things needed to make a budget deal work were "tax revenue increases."

Those last three words had escaped Mitchell's editing, and Sununu believed them to be ambiguous enough to convince Democrats that Bush was accommodating them when in fact the White House could claim it was still holding to the tax pledge. "Don't overreact," Sununu told Newt Gingrich, who had recently been elected to the House's number-two GOP leadership spot and was the party's key House conservative; "it really doesn't mean taxes. We've really got a very artful formulation."

Indeed, some of the very first wire stories out of the White House that morning, written from press releases delivered to the White House press room shortly after the meeting, treated the announcement as nothing extraordinary. Reporters and editors interpreted "tax revenue increases" just the way Sununu hoped they would, as an equivocal construction that could mean something as innocuous as more revenues from the same taxes, something that would happen if the economy picked up.

But as soon as they got back from the White House, Mitchell, Foley, and Gephardt went before the TV cameras in the Senate Radio-Television Gallery to give their version of what had happened, and instantly the story changed. The Democratic leaders left no doubt that Bush had, in fact, dropped his tax pledge. "The statement speaks for itself," said Mitchell. "The president has concluded that tax increases are necessary." Foley, who believed Bush had done the right thing for the country at great political danger to himself, made a gentlemanly call for restraint: "I would hope that this would not be the subject of anybody's effort to create political advantage."

But restraint was in short supply. This was the moment Democrats had been waiting for ever since Bush had stuck it to Democratic presidential candidate Michael Dukakis with the no-new-taxes pledge in the 1988 campaign. "George Bush has announced that he is raising taxes," gloated New Jersey Congressman Bob Torricelli. "The charade is finally over." Arkansas Congressman Beryl Anthony, chairman of the Democratic Congressional Campaign Committee, delightedly trashed the Republicans: "This is an admission that the Republican policies of the last ten years were a dismal failure."

Publicly, Republicans put on a brave front, following Sununu's line. "The statement was worded very carefully," said Pennsylvania Congressman Bob Walker, one of the House's most avidly hard-line Republicans. "It said 'tax revenue increases.' Tax revenue increases can mean a cut in capital gains taxes because that gives you additional revenues." But privately, they were enraged. "They had lied to everybody," said Gingrich. Bush had suddenly jeopardized the chief distinction that Republicans claimed separated them from Democrats: Republicans would always hold the line against the Democrats' tax increases.

Vice President Dan Quayle got the news while he was taking a shower in his hotel room in California, where he was on a fund-raising trip for GOP candidates. "I probably should have looked at the drain, because that's where the Republican Party's best issue— the one that had gotten us elected in 1980, 1984 and 1988; the one that had, more than any other, made the Reagan revolution possible—was headed," he later wrote in his autobiography.

Sununu had grossly overestimated his ability to handle Bush's about-face. Besides being angry, Republicans were mystified: Why was Bush making concessions in June when the end of the budget process was months away, in October? Not only that, but the White House had not done Republicans the elementary courtesy of warning them of what was coming. The reaction was pure fury.

Nick Calio, one of Bush's congressional lobbyists, had no idea what was happening until calls started coming in from infuriated Republicans on the Hill. He immediately went looking for Sununu to find out what was going on, and he found the chief of staff and Darman sitting outside the Oval Office.

"What's the problem?" Sununu demanded.

"This is the problem," said Calio, holding up a copy of the "tax revenue increases" statement. "We just broke the tax pledge."

"We did not," shot back Sununu. "That doesn't change anything. We didn't say we'd go for taxes."

Ignoring that issue for the moment, Calio said, "The secondary problem is nobody on Capitol Hill knew about this; we didn't notify anybody, and people are up in arms."

Sununu said that wasn't a problem, either, and if it was, it was chiefly a problem in Calio's mind. The two argued awhile longer before Sununu angrily called Calio a "pinhead" and insisted one more time that this was not a problem. "I think by the end of the day, his view may have changed," Calio said later with a rueful smile.

Editors and news directors had little trouble picking the day's major story, and the press reaction was quick and savage. That afternoon, the *New York Post*'s front-page headline was READ MY LIPS . . . I LIED. That evening all three networks led with the tax story, and two showed videotape of Bush making the pledge in 1988.

Unhappily for Bush, this faux pas turned out to be a defining moment of his presidency. His trajectory in office is forever described by the liftoff, when he made the pledge, and the beginning of the long downward plummet that began the moment he gave it up. "When Bush rescinded his tax pledge, that day Bush was over," wrote Peggy Noonan, who had crafted the "read my lips" line and fought to keep it in Bush's speech over the strenuous protests of other advisers. "And he was over not only because he had gone back on his central pledge of 1988—the informing pledge, the one that said, 'I'm not an old-style liberal Republican, I'll hold the line as Reagan did'—but because in going back he signaled that higher taxes, higher spending and bigger deficits would continue, which threw a cold blanket over an already shivering economy, which soon enough cooled further."

To conservative Republicans, reneging on the pledge was an act of betrayal and stupidity for which they never forgave the president despite his repeated, abject apologies. "If I had it to do over, I wouldn't do what I did then," Bush would say nearly two years later, when he was deep in his reelection race against Democrat Bill Clinton and the furor still hadn't died down. "I did it, and I regret it and I regret it."

But for most seasoned politicians, including many Republicans, the fundamental mistake wasn't that Bush gave the pledge up but that he made it in the first place. It had been a gross political blunder to box himself unequivocally into the sort of situation where only compromisers—including Reagan, for all his professed opposition to taxes—could survive. "The mistake that Bush made was when he took the no-tax pledge, which we thought was a travesty," said the chief of staff of one of the Hill's most senior Republicans. "You never as a legislator lock yourself into that kind of a position. And in fact, realistically, [the abandonment of the pledge] was bound to come, and it just provided fodder for everybody to go after him. Anything that's that absolute when it's not an absolute world I think is trouble. For anybody who's had to sit up here and get these things done, it was just complete stupidity."

***

Like most budget fights in the bitterly polarized era that began with the 1981 struggle over the Reagan proposals, the 1990 budget summit was not just some exercise in good government where well-meaning members of the two parties sat down to thrash out honest differences. Instead, it was vicious, bitter political warfare in which Republicans fought a deadly battle among themselves for control of the party agenda, and Democrats fought as hard as they could to knock Bush out of the White House. In Congress, the fight boiled down to a struggle between two enormously ambitious leaders out to make their bones. The disengaged, much milder Bush never had a chance.

Although he was technically just the newly elected House minority whip, number-two man in the House GOP leadership, Georgia Republican Newt Gingrich was the first real sign of revolution in this Republican backwater. The House GOP had been under the oppressive heel of the Democrats for thirty-six years, and even moderates were desperate enough for change to vote for a man they might originally have written off as a nut. A charismatic supply-sider with the mesmerizing patter of a tent preacher, Gingrich had edged out the more moderate and accommodating Illinois Republican Ed Madigan the previous March. The victory signaled that House Republicans—outnumbered and pushed around by House Democrats and less valuable to the GOP White House than the more potent Senate Republicans—wanted less conciliation and more confrontation—and guerrilla warfare—from their leaders.

House Minority Leader Bob Michel, a decent, avuncular Republican from Peoria who had held the faction-riven party together behind Reagan's initiatives in 1981, seemed to some now, after thirty-four years exclusively in the House minority, to be too much a man of the institution, too willing to compromise with Democrats on issues that should have defined the differences between the parties. Gingrich, on the other hand, took a revolutionary's view: There was little point in trying to compromise with the House's liberal Democratic majority, with its dedication to the welfare state and its iron-fisted control of House procedure. Those who did were, by implication, weak-willed appeasers who settled for table scraps when they should have been out to change the world.

In his ten and a half years in the House, the forty-seven-year-old former college professor from suburban Atlanta had built virtually no reputation as a legislator, choosing instead to style himself, in the words of one biography, as "an idea factory churning out the Republican agenda of the future." With his doctorate in European history, his omnivorous self-schooling in economic theory ("I've read three hundred volumes on economic development over the last thirty-five years," he bragged to an interviewer), and his limitless, monomaniacal political energy, Gingrich was a formidable intellectual force who relentlessly defined the aggressive, rightward edge of GOP congressional politics.

He was just the sort of Republican that Bush had to be wary of: a smart, angry, hard-line right-winger who instinctively mistrusted the president and intended to watch him closely and hold him to his tax promise. Gingrich's economic convictions were as rock solid as Bush's were vague and situational. Despite the beating that supply-side economics had taken after 1981, Gingrich was an unrepentant believer, fiercely committed to supply side in its broadest manifestation, not just as a means of reducing the tax burden but as a machine that could destroy the welfare state and replace it with a smaller government, remade and market driven. He ran insistently contrary to the Democrats' agenda, demanding not just no new taxes but tax cuts, the more and the sooner the better.

Gingrich had little more than contempt for Bush, whom he considered a far weaker, much more inferior version of Ronald Reagan. Gingrich understood that Reagan was at heart a consensus politician who signed tax bills when he had to and was truer to his supply-side vision in word than in deed. But that was irrelevant. It was Reagan's ability to articulate a vision and lead by inspiration that mattered, and judged against that standard, Bush fell hopelessly short. "The most important thing [a president] can do is be the leader of the people—'read my lips.' The second most important is be the symbol of the nation, and the third is to be manager of the government,"

Gingrich said. "Bush thought number three should be number one."

Gingrich's ferocious and judgmental conservatism was what Bush had at his back; reneging on the tax pledge was almost unforgivable apostasy, but the president could ward off sure vengeance from the right wing if he now held the line against any serious tax increase. Dead ahead of him, though, he faced an equally formidable problem: the Democrats who had forced him to eat his tax pledge and who now wanted to force him to swallow big tax increases for the rich as well. The spiritual leader of this group was every bit as much a threat to Bush as Gingrich was. In late 1988, as they organized for the coming year, Senate Democrats had elected George Mitchell as their new majority leader, elevating an unheralded, deceptively mild-mannered man whom Republicans would come to recognize as one of the toughest, most partisan Democrats in Congress.

After only eight years in the Senate, Mitchell, fifty-six, had become one of the highest-ranking Democrats in the nation. He was the political protégé of fellow Maine Democrat and former senator Ed Muskie, who saw to it that Mitchell was named to fill his vacant Senate seat in 1980, when Muskie succeeded Cyrus Vance as Jimmy Carter's secretary of state. Prior to that, Mitchell's career had been solid if lackluster. He had served as chairman of the Maine Democratic Party, moved on to become state attorney general, and then lost a bid for governor in 1974. With Muskie's help, he had become a federal judge for six months before taking over what was left of the new secretary of state's Senate term.

Mitchell came to Congress an unalloyed liberal whose political sympathies sprang naturally from the experience of growing up in a hardworking, blue-collar family in Waterville, Maine. His background was the antithesis of Bush's silver-spoon upbringing: Mitchell's father was a janitor and his mother a Lebanese immigrant who worked the night shift at a local textile mill while she raised five sons. Bush was a star athlete who became captain of his Yale baseball team; Mitchell was undistinguished at sports and spent his youth in the shadow of his older brothers, who were varsity basketball players. Unlike Bush, who glided through Andover and Yale on family money, Mitchell had to scratch his way through school, putting himself through night law school at Georgetown University by working days as an insurance adjuster.

The first major clash between the two men came in the fall of 1989. Bush had angered Democratic leaders by pushing for a cut in the capital gains tax. Mitchell and others thought the president had agreed during budget negotiations the previous spring not to push such a tax cut, but the White House claimed no such deal had been made. Bush moved ahead, picking up enough support from conservative Democrats in the House to pass a capital gains cut there. The president seemed about to get his way in the Senate, too, where a core group of conservative Democrats was ready to join the Republicans to give Bush the votes he needed. Mitchell was not philosophically opposed to a capital gains cut: He had pushed for one during the 1986 tax-reform fight only to get beaten up by Republican senators who accused him of shilling for the rich. Now that the politics had shifted, however, everybody had conveniently swapped sides. Those Republican senators now backed Bush's insistence on a capital gains cut (they insisted it would boost the economy), and Mitchell was nominally opposed.

Mitchell and other Democrats figured they would ultimately have to agree to a capital gains cut as part of some larger budget deal, but only if it was part of a package that raised other tax rates on the wealthy and left the tax code more progressive, a core Democratic demand. Aside from all that, though, the fight over capital gains in the fall of 1989 had little to do with the budget and much to do with a test of wills between Mitchell and Bush. This would set the tone for the rest of Bush's presidency. Would Bush be able to repeat Reagan's feat of snatching working control of Congress by combining unbroken Republican support with a swing group of breakaway Democrats?

Mitchell played hardball. In private, he asked Democrats one question: "Do you want to give George Bush a win?" He begged his colleagues not to abandon him in his first serious showdown as majority leader, and of the dozen or more who were ready to go with Bush in the beginning, only six finally went. With the Democratic votes he needed in his pocket, Mitchell filibustered the tax cut, forcing Bush to mount sixty votes to break him. The best the White House could do was fifty-one. Mitchell won.

Much later a senior administration official who had gone hand to hand with Mitchell and come away with scars had a scathing remembrance of his adversary, a mixture of respect and contempt:

"When you cut to the core of Mitchell, get down deep, what you get is a very, very, very tough street fighter, gut fighter, alley fighter. You get somebody who'd put a knife in your back. . . . The further down you get with Mitchell, the more anger you get."

As the events of 1990 unfolded, the man Mitchell would most enrage was the ordinarily complaisant Bush, who found himself again and again the subject of Mitchell's relentless attacks on the White House's supposed desire to protect the rich. It was almost as if two Maine kids were slugging it out, working out the insecurities and resentments of their childhoods of fifty or sixty years earlier. The poor, frayed-collar kid from gritty Waterville was making life miserable for the rich kid who summered in his family's seaside mansion in comfortable Kennebunkport. The experience left Bush seething. After his reelection defeat in 1992, when he had gone home to Houston to retire, there was one person in particular whom he wanted to single out for a particularly intemperate slap: "Mitchell's purpose, his goal, was simply to bring my presidency down, and to some degree he deserves credit for that," Bush said.

———

Bush's gamble—that by giving up his tax pledge he could jump-start talks and get a quick agreement with congressional Democrats—did not work. Talks remained stalemated. There would be taxes, but what kind? Sununu, Darman, and Brady dug in their heels, furiously resisting Democrats' demands for a higher top income tax rate. Democrats were just as stubborn. Mitchell, Foley, and Gephardt resisted the Republicans' demands for deep cuts in entitlements and other domestic programs. Artificial deadlines came and went with no conclusion and little movement. By the start of Congress's traditional August vacation, talks had gone nowhere. Negotiators agreed to take a break, but they would come back after the recess and isolate themselves from the press and other distractions at nearby Andrews Air Force Base, where they would—they promised—hammer out a deal in four days.

They had hardly left town when Saddam Hussein invaded Kuwait, spiking up oil prices and providing what economists believed was the final push that shoved a staggering economy into recession. When negotiators gathered at Andrews in September, the world around them had changed: A war loomed, and a recession was clearly under way. The basic goal of the budget summit had not altered, however. Despite fears that major deficit reduction now could worsen the recession, negotiators stuck to their agreed-on target of $50 billion in cuts and tax increases the first year and a total package of $500 billion over five years.

There was a natural deal waiting to be done on the tax side. Bashing Bush's capital gains tax-cut proposal was great class-warfare politics for Mitchell and other Democratic leaders, but a majority of the Democratic rank and file wanted the cut. Privately, Democratic negotiators were willing to accept it, but with one proviso: To maintain a semblance of progressivity in the budget deal and in the tax code as well, they were demanding a hike in the top income tax rate for the richest taxpayers. "They could have had, in my judgment, a significant capital gains reduction as part of an agreement to moderately increase the tax rates," said House Speaker Foley later. "It was a golden opportunity to put into the agreement a very important concession and compromise on tax policy. Every businessman I've ever talked to has said, 'Why didn't you do it?' I said we offered it, we put it on the table, we told them, 'We will give you a capital gains reduction if you just give us a moderate increase in the rates.' I was *amazed* that they didn't do it. I thought, This is just temporizing; this has got to be some kind of stalling for reasons I don't understand. Surely, they won't turn this down."

But they did. "No new taxes" had become "no new tax rates" on the theory that Bush might be able to contain the political damage of dropping "no new taxes" if he drew the line at explicitly raising the income tax. Just about any other construction would get by—excise taxes on gasoline or cigarettes, even some sort of disguised tax on the rich—as long as it wasn't a direct increase in the rates.

At the beginning of the Andrews talks, Texas Democratic Senator Lloyd Bentsen, chairman of the Senate Finance Committee, left the air force base and went on a secret mission directly to the president, to talk Texan to Texan. "I tried to trade with him," Bentsen said. "I wanted to make a deal with him. If he'd go up two percent on the [income tax] rate, I would accept his capital gains proposal; I'd go back and fight for it."

But on his way into the Oval Office, Sununu saw him coming and figured out what he was up to. The chief of staff asked whether

Bentsen wanted him to come in with him to see the president. Bentsen said no. "I said, 'Governor, I've known him longer than you have. I don't need somebody to go with me to talk to George Bush.' I went in there, and I thought I had George convinced. But unfortunately, Sununu followed in afterwards and . . . the trade didn't gel."

The negotiators wound up staying at Andrews not for the four-day-long weekend they had planned but for eleven days as talks dragged on inside the base's officers' club bar with no agreement. After quick consensus on some easy matters in the first few days, negotiations bogged down again over fundamentals. Democrats and Republicans sparred over whether to focus tax increases on wealthier taxpayers or spread the burden to the broad middle class, with higher rates on gasoline, cigarettes, and alcohol. Republicans wanted deeper cuts in entitlements, particularly Medicare and particularly from better-off beneficiaries, not just from doctors and hospitals. Democrats resisted. The differences were motivated by a complex mix of partisanship and a basic disagreement over economic equity, and they were maddeningly difficult to resolve. One participant complained that the talks were so slow the experience felt like "being in a ten-reel Fellini film."

The long hours and the frustrating inability to reach agreement worked on tempers. Sununu's sassy one-liners amused some participants for a while, but his arrogance was beginning to grate on the Democrats. As offers went back and forth, the chief of staff typically sat with his feet propped up on the table, munching on chocolate mints from the bowls that were always set out for the negotiators and reading stamp-collecting magazines. One day he finally went too far. When a Democratic offer failed to please him, he tossed the papers back across the table and barked dismissively at House Budget Committee Chairman Panetta, calling him "Leon" instead of the more deferential "Congressman" or "Mr. Chairman" and snapping that the offer wasn't good enough.

Democratic Senate Appropriations Committee Chairman Robert C. Byrd of West Virginia had had enough. One of the Senate's proudest and most driven men, Byrd was a ferocious protector of the institution of Congress, and the notion that an administration official was treating a member of Congress with such cavalier disregard infuriated him. In a coldly furious dressing-down that instantly hushed the scores of negotiators and aides and left the room so quiet they could almost hear one another breathe, Byrd tongue-lashed both Sununu and Darman for several minutes, calling them "arrogant" and "rude." He told the pair that he had served under eight presidents since coming to Congress, and he could not imagine that President Bush or any other president would tolerate his staff—emphasis on the word *staff*—addressing members of Congress with such disrespect.

When it was over, Sununu put his feet on the floor. No one on the Republican side came to his defense. The Republicans retired for a private caucus and returned with a counteroffer that began to narrow their differences with the Democrats in several areas.

But it was not enough. Although Gephardt, who chaired the negotiations, vowed that the bargainers would not leave Andrews without an agreement, it was not to be. "We had hit the wall," said one participant. They extended the session to include one last Monday-night prime-rib dinner—one thing they all agreed on was that they loved the air base's rich and plentiful food—and then they returned to the Capitol for one last try, winnowing the group down to a "hypersummit" of just three top White House officials (Sununu, Darman, and Brady) and the five top congressional leaders (Foley, Gephardt, Mitchell, Michel, and Dole).

Negotiators had broken every deadline they had set for themselves since beginning the talks in May, but now Bush warned there would be no extensions once they reached the end of the fiscal year, at midnight on September 30. If there was no deal, Bush would refuse to sign the customary stopgap spending bill to keep the government going. With less than twenty-four hours left before Bush's deadline, exhausted negotiators at last agreed to a deal. It would save some $40 billion the first year and $500 billion over five years.

The agreement was a major victory for Darman. In the face of unyielding resistance by the administration, the Democrats had retreated from virtually all their proposals to tax the rich. There was no explicit increase in the top income tax rate and nothing so direct as a surcharge on millionaires, which the Democrats had talked up but finally dropped. All that was left was a luxury tax on cars, boats, jewelry, and furs, a limit on itemized deductions for taxpayers with more than $100,000 in income, and a hike in the income level at which the Medicare tax was phased out. Together these items added up to just one fifth of the overall tax package. Almost half the tax package, by contrast, would hit not the wealthy but everybody: ten cents a gallon more on gasoline, another two cents a gallon on heating oil and other refined oil products, a total of eight cents more per pack of cigarettes, plus higher taxes on beer, wine, and hard liquor.

On the spending side, the negotiators would get huge savings (more than one third of the entire package) by cutting the defense budget. There would also be a large cut in the politically sensitive Medicare program. Republicans had prevailed in that area, too, forcing Democrats to agree to take cuts not just from doctors and hospitals but also from beneficiaries, who would have to pay slightly higher premiums, deductibles, and copayments.

About the only thing Darman had not gotten was a broad capital gains cut, but he had managed to come away with some modest business tax incentives, including a provision that indexed capital gains to inflation for small-business investments.

Democrats had long insisted that any deal be "fair," meaning tilted away from low-income and middle-class taxpayers, placing a progressively tougher burden on higher-income taxpayers. To ensure that they were on track, Democratic negotiators routinely ran tax proposals through a complex computer model at Congress's Joint Committee on Taxation to see how the tax burden would be distributed along the income scale. But getting these critical distribution charts took about twenty-four hours; and when the talks got down to the final hours, there wasn't time, according to Gephardt. Republicans had pressed them for a yes or a no, threatening to walk away from the talks if the Democrats did not agree.

Later, when they finally got the chart that showed the distributional effects of the deal, Democratic negotiators were horrified. Everyone across the income scale would get hit with a tax increase, but it would fall hardest on the lower-income and middle-class voters the Democrats had been trying to protect and lightest on the wealthy taxpayers they were trying to hit: Taxes on those earning less than $10,000 would go up 7.6 percent while those earning more than $200,000 would pay just 1.7 percent more. "When we were in that last negotiation up in Foley's office, we blindly had to accept because we didn't have twenty-four more hours to wait for another run," Gephardt said. "It turned out that the distribution chart got blown to smithereens."

Taxes were not the only area where Darman got the better of the Democrats. Although they had gotten substantial defense cuts out of Bush, Democrats long thought they would get even more in the end; Darman blocked this prospect by sheer force of will. Early in the morning of the final day, he walked into Gephardt's office overlooking the Mall. "Do we have a deal?" he demanded abruptly.

Gephardt thought that now was the time to get a final concession on the defense number. "Where are we on defense?" he asked. "I mean, we've been talking to you about this for five months, and you haven't moved an inch, and you're right where you were. If we're going to go forward, we've got to have something on defense."

Darman exploded. "That's it!" he shouted. "I've done everything I can do!" He said he had just gotten the Senate leaders to agree to the deal and was now worried that he might not be able to sell it to Bush and the advisers waiting back at the White House. "I don't even know if I can get them to agree to what I've done, and if you're telling me we've got to do something on defense, we don't have a deal!" Now Darman looked straight at the shocked Gephardt. "You've got forty minutes. I've got to call the president. You make up your mind. If you want the deal, this is the deal. If you don't want the deal, I'm calling Bush and saying there's no deal."

Then he slammed the door and left the stunned Gephardt alone in his office. The majority leader turned and stared out his office window as the morning sun spread over the Mall. He talked quietly with his top aides, George Stephanopoulos and Mike Wessel. "You're tired. You've been up for three days and nights. You've been doing this for five months," he said. "Like any big negotiation, at the end of it, I think everybody has a really sour taste in their mouth. It is very bitter." He called Darman and said yes.

The deal was a political disaster for the Democratic leaders. The taxes socked their lunch-pail constituency, and the Medicare beneficiary cuts hit the elderly. Opposition immediately formed on the party's left wing, and Democratic negotiators went on the defensive and never got off. Some Senate Democrats were sharply critical of the deal and questioned why Mitchell had signed on to such a regressive package. But Mitchell felt he had had no other choice.

Mitchell said Foley had insisted they take the deal, arguing that at that late hour they could either accept it or get blamed publicly by Bush for blowing up the summit when an agreement was within reach. Just when it looked as if Mitchell and the Democrats would have to swallow a politically damaging budget package, however, they were rescued by the unlikeliest of saviors. Although Gingrich had been part of the negotiations from the start, he immediately disavowed the final agreement and assumed leadership of a critical mass of conservative Republicans who were furious about the tax increases.

Gingrich believed he had given ample warning of his objections a month earlier. Just before negotiators returned from the August recess to seclude themselves at Andrews Air Force Base, Gingrich had made a stunning speech in which he not only warned that he opposed the tax increases the summit was virtually sure to produce but he also demanded a package of tax *cuts* that would cost $134 billion over the next five years. "I think that if you combine this kind of pro-growth tax package with relatively modest spending cuts . . . that you would find over a period of two or three years that we would grow into a balanced budget," he said.

Hardheaded budget analysts thought this was simply nuts. It was as if Gingrich had learned nothing from the disastrous experience of 1981, when precisely the formula he was now advocating—small spending cuts, big tax cuts—had helped unleash monstrous deficits. Even his Republican colleagues repudiated him, including conservative Texas Senator Phil Gramm, who shared many of Gingrich's supply-side convictions. "I'm strongly supportive of trying to reduce taxes generally to stimulate the economy," Gramm said, but there was "not a chance that we're going to do it" with a Democratic Congress.

But Gingrich wasn't trying to please Gramm or Bush or find a deal that would get a majority vote: Legislating wasn't the point, and it wasn't his style. Republican negotiators had gambled that by bringing Gingrich in, they could get his imprimatur on a deal and inoculate themselves against attacks from the right wing. "We had been explicitly led to understand that he was going to be supportive," said one senior GOP summit participant. "We would have had a deal a great deal sooner if we had taken a position of Who gives a damn about Gingrich? . . . We wouldn't have had him in the negotiations. Most people didn't want him in. The whole reason to have him there was to get him to be party to the agreement; and what we got, we thought he would agree to, based on what he said." Negotiators claimed Gingrich reassured them repeatedly that he would posture outside the talks but come through in the end, but the August speech marked the end of any intention he might have had to play along. "I thought that was about as clear a speech as I could give as a member of the summit," Gingrich said later.

He formally rejected the deal just as Bush and the other members of the summit team prepared to go out into the Rose Garden to unveil it. As everyone else went out to announce the budget accord before the TV cameras, Gingrich went straight to the Capitol, to a meeting of the House Republican whips, who broke 3–1 against the agreement when they heard what was in it. Democratic and Republican leaders had promised to deliver half their rank and file to support whatever plan the summit produced, and if Gingrich could keep the count below half among the House Republicans, he had a fair chance of killing it.

While the White House and leaders from both parties tried with increasing desperation to sell the agreement during the week of October 1, Gingrich quietly worked against it, providing a rallying point for angry House members. The heavy-handed Sununu enraged many of them by threatening in a closed-door meeting that any Republicans who voted against the plan risked having Bush campaign against them in the elections now a month away. House Republicans shrugged off the hardball White House lobbying and gradually coalesced around the renegade Gingrich. In a tumultuous, wee-hours House floor roll-call vote on Friday, October 5, both conservative Republicans and liberal Democrats held back their support, and the deal collapsed, 179–254.

The drama would continue for another twenty-two days, but the game was over. Gingrich had blown up the Republican side, and he had no effective means by which to reconstruct it; the Republicans were in utter disarray. When the Democrats reconvened in the Capitol to hash out a replacement deal, House Republican leaders couldn't even agree what orders to give their negotiators and dithered so long they sent no one to the talks. The Democrats were left to put together another deal much more to their own liking.

In the brisk, brutal endgame, Bush appeared clueless and distracted. The president had never been thoroughly engaged in the talks, and now he was focused on his efforts to prepare for war against Saddam Hussein in Kuwait. He had the air of a man who wanted to get the summit over with whatever the cost.

When the capital gains–top tax rate tradeoff suddenly seemed to come alive again after the defeat of the first summit deal, the president vacillated, never giving a clear signal as to where he stood. "That's on the table," he said on October 9. But later the same day, seventeen Republican senators went to see him to argue that the tradeoff was just too controversial, and Oregon Senator Bob Packwood emerged to say that Bush had agreed—no deal.

The very next day, Senate Minority Leader Dole insisted Bush had never agreed to kill the trade. Who was right, Dole or Packwood? Attempts to get Bush to clear up the confusion were unavailing. "Let Congress clear it up," Bush said.

Then came perhaps the lowest moment in Bush's on-again, off-again performance in the months-long budget talks. As the president jogged, a reporter shouted a question about whether he was ready to give up on the capital gains cut. "Read my hips!" he joked, pointing to that part of his anatomy. At a time when many Republicans were still furious at him for breaking the no-new-taxes pledge and while the congressional leaders of his badly divided party were trying to fashion a united position in the budget talks—and were wondering whether he backed them or not—Bush's offhand comment seemed particularly stupid.

With Republicans arguing among themselves and unsure of how to play the hand Gingrich had dealt them, the Democrats had a clear field on which to reshape the package. Although tax increases wound up being just one third of the overall deficit-reduction package (the other two thirds were spending cuts and interest savings), the tax piece drew the most attention and caused the most political damage. Democrats wanted a much better looking distribution table, and they got it, chiefly by raising the top income tax rate, which they had been seeking to do ever since Bush took office. The tax rate on the top tier of taxpayers went from 28 percent to 31 percent. Bush got virtually nothing in return: Democrats refused to give him a capital gains cut.

Meanwhile, the gasoline and alcohol taxes that hit the middle class were sharply scaled back: The gasoline tax hike, for example, was cut in half, from ten cents a gallon to a nickel. The result was a distribution table that looked much more like what the Democrats wanted: Taxpayers with incomes of $20,000 or less would get a tax cut of 2 percent or more; the middle-class tax increase would be held to about 2 percent or less; and taxpayers with an income of $200,000 or more would get socked with a 6.3 percent tax hike.

The final agreement was much worse for Bush than the pre-Gingrich version, but the president signed it anyway. By now, he had little choice: The delays, the foot-dragging, that serenely wasted honeymoon year—all had left him no more time in which to maneuver. When the House and the Senate passed the final deficit-reduction package on October 27, the fall elections were just ten days away, and Bush was focusing most of his time and attention on preparing for a war in the Middle East. He didn't want to have to continue to fight a second front at home, and by accepting this deal, he could make the budget problem go away.

But more important, Mitchell, Foley, and Gephardt now had Bush in the same spot he'd had them in just a month earlier: If the president walked away from the deal now, he would be the one responsible for destroying the summit when an agreement was within reach. "No one got everything he or she wanted," Bush said when he signed the bill, "but the end product is a compromise that merits enactment."

Just a few days later, though, Bush was doing damage control, distancing himself from the agreement and vowing never again to let the Democrats make him raise taxes: "They're going to do it over my dead veto, or live veto, or something like that, because it ain't going to happen; I'll guarantee you."

———

From a strict accounting point of view, the 1990 budget deal was a towering achievement. When the CBO got around to counting up the actual savings, it declared that the package had produced a remarkable $482 billion of the $500 billion in deficit reduction over five years that negotiators claimed. Judged by the lame experience of most previous budget deals, which were much smaller and filled with phony savings, the 1990 package was remarkably big and remarkably gimmick free.

In the only terms the average American voter could understand, however, the deal was a failure. Not only did the deficit fail to get smaller, but it took off like a rocket: From $153 billion in 1989, the red ink shot up to $221 billion in 1990, $270 billion in 1991, and a staggering $290 billion in 1992, the all-time record. Some deficit-reduction package—the deficit set a new record every year after the deal was put in place.

The problem was that the deal was put together in the teeth of a recession and an S&L bailout that simply ate up all its deficit reduction and more. Over time, the deficit was about $500 billion less than it would otherwise have been, but how could Bush explain that to anyone but a budget wonk? Policymakers were on a treadmill; no matter how many painful spending cuts and tax increases they embraced, it seemed, the deficit just got worse.

The 1990 deal had almost no defenders. No one liked the elite, closed-door summit that produced it (Gingrich would forbid use of the "s" word in 1995). Leaders of both parties were badly scarred by the defeat of the first agreement on the House floor, and they promised one another never to abandon the normal budget process again.

Conservative critics blamed the summit deal for Bush's loss of the presidency two years later; they also insisted it caused the nasty 1990–91 recession (a claim most economists rejected for a variety of reasons, not least the fact that the recession began in July, three months before the package was finalized).

Part of the problem with the 1990 deal was that it was disastrously oversold. Bush at first touted it as the end of the deficit problem. On October 2, when he went on evening television in a desperate bid to save the doomed first agreement, he said it "would at last put this budget crisis behind us."

That was an absurd claim, and every negotiator knew it. The numbers had begun to go bad on them during the summer, as a recession loomed and then broke, turning their tax-revenue and spending estimates into hopeless optimism. Early on, negotiators knew a $500-billion package was not going to be nearly enough to make the problem go away. They would have had to do at least twice as much, but Congress and the White House would never have been able to produce a $1-trillion package, and even if they had, the economy would have reeled under the impact.

Bush judged the deal a loser even before he signed it, and instead of touting its positive points, he began backing away from it as quickly as he could. This angered those Hill Republicans who had stuck with the process and walked the plank to support the final package, and it wounded Darman, who had pushed the president to make the deal in the first place and now believed Bush could sell its achievements and come out looking like a winner.

In hindsight, the deal Darman engineered—even the revised, much more Democratic version forced on him when Gingrich killed the first one—stands as the biggest and best such package since the deficit went out of control in the mid-1970s. Beyond providing a very real package of spending cuts and tax increases, the deal radically changed the fundamental budget process itself. The old Gramm-Rudman rules had been useful in that they eventually forced agreement when both sides would rather have walked away in disagreement. This was never clearer than in 1990. But the old rules had also set unrealistic deficit targets that encouraged endless game playing and budget flimflam, which caused real budgetary damage and—even worse—seriously undermined the credibility of Congress and the White House by making those two branches of government look like scam artists. The core problem was that Gramm-Rudman made no accommodation for reality: Hard deficit targets meant that politicians were held hostage by deficits that soared due to forces they could not control—a war, a recession, and an S&L crisis, just to name three factors that pushed the deficit up in 1990 alone.

The authors of the new budget rules dropped the notion of deficit targets altogether and instead substituted strict limits on what Congress and the White House did have control over—discretionary spending, the one third or so of the budget dispensed through annual congressional appropriations and subject to a president's veto. For the first time, budget rules forced Congress to abide by a system of strict, enforceable, long-term appropriations caps. The negotiators privately believed these limits would never hold, especially once the ceilings got dramatically lower in the "out years" of 1994 and 1995. Bush himself complained that Congress embraced the tax increases but never produced the spending cuts. "Congress never came through, never fully cooperated with me on major spending constraints that were promised," he said.

Not true. The appropriations caps locked in by the 1990 budget deal were one of the rare success stories of modern budgeting. The limits were so tight and so scrupulously adhered to by Congress for all five years of the deal that they would later enrage Bill Clinton, who found when he became president in 1993 that he could not spend anywhere near as much as he wanted to on social programs because of Bush's unbreakable appropriations ceilings. By 1995, in fact, appropriations were effectively frozen after a generation of almost unbroken increases.

The deal also imposed a pay-as-you-go rule (PAYGO in budget jargon) that required offsets for tax cuts, for any new entitlement program, or for any expansion of benefits in an existing entitlement. The good news was that this virtually guaranteed that Congress and the president could never get into another disastrous tax-cut bidding war the way they did in 1981, and it ended the practice of running up the deficit to create attractive new entitlements or to add new benefits to existing entitlement programs.

But the bad news was that the 1990 negotiators had completely avoided doing anything about the really big problem: the uncontrolled growth of existing entitlements, especially Medicare and Medicaid. PAYGO grandfathered current entitlements, which left Medicare, Medicaid, and several other big, automatic spending programs free to grow without limit as long as the growth came from such factors as a changing population (more elderly people means more Medicare beneficiaries), a bad economy (more claimants for Medicaid, unemployment, food stamps, and welfare), or the exploding medical inflation rate (soaring costs for Medicare and Medicaid).

In fact, both health entitlements grew far faster than anyone had predicted. This was particularly true of Medicaid, which was hit with everything from the extraordinary expense of caring for crack babies to court orders mandating expanded services and legal but ludicrous scams that allowed state governments to game the system by forcing the federal government to pay a higher share of the program's costs. The result was that a Medicaid growth rate that had been averaging about 10 percent a year (already nearly three times the inflation rate) suddenly jumped to 19 percent in 1990, 28 percent in 1991, and 29 percent in 1992. This blew a huge hole in the 1990 budget deal.

Despite all this, though, Bush could have made a virtue of the package's substantial spending cuts, which outnumbered the taxes two to one and were much bigger than any such cuts Reagan ever achieved (and more than Clinton would wring from Congress three years later). He could also have pointed out that he was the first president to bind Congress to strict and enforceable limits on spending, something Reagan had never managed to do.

"In private, he should have said, I cleaned Tom Foley's clock, and Newt Gingrich stole my victory from me," said then CBO Director Robert Reischauer later. "Gingrich almost single-handedly stole defeat from the jaws of victory. George Bush should have told the rest of the people: I was leader of a country that was slipping into recession, facing a dictator in the Persian Gulf, on the verge of going to war. I could not have this country undergoing substantial budgetary gridlock and sharp reductions associated with heinous spending cuts. That's the difference between leadership and rhetoric."

Although it seemed almost tragically destructive at the time, Gingrich's successful rebellion against a sitting president of his own party was the beginning of the end of Democratic control of Congress. Gingrich wanted an end to Republican ambivalence about taxes, and he got it; from this point on, Republicans closed ranks to oppose tax increases, and this lockstep opposition helped devastate Clinton's budget plan in 1993 and turn the electoral tide in 1994. Not for the last time, Republicans chose perfect politics—no new taxes—over imperfect, incremental deficit reduction.

Gingrich's destruction of Bush established that for Republicans there could be no compromise on matters of principle, no matter what the short-run cost. What Republicans learned from 1990 was never to abandon core principles, never to give in to softheaded good-government impulses to compromise on party-defining issues. The near-religious conviction that they were right would make it tough to compromise with a Democratic president in 1995.

When Clinton and his staff looked back at 1990, they concluded that Bush's fundamental mistake was not necessarily the offer of a compromise—which in the end might have been necessary to get a budget deal of some kind—but the timing. Bush unilaterally disarmed in June 1990, giving up his no-new-taxes pledge in hopes of

getting real negotiations started. Even some of Bush's harshest critics conceded that he probably would have had to bend in the end to
get a deal, but they insist that what he should have done was to get
dragged, kicking and screaming every millimeter of the way, from
no new taxes to okay, a little bit of taxes—but only at the last possible minute and only with the greatest amount of pain and pressure,
with Gramm-Rudman cuts imminent, the Gulf War blowing up, the
budget crashing, and everything else on the brink of chaos. It would
have been much harder to criticize Bush if he had yielded at that
point.

Bush's terrible 1990 experience was the most recent time when a
president of one party faced a Congress dominated by the opposition in negotiating a budget, just as Bill Clinton would do when he
confronted a Republican House and Senate in 1995. The results
were a débâcle; Bush was mortally wounded, and not even the vic-
torious Democrats came away unscathed. No year would resonate
more in the minds of the 1995 combatants than this one, and both
sides drew lessons that determined the way they would act and that
would make the outcome largely inevitable.

Lesson 1: Never mind whether Bush should have made the tax
pledge in the first place; once he was chained to it, politics demanded that he should never have dropped it except under extreme duress. Schooled by that bitter experience, Clinton and
Gingrich both determined not to give so much ground on party-
defining principles that they would lose their core constituencies
the way Bush lost his. This would obviously work to make a deal difficult at best in 1995.

Lesson 2: A weak or indifferent president will find plenty of ambitious people ready to do what he should do himself, to his peril.
Bush was much more interested in global affairs than in arcane arguments over taxes and spending. "When it came to domestic policy, he was pretty much an in-box president," said Thomas Mann, a
senior fellow at the Brookings Institution. "I don't think he had any
clear domestic ambitions other than to do the right thing. As a result, as often as not he was reacting to what fell into his lap." Inside
the White House, his own powerful advisers pushed him in opposite

directions on the critical question of tax increases. Up on Capitol Hill, two ambitious new leaders looking for ways to assert themselves—Senate Majority Leader Mitchell and House Minority Whip Gingrich—were lying in wait to whipsaw him. These two men played the game with a destructive ferocity that made the 1995 budget negotiators look back and shudder—and vow not to live through such an experience again.

Lesson 3: As inadequate as the Gramm-Rudman anti-deficit law was, it had the virtue of embarrassing all sides to the point of deal making in 1990; they simply could not afford to ignore the targets again in an election year. But by 1995, the law had been defanged, there was no external mechanism forcing the two sides to compromise, and both sides could refuse to bend.

Lesson 4: Ross Perot's nostrums notwithstanding, there is nothing easy about deficit politics, especially when the White House and Congress are controlled by different parties. There was no magic wand to wave in 1990 to make deep party differences over the budget go away. Republicans and Democrats disagreed bitterly in 1990 and 1995 over the same things that had divided them for a decade or more: taxes versus tax cuts, spending for the Pentagon versus spending for social programs, and the very role of the federal government in American life. When neither side is strong enough to crush the other, someone has to bend. In 1990, Bush bent.

Chapter 7

THE EDUCATION
OF BILL CLINTON

Although Arkansas Governor Bill Clinton had been anointed the Democratic front-runner in the presidential race in early January 1992, the public didn't know him well. His appearance on NBC's *Meet the Press* on January 5 presented him with an important opportunity to energize his base and expose his ideas to a wider audience concerned about the nation's political future. There was a risk, of course: Politicians who appeared on the program to enhance their name recognition often tripped on the barbed questioning of the program's high-powered journalists. But Clinton economics adviser Rob Shapiro, who was watching the program from his home just blocks from the Capitol, wasn't worried. For Shapiro, Clinton was a dream candidate: a smart, gregarious, telegenic politician as interested in the intricacies of public policy as he was.

It was Clinton's grasp of the issues, as well as his consummate political instincts, that first attracted Shapiro to the Arkansas governor. In a speech at Georgetown University two months earlier, Clinton had methodically detailed his economic proposals, which included a middle-class tax cut and a bold, long-term strategy for reasserting U.S. dominance in the global economy. The speech was heavily laced with new Democratic rhetoric about "growing the economy," "empowering" American workers, and "investing" government spending in education and job training, ideas Shapiro had helped plant with the candidate. Shapiro had gotten to know the governor when Clinton served as chairman of the Democratic Leadership Council (DLC), a group of moderate Democrats determined to pull their party away from traditional liberalism and push it toward a new, more centrist stance. Shapiro was chief economist at the DLC's think tank, the Progressive Policy Institute, and the two men gravitated toward each other, Clinton in search of new ideas, Shapiro drawn to a smart and articulate politician who might one day be in a position of power.

Clinton had hit just about all the right buttons in his Georgetown speech while finessing the most controversial topics—such as a specific plan for lowering the deficit. He declared he could "drastically" cut the deficit in five years as part of a "dramatic budget reform," but he offered virtually no details.

Clinton's deliberate vagueness on such a difficult issue had caught the attention of reporters, however, and the *Meet the Press* questions quickly turned to the deficit. NBC correspondent Lisa Myers wanted to get to the bottom line: "Are you prepared to promise that, if elected, you would balance the budget in four years?" Shapiro smiled to himself and waited for Clinton to knock the question out of the park.

"Well, I don't want to get into a promise that's like 'read my lips,' that I might not be able to keep," Clinton said with a knowing grin. Shapiro silently applauded, then sank back in his chair—it was a good start. But then, inexplicably, Clinton declared that he actually could balance the budget in four years—provided Congress approved his ideas for expanding the economic base and restructuring the government. "But that's not enough!" he added, and Shapiro, now leaning forward on the edge of his seat, groaned. "We're actually going to have to reduce our embedded debt in order to bring down the annual interest payments."

Shapiro was dumbfounded. It was bad enough that Clinton had suddenly promised to balance the budget, a pledge that had come back to embarrass every president who had ever made it. But now he had compounded his problem by suggesting he could somehow produce a surplus in the federal budget—he could actually begin to reduce the national debt. Virtually no serious economist thought such a thing could be done in four years, possibly not in double that many years, and certainly not without changes to the budget far tougher than anything Clinton was calling for. The questioning moved on to other areas, but Clinton's remarks on the deficit created unrealistic expectations that would haunt him well into his presidency.

These off-the-cuff comments were the first hint that the Arkansas governor was woefully ignorant about the depth of the federal deficit problem and what was involved in solving it. Caught up in his own optimistic campaign rhetoric and loath to talk about pain and sacrifice, Clinton—like Reagan before him—was pushing the notion that the country could simply "grow" its way out of the deficit problem by stimulating the economy with tax cuts and well-targeted spending.

This was startling, and not just to Shapiro. Clinton, a former Rhodes scholar and a Yale Law School graduate, was a serious student of public policy, perhaps one of the most knowledgeable men ever to seek the presidency. But like almost anyone who confronts the federal deficit problem for the first time, Clinton seemed to have no grasp of how difficult it really was. Much later, after he had learned the hard way how grim and intractable the deficit could be, he recalled for a close aide his naïve view of the problem when he was governor: "I always thought, Why can't these guys in Washington get their act together and figure it out? It's not that hard."

Clinton had gotten a false sense of confidence from his budget successes in Arkansas: As governor, he balanced his state's budget every year for more than a decade. He had little choice, though, since Arkansas law made it a felony for a state official to run up a deficit. Gene Sperling, a campaign economics adviser who stayed on to become a key aide in the White House, said Clinton boasted during the campaign of his record as a fiscal tightwad and often joked with his campaign aides: "You guys don't know me well. I cut everybody. Education's the only thing I spent a lot of money on in Arkansas."

Clinton presided over a poor, low-tax state that suffered from a third-rate education system, desperate economic problems, and a shrinking industrial base. His response was to stimulate economic growth by investing substantial sums in education, vocational training, and social services. But to do that and still balance the budget, the young governor ruthlessly slashed low-priority programs, decimated the staffs of government agencies, and dismantled the state's

Department of Commerce. "He didn't have trouble cutting other programs to make room for his priorities," said Mahlon Martin, Arkansas's budget director under Governor Clinton from 1982 to 1990. "Generally, he was willing to make the hard choices."

As a presidential candidate freed from the pay-as-you-go shackles of Arkansas's strict anti-deficit requirements, however, Clinton could be far more ambitious in promoting ideas for expanding the economy and enhancing the nation's international competitive edge. Cutting the deficit was a good, sober, worthy public-policy goal, but it did not fit his idea of what would inspire the country. Will Marshall, a domestic policy adviser in the campaign, said Clinton never felt his job was to come to the voters "as a puritanical deliverer of bad news, telling them it was now time to don the hair shirt to make up for the excesses of the eighties."

As manipulated for campaign purposes by Clinton and his advisers, the deficit became a symbol of the wretched excess of the Reagan and Bush years, testament to misguided policies that left the rich richer and the middle class stuck in the mud. On the campaign trail, Clinton evoked populist themes of helping the "forgotten middle class" and sticking it to the well-to-do. Clinton aides reacted with explosive anger to calls for "shared sacrifice"—higher taxes and reduced services for the middle class as well as the wealthy. The old idea that everyone, including the middle class, should shoulder the burden of reducing the deficit was not just wrong but offensive as far as Clinton's advisers were concerned. The budget experts, politicians, and journalists who suggested that notion were "morally wrong, economically wrong, politically wrong," snarled Clinton political consultant Paul Begala, who helped craft the class-warfare rhetoric that would characterize the campaign against George Bush. "They sit there, and they're well paid and well fed and well insured and well educated, and they believe the answer to the pain of the middle class is more pain for the middle class."

Clinton's political handlers and the most liberal faction among his economic advisers warned the candidate against fixating on the budget deficit, arguing that there was another deficit just as worrisome: the "investment deficit," the chronic shortfall in spending for education, job training, infrastructure, and other programs critical to the nation's long-term economic well-being.

The struggle for Clinton's soul on the deficit issue began in earnest during these early days of the campaign. Clinton's far-flung advisers, regularly meeting with the candidate by telephone conference calls, were divided into two camps. One faction, led by Shapiro, was hawkish on the deficit and tried to position Clinton firmly on the side of fiscal conservatism. This camp had a large following, from Bruce Reed, a key domestic policy adviser, to Roger Altman, a wealthy Wall Street financier and a close friend of Bill and Hillary Clinton's. The Harvard- and University of Chicago–educated Shapiro believed that "investments" in education and job training and so on were fine—as long as there was a credible way to pay for them other than by running up the deficit. Shapiro's "cut and invest" plan recognized that even a Democratic president could no longer indefinitely expand the spending universe, that budgeting from now on would be all about difficult tradeoffs. Shapiro proposed to pay for Clinton's investments by slashing away at "corporate welfare," everything from agriculture subsidies to NASA's space station and the navy's hyperexpensive Seawolf submarine.

The other, smaller but more potent faction was headed by Robert Reich, a Harvard University lecturer and prolific author and the most influential policy adviser in Clinton's campaign. Reich and Clinton first met aboard ship as young Rhodes scholars en route to England in 1968. Physically the two couldn't have been more different. Clinton was a tall, handsome Southern kid with wavy hair and easy, disarming charm; the diminutive Reich was just four feet, nine inches tall, the result of a rare childhood disease that had stunted his growth—but had seemingly left his prodigious ego intact. Intense and brilliant, Reich was Clinton's intellectual match, and the two instantly began a lifetime friendship.

In 1991, Reich published *The Work of Nations,* an examination of the new economic world order that became a touchstone for Clinton and his advisers. Reich declared that heavy deficit-spending for investments in the nation's future was far preferable to achieving a balanced budget by deferring or cutting back vital spending on education, job training, health care, and so on. "Debt is only a problem if the money is squandered on consumption," he wrote, meaning everyday government services and operations that did little to promote economic growth.

In the game of one-upmanship and positioning that went on in the Clinton campaign organization, Shapiro let it be known more than once that he was the only formally trained economist in the group, which suggested that his views should carry as much weight as, or more than, those of Reich, who was only a lecturer at Harvard, not a tenured professor, and lacked an economics degree. But Reich had something even better than that: He had the ear of the candidate, and his ideas on "investment spending" carried tremendous weight. James Carville, Paul Begala, and other campaign political operatives fondly referred to Reich as the Professor and soaked up the economic and political lessons he eagerly provided during strategy sessions in Little Rock.

Candidate Clinton translated these notions into policy by proposing to increase spending for dozens of programs he said would produce a better-trained, healthier, and more sophisticated workforce. Clinton would also increase construction of roads, bridges, highways, and high-tech communications systems to help businesses and corporations speed their products to market and take advantage of the latest technology. As a candidate, Clinton did not have to make a final decision between Shapiro's pay-as-you-go demands and Reich's put-it-on-the-cuff recommendations. The beauty of the campaign, at least in the early stages, was that tough decisions like this one could be finessed.

Clinton's willingness to spend money on renewing America had enormous appeal, particularly in New England, where the 1990–91 recession had hit hardest. Americans cared much more about tangible problems, such as unemployment and a stagnant economy, than they did about an abstraction like the federal deficit, and President Bush's stubborn refusal to acknowledge the depth of the problem made him appear brutally callous. Clinton and most other Democratic candidates considered pious harping on the deficit to be a political loser, and they avoided it. Senator Bob Kerrey, a Nebraska Democrat who was also seeking the nomination, frankly conceded that he avoided talking about the deficit because "there were no applause lines" in it.

The exception was Paul Tsongas, a conservative, pro-business former senator from Massachusetts who made a virtue of telling recession-weary New Englanders hard truths about the dangers of misguided tax cuts and uncontrolled entitlement spending. Tsongas favored stiff medicine to bring down the deficit: a fifty-cents-per-gallon increase in the gasoline tax plus tough restraints on the future

growth of Social Security, Medicare, and other entitlement programs. He hammered Clinton's morning-in-America fuzziness on
the deficit and disparaged him for offering an unaffordable tax cut
just to get votes. "I'm not Santa Claus," Tsongas said with more than
a touch of Yankee self-righteousness.

Tsongas's appeal for pain and sacrifice was daring for a presidential contender, and it was tempting to read his first-place finish in
New Hampshire as miraculous proof, as Tsongas claimed, that voters were finally ready to respond to tough talk about the deficit. But
the February 18 victory had more to do with voracious media attention to Clinton's sudden ethical problems—accusations of sexual
misconduct and draft evasion. Practically overnight the campaign
was transformed into a morality play, with Clinton called upon to defend his personal conduct. The real miracle was that Clinton managed to finish second—a performance under fire that revealed a
steely, tenacious side to his character as he toughed it out during the
final days of the primary. His attractive promises of economic re-
newal and security for the middle class got through to voters, and he
escaped political catastrophe largely because the electorate cared
more about his economic ideas than his personal indiscretions.

As the campaign moved south to Florida, the weakness of
Tsongas's strategy became painfully obvious. Clinton pounced on
Tsongas's anti-deficit policies with blistering radio and TV ads that
argued to seniors and low-income voters that the New Englander
was a coldhearted politician bent on cutting their Social Security,
Medicare, and Medicaid benefits and boosting their gasoline taxes.
Under the crush of Clinton's relentless and pointed attack,
Tsongas's campaign collapsed. Later Tsongas lamented that Clinton
had simply turned on him all the deficit-cutting specifics he was so
proud of. "Clinton just used my own club against me," he said rue-
fully.

By now, it was difficult to tell where Clinton stood. In his economic
address at Georgetown in November 1991, he had devoted less than
a minute of his hour-long speech to outlining his concerns about
the deficit. Two months later, in January 1992, he implied on *Meet
the Press* that he could balance the budget in four years. Three
months later, in a major economic address at the University of Penn-

sylvania's Wharton School of Business, he did not mention the deficit once.

Privately, Clinton worried that maybe Tsongas had been right, that maybe he had overpromised by proposing an expensive middle-class tax cut. Seemingly oblivious to the role that character issues had played in so badly wounding his candidacy, Clinton repeatedly complained to his aides that if it had not been for the middle-class tax-cut proposal, he could have won the New Hampshire primary. But if that had been all Clinton had promised, it might have been affordable. In his drive to lock up the nomination, he had also littered the campaign trail with IOUs that would cost hundreds of billions of dollars to redeem: broad new initiatives in education, a program to allow students to trade community service for college tuition, and reforms that would guarantee every American health-care coverage. Tsongas once asked his aides to tote up the cost of all Clinton's promises; the number they came up with was so huge they decided no one would believe it. When Clinton's aides sat down in Little Rock that summer to try to draft a fall campaign plan that would incorporate all the spending and anti-deficit promises, their own math showed that the candidate had proposed to spend a staggering $220 billion on new programs and initiatives over four years. The true figure was surely higher; unable to settle an internal dispute on the cost of Clinton's health-reform plan, his advisers simply factored in the cost at zero.

How would he pay for all that and still reduce the deficit? Like other Democrats, Clinton believed the golden goose was defense spending. During the early 1990s, some Democratic leaders estimated that as much as $200 billion in defense funds could be shifted to domestic programs as part of a post–Cold War "peace dividend." That turned out to be wishful thinking. When politicians went looking for the actual dollars, they found that defense had already been sharply cut back (largely by the 1990 budget deal), that inflation was eating up other potential savings, that the defense lobby was mobilizing against further cuts, and that even rank-and-file Democrats were helping to maintain the pressure to keep building old weapons systems and developing new ones.

Clinton had once suggested cutting the defense budget by as much as a third to free up money for his domestic programs, but

MIRAGE

now he saw that there was no way he could cut that much from the Pentagon without facing accusations that he was undermining the nation's security. As Clinton and his advisers brainstormed, they recognized that something had to give: either Clinton's ambitious package of "investment" spending or his off-the-cuff balanced-budget pledge.

Here the differences among Clinton's advisers that had festered throughout the early months of the campaign came to a head. Shapiro, Altman, Reed, and others argued for preserving a strong anti-deficit component as a means of building confidence on Wall Street and addressing head-on an issue that had become the central focus of Ross Perot's increasingly popular third-party presidential campaign. Although Clinton had locked up the Democratic nomination by June, he still trailed Bush and Perot in the polls and needed to do something dramatic to kick-start his campaign.

But a tough deficit-reduction plan would require sacrificing some of Clinton's investments or his middle-class tax cut. George Stephanopoulos and other political advisers were leery of abandoning a tax-cut proposal that, after all, had been the cornerstone of Clinton's earliest campaign efforts. Meanwhile, Reich and Ira Magaziner, a Rhode Island business consultant and another longtime friend of Clinton's, were pushing for inclusion of massive infrastructure and other "investment" spending on the order of $40 billion to $50 billion a year.

Shapiro had been given an important assignment in the preparation of the overall plan: Clinton had ordered him to go back and tally up all the campaign promises and do all the budget math necessary to determine whether the candidate could make good on most of his campaign pledges and still balance the budget. In his haste to get the job done, Shapiro made a $90-billion error in calculating the potential savings from defense that could be dedicated to Clinton's spending policies and deficit reduction efforts. "My God," he told himself, "we can do it all!" The error was discovered before it was factored in to the final plan, but the mistake weakened Shapiro's standing and gave his rivals an additional edge in making their case to Clinton.

Forced now to choose, Clinton chose spending over deficit reduction in a heartbeat. Instead of pledging a balanced budget in four years, he scaled his proposals back to a promise to cut the projected deficit in half over four years. Even this diminished goal would have required tough cuts in Medicare and Medicaid and other difficult policy choices, but Clinton had a much easier way out: growth. Some deficit reduction would come from scaled-back defense cuts, more from raising taxes on high-end taxpayers, and a big chunk from an illusory plan to capture unpaid taxes from foreign firms doing business in the United States. But most of the deficit reduction would be the utterly painless by-product of huge new economic growth.

Using modified CBO projections, Clinton's aides showed that the deficit would plummet all by itself—from $323 billion in 1993 to $193 billion in 1996—all without a single spending cut or tax increase. That meant that Clinton would have to do nothing more than show up for work in the Oval Office to achieve 80 percent of his goal of cutting the deficit in half. Add in the tepid spending cuts and tax increases the candidate was calling for and factor in even stronger economic growth, and he could slash the deficit down to a quarter of its size in four years.

The plan that finally emerged was aptly titled Putting People First: Spending came first, and deficit reduction was an afterthought. The only program specifically targeted for termination was the government subsidy for honeybee farmers. Clinton himself described Putting People First as an "investment" plan when he unveiled it to a conference of mayors on June 21. Political reporters interpreted it as an attempt by the candidate to back away from the pledges he had made on *Meet the Press* in January. *The Washington Post* reported the following day that Clinton's plan "retreats significantly from his earlier timetable for balancing the budget."

Putting People First became obsolete almost as soon as it was announced, when the happy CBO deficit projections on which it was based suddenly changed. That August, in the semiannual update of its budget forecast, the CBO published gloomy new numbers that showed a 1996 deficit $76 billion higher than its previous estimate. This was a distress signal that the economy wasn't recovering as quickly as the CBO had earlier assumed. Cutting the deficit in half was going to take much deeper spending cuts or bigger tax increases than anything Clinton had so far proposed.

To set things straight, the Clinton campaign would have had to revise its proposal. But with the campaign in high gear and Bush in a political free fall, Clinton's advisers decided they could safely ignore the new CBO numbers. None of the other candidates or the reporters covering the campaign had picked up on them. Gene Sperling, who had been brought into the campaign from the staff of New York Governor Mario Cuomo to assemble the plan, shrugged off the new CBO forecast as a "non-event." Instead, Putting People First would stand as written, a cheery but baseless piece of fiction.

On the campaign trail, where issues were discussed in broad strokes and inspiring rhetoric, Clinton could afford to be vague about his plans to cut the deficit. But the subject was taking on a much sharper edge in Washington. In the year and a half since the 1990 budget deal, the deficit had gotten worse, not better. Congress and the White House had taken the traditional year off from further deficit reduction in 1991, but now there was a restless, edgy feeling among members of both parties that they had not done enough. They wanted more, but it was a presidential-election year, and leaders wanted to avoid a draining budget fight. Nonetheless, Gingrich and the Republicans were raising the temperature on the issue as self-styled "pork busters" held repeated press conferences to slam "tax-and-spend" Democrats for pork-barrel spending.

Democratic leaders saw no need to act against the deficit. What they did see was a terribly vulnerable Republican president who was refusing to acknowledge what every working family knew: The country was in the midst of an economic slowdown that, if it did not technically qualify as a recession, had still put many people out of work and had made still more of them deeply worried about their future. Leaders figured this was no time to worry about the deficit; instead, they should begin working the levers of government to jump-start a tired economy, something Bush flatly refused to try. "I think his kind of waiting for events to restore the economy was a devastating mistake; it gave the Democrats a chance to say that he doesn't do anything because he doesn't care, really," said then House Speaker Tom Foley. "President Bush was a sensitive and caring man, but he needed to demonstrate that fact in a public way."

Foley might have been right about Bush, but he was missing an equally important dynamic in his own backyard. The conservative

Democratic deficit hawks who had given their party's leaders so much trouble in 1981 by helping Reagan get his budget and tax cuts passed were going militant again, demanding an agenda that ran directly counter to the line Foley and Senate Majority Leader George Mitchell wanted to take.

Texas Congressman Charlie Stenholm was typical of the Democratic hawks who had last enjoyed real clout during the 1981 fights. Ever since, hawks like him had regretted their role in unleashing such big deficits and worked away at the deficit to atone. Since their eclipse after the 1982 elections (which shifted power back to more liberal Democrats), the hawks had gradually had their ranks filled out again by latecomers, more socially moderate Democrats from swing districts who had gotten elected at least in part on pledges to take on the deficit and were just as avid about the issue as their old-line brethren were.

Democratic leaders had ignored or browbeaten conservatives like these for a decade. In 1983, Minnesota freshman Congressman Tim Penny—who had been sent to Congress from a Republican district on the strength of his promise to clean up the deficit mess—led fellow deficit hawks in an unprecedented floor revolt against a leadership-backed spending bill and temporarily stopped it. Then–House majority leader Jim Wright reacted with rage only barely disguised with humor. Penny's action, Wright told him at a private breakfast the next day, had been a little like a trainer coming into the ring when his fighter almost had the fight won and clobbering him from behind with a stool. Chagrined, Penny immediately backed off and allowed the bill to pass, but he concluded later that he should have stood firm. What the incident revealed was that lowly conservative Democrats had the power to use against their domineering leadership—if only they had the nerve to wield it. Now they would.

By 1992, the conservatives' ranks had grown to the point where they once again formed a critical mass within the majority. As much as a quarter of the House's 268 Democrats were now loosely in the deficit-hawk camp; if every one of them joined with a united GOP bloc, they would have more than enough votes to defeat the Democratic leadership.

The turning point came on an obscure vote in March 1992, when Democratic leaders tried to tear down the "firewalls" erected by the 1990 budget deal to stop the raids Democrats traditionally made on defense spending to shift money to domestic programs. Senior Democrats assumed they would win no matter what happened: Either they would get more money for their priorities, or they would lure Bush into vetoing the bill, which would allow them to attack the president for shortchanging domestic needs during the recession.

What they did not see coming until too late was a revolt in their own ranks. Led by deficit hawks who refused to abandon the discipline of the 1990 agreement, seventy-six Democrats defected to join with Republicans, humiliating Democratic leaders on an overwhelming 238–187 vote to preserve the firewalls. In the insular world of Capitol Hill, this was a strong signal that deficit fever was much hotter than leaders or candidate Clinton imagined. The leadership rarely got defeated when it brought major initiatives to the House floor; Tim Penny called this "the single most important vote of the year."

Out on the campaign trail, though, Clinton was oblivious. He wanted the firewalls down to make room for domestic spending, and he even rejected a compromise that would have devoted half the savings to cutting the deficit: He wanted *all* the money for his domestic programs. The message was clear to moderate and conservative Democrats who had been sizing up the candidate: Bill Clinton was no deficit hawk.

It was just at this time—with congressional concern over the deficit high but the issue dying on the campaign trail—that Ross Perot, the billionaire Texas businessman, strode onto the nation's political stage and snatched the issue from under the noses of his Democratic and Republican rivals. Perot wasn't merely a deficit hawk, he was a megahawk, a larger-than-life figure who not only passionately believed the deficit was the most critical issue of the day but also had the wealth to carry the message to nationwide TV and the charisma to get voters fired up about it to a degree no other candidate had ever managed. Before Perot's arrival, barely one in ten Americans believed the deficit was important, according to a Gallup poll. Once the networks began beaming Perot's eagle-beaked, jug-eared visage into the living rooms of millions of American TV viewers practically every night, the deficit came to dominate the political debate. With Perot on the scene, it became much tougher for Clinton and Bush to get away with throwing bromides at the issue.

When he had turned up on *Larry King Live* on February 20, just forty-eight hours after Clinton limped to a second-place finish in New Hampshire, Perot was determined to build an instant reputation as an expert on how to cut the federal budget. But while he was a genius at selling voters on the seriousness of the problem, his plans for fixing it were at best half-baked. He regaled an American Society of Newspaper Editors meeting in Washington with his proposal for cutting $480 billion out of the deficit: $100 billion would come from denying Social Security benefits to wealthier Americans such as himself; a whopping $180 billion would come from eliminating unspecified "waste, fraud, and abuse" (that chestnut of the Reagan era); our European and Asian allies would be forced to pay $100 billion as their share of joint security operations overseas; and finally, upgrading IRS computers and streamlining the tax-collection system would produce $100 billion. Presto, he bragged, you've eliminated the deficit, "and you haven't even broken a sweat."

In truth, Perot was flying by the seat of his pants. His understanding of the intricacies of the federal budget—or the consequences of his own proposals—was painfully shallow. He assumed that his mastery of corporate finance automatically qualified him as an expert on the federal budget as well, but those who early on plumbed the depths of his knowledge discovered that he was, as Texans like to say, all hat and no cattle.

On May 3, NBC News Washington bureau chief Tim Russert coolly dismembered Perot's plan during a broadcast of *Meet the Press*, the same program that had made Clinton an early victim. Did Perot realize, Russert wondered, that ten million people would lose their Social Security and Medicare benefits under his plan, including people who earned as little as $15,000 a year? As for Perot's idea for eliminating waste, fraud, and abuse, that would require 20 percent across-the-board cuts in just about everything the government did, a wildly absurd figure.

"Now then, this is an interesting game we're playing today," snapped the suddenly flustered Perot. "It would have been nice if you had told me you wanted to talk about this and I'd have had all my facts with me, but you didn't, right?" Embarrassed by his weak answers to Russert's questions, Perot finally backed down. "Give me a little time to get all this nailed down," he said in retreat, "and I will give you the very specific ways we will do this."

Perot was the embodiment of all the wrongheaded notions Amer-

icans have about the deficit, especially the destructively simple-
minded idea that it would be easy to fix if only those idiots in Washington would get out of the way and a man with common sense
could attack the problem with sound business practices and a little
tinkering under the hood. But Russert's tough inquisition had
wounded Perot's pride and forced him to grapple with the dimensions of the problem. Perot went back to Texas and hired John
White, a vice president of Eastman Kodak and a onetime Office of
Management and Budget (OMB) official under Carter, to put together a credible package. During meetings, White was shocked by
Perot's ignorance of the federal budget. Perot, he said, "was really
quite surprised at how hard it was" to put together a real deficit-
reduction plan. "It was quite remarkable," White said.

White's hardball plan, far tougher and more credible than anything Bush or Clinton had proposed, aimed to cut the deficit by
$744 billion over five years, essentially by goring the ox of every spe-
cial interest group in the country. It would raise $300 billion in new
taxes, slash defense spending more deeply than Bush or Clinton
would ever dare, and launch a frontal assault on America's most
cherished entitlements. Striking at the very heart of the deficit problem, Perot's plan curbed COLAs for federal retirees, raised taxes on
Social Security recipients, raised premiums for Medicare, and imposed strict cost-containment measures on federal health-care programs. In short, it was the type of plan that no serious political
candidate would have dreamed of offering. But what Perot's plan
lacked in political realism, it made up for with fiscal credibility. Balancing the budget wouldn't be easy after all, Perot was learning, and
it would require painful choices and sacrifice. "Now, if you can't
stand a little pain and you can't stand a trip across the desert with
limited water, we're never going to straighten this country out," he
said during an appearance on NBC's *Today* show on June 11. "So if
you want Lawrence Welk music, I'm not your man."

―――――――

Bill Clinton's victory five months later had little to do with his
stance on the deficit or specific plans to fix it; Clinton the candidate
had built no broad public consensus on the major pieces of a serious deficit-reduction plan. As the exhilaration of victory began to

fade, President-elect Clinton and his top advisers were finding the transition from campaigning to governance unsettling. On the evening of December 7, a little more than a month after Clinton was elected the forty-second president of the United States, Robert Reich convened a meeting with Clinton and a half-dozen aides at Blair House, the historic building across Pennsylvania Avenue from the White House, to review the budget picture. The numbers were not good. The grim CBO report from August (that "non-event" in the words of economics adviser Gene Sperling) was now assuming far larger importance. Worried advisers had concluded that the only way Clinton could keep all his campaign promises and still meet his goal of slashing the deficit in half was to find half again as much deficit reduction as they had proposed during the campaign. Worse, the numbers had to be real.

When Clinton and his aides gathered that night, they laid out the problem using a chart entitled "Budget Deficit Forecasts Under PPF [Putting People First] Policies." It graphically showed the serious flaws in the campaign document: The economic assumptions and deficit projections had been far too optimistic. Clinton was first amazed, then angry. "What the hell happened?" he demanded to know.

The problem was largely that the sluggish economy still wasn't performing as they had hoped, but there were other complications. Some of the "savings" that Clinton's advisers had claimed in Putting People First were sheer fantasy—notably the $45 billion that Sperling had said could be saved by closing tax loopholes for foreign corporations. In fact, the government would be lucky to pick up a small fraction of that. Clinton's advisers also assumed they could reduce "administrative" costs by $22 billion, but that promise now seemed as airy as Reagan's pledge to eliminate government waste.

What Clinton's advisers were telling him, in effect, was that his economic program was an illusion, rendered inoperative by phony savings and a major new deficit forecast that they had chosen to ignore. "When you stripped away the optimistic projection, we didn't have much deficit reduction in Putting People First," domestic adviser Bruce Reed later explained. "The document had been a highly effective campaign tool, but as a road map to govern, it was close to useless."

Clinton was confronted with a troubling dilemma: He had cam-

paigned for the White House as a New Democrat, advocating generous "investment" spending and middle-class tax cuts to create a
more vigorous economy, but at the expense of more aggressive anti-
deficit policies. Even after retreating from a balanced budget to a
pledge to cut the deficit in half, he and his advisers had been unable
to commit themselves to the necessary spending cuts, for fear of
alienating his core Democratic constituency. Instead, he had assumed away the problem, banking on the economic recovery to
make most of the deficit problem disappear.

Only now the economy wasn't cooperating, and the campaign's
gauzily hopeful view of the world was colliding with the bleak reality
inside the Beltway. Clinton had no choice but to go ahead, even if
that meant sacrificing the middle-class tax cut and drastically scaling
back his investment plans.

Clinton was far more interested in domestic policy than Bush had
been; if he was ever going to get the deficit out of the way so he
could do other things, he would have to begin at once. Bush had let
his honeymoon year, the time when a president is most powerful,
slip away without taking any action on the deficit, a mistake that left
him with a much weaker hand later, when he was forced to act. Clinton would not repeat Bush's mistake.

Clinton was also being pushed by his personnel decisions. He had
filled the top jobs in his new administration with some of Washington's most celebrated deficit hawks, so when his new economic team
argued about whether to be real about the deficit or to punt, the
hawks had superior firepower.

The two senior posts at the White House's all-important OMB, the
agency that keeps the numbers and draws up the plans, went to
House Budget Committee Chairman Leon Panetta and Brookings
Institution gadfly Alice Rivlin, both of whom had openly disparaged
Putting People First for not taking the deficit seriously enough.
Panetta had a reputation among his fellow congressional Democrats
as a tireless (tiresome, to some) crusader for deficit reduction.
Rivlin, the first director of the CBO, was so intent on deficit reduction that she used her job interview to make sure Clinton was seri-
ous enough about it to make the job he was offering worth taking.
He took her by surprise by telling her right off that he had reread
her latest book on the subject. "I agree with the way you set out the
problems," he told her. "This is the way I'm thinking about it, too."

Clinton was out to win credibility in Congress, where Panetta and Rivlin were the gold standard on deficit matters. Just days after he was elected, Congress's top Democratic leaders—Senate Majority Leader George Mitchell, House Speaker Tom Foley, and House Majority Leader Richard Gephardt—had flown to Little Rock for a get-acquainted dinner. Foley and Gephardt had been shaken by their recent initial meetings with the large new class of Democratic freshmen, many of whom had won election by talking tough on the deficit and had warned the House leaders they meant to follow through. Just as freshmen would assume a special role as ideological shock troops in the Republican revolution of 1995, freshmen Democrats elected in 1992 were perceived by their party elders as the vanguard of change, the members most closely attuned to public sentiment. Watch out, the leaders told Clinton over dinner. "The first most major issue you've got to deal with is the deficit and the budget," Gephardt said. The Missouri Democrat added that a serious deficit-reduction plan was "the ticket of admission to the park to play the game." If Clinton did not bring a plan to Congress, restive Democrats would impose one on him, and he would lose control of the agenda from the outset.

Clinton had another key constituency to worry about as well. He had to signal Wall Street early on that he was in fact a New Democrat, not the spendthrift liberal bogeyman many conservative money managers imagined him to be. Cooperation from the markets was critical; lower interest rates would cut the costs of mortgages and car loans and do more than tax cuts or a dozen spending programs to juice up the economy and get the shaky recovery moving. As his Treasury secretary, he picked Senate Finance Committee Chairman Lloyd Bentsen, a veteran senator trusted by the financial community. From the Street itself, he brought former Goldman, Sachs co-chairman Robert Rubin to run the brand-new National Economic Council and former Lehman Brothers wunderkind Roger Altman to serve as Bentsen's number two at Treasury.

Appointments alone would not be enough, though. To show the markets he was serious, Clinton would have to come through with a serious deficit-reduction plan. "You had to show the bond market we were serious about deficit reduction," said senior adviser George Stephanopoulos.

They were also playing to public perception. Perot had dramatically raised the public's awareness of the deficit, driving home the point not so much that it was a direct threat to day-to-day life but that it was a huge symbol of the federal government's incompetence.

All this—Clinton's own predilection for action, his new cadre of tough-minded advisers, a Congress waiting for a plan, and a public spring-loaded by Perot to demand action—was combining to make it impossible for Clinton to do anything but offer a serious deficit-reduction proposal. Then came the coup de grâce.

Just as Clinton's economic team was getting used to the CBO's awful August deficit estimate, the outgoing Bush budget office released its own, even worse deficit projections that January. Not only did OMB Director Dick Darman's numbers confirm the deteriorating trend the CBO had identified, but they also added about another $80 billion to the deficits in Clinton's first four budget years, from 1994 through 1997. Now there was no question of doing a minimalist plan; it would take everything Clinton's staff could come up with just to get close to the president-elect's pledge to cut the deficit in half in four years. The deficit projected for 1997—the year by which Clinton had promised to cut the deficit in half—had ballooned from a manageable $226 billion in January 1992 to $305 billion now, according to the latest OMB numbers. Even worse, when the Clinton staffers looked more deeply into the numbers and ran their own private calculations, they were stunned to find a 1997 deficit in the range of $350 billion or more. The CBO's August forecast had "made life rougher," Sperling said, "but that didn't break our back. It was the OMB numbers." Now they simply had no choice.

Hovering over all the deliberations as the Clinton team assembled its economic plan was the dour visage of Federal Reserve Board Chairman Alan Greenspan, a Republican appointed by Reagan. As chairman of the nation's central bank, Greenspan held critical power over the economy and, by extension, over the success or failure of Clinton's presidency. Greenspan's approval of Clinton's plan could make a huge difference with Wall Street. Both privately, in two meetings with Clinton, and publicly, in testimony on Capitol Hill, Greenspan pushed the White House to stick with serious deficit re-

duction, saying it was essential to winning the confidence of the markets and bringing down the long-term interest rates that mattered to
businesses with large debts and to people paying mortgages. In their
second private meeting in late January, Greenspan again urged Clinton to be aggressive, warning that failure to address the problem
now virtually ensured a financial catastrophe, possibly before the
end of the new president's term.

Greenspan was preaching to the choir. Clinton had already decided to be bold, yielding almost completely to the insistent advice
of hawks like Panetta, Rivlin, and Vice President Al Gore, who had
all pushed him hard in two key meetings in Little Rock in January to
put together a big deficit package. Panetta had warned Clinton that
if he was too timid, he would lose control of the agenda, something
a rookie president might never recover from. "What will happen is
the Republicans will pick up the pieces, you'll get a balanced-budget
amendment rammed down your throat, and ultimately they will determine what happens with your administration, not you," Panetta
said.

But Clinton's senior economic advisers shot back that he had
better watch out lest this enthusiasm for deficit reduction knock
the fragile economy right back into the ditch, a disaster that would
cripple his presidency just as surely. Laura D'Andrea Tyson, the
University of California trade specialist Clinton had plucked from
relative obscurity to be his chief economist, warned that a big
deficit-reduction plan would inevitably dampen the economy and
might even touch off another recession. Princeton economics professor Alan Blinder, Tyson's number two at the Council of Economic Advisers, cautioned Clinton to remember that all the
guaranteed benefits of deficit reduction were out somewhere in the
future (a more stable and productive economy, less foreign debt, a
better life for their children, and so on), but all the risks were immediate (pushing the economy back into the ditch and stirring up
a political backlash against specific fixes), which argued for doing
less.

The owlish, chatty Blinder suggested a paradigm that helped focus the debate: Instead of worrying about balancing the budget or
taking a major chunk out of the deficit, what they really had to worry
about was making sure the nation's debt grew no faster than the na-

tion's economy. If the debt grew too fast, Blinder explained, the annual interest payments would devour bigger and bigger shares of the federal budget—an unsustainable path. If they cut deficits just enough to slow growth of the debt to the same rate as the growth of the economy, the situation would stabilize.

In the end, the argument boiled down to one big number: By how much would they cut the $350-billion deficit they were privately forecasting for 1997, the fourth budget year of Clinton's presidency and the year by which Clinton had promised to cut the deficit in half? Blinder proposed a $117-billion cut, just enough to stabilize things. Reich urged a $110-billion cut, to leave a little more room for investment spending. Rivlin, the most hawkish of them all, called for a $160-billion cut. By the middle of January, Clinton had made up his mind. He opted for a cut of $145 billion from the 1997 deficit, not quite as harsh a reduction as Rivlin had called for but much closer to her end of the spectrum than to Reich's and more stringent than what Blinder had warned was bland but safe.

This was fine with Greenspan. Later on the same day that he had gone to see Clinton privately at the White House, the Fed chairman went to the Hill to urge Congress to adopt a "hardwired" anti-deficit package with no gimmicks, its cuts locked in by law. Greenspan spoke carefully, in sepulchral tones, suitably fastidious for a man whose slightest utterance could move the markets.

Fishing for specifics, Democratic Senator Kent Conrad of North Dakota pushed the inscrutable chairman, trying to see whether he would make a more categorical endorsement of the Clinton effort.

"Are you looking for a number, Senator?" Greenspan finally said. "Let me just say to you I don't find that the number that President Clinton has indicated to be off base. It sounds to me as a rough order of magnitude, I would say as a starter, probably—"

"Which number?" interrupted Conrad.

"The $145 billion, as I remember it," he said, effectively locking Clinton in.

With a crash of chairs, financial reporters burst from their seats like a covey of startled quail and bolted through the crowded hearing room for the hallway to flash the news that Greenspan approved Clinton's number. After a shocked pause, the audience broke out laughing.

"I think you just made news," cracked Tennessee Democratic Senator Jim Sasser.

"Splendid," said Greenspan.

———

In late January, shortly after Clinton was inaugurated, Bob Dole went down to the White House to give the new chief executive some bad news. It was no secret by now that Clinton's big deficit-reduction package would contain major tax increases. Just two days earlier, Treasury Secretary Bentsen had said on *Meet the Press* that everybody would be paying higher taxes of some kind: Rates would go up for the rich, and even the middle class would probably pay some sort of a broad-based tax on energy. The Senate minority leader got right to the point. "You're not going to get any Republican votes for this," Dole told Clinton, warning that Republicans would walk away from any package with taxes in it.

This was a critical turning point that would dictate events for the rest of the year and trouble Clinton for the rest of his term. Neither man had a choice. Clinton had to have a major tax piece in his deficit-reduction plan; Democrats had burned to get even since 1981, when Reagan—they believed—gave away the store by cutting taxes for the rich. Dole was also locked in by party doctrine: Gingrich had established in 1990 that Republicans did not support tax increases.

Barely two months past the presidential election, Dole was already looking down the road to 1996, when he expected to duel for the GOP nomination with Texas Senator Phil Gramm, a visceral anti-taxer who would hammer Dole if the Senate leader waffled on the tax issue. Ever the deal maker, Dole did not rule out taxes when he appeared on *Meet the Press* the following Sunday. But Dole set the price for GOP support so high that Clinton could never hope to meet it. Any package with taxes would have to have at least a 2:1 ratio of spending cuts to tax increases, he said, and "if you don't have too many new taxes involved or if you have zero taxes involved, it'd be better."

Under enormous pressure from the Republicans in 1990, Democrats had swallowed a 2:1 ratio, but they had gotten that chiefly by taking the first big post–Cold War cuts out of defense spending, a huge piggy bank that was much smaller now. They could not make 2:1 again without going hard at politically volatile entitlement spending or at the very domestic programs Clinton was determined to bulk up.

The end of any hope of bipartisan support was the end of any chance that Clinton would seize this opportunity to put together the sort of radical, good-government deficit-reduction plan that reformers insisted was necessary. The heart of any such plan had to be major changes in entitlement programs such as Social Security, Medicare, and Medicaid, the big budget engines that were driving the deficit. But if Republicans would not join with Democrats to cut entitlements, doing it alone would be pure suicide for Democrats, who had proved that point over and over again in the 1980s by crucifying Republicans for their proposals to scale back Social Security.

This equation defined reality in the White House's Roosevelt Room, where Clinton and his senior economic aides were now meeting intensively to hammer out their budget package. The narrow options for major spending cuts strengthened the hand of deficit doves who did not want to go overboard on a big deficit-reduction package, but it was terribly frustrating for hawks like Panetta and Rivlin, who had been waiting for years for a chance to write a real plan.

Panetta refused to give up. The same earnest budget balancer who had so annoyed Mitchell and Sasser in 1990 by pushing to make a budget offer to Darman now found a way to annoy a whole new set of allies by pushing for spending cuts most political veterans thought were crazy. If they wanted to be taken seriously, if they really wanted to make a serious dent in the deficit, Panetta argued, they should take this opportunity to freeze the Social Security COLA temporarily, a simple step that would make little difference to beneficiaries (a few dollars a month at worst) but would save an impressive $12 billion to $15 billion over five years. There were any number of good arguments for it: It would show that everyone had to pitch in to get the deficit down; COLAs had cost the government trillions while making Social Security recipients virtually the only Americans immune to inflation for the last two decades. Many senior members of Clinton's brain trust agreed with the COLA-freeze idea, at least in theory. "On pure equity, Social Security recipients had done better than almost every other group in society for the previous twenty years," said a senior administration official who sympathized with Panetta. "About the only exception to that was corporate CEOs."

Panetta had long urged politically difficult steps like this, ostentatiously including Social Security in the multiyear plans he developed as chairman of the House Budget Committee, sometimes as a serious proposal, sometimes seemingly just to shock his colleagues with what balancing the budget would really take. "I always knew what the politics of it would involve," Panetta said later, "but I also knew that in a huge package for deficit reduction, where we were trying to get everybody to sacrifice, that you could, in fact, maybe touch the third rail."

At an Oval Office meeting on January 27, Panetta and his House allies tried to talk Clinton into the COLA freeze. "We're going to have to go there one day," said House Ways and Means Committee Chairman Dan Rostenkowski, who had long agreed with Panetta about the need to take bold steps against the deficit. "I think Clinton wanted to do that until everybody in the room frightened him," Rostenkowski said later. The chief worrier that day was Senate Majority Leader George Mitchell, who had lived through the 1985 experience, when Dole had persuaded his colleagues to vote for a COLA freeze only to lose the Senate the next year. Mitchell and other Democratic senators thought this was a death wish, and they were horrified that Panetta seemed to be convincing Clinton. "I thought Mitchell was going to have a baby," Rostenkowski said later.

Again and again on the COLA issue and in making other critical judgments about entitlements, Clinton and his advisers looked into the abyss but decided not to jump. Clinton had built no momentum or mandate for reforming entitlements during the campaign. Indeed, Putting People First called for a meager $4.4 billion over four years in "entitlement reform" by raising the costs of the doctor-care portion of Medicare (Part B) for seniors with an annual income of more than $125,000.

Panetta and Rivlin were relentless, however, urging repeatedly that Clinton go to the heart of the deficit problem by tangling with the entitlement programs that were the chief source of the big deficits. Their last fight came over making a comparatively tiny increase in the Part B premium for all beneficiaries, who then enjoyed a huge subsidy from non-elderly taxpayers. Under current law, se-

niors paid just 25 percent of the cost of Part B, which provided almost all of Medicare's nonhospital care, and taxpayers picked up
the other 75 percent of the premiums. This law called for a gradual
rise in the seniors' premium, to 27 percent of the cost. Panetta and
Rivlin urged bumping that up to 29 percent. Again there were all
sorts of equity arguments for doing it, but just as with Social Security, a majority of Clinton's advisers banded together to insist he
would be foolish to embrace such a plan; it would be much safer to
extract cuts from Medicare providers, the doctors and hospitals who
served the beneficiaries, than from the beneficiaries themselves.

"That thing came up three or four times, and in the end we went
with twenty-seven percent," said a senior administration adviser who
helped fashion the plan. "If we lost our virginity on the beneficiary
side," by taking any of the savings from Medicare recipients, the adviser said, Republicans would certainly distort the issue by accusing
them of taking *all* their cuts from beneficiaries.

This was not paranoia. Deficit politics was so polarized that anyone who took on real reductions—Democrats or Republicans—had
to assume the other side would exploit any opening to demagogue,
distort, and misrepresent the effort. Democrats should know, of
course, since they had used this tactic for years on Social Security.
Clinton decided to give the Republicans no opening on Medicare,
but he offered them a huge one on taxes.

Deciding to whack upper-income taxpayers was not difficult, but
even the bracing increase in the top tax rates for the wealthiest
Americans did not give the budget drafters nearly the savings they
needed to make their plan work. Even lowering the annual income
threshold for higher taxes from $200,000 to $140,000 was not
enough. The upper crust of America is rich but thin; to get real
money, it is necessary to go after the enormous middle class, where
even a modest tax can generate huge revenues.

For years, members of both parties had advocated a big energy tax,
but Congress had never managed to get it off the ground. Such a tax
had multiple pluses: It was broad based and therefore presumably
fair, it could be engineered to discourage use of environmentally destructive fuels, it would satisfy the Clinton team's desire to mount a
"bold" attack on the deficit, and it would raise pots of money. But
there were reasons Congress had never managed to make such a tax

work, beyond the simple fact that it would be unpopular with consumers. First, it was fiendishly hard to write it without penalizing various regions of the country (a coal tax would hit the coal-producing Midwest; an imported-oil tax would hurt the Northeast, and so on); also, the minute the government began taxing energy sources, it tangled with big energy producers and big users, some of the best-connected special interests in Washington.

But with the hubris of the newly elected, the Clinton team decided it could make this work. Gore in particular was intrigued by the potential environmental benefits, and he managed to override Bentsen's concerns about writing a complex new tax that would very likely get bogged down in Congress. Bentsen suggested a simple four-cents-per-gallon gasoline tax, but the group eventually devised a complex mechanism that would tax virtually all forms of energy according to their heat value, measured in British thermal units. The Btu tax was launched with great fanfare and high hopes: It would raise an astounding $72 billion all by itself, a huge chunk of the money that was needed. Sadly, it was a political disaster.

As Bentsen had warned, the tax was much too complicated for Congress to digest. There were scores of problems, and fixing them just made them worse. "It was like a progressive disease," said one Treasury official who tried in vain to make the tax work. "You deal with one thing, and in dealing with one symptom, you get another symptom." Did they really mean to make hardworking farmers pay the same tax on gasoline that casual drivers paid? Of course not; farm fuel would be dyed to distinguish it from taxable fuel for non-farm cars and trucks. Aluminum manufacturers, who used enormous amounts of electricity, complained bitterly and got a big exemption. Exporters protested and got the tax lifted from products headed overseas. "We would look up at the bookshelves and think, How many bookshelves are they going to have to build just to describe this in the tax code?" said Lawrence O'Donnell, chief of staff for the tax-writing Senate Finance Committee.

In the end, no one liked the tax, not even the environmentalists Gore had hoped would embrace it; they complained that it did not hit high-polluting fuels, such as coal, hard enough. But the administration could not hit coal without alienating key coal-state Democrats whose support they needed to pass the overall budget package. The coup de grâce came when energy-state Democrats rose up

against it and threatened to walk out on the budget altogether unless Clinton killed off the Btu tax.

With the Btu tax went that huge chunk of revenue—$72 billion.
Desperate for money, the staffers dusted off Bentsen's original idea
of a tiny increase in the gasoline tax, but by then they were so sensitive to charges they were raising taxes on the middle class (instead
of cutting them, as Clinton had promised during the campaign) that
they fought bitterly over tenths of a penny.

The Senate Finance Committee was coalescing around a proposal
for a 7.3-cents-a-gallon increase in the tax on gasoline and other
transportation fuels but had to settle for only 4.3 cents a gallon, the
maximum Montana Senator Max Baucus would accept. The decision to push the package through Congress with Democrats alone
effectively gave recalcitrant Democrats a veto at critical points;
dozens of times in the seven months it took to work the budget plan
through the House and the Senate, its entire fate would come down
to a single member like Baucus, and Clinton or other Democrats
would have to go to extraordinary lengths to budge him or her.

Baucus was motivated in part by parochial concerns, since many
Montanans drove long distances across the Big Sky state and would
not care much for a bigger bite at the gas pump. Baucus was also
concerned about the way Clinton's formerly progressive package
was unraveling; the corporate tax rate increase had been cut from
two percentage points to one, and now business and industry were
skating out from under the Btu tax. Where was the equity in that?

To restore the revenue they lost by junking the $72-billion Btu tax
in favor of a $24-billion gasoline tax, Democrats had to do surgery
on the rest of the package: Out went $10 billion—about one third—
of Clinton's plan to expand the earned-income tax credit for the
working poor, and the Medicare cuts would go up another $17 bil-
lion. The final plan raised dozens of separate taxes, but only one—
the gasoline tax—was a direct hit on low-income taxpayers. Roughly
ninety cents of every dollar of Clinton's new taxes would be paid by
families earning more than $100,000 a year. Fewer than 2 million of
the nation's 115 million taxpayers would get socked by the new
higher income tax rates, and poor families would actually get a tax
cut from the expansion of the earned-income tax credit. This was
clearly a soak-the-rich plan, but that was not how Republicans por-
trayed it. Critics so willfully misrepresented the tax provisions that

many Americans who would pay nothing more than the gasoline tax increase believed their income taxes would rise. It was a devastatingly effective campaign and an ominous harbinger of what was to come for Clinton and the Democrats.

Even deficit hawks were vulnerable. Charlie Stenholm was being pounded back home in West Texas by a relentless campaign organized by the Christian Coalition, Citizens for a Sound Economy, and the Republican Party. Full-page newspaper ads, radio spots, and a boiler-room telephone operation all built voter pressure on him to vote against the Clinton package, and the pressure was ferocious. Calls to his Washington office were running 90–1 no.

One day, Stenholm randomly picked one of the callers and returned her call to find out why she was so opposed. She was a retired schoolteacher in San Angelo who admitted she called simply because "they told me to." Who were "they"? Stenholm politely asked. After some hemming and hawing, she said it was the Christian Coalition.

"I don't want my taxes to be raised," she told Stenholm. "They" had told her that her taxes would go up.

"I said, 'Well, if you mind me getting personal, just stop me at any time, but is your income over $180,000?'

" 'Oh, heavens, no!' she said. 'I'm a retired schoolteacher.'

"And I said, 'Well, is your income over $140,000?' She said, 'I told you, I'm a retired schoolteacher.' It turned out her income was less than $20,000. I said, 'Would it make any difference to you if I told you your taxes were not going to be raised?' And she said, 'They're not?' And I said, 'No, ma'am, at your income, your taxes aren't going to be raised. Let me ask you this. If I told you that the only people's taxes that basically were going to be raised were those making $180,000 and above, how would you feel about that?'

"She said, 'Well, I agree with that. Those folks can afford to pay more taxes. I can't afford to pay more taxes.'

"And I said, 'Well, you're not.' "

One constituent set straight. But Stenholm couldn't convince voters one by one that they were being lied to, and the tax issue was killing him. Just a day before the vote, one of the most consistent and fearless deficit hawks in Congress told Clinton that he would not vote for the package.

Given all the pressure on Clinton not to act at all—not to raise taxes on anybody, not to cut anyone's entitlements, not to cut the scores of other big programs that were the only place to go to get big savings—it is almost a surprise that he did push to assemble his budget package and then get it passed. The risks for a brand-new president were enormous. Had he lost at any point, the markets would have punished both him and the economy, his agenda (particularly health-care reform) would have been in tatters, and his prestige and ability to affect the national political debate would have been badly weakened. "I think he would have been finished," said George Kundanis, senior adviser to House Speaker Tom Foley. "How could he have with a straight face told Republicans that he was going to pass a health-care bill, which is thousands of times harder?"

For all the political problems in Clinton's deficit-reduction package, the first four votes on it were a breeze. The House and the Senate both passed their own versions of the Clinton budget and then approved a compromise House-Senate version with comfortable margins that never fell below fifty-six votes in the House and nine votes in the Senate, a virtual landslide on something this difficult. Anyone who had been through this before knew it meant nothing, however. The next four votes were the killers. Where a budget simply promises spending cuts and tax increases, the "reconciliation" bill actually does it, "reconciling" tax-and-spending policy with deficit-reduction goals by making sweeping spending cuts and/or raising taxes. A member who votes for a budget can always say that it was just a blueprint and claim not to have agreed with half of it, but there is no such wiggling on a reconciliation bill. Once a member votes for that, he or she is liable for every single spending cut and tax increase in it. "Now we're shooting with real bullets," Dole liked to say of these big anti-deficit bills. Those bullets would be flying right at Democrats' heads in the next election.

When it came time for the first vote on the reconciliation bill in the House on May 27, moderate and conservative Democrats were rebelling, angry that they had been treated like second-class citizens all year as Clinton stroked the party's liberal majority, resisted New Democrat budget ideas, and stuck with the Btu tax, which particularly galled the energy-state members.

The rebels set up shop in Stenholm's office, where they were impor- tuned in conference calls and individual sessions by Chief of Staff Thomas "Mack" McLarty, Treasury Secretary Bentsen, Budget Director Panetta, and Clinton himself. Back at the Capitol, Democratic leaders Foley and Gephardt were getting frightening vote counts showing they were short, but they feared that waiting would only make things worse. As the chamber darkened and the illuminated tote board began to reg- ister the yeas and nays, Clinton had what Oklahoma moderate Dave McCurdy later called a "near-death experience"—he was losing.

McLarty frantically spoke to McCurdy by phone as time began to run out. He admitted that the White House had been wrong, had pursued the wrong strategy, had built the wrong coalition, had for- gotten its true friends. "He finally gets it; the president finally gets it," the chief of staff told McCurdy. Clinton would hire former Reagan aide David Gergen as a top adviser. The Btu tax would be gone. Al- most anything they wanted they could have if they would just vote yes.

The bill carried by a vote of 219–213. Clinton's comfortable vote margins had suddenly shrunk to just six votes or fewer. Had just three more Democrats voted no (joining the thirty-eight who did), Clinton would have lost. This was obviously a new ball game. There were three more roll-call votes to go.

Even after the Btu tax was gone, passing the bill in the Senate the first time was no easier. In fact, it was harder. The bill had been re- shaped to please conservatives, chiefly by dropping the Btu tax, but solving that problem created others: Now liberals were angry about the bigger Medicare cuts, and moderates were displeased that busi- ness tax breaks had been dropped, both necessary changes to re- plenish the savings lost by killing the Btu tax. Numerous Democrats were threatening to vote no. Leaders, sensing trouble, warned that killing the reconciliation bill would hurt or cripple the president, but many Democrats were more anxious about their own political future than they were about Clinton's. "It's not the president; it's the class of '94," said Louisiana Democrat John Breaux of the twenty-two Democratic Senate seats that would be up for grabs the following year.

When the Senate finally voted, at about 3:00 A.M. on June 25, six Democrats and all forty-three Republicans present voted no, tying the roll call at 49–49 (a senator from each party was out sick). Vice

President Al Gore broke the tie, squeaking out a win, 50–49. In a wee-hours press conference, Minority Leader Dole wore his trademark wolfish grin despite the loss. "It reminds me of 1985," he told reporters. "The next year we lost six seats"—and control of the Senate.

There *was* an eerie similarity between the two late-night votes. In 1985, Dole and Domenici had passed their tough plan on a tie vote that was broken by Vice President Bush at around 1:00 A.M., only to lose the Senate the next year. Eight years later the wounds were still fresh. Did Dole expect history to repeat itself? "That's my hope," he said. "If everything else is the same, why not [have the Democrats] lose eight seats?" Such a loss would shift control of the Senate back to the Republicans once again. There were two more votes to go.

The final vote in the House on August 5 gave Democrats an awful choice. Vote no: Kill the package, send the financial markets reeling, and quite possibly destroy the effectiveness of the first Democratic president in twelve years. Vote yes: Support the president, and take a flier on a horribly risky plan full of politically damaging taxes and spending cuts, a plan that might not even work. There were plenty of perfectly good excuses to vote no: The taxes were too big, the spending cuts were too small, the plan was unfair. The easiest thing to do—and this was true anytime Congress voted on a real deficit-reduction package—was to vote no. No wonder congressional whips and White House lobbyists were having such a terrible time rounding up the votes to pass it. But leaders had to win or die. There was no fallback strategy, no Plan B. If they lost this vote, they would have to improvise a new package to attract the mostly conservative Democrats who were walking away, but any concessions to them would just drive down support on the left.

At 1:00 P.M. on August 5, with the House vote now just nine hours away, the count stood at 198 yeses plus 10 leaners, for a shaky total of 208, still 10 votes short of the magic 218 it would take to win.

Two Democrats had signaled that they might be there at the end if Clinton absolutely needed them. Freshman Congresswoman Marjorie Margolies-Mezvinsky of Pennsylvania was a fifty-one-year-old former TV reporter who had narrowly upset a Republican in a heavily GOP district that included Philadelphia's old-money, Main Line suburbs. She had voted no in May, preserving a campaign promise to oppose taxes. She hoped to vote no again and had even told her hometown paper the day before that she would oppose the plan. Montana Congressman Pat Williams also planned to vote no. The fifty-five-year-old former schoolteacher had earlier talked up the Btu tax, arguing at a town meeting that it was a much better deal than a gasoline tax for Montana. Now that leaders had dropped the Btu tax and replaced it with a gasoline tax, Williams thought he would look like an idiot if he voted yes. But he was there if Clinton needed him.

A third possibility was Ray Thornton, an Arkansas Democrat who was a close friend of White House Chief of Staff McLarty's. The whips had been carrying Thornton as a yes for weeks, but just that morning he had called a deputy whip to warn him that he wasn't a solid yes at all. He had told his constituents he would not vote for a gasoline tax. Foley and other Democratic leaders were aghast that Thornton and others were seizing on the pathetically small increase in the gasoline tax as an excuse to vote against the president's plan.

Clinton was working the phones steadily now, trying to round up votes that only a direct call from the president could bring. Early on, the House's hard-nosed vote counters complained that Clinton would call members only reluctantly and then engage them in a sort of Socratic dialogue that ended without his directly asking for their vote. "He was not enthused about making a lot of phone calls to people originally," said a senior Democrat. "Then when he started to do them, he'd spend fifteen, twenty minutes on a call to someone, and then he wouldn't close the deal." But now that they were down to the wire, Clinton was at last getting tough and direct. When he called Williams that afternoon, he got right to the point: "Pat, I need you on this. It will not pass without your vote. My presidency is at stake."

With time running out, the yeses would not move above 212—a stubborn 6 votes from the needed 218. Majority Leader Gephardt was deeply worried. "I was the one in the leadership who was saying, 'We've really got a problem here. I mean, this thing well may not pass,' " he said. There was talk of postponing the vote, but Gephardt said they had no choice but to go: "These votes have kind of a rhythm to them, and you get down to the moment of truth, and you've got to go into the machine guns. I mean, you've got to go; you've got to try to make it happen. There's no other way to do it."

The vote began at 9:55 P.M., and with all time expired fifteen minutes later—the nominal time allowed for a House floor vote—the count was tied, 210–210. Now, thought New Mexico Democrat Bill Richardson, now we're going to lose. It's really going to happen. Richardson was chief deputy whip for the Democrats, and he had done little for the past several days but live and breathe this vote. Things looked very bad.

The tally moved to 211–212, and as it looked as if Clinton really would lose, cheers erupted on the Republican side of the chamber, punctuated by shouts for "regular order," a demand that the presiding officer bang the gavel and bring the vote to an end, recording it as a loss for Clinton. But more votes trickled in, and the count see-sawed for several minutes before it finally stuck at 216–215. Three Democrats had still not voted; two had to vote yes, or the bill would lose on a tie, 217–217, or outright, at 216–218.

The chamber was in pandemonium. To the whips and the Democratic leaders, what had to happen was clear. Williams and Thornton would have to vote yes so Margolies-Mezvinsky could vote no. It was time for Thornton to deliver, but Richardson could tell from the Arkansas representative's face that he wasn't going to do it. Shortly after the fifteen minutes that are usually set aside for a House vote expire, the automatic voting machine is shut down, and the only way to vote is with a cardboard card, a red card signifying no, a green card for yes. Thornton held a green card and a red card as he walked toward the dais. But as members crowded around him to make sure he would vote for the package, he signaled that he would vote no.

The beefy Richardson intercepted him. "Ray, you told the president that you were with us," he said. "Ray, you've got to do this." Thornton, a former Arkansas attorney general, shook his head. His face was ashen. He was shaking. "I promised my constituents I couldn't do this," he muttered. "I told the president that the gas tax would kill my constituents."

If Thornton voted no, Margolies-Mezvinsky would have to vote yes. Foley, normally a placid, gentle soul, grabbed Thornton's arm and angrily reminded him of what he was doing. "You can't let her make this vote!" he shouted. "You've got to be with the president; he's from your state!"

It was no good. Thornton handed in his red card. The vote was

216–216. If the tie held, the bill would die. It was clear to everyone in the well what was going to happen next, and the Democrats were furious. Tim Penny accosted Richardson and shook him angrily. "You've killed her; you killed this woman with this vote—you can't do this to her." But there was nothing else they could do, Richardson told him. "We don't get her, we lose," he said simply.

Margolies-Mezvinsky was waiting thirty feet away, next to the vote computer on the Democratic side of the chamber, where nervous members and aides were anxiously watching the count. To anyone looking down from the spectators' galleries high above the floor, Margolies-Mezvinsky was instantly noticeable. Around her, people swirled in constant motion, conferring, shouting, grabbing arms, and yelling in one another's ears. She alone seemed to stand stock-still, her face ghostlike, her eyes wide and fixed in the middle distance, contemplating what must have seemed like the imminent end of her short career as a House member. Foley walked up and told her they needed her. Barely glancing at him, she hesitated and then began to walk slowly down the aisle toward the well. She had the look of someone on the way to her own hanging. A Democrat handed her the green card she would need to vote yes. She joined Williams at the desk at the foot of the Speaker's dais. Williams signed his card and handed it in, and finally, agonizingly slowly, Margolies-Mezvinsky did the same.

After a few seconds' delay, the orange lights displaying the vote total blinked out the changes: from 216–216 to 217–216 and finally to 218–216. It was over. Cheers swelled from the Democratic side of the chamber. Republicans hooted derisively. "Good-bye, Marjorie," they shouted, pantomiming extravagant good-bye gestures. Margolies-Mezvinsky was in tears. Michigan Democrat Sander Levin kissed her on the cheek and gently guided her off the floor into a small holding area called the Red Room, where California Democrat Anna Eshoo comforted her. Richardson came hustling in and thanked her for her vote. "But I may have lost my seat," she protested, choking back tears. Eshoo flashed a venomous look at Richardson. "I can't believe you guys did this to her," she said. Outside, GOP aides eagerly distributed Xerox copies of *The Philadelphia Inquirer* article that quoted Margolies-Mezvinsky as saying she would vote no.

In sharp contrast to the wild, all-elbows roller-derby match in the House, where the winning margin came from a fissionable group of a half-dozen or more members, the Senate was a master-level chess match, where in the end just one person was in play: the stubbornly independent, capricious Senator Bob Kerrey, the Nebraska Democrat who had fought Clinton for the presidential nomination and lost in the early running. Now he had the fate of a president he did not much care for in his hands. Kerrey had voted for the president's plan the first time, chiefly to keep the process going. But now, he signaled, he was unhappy with the finished product and warned he would vote against it.

Kerrey and the handful of other Democrats determined to vote no insisted the package just wasn't good enough. Yet each of these politicians was a self-styled deficit hawk who believed the deficit was the government's single most important problem. Each had proposed a different approach, but each had failed to attract sufficient support to adopt his scheme. Now all of them were turning their backs on the only proposal that had a chance of passage. They were saying, in effect, that no deficit reduction was better than what Clinton was offering.

The day before the vote, Clinton got on the phone to try to persuade Kerrey to vote yes. Kerrey told Clinton the plan wasn't good enough. Both men's tempers began to rise. Clinton complained that he had tried to do the right thing and now Kerrey was going to make it impossible. "I shouldn't have even done this. I try to do the right thing, and I just get beat up," Clinton said. Kerrey was disgusted at Clinton's whining and told him so. The two men hung up angrily.

Few knew what Kerrey would do until shortly before he finally came to the Senate floor at about 7:00 P.M. the next evening to speak. The situation was so fluid that Dole went to Kerrey with a last-minute scheme to defeat Clinton's package and then work together on a bipartisan plan. Kerrey turned him down. When he finally took the floor, the chamber quickly hushed. In a strong, clear voice, Kerrey said that while he regretted it, he would vote for a bill that "challenges America too little" because he did not trust Republicans to do any better if he voted no. He reserved his strongest criticism for Clinton. In a gesture that was part shameless theatrics and part riveting oratory, he directed the rest of his speech at Clinton, looking into the TV cameras that ringed the chamber. "President Clinton, if you are watching, as I suspect you are, I will tell you this: I could not and should not cast a vote that brings down your presidency," he said. "Get back on the high road, Mr. President," he said, reminding Clinton of the "shared sacrifice" the president had called for months earlier in announcing the plan. "It is not shared sacrifice for us to brag that we are only raising taxes on those who earned over $180,000 a year. It is political revenge.

"You had the right idea, Mr. President, with the Btu tax. And when we came after you with both barrels blazing, threatening to walk if you did not yield, you should have let us walk," he said. "Instead, we find ourselves with a bill that asks Americans to pay 4.3 cents a gallon more. If they notice, I will be surprised. And if they complain, I will be ashamed."

An hour later Kerrey voted yes, the roll call tied at 50–50, and Gore again cast the decisive vote, allowing the plan to pass the Senate and go to the White House. Shortly afterward Senate leaders gathered for the ceremonial phone call to tell Clinton what he already knew. With exhausted staffers looking on, they told Clinton that his long roll of the dice was over, that he had won. Clinton's voice, husky and relieved, came back to them over the phone. "Thanks," the president said to the senators. "Now I can govern."

———

During the bitter fight over passage of the plan, not a single Republican voted yes in any one of the eight critical votes, and GOP leaders consistently predicted that Clinton's tax-heavy proposal would fail. "This plan is not a recipe for more jobs; it is a recipe for disaster," declared then–House Republican conference chairman Dick Armey in 1993. "Taxes will go up, the economy will sputter along, dreams will be put off, and all this for the hollow promise of deficit reduction and magical theories of lower interest rates." GOP doctrine taught that raising taxes would increase the deficit and tank the economy. "We'll come back next year and try to help you when this plan puts the economy in the gutter," sneered House Budget Committee ranking Republican John Kasich.

Six months later, in early 1994, however, jobs were up, and the economy was beginning to surge. Clinton's gritty work to bring down the deficit had combined with the luckily timed upswing in the business cycle to produce handsome economic growth: a robust 3.5 percent during his second full year in office. The financial markets, impressed that Clinton had spent his newcomer's political capital on deficit reduction, had pushed down interest rates, and the lower rates accelerated the recovery. Ironically, the boom was so strong that the Federal Reserve had begun pushing interest rates back up, fearful that the economic surge would reignite inflation. Except for interest rates, though, all the indicators a president usually lives or dies by were headed the right way: household spending, retail sales, and job creation—all up; unemployment and inflation—down. By the end of Clinton's first year in office, the booming economy had created more new jobs—2.1 million—than in all four years under Bush. Interest rates in the early months of that first year were so low that five million families refinanced their home mortgages, adding a huge wallop to consumer spending.

For all of its shortcomings, Clinton's budget plan had one saving virtue—it worked. With a big push from the recovering economy and the groundwork of the much-maligned 1990 budget deal (both of which Bush should get substantial credit for), the deficit fell steadily for the next four years. The chronic $300-billion-a-year deficits projected when Clinton took over from Bush eventually shrank to less than $110 billion in 1996. True, Clinton had not made the structural deficit go away; thanks largely to persistent growth in the two large health entitlements, Medicare and Medicaid, the deficit was projected to head back up again by the end of the decade. But for the time being, deficits would continue to hover a lot closer to $100 billion than to $300 billion.

Despite the good news, though, Republicans continued to hammer away at Clinton's plan; in the fall of 1994, they used public animosity toward his deficit-reduction package to help end Democratic control of both the House and the Senate for the first time since 1954. How they did that says a lot about the political payoff for reducing the deficit.

Attacking any real deficit-reduction plan is always easier than defending one (as Republicans would learn in 1995), and selling partial victory is tough. The deficit was down, but it was still projected to stick somewhere between $100 billion and $200 billion a year. Clinton quickly lost the public relations battle. He could have said, The economy is getting better, the deficit is coming down, and Bill Clinton did it. Instead, the political discourse was all about his tax increases, which drowned out the president altogether.

The GOP launched a remarkably effective nationwide campaign to redefine Clinton's deficit-reduction program as the largest tax increase in history. It was certainly a big tax package—self-destructively big for Clinton and the Democrats, as it turned out. But it was not the largest tax increase in history, only the *second* largest since the end of the Second World War. The largest since the war was the TEFRA legislation ushered in by Bob Dole and congressional Republicans to try to counteract Reagan's ballooning deficits in 1982: Updated to 1993 dollars, TEFRA raised taxes $268 billion over five years versus Clinton's $223 billion over the same period. Tax historians agree that tax increases during the Second World War and the Civil War were much larger than either TEFRA or Clinton's package (when compared on an inflation-adjusted basis).

Clinton compounded his public relations problem by completely rejecting any further deficit reduction, no matter how modest, arguing that it might hurt the economy or cripple his investment spending. Once Republicans realized the president would fight anything, they simply kept pitching balls for him to hit. Kasich and deficit-hawk Democrat Tim Penny proposed a $93-billion package of spending cuts in the fall of 1993; Clinton beat it. In early 1994, Clinton proposed a stand-pat budget with no new deficit reduction; when a bipartisan group in the Senate called for just $13 billion more in spending cuts, Clinton fought that and lost. Republicans dragged up the balanced-budget amendment again in 1994; Clinton beat it back. Repeatedly in the months after he signed the big budget package in August 1993, Clinton got sucked into battle after battle against deficit reduction—who could believe he was for it?

Finally, the White House lost much of its remaining credibility in a vain battle for a health-care reform plan that was grotesquely overcomplicated and far too big for Congress to ram through in the single year Clinton and First Lady Hillary Rodham Clinton had mapped out for it. The Congressional Budget Office analyzed the Clinton proposal and concluded that it might save money someday, but nowhere near as soon or as much as Clinton was claiming. The proposal simply added to the impression that the president was for big government and big spending.

With the administration badly distracted by its wasting fight over health care, Republicans clubbed away at Clinton's wimpishness on spending cuts, bashing the president in floor speeches, in committee debates, in television appearances, at rallies, and in attack material faxed to GOP governors, legislators, and party operatives throughout the country. From local officials to congressional leaders, Republicans stuck relentlessly to their strategy of keeping the tax issue before the public. "We just steadily stayed on point," said Haley Barbour, chairman of the Republican Party. "Clinton gave us the issue to win back our position in the country as a party of principle. He put on the table the best issue to show the difference between Republicans and Democrats."

It worked. Between January and June of 1994, public support for Clinton's handling of the economy dropped from nearly 60 percent to less than 40 percent, according to a Washington Post/ABC News poll. And even though the deficit was as low as it had been since the end of the Reagan administration and was projected to drop three years in a row for the first time since the Truman administration, poll after poll showed that only about 25 percent or less of the public realized that anything had changed. Against all evidence, three quarters of the American people believed that the deficit had stayed the same or gotten worse.

The experience often left congressional Democrats and White House officials seething with frustration. All their work, all their political sacrifice, all these undeniably good results—and still they were demonized. Massachusetts Democratic Congressman Barney Frank said the Republicans' complaints reminded him of the lifeguard who jumps into the sea to save a drowning boy, fights off sharks, and safely delivers the boy to his father only to have the father ask, "Where's his hat?"

During a February 1994 appearance before the House Budget Committee he had once chaired, Budget Director Panetta came under fierce attack from Kasich and other committee Republicans: Domestic spending was still going up, wasn't it? And while the deficit might look okay now, it was going up again by the end of the decade, wasn't it? It was all too much for the hot-tempered Panetta. So furious his voice was shaking with rage, he barked that if a Republican president had brought the deficit this low, "you'd kiss the ground! Does it really hurt that much to admit we are impacting the deficit?"

Chapter 8

TRAIN WRECK

On September 14, 1995, shortly after Congress returned from its August recess, Gingrich and Dole summoned House and Senate Republicans for a rare joint meeting in the cavernous hearing room of the House Ways and Means Committee, one of the few indoor spaces anywhere in the Capitol complex big enough to comfortably accommodate every single Republican from both houses. The theme of the mass meeting was unity, and not since an almost identical gathering fourteen years earlier—when Ronald Reagan had come to rally the troops for his supply-side assault in 1981—had practically every Republican from both chambers sat together, side by side, in a show of party fidelity.

Dole and Gingrich were worried that the Republican revolution might stall out now, when they were on the verge of success. Downtown at the White House, there was a strong expectation that Republicans were entering a difficult time and might well fail to make good on their promise of converting their budget resolution into reality. Democrats sensed vulnerabilities everywhere, opportunities to peel the more moderate, more cautious, more pragmatic Senate away from the reckless House and split the coalition. "There had been continued attempts to break the House and Senate apart— separate Dole from Gingrich," said Dole chief of staff Sheila Burke. "The only way we could succeed is if we prevented ourselves from being torn apart, and that rally was an important part of that," she said.

At the outset, Gingrich summoned up the spirit of the Gipper, deftly linking himself to the GOP icon. As they girded for the toughest votes and decisions of the year, he invoked the spirit of Reaganism to see them through. "It's hard to explain, if you weren't here, how, when we got tired and we got frustrated and we got stupid and we would be arguing with each other, Reagan had a magic ability to reach beyond us . . . and touch the American people," he said, staking a claim to the former president's leadership mantle. "Now we don't have Ronald Reagan as president to carry us through this challenge, so we're going to have to do it on our own."

They had a prodigious amount of work to do, very little time in which to do it, wavering public support, and uncertain agreement among themselves about how to move ahead. Their chore was stupendous: completely remake most of the low-income end of the federal government (Medicaid and welfare), transform its second-biggest middle-class entitlement (Medicare), overhaul the nation's agriculture policy, and cut taxes more deeply than had been done since Reagan's first year in office. The spending programs Republicans meant to radically change had been constructed over decades, affected millions of people, and often relied on complex formulas that had been written, rewritten, and further refined for years. "To overhaul any one of these programs is a year's work," observed California Democratic Congressman Bob Matsui. The Republicans had a couple of months.

For the Republicans, passing the budget had been, in retrospect, a snap. But now they were at the stage in the legislative process where things had gone so desperately bad in 1993, when Clinton's easy march to a deficit-reduction package had turned into agonizing negotiations and nightmarishly close votes. Turning a purposely vague budget into a numbingly detailed reconciliation bill that laid out all the spending cuts was the single hardest and most ambitious thing Congress did.

In the hearing room that morning sat many of the key Republican veterans of the last two decades' budget wars, members of Congress who knew just how bad it was about to get, survivors whose mistakes and miscues had helped lose elections and polarize a process they now thought they had finally mastered: Gingrich, whose fiery opposition to the 1990 budget deal had helped kill George Bush's presidency; Dole, who had been a key player in constructing Reagan's 1981 tax and spending cuts only to labor thanklessly for the next four years to try to repair the damage; Domenici, the old-school budget balancer who had instinctively resisted supply-side magic in 1981 and had warned his colleagues in vain against being seduced by tax cuts in 1995; and Kasich, the youngest of them all, eager and optimistic. Unlike the others, though, Kasich had not lived through—and in some cases had never learned—the history that had scarred the older men and made them cautious. Kasich's limited knowledge of budget history could be disconcerting. He appeared to know little about the Republicans' catastrophic 1985 gamble to freeze Social Security COLAs, which helped cost the GOP control of the Senate. And he seemed to have only a passing knowledge of the watershed 1990 budget negotiations. In many ways, for Kasich, history began in November 1994, when the GOP won control of Congress.

Here, inside this room, Gingrich was at the height of his powers, still indisputably in charge of the revolution that had brought them this far, still the spark plug, the visionary, the chief strategist who decided how far they would go and when they would move. Dole was increasingly distracted by his presidential campaign, which was now building toward the early 1996 primaries, and he was locked into a wasting set of skirmishes with Texas Senator Phil Gramm for the title of the Senate's real conservative. Gingrich himself was frequently rumored to be a presidential contender; he did little to stifle the rumors, as if he relished keeping Dole off balance. He had drawn a mammoth horde of reporters when he traveled up to New Hampshire in June, ostensibly to look for a moose. Was Dole annoyed with the man he had to work with so closely every day? The inscrutable Kansan gave no hint.

By now, actually, after they had worked together through the year, much of the early tension between the two had dissipated. "I don't think Newt and Dole would be natural fishing buddies," said Gingrich spokesman Tony Blankley, "but both of them came to appreciate aspects of the other." Gingrich, Dole understood better now, was prisoner as well as leader of his freshmen-driven conservative core; Dole, Gingrich realized, had the opposite problem with a Senate where old bulls were wary of the House's insistence on heedlessly rushing ahead.

The leaders might have begun to warm to each other, but still there was strain between the two chambers. The House had moved at near light speed all year to enact all manner of legislation only to see bills stall and break down in the Senate. The Senate's insistence on shrinking the House's $350 billion in tax cuts to $245 billion marked the fundamental difference between the two chambers: House revolutionaries saw it as proof of the Senate's essential wimpishness; senators characteristically viewed it as practical politics. To the House, everything about the Senate was maddeningly slower and more cautious, including Dole's ponderous, wooden manner, a striking contrast to Gingrich's exuberance, his wordy playfulness, and his energy.

With Gingrich, almost everything that went on in his head seemed to come out of his mouth; he rarely seemed to have an unexpressed thought. When a white woman in South Carolina drowned her two sons and for days placed the blame on a nonexistent black man, Gingrich linked the terrible incident to Democratic values. His interior monologue often went public. Typical was a minisoliloquy during the September 14 GOP rally in which he mentioned, in the same breath, the movie *Gettysburg*, General George Pickett's charge, Colonel Joshua Chamberlain's heroic stand, the beach at Normandy, and balancing the budget, wrapping up by admonishing members that if they couldn't explain that the Medicare Part B premium would be a mere $7 a month higher in 2002, "there ain't no point in your serving in the United States Congress."

Dole, by contrast, was virtually mum. At joint press appearances, he usually stuck to a few stiff comments and turned the podium over to Gingrich to run free. As Gingrich's poll ratings sank lower and lower, Dole shrank farther and farther away, sometimes all but hiding behind the charts the two men brought to illustrate their points. Dole's leadership style in the Senate was the antithesis of Gingrich's wide-open inclusiveness in the House; Dole, said House GOP Conference Chairman John Boehner, "just runs that place with his cards right up against his chest." In private meetings, Dole usually said as little as he could, leaving other leaders with little sense of where he stood. "Bob Dole is a very, very circumspect person," said House Majority Leader Dick Armey. "I'm not sure that I can tell you much of a read on Bob."

Dole's problem now was so obvious that he need not have articulated it. If the revolution was going to fail, chances were it would fail in the Senate, where the huge reconciliation bill had to pass through the narrowest gap: the Senate Finance Committee, where the bare, one-vote Republican margin made the majority party extremely vulnerable. One man could stop the train, just as Montana Democratic Senator Max Baucus had when he forced Clinton and the Democrats to accept a much smaller gasoline tax in 1993. Now the man in that narrow gap was moderate Rhode Island Republican Senator John Chafee, who had misgivings about GOP proposals on Medicaid. "This bill goes too far," Chafee warned.

At the September 14 rally, however, the message was to keep going the way they had been. Haley Barbour, the Republican Party chairman, warned the assembled Republicans against any impulse to ease up. Citing internal Republican National Committee polling, he insisted the public was much less worried that the Republicans would go too far with their reforms than that they might not go far enough. "Stay united," the Mississippian urged. "We're close, close, close."

As he wound up his remarks, Gingrich, the former college history professor, sought to cast the struggle in epic terms. The upcoming votes, he said, would be the legislative equivalent of the Allied invasion of Normandy in the latter days of the Second World War. "In the next sixty to ninety days, we're going to prove whether or not we're worthy of being truly historic," he told them. "The real challenge isn't the left, it isn't the Democrats, it's us."

———

But Gingrich was wrong. The danger was not "us," not that the Republicans would fall apart or lose their nerve. They had come too far, their discipline was too strong, and there were still too many of them who had never tasted the political reward for real deficit reduction. In the end, Chafee would find it impossible to cross his old comrade Dole by stopping the balanced-budget bill in committee or on the floor. Members with objections would be mollified or simply intimidated, warned not to be the one whose vote would go down in history as the vote that stopped the revolution—or undermined Dole's presidential campaign. That was the virtue of rolling almost the entire year's agenda into one huge bill: It was an all-or-nothing vote. "You've got to remember one driving force that is pushing this: We've got to get these deficits under control," said Chafee. "So we've been able to swallow a lot of things to achieve that goal."

The danger was not that they would fail to go far enough but that they had already gone too far and did not realize it. The mandate they thought they had, the huge political push they had gotten in the elections almost a year before, had vanished.

Anyone who cared to look at the polls knew things had already gone seriously awry. Months earlier the numbers had begun to slip as Republicans made inevitable rookie mistakes. Their politically disastrous drive to scale back the school-lunch program was on a strategic par with Clinton's decision to tackle the gays-in-the-military policy in the first month of his presidency: Both decisions gave their opponents huge openings for an attack. Democrats who had been rattled and demoralized by their awful loss in the November 1994 elections took heart and went on the offensive.

Even before Michigan Governor John Engler warned House Republicans in May that they should brace for inevitable bad news, polls had begun to plummet. By March, barely two months after Republicans took formal control of Congress, a Washington Post/ABC News poll was already showing that most Americans feared the new majority was going too far in cutting programs that helped the elderly, children, the poor, and the middle class. Asked whether they agreed with the statement "The more I hear about what Republicans do in Congress, the less I like it," 52 percent said yes. Nearly six in ten agreed that Republicans "will go too far in helping the rich and cutting needed government services that benefit average Americans as well as the poor." Ominously, the 59 percent who agreed with that statement marked a fourteen-point rise just since January.

Republicans had expected heavy weather. What they did not expect, and what particularly galled and worried them now, was that as they fell, Clinton was rising. Asked whether Clinton or the GOP Congress would do a better job helping the middle class, respondents chose the president, 52 to 38 percent. Asked whom they trusted to protect Social Security, they favored Clinton by nineteen points, 53 to 34 percent. Barely two months earlier, Republicans had won that matchup by seven points.

Pollsters zeroed in on the Republicans' core problem: the $270 billion they wanted to cut from projected spending on Medicare over the next seven years. In a May NBC News/Wall Street Journal poll, 69 percent of respondents said they would rather leave Medicare spending at current levels than cut it and use the money for deficit reduction. Even if it was a question of keeping Medicare solvent, respondents would rather cut programs other than Medicare to find the money. "It's a tough political problem," conceded GOP pollster Robert Teeter, who helped conduct the poll. It's "school lunch times ten," said Democratic pollster Stan Greenberg.

About a month before the unity rally, when Congress quit work for the August recess, the poll-to-poll results had solidified into a trend. "No opposition Congress and House leadership (at least since the invention of polling) has lost so much credibility so quickly," wrote political analyst Kevin Phillips. Citing a variety of polls, Phillips said Republicans had misinterpreted and mishandled their 1994 mandate, substituting their own agenda—gun control, regulatory and financial relief for business, radical cuts in social programs—for the more moderate, pro-environment government and political reform voters wanted. Worse, Republicans had put a single face on their effort, raising up an easily demonized villain who personified the mean-spirited excess Democrats now charged them with. Gingrich, adored by the party faithful, had in just eight months become "Typhoid Newt" to the public, Phillips wrote, managing "to garner negative ratings at a pace heretofore matched only by mass murderers."

Increasingly jittery and unpredictable as pressure mounted, Gingrich sometimes seemed to be two different people. One was the calm, brilliantly articulate leader who could make even Democrats nod in agreement as he spun out his compassionate vision for the future. The other was a strident attack artist who could not resist the sort of personal vengefulness that a leader at his level ought to have avoided. Gingrich regularly salted his remarks about Democrats in general and Clinton in particular with the words *lie, cheat, steal, dishonest,* and *shameful.* Speaking to the Republican National Committee in July, he called Clinton "a wonderfully engaging, fabulously glib, terrifically good talker whose words have almost no meaning."

But Republicans had larger problems than Gingrich's growing unpopularity. They were now stuck in the destructive deficit-reduction trap familiar to all their predecessors, the snare they had thought they could somehow avoid. Polls showed that voters approved of the Republicans' general plan to cut the deficit and balance the budget but did not approve of the specific plans to go after huge reductions in programs like Medicare and Medicaid. But as Kasich and the rest understood, it was impossible to cut the deficit and go easy on those big entitlements. Here was the serene voter ambivalence, the rock-headed insistence on believing two mutually exclusive things at once that had made deficit reduction so impossible for so long. Over the August recess, voters told the Republicans to go after savings in Medicare—but in fraud, waste, and abuse, not by cutting benefits or raising premiums. Reagan's soothing reassurances of a decade ago now haunted his congressional heirs: The public believed that deficit reduction could be painless—Reagan had told them so. Of course, the trouble was that there were nowhere near enough savings to be had from Medicare just by squeezing fraud, waste, and abuse. They needed $270 billion; Republicans deployed their sharp pencils and found that fraud, waste, and abuse would get them—maybe—$20 billion, less than 10 percent of what they needed.

Very early on, the Republicans sensed how the Democrats would attack them over their plans to cut Medicare by $270 billion and taxes by a similar amount—$245 billion. "They would pull out Medicare and tax cuts, link them up, and make a federal case out of it, which is exactly what they did," said House Majority Leader Dick Armey. If the Republicans knew this, why did they proceed? First, the numbers left them no choice; if they wanted to balance the budget and cut taxes, they would have to go where the money was. Beyond that, they were propelled by responsibility and self-delusion. Medicare really did need an overhaul: Every trustees' report since 1970 had raised the specter of bankruptcy, and Congress was running out of Band-Aid fixes. It behooved the party in power to do something.

But what made the Republicans think they could do it without somehow involving the Democrats from the beginning? That defied the basic law of modern deficit politics: Those who do the heavy lifting get attacked by those who do not. Republicans had done that to

Democrats over taxes; Democrats had done it to Republicans over Social Security. Winning big elections and ousting the incumbent party can make politicians pathologically sure of themselves. The Republicans were convinced beyond any doubt or caution that they were right.

For years, Congress had chipped away at Medicare as part of larger deficit-reduction efforts, but never on so huge a scale. The $270 billion that the Republicans wanted was nearly a third of their entire balanced-budget plan and more than four times the record Medicare savings that Clinton pushed through in 1993.

In the past, Congress had rarely taken direct aim at beneficiaries, preferring instead the safer course of squeezing funds from the system at the expense of doctors, hospitals, and other medical-care providers. The new GOP plan called for another round of deep provider cuts, but the Republicans needed so much money this time that planners scrounged for ways to make beneficiaries pay more. One was to keep the Part B (doctor-care) premium for all beneficiaries at the current 31.5 percent of the cost of the program rather than letting it drop back to 25 percent, as scheduled for the coming year. They also nicked better-off beneficiaries by raising their premiums even higher.

The Republicans were convinced they could extract significant further savings by introducing a much greater degree of marketplace competition, opening Medicare more aggressively to a variety of competing plans that they believed could provide health care more efficiently than traditional fee-for-service medicine. From now on, Medicare would act a lot more like private business, which was moving workers into HMOs and other "managed care" institutions that could rigidly control costs and—in theory—provide the same amount of care for less money.

The Republicans did not want to overtly force seniors away from their familiar doctors and herd them into HMOs and other private programs; that would be political poison. But if they couldn't push the patients out, they could slowly starve the old system until it became unattractive for both doctors and patients to stay in it. Squeezing payments to fee-for-service Medicare providers would eventually force the providers out; patients who chose to stay would find fewer doctors and fewer hospitals willing to provide them with care. In a controversial speech that critics said revealed the Republicans' true

intentions, Gingrich told an insurers' group that fall that he believed the federal agency that traditional Medicare—and by implication, traditional Medicare itself—would eventually "wither on the
vine," though, he confided, he didn't think it was "politically smart"
to kill it right away.

Republicans would squeeze Medicare costs and force efficiencies
by capping total Medicare spending for the first time in the program's thirty-year history. The program would remain an entitlement, but it would no longer be open-ended; if Medicare costs rose
faster than projected, as they almost always had, providers would
have to make up the difference. There were complex rules about
what costs could be passed on to beneficiaries, particularly in fee-for-
service Medicare. But the bottom line was that if costs rose beyond
the preset annual limits, beneficiaries with traditional Medicare or
those in the new HMO world would either pay more or get less—or
lower-quality—medical care. What the Republicans were doing was
taking government out of the equation when it came to sharing the
costs of excessive medical inflation. From now on, providers and
beneficiaries would bear that risk.

From a strictly good-government, balance-the-budget point of
view, the Republicans were right to propose this change. There was
no way to get Medicare under control without beginning to shift at
least some of the rising costs to beneficiaries. The public debate
never focused on this little-understood change, but it was the single
most important difference between the Republicans and the Democrats, who would keep that risk with the government.

The Medicare proposal was so fraught with political danger and so
critical to the overall success of the Republican plan that Gingrich
assumed personal charge of it in the House, literally drafting the legislation in the Speaker's office instead of entrusting the job to the
two committees that would ordinarily have handled it. Gingrich saw
no one else with the brainpower to handle the complex technical
decisions and with the strategic vision to chart a safe political course.
"He was," press secretary Tony Blankley declared, "the only guy who
could have pulled that off."

Gingrich's chief problem was the big, independent interest
groups—doctors, hospitals, insurers, seniors—that stood to gain or
lose so much from any Medicare proposal. If Gingrich could not co-

opt most of them, he would fail. He went about it by summoning representatives of these groups, one by one, and giving them the choice of helping to shape and pass the legislation or getting bulldozed by it. "Their style is you're with them or against them," said Tom Scully, president of the Federation of American Health Systems, a hospital group. "If you're against them, they'll beat the shit out of you."

When the American Hospital Association took out newspaper ads that spring to warn that many community hospitals would be forced to close if the Republican plan took effect, irate GOP leaders quickly excommunicated the group, denying it any further input in shaping the legislation. "Rather than engaging in a dialogue about the program, they went into attack mode, and they now find themselves on the outside looking in," Barry Jackson, executive director of the House Republican Conference, told reporters.

John Rother, legislative director for the American Association of Retired Persons (AARP) and a former GOP health-care staffer himself, was attacked and ostracized by Gingrich's operatives for publicly raising concerns about the Republican Medicare plan. Rother had already committed the unpardonable sin—in Republicans' eyes—of heading a coalition in 1994 that promoted a universal health-care plan in Congress along lines favored by President Clinton. Now he ran afoul of Ed Kutler, a Gingrich health-care aide who aggressively enforced the GOP line and had no compunction about intimidating lobbyists. Although he had never met or spoken with Rother, Kutler wrote him off as a Democratic political operative and signaled to other AARP senior officials who were negotiating with Gingrich that their legislative director was not welcome in the Speaker's office. "They impugned my credibility and reputation," Rother said. "It all became so personal and so polarized and unpleasant." Gingrich and his aides made no apologies for their tactics. "I'm not suggesting this was the lion lying down with the lamb," said Tony Blankley.

Republicans kept the details of their Medicare plan vague as long as they could, in part because they had not worked them out and in part because doing so deprived critics of a hard target to shoot at. Even so, Democrats were making headway by relentlessly linking the Medicare cuts to tax cuts. More important, the Democrats were scoring with shrill attacks that often grossly exaggerated the harm that might realistically come from the GOP proposals. "Those who want to gamble with Medicare are asking Americans to bet their lives," declared Clinton in a typical attack; "not to balance the budget, not to strengthen the Medicare trust fund, but simply to pay for a big tax cut for people who don't need it."

The issue lit a fire under Democrats and their traditional allies in seniors groups and labor organizations. In a particularly effective move, a coalition of labor groups spent millions to air TV commercials that were as slick and as manipulative as the "Harry and Louise" spots that had helped devastate Clinton's health-care plan in 1994. A typical labor-backed anti-GOP spot showed a middle-aged husband and wife having an urgent discussion about what to do with Grandma if federal health-care spending is cut—while Grandma sits listening in the next room, in tears. On Capitol Hill, the same sort of activist seniors who had forced Dan Rostenkowski to flee down North Milwaukee Avenue in 1989 now invaded hearings in T-shirts with the word SHAME emblazoned across the front and got themselves arrested while TV cameras rolled.

The Republicans had gone home for the August recess in a defensive crouch, braced for attacks from their constituents. Elderly voters were nervous about changes. "Managed care does not go over well," admitted Jon D. Fox, the freshman Republican from suburban Philadelphia who had ousted Democrat Marjorie Margolies-Mezvinsky. "The great majority prefer the system they have." Back home in Wisconsin, freshman Republican Mark Neumann found open hostility. "I don't want any HMO or any of that crap," eighty-five-year-old Hazel Ann Helgesen warned him at a town meeting where he was giving the GOP sales pitch. "If you vote for it, I'll vote you out."

Democrats could gauge the political effectiveness of their attacks by watching how angry Gingrich was getting. Gingrich repeatedly called House Minority Leader Dick Gephardt and other Democrats liars and worked himself into a rage over the Medicare campaign. "I mean, think about a party whose last stand is to frighten eighty-five-year-olds, and you'll understand how totally, morally bankrupt the modern Democratic Party is," he fumed.

Much of what the Democrats were saying was, in fact, pure demagoguery, but both sides lied and misrepresented their way through the entire debate. Democrats jumped on Republicans for raising premiums, but the Democrats were doing that, too: At the end of seven years, the Republicans would raise the monthly Part B premium from the current $46.10 to $87.60. Clinton's proposals would raise it to $82.80.

In the end, the debate had nothing to do with substance and everything to do with political advantage. Both sides agreed that Medicare could not go on as it was. Republicans proposed ways to control ever-rising costs and begin to split those costs more rationally between the federal government and beneficiaries. "While the details left something to be desired, the basic structure of the Republican proposal was sound," said former CBO director Robert Reischauer, a Democrat who was known for being equally tough on the health-care proposals of both parties (his assessment of Clinton's health-care plan in 1994 found that it overestimated future savings, a critique that turned out to be a serious blow to the proposal). If Republicans were guilty of anything, it was duplicity. They insisted they wanted to preserve traditional Medicare when their policies were aimed at slowly starving it to death.

Democrats, on the other hand, were offering no proposals to begin solving the long-run problem. Clinton simply wanted to stay in the game, but without political risk; his proposals focused exclusively on providers, piously sparing beneficiaries even the modest premium increases he had advocated a year earlier (his 1994 health-care reform plan included higher premiums for better-off seniors). He was using Medicare the same way Democrats had used Social Security in the 1980s, and just as effectively.

As the Democrats' save-Medicare campaign wore on, polls showed the Republicans in deep trouble. Gingrich privately conceded that the upcoming votes on Medicare and the rest of the budget agenda would test the Republican majority's ability to survive. Medicare, he said, "was the only thing we touched this year that could kill us." In fact, they were already dead. They just didn't know it.

———

From the first, the Republicans had acted as if Clinton were irrelevant to their drive to balance the budget, and for a long time he was. The 1994 election had stunned the president and left Congress's new Democratic minority shell-shocked and confused. For weeks afterward, the White House seemed shrouded in an atmosphere of gloom and indecision. At one point in late December, to great derision around Washington, Clinton searched for direction from a group of New Age gurus and self-improvement authors he convened at Camp David.

Congressional Democrats were in even worse shape than the president. At least Clinton still had a job. Power shifts in Congress are brutally wounding in dozens of humiliating ways. Defeated members—particularly ones like suddenly former House Speaker Tom Foley and newly ex–Ways and Means chairman Dan Rostenkowski—were transformed virtually overnight from exalted beings to nobodies, expected to clear out their offices, fire their staffs, and be gone as soon as possible. (The once-mighty Rostenkowski also had to deal with criminal charges that he misused government money and property; he later pleaded guilty and was sentenced to prison.)

Those who had managed to hang on had to give up most of their former perks; in some cases, that meant putting loyal, longtime aides on the street, losing the immense power that went with being a committee or subcommittee chairman, and moving into a smaller office formerly occupied by a Republican. The triumvirate of Democrats who had once written most health-care legislation in the House—John Dingell, Henry Waxman, and Pete Stark—suddenly had no role in the effort to completely remake the programs they had helped shape for years. Dick Gephardt went from the second most powerful man in the House to leader of the ravaged Democratic minority, so far down on the food chain that he now couldn't even get Gingrich to return his phone calls. "We were dealing with the walking wounded," recalled House Democratic aide George Kundanis, who stayed on after Foley's defeat. "Careers were shattered. We were laying off staff. It was like a family in mourning."

Clinton and the Democrats were in no shape to mount an effective counterattack against the new Republican majority, and at least in the early going there would have been no point. Gingrich and the Republicans were on a roll, bathed in nonstop media attention and widely expected to transform Washington and the nation itself. By mid-April, when Gingrich had pushed the Contract with America through the House and was rolling up his sleeves to begin balancing the budget, the president was reduced to plaintively reminding reporters that he still had a role to play. "The president is relevant," Clinton insisted at a press conference. "The Constitution gives me relevance." The fact that he had to say it made it seem doubly beside the point.

Even in this weakened state, however, Clinton was far from powerless, as Gingrich well knew. In moments when they looked more than a few weeks into the future, the Republicans reminded one another that Clinton still had the power to veto the bills they would send him. With one stroke of his pen, the president could undo all that they had worked so hard to achieve.

The Republicans wanted radical transformation of government, a balanced budget in seven years, and huge tax cuts, and every day they got more adamant. Gingrich could not offer them a typical, split-the-difference compromise and expect to get even a majority of the votes of his own House Republicans; if he split his rank and file, he would lose his leader's job. It was the same for Clinton; if he signed anything like what the Republicans were demanding, he would become a pariah among House and Senate Democrats. For them to get a deal at the end of the year, somebody was going to have to abandon his base—and Gingrich had to find a way to make Clinton be the one to do that.

For the past two years, the Republicans had watched Clinton but had no clear sense of him. They had never had to deal with him as anything but a caricature, the enemy, a politician to be derided and criticized. House Majority Leader Dick Armey said he got much of what he knew about Clinton not from close observation but from reading *The Agenda,* journalist Bob Woodward's book about Clinton's first year in office. Now Armey, Gingrich, and the rest had to get inside Clinton's head, figure him out, divine a way to make him do what he would certainly not want to do: sign the budget and tax-cut bills they planned to send him. "It wasn't like we were sitting around playing Freud, but we were trying to figure out what would make him respond one way or another," said Gingrich budget aide Arne Christenson. Not unlike FBI psychologists who try to help catch serial killers by getting inside their heads and predicting their moves, they started to piece together a psychological profile of the president. What made him tick? How could they bend him to their will? If Clinton saw that his political future depended on it, would he be inclined to cut a deal with the Republicans?

Clinton had shown flashes of toughness and resolve, as in 1993, when he held a bare majority of Democrats together in the face of complete GOP opposition to his deficit-reduction package. But the president also had a record of backing down under pressure: He had supported high-profile nominees for attorney general and other top administration posts only to drop them, and over and over again he had watered down tough principles on issues such as gays in the military and the protection of old-growth forests to make middle-ground deals.

Republican analysts talked to people who had known Clinton well in Arkansas. "They said he worked hardest to bridge differences with his enemies, and he was toughest on his friends," said Christenson. "They said he would want a deal and would not want a *High Noon* showdown." The Republicans concluded that Clinton was fundamentally weak, prone to give ground at the critical moment. Even better, he had now been further weakened by the Republicans' stunning takeover. All this confirmed the low opinion most GOP leaders already held. "We kind of felt the president was so comfortable with the I-feel-your-pain '90s role of the sensitive man that he'd never be able to get in touch with a fellow like John Wayne," said Armey.

But Republican Congressman Tim Hutchinson, a former Arkansas state legislator, offered a word of caution: Clinton might be pliable, but he was also dangerously slippery, with a lawyer's adroitness at finding loopholes through which to wiggle out of an agreement. Hutchinson told them a story: When Arkansas Republicans threatened to shut down part of the state government in 1991 unless Clinton signed a new budget that included a ban on the distribution of condoms in high school health clinics, Clinton balked at first and threatened to force the legislature into a special session. On the last day of the regular session, though, he relented and signed the budget. But even as the Republicans and their Christian Coalition allies celebrated the victory, Clinton announced that he had found a way around the ban: Although the clinics were built and maintained with state funds, the nurses who staffed them were paid with federal funds and were not subject to the state prohibition. Distribution of condoms would continue.

Forewarned, Republicans now set about designing a nuclear option that would leave Clinton no room to slip away. They had a problem: The veto gave Clinton the power to wipe away their proposals and leave things as if the GOP revolution had never occurred. Entitlement programs they wanted to radically transform would remain unchanged, doling out benefits as before. The tax system, too, would roll on unchanged, levying taxes at the old rates, with none of the GOP cuts. It would be as if nothing had ever happened, except in one area: The federal bureaucracy could not continue to operate without appropriations, and it is Congress that has the power to write and pass those money bills. Republicans could opt to send Clinton no appropriations bills, guaranteeing that the government would shut down until he met their terms. Or more likely, they could send him appropriations bills with conditions so onerous that signing them would mean knuckling under to at least part of their agenda. "You had to find a trump to match his trump," Gingrich explained, "And the right to pass money bills is the only trump that is equally strong."

Very early on, Republicans began laying down threats and acting tough. They had no fear of a government shutdown, a "train wreck" in Washington parlance, if that's what it took to bring Clinton and the Democrats around. "We'll go through a dance," Gingrich confidently explained to *Time* magazine in late May. The Republicans would offer a series of spending bills that would surgically remove or pare down agencies and programs the Republicans did not like. Clinton would then have to choose between two unpleasant alternatives: He could sign the tough Republican bills and run "the parts of government that are left," or, the House Speaker said with obvious relish, "he can run no government." Either way was fine with the Republicans. "Which of the two of us do you think worries more about the government not showing up?" Gingrich asked.

Part of this was macho posturing, part was careful calculation. As they sketched the psychological profile of their adversary, GOP leaders had called in former Reagan and Bush staffers to help them try to understand what it was like for a president to preside over a government shutdown. Very unsettling, the former aides reported. A president's job is to run the government; all those hundreds of thousands of federal employees work for *him*. Republican or Democrat, it is tough for a chief executive to sit by while federal workers are locked out of their offices, while the government *he* is responsible for smoothly running grinds to a halt. Bush had been disconcerted by even a three-day shutdown—the longest ever—during a budget impasse in 1990.

The Republicans received one other piece of advice from Kenneth Duberstein, a prominent GOP lobbyist and a former congressional liaison and chief of staff in the Reagan administration: No matter what they thought of Clinton personally, no president is ever irrelevant, just by the nature of the office and the bully pulpit it offers. Duberstein was troubled by Gingrich's open threats to shut down the government if Clinton didn't bend to his wishes, and he said so. "You never want to back a dog into a corner because the only way for the dog to get out is to attack back," he told Gingrich and Armey. The Republicans thanked him for his advice and promptly ignored it.

GOP planners were so confident Clinton would ultimately give them what they wanted that they saw no need to construct a Plan B. Sheila Burke, Dole's chief of staff, said there were no contingencies for how to deal with a veto and a Clinton refusal to come to terms in subsequent talks. It was simply inconceivable that this would not work. "I kind of just felt if we get this done, somehow it'll all work out," said Kasich. "We just assumed that given enough pressure, Clinton would do what he always had done," said House Republican Conference Chairman Boehner, "—cave and cut a deal."

The Republicans had underestimated Clinton, discounting at least two signs of the core toughness that would eventually shock them. In 1992, his steely performance in New Hampshire demonstrated his refusal to go down without a fight; his response to devastating attacks on his moral character was to go—with his wife—on CBS's *60 Minutes* to confront charges of infidelity. A decade earlier, in 1982, others had similarly written Clinton off as a one-term governor when he lost his first reelection race in Arkansas. But after brooding awhile, Clinton figured out what he had done wrong, readjusted his strategy, and clawed his way back to the governor's mansion two years later. He had not gotten where he was by being weak willed. Republicans badly misread him when they concluded that they could push him around or that he would find no way to recover from the shock of the 1994 election. Clinton "could get back on his feet as fast as anyone I know," said James Carville, Clinton's 1992 campaign manager. Within a few days of the 1994 shock, said adviser Gene Sperling, Clinton had recovered some of his former energy, telling aides that he had gotten up in the wee hours to scribble notes to himself about what to do next.

The first sign of life from the White House was an odd one. After abandoning his promise to cut taxes for the middle class in 1993 on the grounds that such a cut would make it harder to reduce the deficit, Clinton did an abrupt about-face in December 1994 and called for $60 billion in tax cuts. Critics immediately attacked this as a transparently imitative, wimpy, me-too move, a pale version of the much bigger GOP tax cuts. Reaction from Hill Democrats was mixed but mostly negative: Senators opposed it; House members divided—most Ways and Means Democrats were against it, as were centrist and conservative Democrats, who believed (absolutely correctly) that tax cuts would just push them backward on deficit reduction.

But this wasn't about deficit reduction or being responsible; this was pure politics, and it was much smarter than it looked at first. Gephardt got it as well, upstaging Clinton by proposing his own tax-cut package two days before the president announced his. What Clinton and Gephardt both intuited was that they needed inoculation against the Republicans' charges that all they wanted to do was tax and spend. They also needed to draw sharp distinctions between themselves and the GOP: Democrats were for tax cuts, too, but for the middle class, not for the rich taxpayers who would get most of the Republicans' tax relief. And on the most basic level, they had to keep fellow Democrats from being frozen out of the debate and forgotten in the heady rush toward the new Republican future. Quite simply, they had to do something. "Here you had a situation where essentially we were being perceived as irrelevant," said a senior administration official. "Those tax cuts were an effort to try to get ourselves back in the game."

Clinton's next move was not an optional one, since the law required him to produce a budget every year. Here was a critical turning point: How would the president respond to the Republicans' determination to balance the budget? His answer was budgetary rope-a-dope, a you-go-first proposal that made virtually no serious attempt to cut the deficit further, leaving all the heavy lifting to the Republicans and projecting $200-billion deficits to 1999 and beyond.

Administration strategists had opted to punt because it made no sense to them to lay out a big, ambitious package of spending cuts that Republicans would only top. For one thing, Clinton had taken a great risk in 1993 to propose and pass a major deficit-reduction plan only to have Republicans demonize it. Why should he stick his neck out again? For another thing, there was wide skepticism among Democrats in the White House and on Capitol Hill that Republicans could actually fulfill their campaign promises to balance the budget and cut taxes while leaving Social Security and defense off the table. Instead of offering up spending cuts to help the GOP do that, why not give them no cover and force them to show where they would cut? There were only a few places Republicans could go to get the kind of money they needed. "We knew they couldn't do it without deep cuts in Medicare, and that's why we laid the trap in Medicare in the first budget," said senior Clinton adviser George Stephanopoulos. "Make them go first. Call their bluff."

The Republicans reacted largely with contempt. Kasich called Clinton's offering "a tragedy" and accused the president of abdicating his leadership role. Characteristically, he could not resist a sports metaphor: He said it was as if the president were a ballplayer who had finally gotten a chance to get up to bat in Yankee Stadium but was trying to get hit by a pitch. "When you're president of the United States," he said, "you better swing at the fences."

In all the bristling rhetoric Republicans fired at Clinton's budget, though, there was a lone note of regret and caution: "Frankly, without the president's leadership, I don't know where we are going," said Domenici, who had been to the end of budget roads before and could see to the end of this one. "You will not get a balanced budget unless the president wants to cooperate with the Congress."

———

Throughout the 1980s and into the 1990s, congressional Democrats had grown used to fighting presidents, but the targets had always been Republicans: Reagan and Bush. Now they found themselves in the curious position of skirmishing with Clinton, the guy who was supposed to be on their team. The heady vision of a united Democratic government had been blasted apart by the 1994 elections, and both sides were pointing fingers at each other. No longer chained together to pass difficult legislation, they had much less to force them to agree, and Clinton suddenly seemed to be taking advantage.

On February 22, the midpoint in the House Republicans' one-hundred-day wind sprint to pass their Contract with America, Clinton came to the Hill for a private meeting with the House Democrats. While the president tried to boost their spirits with a pep talk, he also warned them bluntly that they should no longer assume he would support them on every major issue. "There will be times when I have to move to the center, which may be a problem for some of you," Clinton told them, according to Chief Democratic Deputy Whip Bill Richardson. The president asked for their help—or at least their understanding—on those issues. Some Democrats left the meeting confused or suspicious, unsure of exactly what Clinton had in mind. There was no way for them to know that the surreptitious hand of Dick Morris, a forty-seven-year-old political consultant from Connecticut little known in Washington, was manipulating the White House and charting a new, more independent course for the president.

Clinton and Morris were bound by the past: Morris had helped the Arkansan rise from the ashes to mount his political comeback in 1982 after Clinton lost the governorship. Morris later went on to advise a string of Republicans, including hard-rock conservative Trent Lott, now Senate Majority Whip, number two behind Dole in the GOP hierarchy. To Democrats who preferred that their consultants show allegiance to the party, Morris was an untrustworthy hired gun, arrogant and prone to grandiose self-inflation: He would soon boast that he was Clinton's "chief adviser" and, as such, was "running the country."

Clinton had turned to Morris for counsel in the bleak, waning days of the 1994 campaign. The president had lost confidence in the advice he was getting from some of his aides, and Morris encouraged that view, telling him that his staff was the source of his problems. At first, Morris's role was a secret; Clinton wanted to avoid an angry confrontation with Panetta, who by now had been promoted to White House Chief of Staff, and the rest of his advisers. Only after it became apparent that an outsider had rewritten large chunks of the president's State of the Union Address in January and another major speech in April was Morris formally brought in to the White House operations as a paid consultant.

Morris was concerned that Clinton had strayed from the political center, where he had run for president in 1992. In doing so, the president had become too much the creature of his party's congressional left, too predictable in his rejection of all Republican proposals, and too stuck in the increasingly polarized backbiting that now characterized congressional debate. Morris's goal was to reposition Clinton at the apex of an imaginary triangle, above and apart from the squabbling congressional parties. "Triangulation," as Morris called it, meant that the president would no longer automatically embrace Congress's liberal Democratic leadership or automatically reject what Gingrich and Dole proposed. "He's free of an overly rigid Democratic caucus," Morris said of Clinton after the plan had operated for a while. "He's transcended them. He's liberated."

Clinton's new go-it-alone approach pushed his fragile relations with his congressional allies to the brink; House and Senate Democrats grew increasingly unhappy that the president was so publicly distancing himself from them and cozying up to the enemy. Other advisers fought to keep the situation from getting even worse: When Morris wanted Clinton to run a TV commercial blaming Congress (not just the Republicans) for cutting Medicare, it took frantic internal lobbying by Panetta and Stephanopoulos to convince the president that that would enrage Hill Democrats to the point of an outright rupture with the White House. (Morris resigned his White House job in disgrace in August 1996 after a supermarket tabloid reported the accusations of a prostitute who claimed she'd had an extended liaison with Morris.)

Despite his misfires, though, Morris hit on at least one winning piece of advice. With no balanced-budget plan of his own, Morris advised, the president wasn't really a player in the year's most critical debate. The only way Clinton could effectively counter the Republicans' balanced-budget proposal—and simultaneously silence their attack on him for refusing to lead—was to lay out a plan of his own in which he insisted on maintaining his priorities.

Beginning in mid-April, Morris's idea turned the Clinton White House inside out, just as it would disconcert congressional Democratic leaders once the president's intentions became known. Both

Clinton and Vice President Gore embraced the idea of offering a balanced budget, which should have been enough to settle the matter. But practically all the rest of Clinton's senior advisers, including Panetta, Stephanopoulos, Treasury Secretary Bob Rubin, and chief economist Laura Tyson, opposed it.

Their key objections were the same as those that would quickly be voiced by Hill Democrats: It was better to keep attacking the Republicans than to put up their own plan, which—since it would have to include at least some Medicare cuts—would undermine the Democrats' ability to keep hammering the Republicans on the Medicare issue. Plus the timing was all wrong: The Republicans hadn't even finished their own budget yet; all the really tough votes were still to come, and a Clinton proposal would just let them off the hook.

Gene Sperling described the dynamic inside the White House as Clinton, Gore, Morris, and Deputy Chief of Staff Erskine Bowles "against the world." To recalcitrant staffers who continued to argue with him, a testy, sarcastic president replied, "You guys want me to go out and criticize the Republicans, and then when they say, 'Where's your plan?' you want me to say, 'Well, who am *I*? I'm just the president of the United States. *I* don't have a plan!' "

The real reason Clinton's advisers resisted the balanced budget as strenuously as they did was that they knew that drafting one would be only a little less difficult for them than it had been for the Republicans. Despite their attacks on the GOP cuts, the Democrats tacitly accepted all the political restraints that had forced the Republicans to go after Medicare and Medicaid. The White House was no more willing than Gingrich and Dole to raise taxes or go after deep cuts in Social Security, and Clinton was only slightly more willing to cut defense spending. The big difference between the two sides was that Clinton's tax cuts were less than half the size of the Republicans', which would allow the president to make somewhat smaller cuts in Medicare and Medicaid; he would still have to cut those programs if he wanted a balanced budget.

"The problem always is the math," said Stephanopoulos. "The reason we resisted [a balanced budget] for so long was it was hard to make the numbers work. In the end, the only way we could make it work was with OMB," the White House's Office of Management and Budget. The OMB's projections for economic growth, inflation, revenues, unemployment, and so on were slightly more optimistic than the CBO's projections that congressional Republicans insisted on using to "score," or measure, their budget proposals. The differences were tiny—OMB's 2.5 percent long-range economic growth projection versus CBO's 2.3 percent, for instance—but even such small disparities could generate huge variations when compounded over the seven years it would take to balance the budget.

Using its slightly more optimistic economic assumptions, the OMB projected cumulative deficits from 1996 to 2002 that were an astonishing $425 billion smaller than the CBO's. Smaller deficits meant that smaller spending cuts were needed to balance the budget, and that made it much easier for Clinton to balance the budget than it was for the Republicans. Not only that, but Clinton would stretch the exercise out over ten years instead of seven, postponing the biggest cuts until long after he would leave office. Now that budget technicians had figured out a way to make it much easier, Clinton pressed them to put together a plan as soon as they could.

In mid-May, the president ended the internal debate by disclosing on New Hampshire Public Radio that he was on the verge of offering a balanced-budget plan. Anguished Hill Democrats and White House staffers urged the president to hold off, arguing that the relentless Democratic attacks were finally having an impact. "From a timing point of view, it was critical that we stay together," said Senate Minority Leader Tom Daschle. It was not to be.

Although White House officials had promised to warn the Democratic leaders before the president announced a final decision, Gephardt and his staff first heard the news when CNN correspondent Wolf Blitzer went on the air around 9:30 A.M. on June 13 to report that the president would go on television that evening to announce his plan for a ten-year balanced budget.

Judged strictly on the raw numbers, Clinton's proposal was the GOP's writ smaller: Medicare would be cut $128 billion instead of the GOP's $270 billion; Medicaid would be cut $54 billion in place of the GOP's $180 billion; and so on. The numbers were misleading, though, since the two plans worked off separate OMB and CBO baselines (projections of future spending) and could not be directly compared.

The most important difference between Clinton and the Republicans had nothing to do with numbers, however, but with sharply divergent views of the role the federal government should play in society, particularly in running its biggest and most important programs. Republicans trusted the marketplace to transform Medicare and would leave state and local governments to run Medicaid and welfare. All the government's open-ended guarantees in these areas would end, whether to pay ever-rising medical bills for seniors or to provide basic health care and cash assistance for the poor. Clinton would preserve these expensive guarantees, and he would keep most responsibility for running programs at the federal level. Now, at last, the battle was fully joined.

The reaction from Hill Democrats was scathing. In a remarkable statement for a senior Democrat, even one with a notorious temper, Wisconsin Congressman Dave Obey said, "I think most of us learned some time ago if you don't like the president's position on a particular issue, you simply need to wait a few weeks. If you can follow this White House on the budget, you are a whole lot smarter than I am." Gephardt and Daschle bit their tongues but admitted they had strongly urged the president to hold off. Clinton appeared to have touched off a dangerous internecine war.

Inside the White House, some aides were terrified that Clinton had walked them right into a Republican trap. Stephanopoulos said he and other liberal Democrats in the White House and on Capitol Hill held their breath for days, fearing that the Republicans might seize the opportunity to call for a budget summit. "Had they done that," Stephanopoulos said later, "I think we'[d have been] dead." The protocol of a summit would have required both sides to do their talking inside the room; Democrats would have had to shut down their scathingly effective TV commercials and their verbal attacks on Republicans for cutting Medicare. "The room prevents you from making a public case," Stephanopoulos said. "We wouldn't have been out there with the president on the bully pulpit defining the issue." The Republicans, completely united, would have entered into negotiations at a time when the Democrats were at odds with one another, giving the GOP a huge advantage. "Instead, what we got was six months to unify our party," Stephanopoulos said. "They made a terrible mistake."

In retrospect, though, Stephanopoulos had been worried for

nothing. The Republicans were nowhere near ready to talk with any-one but one another. There was zero desire to work out a compro-mise with Clinton that would spare rank-and-file Republicans tough votes or head off a train wreck. Too many of them *wanted* the train wreck and the tough votes. How could true revolutionaries cut a deal now? They were convinced they could have it their way if they could only hold out long enough. "To tell some of these freshmen they have to come more toward the middle is like telling them they have to shoot their daughters," said moderate Republican Con-gressman Sherwood Boehlert.

Although it would not be clear for weeks, both sides had won im-portant victories. By now, Republicans had dragged Clinton an enor-mous distance from where he'd stood the previous fall, when he would have flatly rejected the idea of balancing the budget. Now he was fighting on their turf. For his part, the president had found the strategy that he would perfect as the year went on. He was learning that the most effective way to deal with his GOP adversaries was to co-opt their proposals, buff them to a more moderate Democratic gloss, and make them his own. Let them whine that he had stolen their ideas; it worked. As the weeks went by, his shallower cuts in Medicare did nothing to undercut Democratic attacks on the much bigger GOP cuts, and the fact that he now had a budget—even a pal-lid one—all but ended the GOP accusations that he was refusing to lead. Grudgingly, Hill Democrats admitted Clinton had been right. "If he had not come out for a balanced budget last summer," said Massachusetts Congressman Barney Frank, "he and we would have been in a much weaker position."

For all his give-no-ground rhetoric, Gingrich wanted to avoid a con-frontation with the White House if he could. For months, the Speaker had pursued secret, back-channel talks with Clinton and Panetta, searching for at least the basis of a deal that would give both sides a viable bargain without having to go through the drama and uncertainty of tough votes, a veto, and subsequent negotiations. "If they could [have] reach[ed] an accord without a brawl, that would have been better," said Gingrich spokesman Tony Blankley. "That's sort of Politics 101."

There was nothing formal or conclusive about these occasional conversations, most of them over the telephone, but as they proceeded, Gingrich was getting a good feeling that Clinton wanted a deal. In July and August, both his direct contact with the president and various back-channel communiqués—chiefly word passed from the inner councils of the White House by adviser Dick Morris via his pal Senate Majority Whip Trent Lott—convinced the Speaker that things were drifting in the right direction. In retrospect, even Gingrich himself conceded that he had been reading too much into his talks with Clinton—not the last time this would happen between the two men. Both loved to talk policy, but when it came to negotiating, the two were on entirely different wavelengths. Gingrich was very up-front about what he wanted, and to his own detriment he would often lay out his position from the start, including his bottom line. Clinton was far more sophisticated and indirect. He often left people believing he had agreed with them when he meant only to be affable. That was how he left Gingrich.

The Speaker got a rude shock in early October when the White House he thought he was making progress with suddenly turned on him. First, word came that administration officials were talking up their belief that Gingrich might never be able to pass the GOP reconciliation bill, that the effort would collapse. Then, in his Saturday radio address of October 7, Clinton charged that the Republicans were pushing a backdoor tax increase on the working poor (by scaling back the earned-income tax credit). To be accused of raising taxes particularly galled the Republicans, and they felt the earned-income credit—much of it payments to workers whose incomes were too low to be taxed—did not constitute taxes. The coup de grâce came that same weekend, when Vice President Gore made a speech in which he attacked Republicans as "extremists," a word that pushed all Republicans' buttons. Democrats had begun attacking the GOP as extremists right after the Oklahoma City bombing in April, and the implication that harsh GOP rhetoric had provoked that awful massacre enraged Republicans, who could not hear the word *extremist* after that without erupting in renewed fury.

The notoriously thin-skinned Gingrich, who had spent much of the year demonizing the Democrats and their policies as variously "pathetic," "sick," and "morally and intellectually corrupt," felt abused. He summoned the leadership and his top advisers to an unusual holiday meeting in his office on Columbus Day, October 9, to denounce Clinton and declare an abrupt end to any back-channel talks. The Speaker said he was tired of getting trashed by the White House while trying to negotiate in good faith. He thought he had established a relationship with Clinton; he had repeatedly told colleagues a deal was in the works—and now he felt as though he'd been betrayed. "We have to stop all this crap," he snarled. It was a syndrome that would become familiar to Gingrich's colleagues. "He thought he was getting somewhere [with Clinton] and tried to reach out," said Boehner, "only to have the president and the administration kick him in the teeth. And he got angry."

There was a lot more going on than mere pique with the administration, however. Word of the back-channel explorations had leaked to the press, and the ever vigilant freshmen had become alarmed that Gingrich might negotiate a compromise unacceptable to them. They quickly drew lines in the sand: Don't weaken any further on tax cuts; don't give up the thrust of their Medicare, Medicaid, and welfare overhaul plans; make sure the final plan includes the death of at least one Cabinet department. The absolute bottom line, though, was that there be no retreat on balancing the budget in seven years. Yield on that, warned Congressman Sam Brownback of Kansas, a freshman leader on budget matters, and "the same thing will happen here to our leadership that happened to George Bush when he broke his promise of no new taxes: You will have an internal revolt."

The freshmen and other conservative Republicans had enormous admiration for Gingrich for masterminding the GOP takeover of Congress, but they harbored a nagging sense that at heart he really wasn't one of them. They kept watch, worried that he might be too willing to bend on principle to get a deal, and they looked increasingly to Kasich, who was younger and more hard-nosed about sticking to GOP revolutionary principles.

To signal that he had no such intention, Gingrich lashed out at Clinton and Gore on October 10, warning that their personal attacks on Republicans were undermining chances for any agreement. The Speaker called Clinton's balanced-budget proposal a "joke" and said he knew of "no serious offer by this administration" to reach an accommodation with the Republicans. Clinton's and Gore's weekend attacks made it "inconceivable" that the administration was interested in bargaining in good faith, he said.

Gingrich was embarrassed—Clinton had obviously strung him along. Once the unquestioned leader of all factions of the party, Gingrich was now on a short leash. The big, angry dog he had been walking—hard-core conservatives out to change the world—was now walking him. Gingrich and Clinton shared the same problem: Each was mistrusted by his core supporters, who worried that the man at the top was a little too eager to make a deal with the enemy. Eventually, Gingrich even felt compelled to defend his radical credentials. "I'm a revolutionary, too," he told the rank and file; "there's no one more revolutionary than me." The line sounded jarringly like Clinton's insistence earlier in the year that the president was "relevant" to the budget process.

If there was ever to be a budget deal, someone was going to have to move away from his political base to get it, and the GOP strategy was based on the belief that Clinton would do that. But here was an object lesson for Gingrich in how hard it would be for either of them to compromise: The merest hint that the Speaker had been dallying with the opposition provoked an angry reaction from his political core.

Gingrich's waning power to rein in the conservatives and keep them focused on the balanced-budget prize was nowhere more evident or more critical than in the appropriations process. All year long the conservatives had had a problem deciding what they really wanted. They thought they could have everything: not just a balanced budget and tax cuts but a radical transformation of big-government programs and a dramatic rollback of a generation of environmental and workplace regulation. Now their indiscriminate appetite was giving the legislative system indigestion, especially in appropriations.

Long a clubby oasis amid the partisan backbiting that afflicted most other committees, Congress's Appropriations panels traditionally treated party warfare as a distraction its members had to minimize if they wanted to move the thirteen major spending bills they were responsible for every year—a workload that committee members proudly noted was the heaviest of any committee. But now the bipartisan atmosphere was gone, particularly in the House, where

Gingrich saw appropriations as key to remaking government. Not only could the GOP kill or starve departments, agencies, and programs it disliked by withholding money, but the Republicans could also attach policymaking riders to the fast-moving, must-pass appropriations bills and get them into law much more quickly than they could if they took the usual route on slow-moving authorization bills. A typical rider sought to ease industry fears of new regulations by barring the Labor Department from even researching methods to prevent repetitive-stress injuries in the workplace. "We knew from the beginning that Appropriations would have to carry much of the load of what had to be done," said House Majority Whip and Appropriations Committee member Tom DeLay. "It was our first year in the majority, and there were a lot of things we wanted to accomplish."

Gingrich had begun sharpening the political focus of the spending committee right from the start, elevating the combative Bob Livingston to the chairman's job, forcing him and every Appropriations subcommittee chairman to sign a letter pledging fealty to the revolution, and giving six hard-edged freshman members prized seats on the committee. But instead of speeding up the revolution, Gingrich's efforts almost ground it to a halt. By midyear, this aggressive new partisanship and the weight of the riders were causing the once well-oiled appropriations process to break down. Bills that had formerly moved efficiently were now stalled by angry fights over radically lower spending levels and bold attempts to hamstring federal regulators (one bill, for example, contained more than a dozen separate riders to bar the Environmental Protection Agency from carrying out many of its traditional enforcement duties).

Livingston was a faithful revolutionary, but he was also a pragmatist in charge of making the appropriations process work, and now he saw it bogging down. The riders were provoking fights not just with Democrats but with moderate House Republicans and with the Senate GOP as well. This was stupid, Livingston thought. House leaders could have their slimmed-down spending bills, but if they didn't call off the hard-liners and free up the bills, they risked getting nothing. The process was on the edge of disaster. An increasingly frantic Livingston began appealing to Gingrich to get the hard-liners to back off. "I just kept warning him that we were going to run into a buzz saw," he said.

But Gingrich was in a bind. Even if he had agreed with Livingston, an order to the hard-liners to back off meant risking revolt. And other House leaders were just as avid about pushing pro-business, anti-regulatory riders as the rank and file were. DeLay, a former small-businessman himself, saw the anti-regulatory riders as a critical part of what the revolution was all about. As far as he was concerned, Livingston was representing the old log-rolling appropriations ethos. "I'm sick and tired of your bellyaching," DeLay snapped at Livingston during a tense meeting in Armey's office. "We're trying to change America here."

"Fuck you!" snarled a furious Livingston.

Livingston's continuing humiliation was a particularly pointed illustration of how chairmen had been downgraded under the new Gingrich-run system. Democratic chairmen had been virtual autocrats; their GOP successors were subject to second-guessing and micromanagement not just by Gingrich but by the aggressive freshman class. Just how much things had changed became clear in an incident that October, when Mark Neumann, one of the GOP freshmen Gingrich had placed on Appropriations, defied both Livingston and the longstanding committee tradition by opposing the defense appropriations bill on the floor. It had long been settled practice that committee members made what changes they could in subcommittee or committee but closed ranks when a spending bill got to the floor. The freshmen saw no reason to abide by the old rules.

Livingston lashed out at the freshmen as the bill went down to embarrassing defeat, and to make a point, he transferred Neumann from the powerful defense subcommittee to the much less important panel that oversees the construction and maintenance of military buildings. Gingrich had been consulted in advance and approved. But when a group of freshmen complained and threatened mutiny, Gingrich backed down and declared that Livingston had gone too far. Humiliated and furious, Livingston threatened to resign his chairman's job. The Speaker concocted a face-saving compromise that upheld Livingston's disciplinary decision but gave Neumann a prized seat on the Budget Committee as a peace offering. For anyone trying to make sense of the House GOP power struggles, the message was unmistakable: A freshman had defied the chairman of one of the most powerful committees in Congress, gotten away with it, and been rewarded for his disloyalty with a promotion.

Unwilling or unable to exercise party discipline, Gingrich let the appropriations process drift to the point where Congress had sent just two of the thirteen bills to the president by the October 1 start of the new fiscal year—the deadline for enactment of all new spending bills. Leaders had long talked tough about shutting down the government to bend Clinton to their will, but now they had to ask him for a six-week extension or risk closing the government because they couldn't get their work done on time.

It was here, some felt, that the revolution began to unravel. Top advisers, including former Reagan chief of staff Duberstein and Republican National Committee Chairman Barbour, had been counseling House leaders that the key to pressuring Clinton lay in getting the spending bills done on time. "The best advice was given in August," said a GOP strategist. "Set arbitrary, hard deadlines. Pass the appropriations bills before the end of the fiscal year, and send them to Clinton to sign or veto. Pass short CRs [continuing resolutions, to keep the government open], each one a little tougher, . . . bring the matter to a head early, keep the pressure on all the time."

Instead, leaders let the process run almost out of control. In retrospect, GOP critics said, the six-week CR was a disaster. It gave the White House and congressional Democrats that much more time in which to make their case and rally public support before the big budget confrontation took place. Yes, the hard-line Republican House members might have fought orders to abandon their riders. "That's why you have leadership," said a senior Republican. Ultimately, the leadership forced agreement by pushing the riders off the bills. "It was no easier later than it would have been earlier," he said.

———

The hard-liners were on Gingrich's mind when he and other Republican leaders went to the White House on November 1 for a sit-down with Clinton to discuss what lay ahead. There were now just thirteen days to go before the lengthy CR ran out, raising the prospect of a government shutdown. The White House wanted another no-conditions extension to allow more time for the two sides to come to terms; the administration was also demanding a conditions-free extension of the limit on the federal debt, vital fiscal housekeeping that would let the Treasury go on borrowing money to meet government obligations. But Gingrich warned Clinton that rank-and-file members were spoiling for a showdown and unlikely to let the White House off without demanding conditions. It was time for Clinton to stop posturing and agree to negotiate a seven-year balanced-budget plan.

The president was polite but far from compliant. He said there was no way he would sign anything but clean, unconditional extensions of the CR and the debt ceiling. He would not be "blackmailed" by the Republicans. When Gingrich replied that "you have to understand the situation we're in," meaning hard-line Republicans would never go along with that, Clinton waved them off. The president argued that since June he had accepted most of the Republicans' principles—balancing the budget, reforming welfare, saving Medicare, and so on—but the Republicans had yet to accept a single one of the Democrats' underlying principles. While the Republicans had a Contract with America, Clinton said, he had a contract of his own with the American people to guard against an unreasonable assault on important domestic programs, such as education, job training, and Medicare. Turning to Gingrich, he said, "Look, you guys don't get it. If you want a president to sign your budget, you're going to have to elect someone else to do it." Then, pointing across the room to the chair at his desk, he added, "You may not believe this, but I'm willing to lose this seat rather than take a budget like this. . . . I'll let Bob Dole do that if he's in that chair."

The tough-guy stance took the Republicans by surprise. The president had been so widely perceived as spineless that his confrontational manner seemed completely out of character. Gingrich and Dole were now in a difficult spot, caught between Republican members who would not stop pushing and a president who would not yield.

Now the Republicans made a huge mistake. In drafting a new CR that was to be much tougher on spending levels, House Ways and Means Committee Chairman Bill Archer insisted on adding a seemingly straightforward provision to extend the Medicare Part B premium at its current rate, 31.5 percent of program costs. From a pragmatic point of view, this made perfect sense: Any reasonable Medicare deal had to involve keeping the premium right where it was rather than letting it drop back to 25 percent of the cost of the program in January 1996, a quirk prescribed in a 1993 bill. If Congress did not act now, they risked having the premium fall in January and then rise again whenever a new budget deal went into effect—bad politics. When the Senate got the bill from the House, things were moving fast. Kasich had flagged the premium rider as a problem, but few others saw it as a big deal. "It was such a logical thing," said Domenici, that nobody thought to challenge it.

At the White House, aides took one look at the Medicare provision and rejoiced. "They gave us our line," Stephanopoulos said. "They're saying, If you don't cut Medicare, we're going to shut down the government. That's blackmail." The CR also slashed spending for some of Clinton's highest-priority programs by as much as 40 percent. Clinton used both GOP actions to justify his veto, but it was the Medicare-premium rider that gave him a clean kill. "If they had not done that, they would have had a better fight," said Stephanopoulos. "They could have said, Clinton wants bigger spending." The president still would have vetoed the CR, "but it would have been a tougher veto."

Republicans looked back at this and grieved. They shot themselves in the foot *and* handed Clinton the chance to play the hero. "Putting that rider on the first CR turned the tide," said Domenici. "When we sent that rider down, that closed [the] government. That's about the time he became a man."

There was still time for last-minute statesmanship to somehow avert a government crisis—the long-prophesied train wreck—but that would have required a willingness to compromise and a degree of good faith that simply did not exist. The White House and the GOP leaders had spent so much time demonizing each other that the few promising relationships had soured. Both sides made one last stab at a compromise at a meeting at the White House on Monday evening, November 13, just hours before the midnight deadline when funding would run out. But by then, the lines had been firmly drawn, and there was nothing left to do but exchange recriminations.

House Majority Leader Armey got into an angry exchange with the president. There was no love lost between the two men; Armey had led the tough, often personal attacks on Hillary Clinton during the 1994 fight over the president's health-care proposals. Now it was Armey who was aggrieved; he complained that the president and his men were frightening old people with claims that the Republicans were out to destroy Medicare and Medicaid. Armey said his wife's grandmother had refused to move out of a run-down nursing home and into a more modern facility because she had heard a Democratic ad and was afraid she would lose her Medicare benefits. "You all just scared the hell out of her," Armey lectured the president. "And you're ruining a lot of peoples' lives with your scare rhetoric."

The president responded that while he felt sorry for Armey's relative, "there was nothing said about your budget that's half as bad as the lies you told about my health-care plan last year, and there is no scare tactic we've used that is half as bad as the lies that you used." Clinton ticked off four or five examples of Republican distortions of his health-care plan. Then, turning to the House majority leader, he added, "And another thing, Mr. Armey. In this debate, I never once attacked your wife. I never once called your wife a name."

Armey shot back, "I appreciate your outburst, Mr. President, but I'm not impressed."

Republicans left the meeting surprised again at Clinton's tough-guy posture. They had expected him to weaken at the critical moment and sign their CR. "I just didn't believe this president would shut down the government over a matter of principle," Armey said. A little earlier than they had expected, they now had the shutdown they had threatened with such bravado in the spring. It would be their undoing.

The following day, roughly 800,000 federal workers all over the country were involuntarily sent home. The military, the FBI, the Federal Aviation Administration, and other government services essential to protecting lives and property could keep running, but hundreds of other government activities, from processing applications for passports and Social Security and veterans' benefits to cleaning up toxic-waste sites and making grants to schools and colleges, came to a standstill.

Republicans gloated that nobody noticed or cared, but the effects of the partial closure of government were quickly felt in every corner of the nation. The Defense Department and various agencies immediately put a hold on billions of dollars' worth of government contracting, affecting thousands of private businesses. Concessionaires and small companies that flourished in and around national parks and monuments were forced to close. In Arizona, the Grand

Canyon was closed for the first time in its seventy-six-year history as a national park, a mute symbol of a federal government in crisis.

The spectacle of government adrift was appalling to voters, who saw not high principle but petty squabbling and arrogant intransigence. With Thanksgiving coming, nearly a million federal employees suddenly faced the prospect of no paychecks. "People got bills, finances and debts to meet. I think they should let everybody come back to work and stop acting like a bunch of kids," Darnell Hayward, a thirty-four-year-old custodian at the FBI Building in Washington, told *The Washington Post*. "Why do we have to lose our money and they ain't losing a dime?"

Clinton masterfully kept to the high road, deliberately acting presidential, canceling an important trip to Japan to stay on top of the situation, speaking in measured tones, and calling for restraint. Gingrich, by contrast, railed against the administration and pouted that the White House wasn't showing him the deference and the respect he deserved. For days leading up to the government shutdown, he had fumed privately about the treatment he and Dole had received on November 6–7 aboard Air Force One during the round trip to Jerusalem for the funeral of Yitzhak Rabin, the slain Israeli prime minister. Not only had Clinton passed up an opportunity to confer at length with the two GOP leaders on the budget crisis, Gingrich complained, but the Republican leaders had been directed to leave the plane by the rear exit.

Ignoring the advice of press secretary Tony Blankley, who paced uneasily at the back of the room, Gingrich brought up his grievances publicly during a breakfast meeting with reporters on Wednesday, November 15, two days after the shutdown began. In a bizarre, rambling tirade, the Speaker declared that his treatment on the plane was "part of why you ended up with us sending down a tougher interim spending bill. . . . This is petty. I'm going to say up front: It's petty . . . but I think it's human."

Disaster. Suddenly, the public perception was not that the shutdown was a critical struggle over the sweeping issue of whether to balance the budget but the hissy fit of a self-important politician. Gingrich had a valid complaint—the administration was just not interested in negotiating—but that was completely overshadowed by his petulance. The Speaker's comments caused an uproar: The next morning the front-page headline of the New York *Daily News* screamed CRY BABY above a cartoon of a bawling baby Newt in diapers. Gleeful House Democrats rushed to the floor to blast the Speaker for triggering a massive government shutdown out of sheer spite. Republicans were embarrassed and furious with Gingrich. "It's incredible, petty childishness. Nobody in America gives a damn where he was on Air Force One," New York GOP Congressman Peter King told the *New York Post*. "It's total egomania to think anybody cares."

Republicans weren't the only ones with troubles. The same day Gingrich stunned the reporters' gathering, Democrats began to abandon Clinton. House GOP tacticians had smartly updated their CR, dropping the disastrous Part B premium language and adding only a requirement that Clinton produce a seven-year balanced budget based on CBO numbers. This was designed to lure Democrats who favored a balanced budget and were uneasy about the shutdown, and it worked: A stunning forty-eight House Democrats voted yes, which, when added to the united GOP bloc, allowed the Republicans to get within just nine votes of the two-thirds majority needed to override the president's veto. This was a warning that Clinton was now getting dangerously out of sync with his own party. Only frantic White House lobbying had kept the Democratic votes to just forty-eight. Senior aides privately concluded that they would lose enough Democrats the next time that Clinton would, in fact, suffer a humiliating veto override. As the third day went by with much of the government shut and the closure setting an all-time record, both sides began to get anxious about finding a way out.

Meanwhile, all but unnoticed, House and Senate Republican negotiators worked out contentious differences between their two versions of the huge budget-balancing reconciliation bill and passed it in both chambers. To be sure, the bill was only an agreement among Republicans, and Clinton was certain to veto it. But it was a historic achievement nonetheless, the first time since the deficit went out of control in the 1970s that Congress had passed a bill with a legitimate chance of balancing the budget. But who noticed or cared? By precipitating the shutdown when they did, Republicans—amazingly—obscured the most remarkable thing they had done all year long.

All the focus was on the shutdown and how to get out of it. Panetta came to Capitol Hill late in the week and searched frantically for Kasich, hunting him down in the House gym to test options.

Both sides began to write up language that would extricate them from the mess. The Republicans were determined to force Clinton to commit himself to a balanced budget with CBO numbers. Administration officials knew they would eventually have to put a seven-year budget on the table to replace their ten-year proposal, but they needed wiggle room. White House aides were desperate to keep Clinton out of the CBO box.

As the shutdown ground through its fifth day, a Saturday, the mood in the Capitol turned ugly. A fistfight broke out in the House chamber between two hot-tempered congressmen, and Republican Congressman John Mica of Florida ignored decorum by calling the president a "little bugger" during a speech on the House floor. Into the midst of this rapidly deteriorating atmosphere came Dole, fresh from a presidential straw-poll victory in Florida, the adult in a room full of squabbling children. Summoning Gingrich and other GOP leaders to his office that evening, Dole said the shutdown was getting out of hand and allowing it to continue past the weekend would be a serious mistake. The longer they waited, the less they were likely to get from the administration. "Dole has a sense of gut instinct," Kasich said later. "He's been around a long time, and when he makes a statement like that, you listen to him."

Dole set in motion intense negotiations over the next twenty-four hours that brought the crisis to a resolution. The trick for both sides now was to find language that would allow the White House to sign onto the GOP's bottom-line seven years and CBO. The administration wanted to pair CBO and seven years with language that incorporated their mantra: Any budget deal would protect Medicare, Medicaid, education, and the environment and not raise taxes on working families. Faxes went back and forth between the Hill and the White House.

That Sunday, day 6, Stephanopoulos and other aides were convened in the White House, war-gaming their alternatives. Things looked bleak. The forty-eight Democrats who had voted with the Republicans on Wednesday "were gone," Stephanopoulos said. An eventual veto override was all but certain. After chewing over the options, they realized there wasn't much they could do besides let it happen. "How should we handle it? We didn't have a good answer when the fax came in," said Stephanopoulos.

The fax from Capitol Hill showed that the Republicans had accepted the White House mantra with one important change: The GOP's CBO and seven years and the administration's mantra language would not be joined by an ironclad "if and only if," as the White House had asked, but by a simple "and." Clinton had just come back from a run and joined his aides, still wearing his jogging clothes. As they digested the fax, the reaction was immediate. "We took one look, and everyone said, 'Oh, my God! Let's take it and run!' " said an official.

Within hours, the deal was done. The Republicans were ecstatic. At last, after months of tough votes and struggle, maneuvering, jawboning, and pressuring, they had roped Clinton in, gotten him to sign on to their bottom-line demands to balance the budget with the "honest" numbers of the CBO. As they walked into the Senate TV studio to announce the agreement, Kasich, Gingrich, Dole, and Domenici were smiling giddily. Kasich pumped his fists in the air in a show of glee and triumph. "I think it's a wonderful day for our country—that's why I've been so excited. We no longer have the balanced budget as a goal or a dream; it's going to be a reality," he said. Elsewhere Livingston summed up the Republicans' view of the deal: "The president of the United States," he said, "has capitulated."

Chapter 9

ENDGAME

The White House counteroffensive began the very next morning. Panetta went on early-morning TV and immediately began backing out of the trap the Republicans thought they had caught the White House in. Balance the budget? "We can do it in seven years or eight years," he said casually on NBC's *Today* show, instantly raising GOP blood pressure. "I don't think the American people ought to read a lot into what was agreed to last night. I think the important thing was that we put America back to work. We stopped the crisis. We protected the options of both sides. . . . We developed a framework for the negotiations."

This was not what the Republicans had so giddily celebrated the night before. And just as bad for the Republicans, this was not the same earnest, hyperreasonable Leon Panetta who had earned the contempt of Senate Democrats in 1990 for his eagerness to put budget offers on the table for President Bush and Budget Director Dick Darman. Now a much tougher Panetta set about enraging Republicans with precisely the opposite behavior, displaying an infuriating unwillingness to be drawn into negotiations on GOP terms.

The difference in style was deliberate. Darman and Bush had been the sort of pragmatic, non-ideological Republicans with whom Panetta could do business, cut deals, reach an agreement that both sides could live with. Each understood the other, and they had all played the game for years and knew the rules. But Gingrich and Kasich and the rest of the House GOP were a different breed, ideologically driven, on a government-altering mission in which compromise amounted to capitulation. The two sides viewed the exercise completely differently. "We're thinking diplomacy," said White House economics adviser Gene Sperling, "and they're thinking war."

At one point in the budget talks that were about to begin, Panetta brought out an easel and displayed a chart on which he had written down the ten big-ticket items in play: balanced budget, seven years, CBO scoring, Medicare, Medicaid, and so on. "Look," he told the Republicans, "if we're going to get a deal, each side has got to claim some wins. We each have to give in some areas, and there has to be some splits." He walked through the ten items one at a time. "On this issue, balancing the budget, we'll give to the Republicans. Seven years we'll give to you. CBO we'll give to you. Come to us on Medicare. . . . You get three wins, we get three wins, we split the difference on other things, and that is the context in which we get a deal."

That kind of language made sense in 1990, but in 1995, Panetta might as well have been speaking Martian. Kasich was adamant that he wanted no "phony Washington deal" that failed to transform the federal government in ways the Democrats simply could not abide. House Republicans had built the budget crusade to the intensity of a jihad. Every day that went by, every tough vote the Republicans took made it harder to move back toward the middle.

The same morning that Panetta went on the *Today* show, Gingrich did as well, but to radiate conciliation, downplaying the Democratic message that the two sides remained far apart. "The administration is legitimately saying they don't want to . . . give us a blank check for what kind of seven-year balanced budget, just as we wouldn't give them a blank check," he said. But when word of Panetta's finagling on the seven-years question hit Capitol Hill, House Majority Leader Dick Armey flared, firing off a letter to Panetta complaining, "Words have meaning, Leon. Seven years is seven years, not 'seven years or eight years.' "

So brief a victory. Less than twelve hours earlier, the shutdown had ended in Republican triumph. GOP negotiators had finally corralled Clinton in what they thought was an inescapable box. Now the

White House was dancing outside the box. Read carefully, the vague protect-our-priorities language that the Republicans had believed was meaningless in fact gave the administration enormous freedom to back away from anything that squeezed their programs too much, a heads-I-win, tails-you-lose loophole.

With the anger of the newly conned, the Republicans tried to firm up the deal with jawboning: "There is no wiggle room here," insisted House Rules Committee Chairman Jerry Solomon, "no smoke and mirrors." In fact, there was little but smoke and mirrors. It was a lawyer's dream, written to be read at least two ways, a nice-sounding statement that provided both sides a face-saving exit from a shutdown that had become a destructive problem for everybody while binding them to little that was enforceable. That the Republicans read it as cow high and pig tight, as they say of Texas fences, made it seem as if they had not checked with their attorneys. Though Solomon and Kasich and Gingrich and Dole and the rest of the Republicans would insist it bound the president to a deal, they steadfastly ignored the critical fine print, which drilled holes in the boat constructed by the first phrase.

Yes, the agreement bound them to enact a seven-year deal, signed by the president, to balance the budget using CBO numbers by the end of the first session of the Congress, early in January 1996, now less than two months away. This was the part the Republicans clung to, and if it had stopped there, it would indeed have been binding. But the agreement went on to say that everybody agreed "that the balanced budget must protect future generations, ensure Medicare solvency, reform welfare, and provide adequate funding for Medicaid, education, agriculture, national defense, veterans, and the environment. . . ." This was hortatory fluff that meant whatever anyone chose it to mean. The biggest weasel words of all were "adequate funding." Who got to define *adequate*? The agreement did not say. What Gingrich considered adequate would surely strike Clinton as inadequate, and vice versa. They had agreed, in effect, to nothing.

"One of the things the president stressed today is we shouldn't gloat," said White House spokesman Mike McCurry with a straight face the day after the deal was signed. "And the president also instructed the staff not to make too much of the polls."

The polls. The Democrats had to pinch themselves. Could they be dreaming? Public reaction to the shutdown was devastating for the GOP. Three major polls taken on the last day of the shutdown (Washington Post/ABC News; Wall Street Journal/NBC News; New York Times/CBS News) showed that Americans blamed Republicans roughly 2:1 over Clinton for the impasse. Seven of ten disapproved of the way the Republicans were handling the budget dispute, *including 55 percent of Republicans.* Asked whose budget position was closer to their own, respondents picked Clinton's over the Republicans', 56–36. Asked what Clinton should do with the GOP's big budget-balancing reconciliation bill, 56 percent said veto it; just 36 percent wanted him to sign. Six in ten said they were more worried that the Republicans would go too far than that they would fail to make necessary changes. In the three-way personality struggle between Clinton, Dole, and Gingrich, Clinton trounced his rivals. His job-approval rating was a strong (for him) 54 percent, while Dole had fallen to 45 percent (from 60 percent in March), and Gingrich had dropped to an abysmal 27 percent. Gingrich's number, noted *Washington Post* poll expert Richard Morin, "rivals that of President Richard M. Nixon at the height of the Watergate scandal."

Republicans derided Clinton's fixation on the polls and claimed they didn't care whether their own ratings went through the floor. But they were heading into a period where public opinion was the only tool they had to help them get an agreement from the White House. With one exception—nervous financial markets—there was no other external pressure with which to force a compromise. The last time a divided government had gone to negotiations like these, in 1990, a Republican president and a Democratic Congress had been pushed hard to an agreement by powerful external forces. The economy was souring, a war was brewing in the Persian Gulf, and the inflexible Gramm-Rudman targets were pressing. None of that applied now. The economy was healthy, there was no serious war in the offing, and Gramm-Rudman was gone. Public opinion could push the parties to reach an agreement, but right now Clinton was winning the public relations war. Why should he compromise with Republicans he had successfully characterized as extremists? And if he did make a deal with them, why should he make it on their terms? Very bad news for the Republicans, and for a balanced budget.

Gingrich remained publicly upbeat. "In the long run," he said, "people are going to say the Republican Congress produced the first balanced budget in a generation." There was only one hitch. The only way the Republicans could do that was by getting Clinton's signature.

———

All year long Gingrich had flatly rejected the idea of a budget summit with the White House, insisting it was unnecessary and a terrible way to do business. No one wanted a repeat of the awful 1990 experience; the notion of a group of elite-level politicians working up a plan behind closed doors and then trying to force it on the rank and file was anathema. Orders went out striking "summit" from acceptable Republican vocabulary, along with the forbidden "cuts." "Not the 's' word," said Kasich, retreating in mock horror one day when reporters asked him about the possibility. "For Republicans, 'summit' is a dirty word," explained Armey press spokesman Ed Gillespie. "Summits are inherently smoke-filled rooms—or Perrier-filled rooms, anyway." And yet—here they were. Gingrich's refusal to agree to a summit was a sustainable position only as long as Clinton was irrelevant. Now that the president was a player, there was no other way to get this done.

When the parties returned from the Thanksgiving break to start talks on Tuesday evening, November 28, the plan was to convene a manageable group of high-level officials from the White House and Congress and work as close to a deal as possible. There was little chance of getting everything done, since they had an absurdly large amount of work to do and little time to do it in. The expiration date of the new CR was December 15, just seventeen days away. By now, the Republicans had spent the last eleven months coming to terms among themselves over the sweeping tax and program changes in their big budget-balancing reconciliation bill. Now they expected to reach agreement with Clinton in two and half weeks. The two sides remained separated not by numbers but by the same deep divisions over the proper role of the federal government that had dogged them all year long. Now these questions had to be decided in one bill in seventeen days.

The talks were held in the Mansfield Room, a handsome, wood-paneled space just across the hall from the Senate chamber and a few steps from Dole's office. The room was named after legendary Montana Democrat Mike Mansfield, the longest-serving Senate majority leader in history, the man who succeeded the imperious Lyndon Johnson in 1961 and replaced Johnson's bullying style with self-effacing accommodation and bipartisanship, for which he was revered. The negotiators could have used more of any of those qualities themselves. From the start of the talks, all the signs were bad.

In a bit of gamesmanship they would repeat again and again, the Democrats insisted at the last minute on bringing in more people than the five per side originally agreed to; the negotiating group quickly expanded from the agreed-on ten to an unwieldy sixteen, far too many to make a deal or even to bargain meaningfully. Each negotiator brought one or more staffers, who kept notes for their principals, themselves, and—a bad sign—reporters, who were leaked selective blow-by-blow accounts after every session. The press also had the benefit of full statements from the principals themselves, who walked into a huge floating press stakeout just outside the doors to spin the proceedings from their point of view every time the talks recessed.

The negotiators were not the top leaders who would ultimately approve the deal—Clinton, Dole, Gingrich—but second-tier officials: Panetta, Kasich, Domenici, White House Budget Director Alice Rivlin, the top Budget Committee Democrat from each chamber, and a changing cast of other leaders and White House officials. Also present were the two House party whips, Republican Tom DeLay and Democrat Dave Bonior, scorpions in a bottle sent to monitor the proceedings on behalf of polarized factions of the House. DeLay represented the House's most conservative Republicans, who would accept very little short of the full GOP demands. Bonior was an emissary for the House's most liberal Democrats, who wanted no balanced-budget deal at all.

Things went wrong immediately. At the first session, the two sides instantly fell to squabbling over which organization should score the agreement—CBO or OMB—and when and how. The Republicans had assumed this was a settled issue, but the Democrats said they read the agreement to mean that the CBO would score the deal only *after* it was done and after working out a compromise baseline with the OMB. The baseline—the projection of spending, revenues, and deficits over the next seven years—was all-important; if they worked from the OMB's more forgiving baseline, the job would be $425 billion easier. The White House had to have some middle-ground base-line between the OMB and the CBO, or the spending cuts it would be forced to make would be too deep.

Reporters stood in hallways outside the Mansfield Room for hours on end, aching to be inside for just a minute to listen to the talks. But reconstructions based on notes kept by participants revealed bickering that was strikingly banal and unproductive. It was little wonder the negotiators emerged in such bad moods, and no wonder the talks went nowhere.

At the beginning of the first session, Domenici suggested putting together a group to work out a common baseline with the CBO. No, Panetta said, it was important to preserve maximum flexibility and work out a baseline when they got close to a deal; the idea was not to cook the numbers but to use adjustments to the numbers as a last gap-closer once they were close on policy changes.

Kasich objected. They had already agreed to use CBO numbers up front, had they not? Panetta insisted: It was wrong to lock up the baseline at the outset. Domenici asked, "How will we know what we're doing if there's no baseline?"

Kasich deployed one of his famous analogies. This was like driving to Los Angeles without a map and without any idea of how far away it was, he said. "If we don't have a baseline, how are we going to get there?" Senate Majority Whip Trent Lott observed that the two sides needed to be talking about apples and apples. No, said Panetta, they needed to be talking about policies that protected people—education, environment, and the rest of the administration's priorities. Domenici said the Republicans would be happy to talk about policies once they got the baseline out of the way. Since they had all agreed to balance the budget in seven years, Kasich put in, it would be helpful if the administration disclosed how they planned to do that.

At this point, Republicans said later, Panetta blew up and accused the GOP negotiators of being uninterested in how Republican policies affected real people. The Republicans rolled their eyes; they felt they were hearing a campaign speech. "Leon," Armey said, "this is no place for you to blow your stack. If we were to suggest to you that you don't care about kids or taxpayers, you'd say that was unacceptable." Panetta apologized for questioning their motives. Discussions resumed.

There was a crucial question from Kasich: Could the White House team write a plan that balanced the budget in seven years using CBO numbers? Panetta said he thought they could. Kasich asked whether Panetta would do that. Panetta made a vague promise to do it. Kasich objected, though, that he had never known anyone to put together a budget without having a baseline first.

It was about now, Kasich said later, that he began to sense there would be no deal. "I knew right off the bat when we sat down with Leon and he started hedging on all of this that they weren't serious. . . . The longer we met, the more convinced I was that they were just really completely jerking us around." In the following days and weeks, White House aides would reassure him that this was just part of the mating ritual. "In fact, I had several of them tell me, 'Don't get frustrated here, because we really are going to get this done. We just have to go through this.' But then my attitude changed when I finally realized that this was a total charade and that they had literally no interest at all in working anything out."

In fact, this was beginning to feel eerily like what came to be known as the "walk through the fields" in 1990, when the Democrats set out deliberately to stall the Bush White House until they provoked a desperate Bush to break his no-new-taxes pledge. Then, Democrats had frustrated Republicans intent on serious negotiations by sending up one Democratic committee chairman after another to talk on and on about how important his programs were and how critical it was not to cut them. The plan was to stall until Bush realized there would be no deal without tax increases. Now the plan seemed to be to prenegotiate endlessly over baselines and discuss policy forever. The plan seemed to be to stall until the Republicans realized there would be no deal without a new baseline that was more to the White House's liking.

At the same time Democrats were trying 1990 tactics on the Republicans, however, Republicans were doing the same thing with Clinton, pushing him to make a mistake like Bush's that would pull him away from his base and open up the possibilities of a deal on GOP terms. Panetta, Stephanopoulos, and other top White House officials who had lived through the 1990 débâcle were determined not to repeat Bush's fatal mistake. The Clinton equivalent of Bush's no-new-taxes pledge was Medicare, and the moat around Medicare was the OMB baseline. The OMB's easier numbers meant shallower Medicare cuts, and that Clinton could live with.

All year long Clinton had retreated from his initial resistance to a balanced budget in little baby steps, and only when he absolutely had to. There would be no sudden, unilateral disarmament, as when Bush had suddenly dropped his tax pledge. If Clinton had to move toward a balanced budget, a step that would antagonize his liberal base, he would make it look as if he were being dragged at gunpoint. "Every step of the way they were trying to get us to do the equivalent of George Bush," said Stephanopoulos. "They just wanted us to go into a meeting and agree to give them something which they could construe as going back on a 'read my lips' pledge, and we were well aware of it and would never let it happen."

On November 30, the first round of negotiations blew up after only three days, with righteous indignation on both sides. Inside the room, Republicans pushed the White House officials to lay down a plan that would achieve a balanced budget in seven years, scored by the CBO. Treasury Secretary Bob Rubin countered that the White House had a plan that achieved balance in ten years. Kasich said the White House plan led to a $200-billion deficit in 2002, by CBO calculations. Where was the seven-year plan the White House said it could produce? "That's what we're waiting for," Kasich said.

"We're waiting for you to talk about policies," snapped an angry Panetta, suddenly rising to leave and putting on his jacket. "Call us when you're ready to talk about policy!" As he turned, however, he came face-to-face with Stephanopoulos, who quietly told him he could not be the first to leave. Panetta resumed his seat and continued talking, but the session went nowhere.

Outside, both sides traded angry accusations in front of the TV cameras. "If we're the only ones with a plan and they refuse to put a plan on the table, how can you have a negotiation?" asked Kasich. "I cannot negotiate unless we can talk about two documents with the same beginning and the same end. . . . They can't say, No, I hate your budget but not show us theirs. I'm not going to sit in the room burning calories, getting worked up about their silly arguments, until I see a balanced budget from them."

"We have a budget on the table," said Panetta. "The problem is they don't want to discuss these issues. . . . If all we're going to do is have speeches on both sides, this isn't going to work."

The two sides canceled sessions set for the next two days and made plans to reconvene the following week.

For the first time, the prospects that there would be no deal began to get a serious public airing. Dole said he thought the chances of a negotiated settlement were 50–50 at best. White House press secretary Mike McCurry said on Fox *Morning News* on November 28 that it might take an election to decide who was right: "There are big differences between the president and the Congress, and I suspect that those kinds of issues will have to be settled in November of 1996."

"I've gotten the impression that the unthinkable could be thinkable—that is, the notion of passing nothing," said conservative Alabama Democratic Congressman Glen Browder. Both sides "are seriously looking at the advantages of not having a budget," he continued. "Both sides are having people telling them it's a winning strategy."

While Clinton and his aides insisted publicly that the White House wanted a deal, the president was a winner either way. If he negotiated an agreement that he could sell to a majority of congressional Democrats, he could also sell it to voters as proof that he could tame a Republican Congress that would otherwise be dangerously extreme. If talks collapsed, he was positioned to claim that he would have balanced the budget except for the extremist Republican Congress, which wanted to balance the budget on the backs of the poor and the elderly.

Some advisers argued that Clinton would do better without a deal. Unless the president could get an agreement on his terms, with wins on Medicare, Medicaid, education, and the environment, former campaign manager James Carville said on *Meet the Press,* "I would rather there be an election." "There's nothing wrong with having some differences and distinctions here, and we have them, and let's go to it."

Polls seemed to reward Clinton for orneriness; the numbers slumped or stayed flat when he reached for middle ground with the GOP but spiked when he took a confrontational approach. His numbers had sunk when he seemed to make peace with Gingrich at a senior citizens' forum in New Hampshire on June 11 and when he unveiled his balanced-budget proposal two days later. But when the president faced off with Gingrich over the government shutdown in mid-November, his numbers shot up higher than they had been in almost two years.

Maybe what the negotiators were attempting to do was impossible after all. Trying to get a divided government to agree to a compromise on the very issues that led its members to join different parties in the first place was hard work indeed. The differences seemed irreconcilable. In an irony lost on most of those who filed quickly into and out of the Mansfield Room for the first round of fruitless budget talks, looking sightlessly at the room's back door from an alcove just outside the Senate chamber was a marble bust, an image of George Bush, the last president to cut a budget deal with an opposition Congress. The bust's smooth stone gave Bush's face the look of a death mask, imparting a mute message to Republicans and Democrats alike, reminding them of the costs of dropping party principle to get a deal in the name of good government: Don't do it. You'll be sorry.

On December 6, the president issued his long-expected veto of the Republican balanced-budget plan, and a year's worth of work was suddenly gone. In a pointed bit of political knife twisting, Clinton killed the Republicans' Medicare cuts and everything else with the same pen President Lyndon Johnson had used thirty years earlier to sign Medicare into law. Now Republican hopes for a balanced budget and the heart of their agenda—welfare, Medicaid, Medicare, farm policy—all hinged on the success of talks with the White House, which were going absolutely nowhere. Kasich had known the veto was coming, but even so the news was a blow. "I felt like I'd just lost my best friend," he said.

The very next day—Pearl Harbor Day, Republicans noted grimly—Clinton finally unveiled a proposal that would balance the budget in seven years. It was an effort to deflect criticism that all he could do was say no, and the White House headlined the fact that the president had added $141 billion in spending cuts to his ten-year June budget. But all Republicans saw was that he was still sticking with OMB score keeping, as if the November deal on that subject had never happened. By Republican math, he was still about $400 billion short of what it would take to balance the budget.

Although there were any number of reasons now why they could not get to a deal—deep philosophical differences, both sides' stubborn unwillingness to move, some advisers' creeping conviction that no deal might not be so awful after all—it was not crazy to think they would find a way. Pressure to reach an agreement still seemed to outweigh all the negatives: There was growing fear that the markets would erupt if they failed (Gingrich was warning that the stock market would "crash"), newspaper editorials were urging compromise, and the prevailing view on both sides was that an agreement would give everyone a political boost. The Republicans would walk away having achieved their number-one priority, able to claim correctly that Clinton never would have done this had they not dragged him to it. Clinton could use the bully pulpit to take credit for balancing the budget, claiming—provided the deal bent in his direction—that the Republicans would have scorched the earth had it not been for his intervention. A plausible win-win.

The easiest and most sensible way of finding an accommodation was to get beyond the Republican hang-up over the CBO numbers and essentially split the difference—and why not? A dispassionate look at the track record of the two agencies showed that the CBO was more accurate than the OMB—but not by much. In sixteen separate two-year forecasts from 1976 through 1992, the CBO had missed the actual economic growth rate by an average 0.8 percentage points while the OMB had been off the mark by a full percentage point—a difference of two tenths of a point. More important than who was less wrong, though, was that both agencies missed the mark by about a full point—and this was just for two-year forecasts. Now Republicans and the White House were prepared to shed blood over who was right over *seven years,* where a full one-percentage-point error could skew the projection by hundreds of billions of dollars. It had a touch of the ridiculous to it.

Former CBO director Rudolph Penner, a Republican himself, said there was nothing wrong with a compromise between the CBO and the OMB; the Republicans' decision to elevate the CBO's numbers to "religious significance" was silly, he said, since most of the dif-

ferences between the two agencies were small and well within the
scope of legitimate disagreement by economists. But the Republicans had dug themselves in on this issue. Kasich had all but accused
mild-mannered OMB Director (and former CBO director) Alice
Rivlin of lying when she stuck up for her agency's projections at a
House Budget Committee hearing, and Gingrich had said the suggestion that negotiators should compromise on the two baselines
was "what's sick about this city. . . . Let's find one more excuse to lie
to the American people." So much for that.

But then a huge break came in early December, when the CBO
lowered its seven-year deficit projection by a whopping $135 billion,
demonstrating again how volatile and unreliable even the CBO's
numbers could be. The new forecast replaced one the CBO had
made just eight months earlier, in April; since then, the agency's analysts had noted better economic growth, had re-estimated the likely
impact of balancing the budget, and had recalculated future spending for Medicare and other entitlements. At the same time that the
CBO discovered a lower deficit number, the agency's recalculations
also changed the size of the GOP's headline spending cuts:
Medicare cuts shrank from $270 billion to $226 billion, Medicaid
cuts from $163 billion to $133 billion. The new numbers offered
both sides a chance to narrow the gap between them, and Republicans and Democrats repaired to their calculators to incorporate the
new projections into their proposals. The emotional weather of the
talks, sullen and overcast, suddenly broke for a ray of sunshine.

After weeks of unproductive backbiting with the White House, Kasich's and Domenici's hopes were now sky-high. In a three-way
phone call with Panetta, the White House chief of staff led the two
Budget Committee chairmen to believe that the administration
would at last be making them a serious offer. Kasich pushed Panetta,
demanding to know whether this meant the White House would finally lay down the magic, CBO-scored plan to balance the budget by
2002.

"Leon, I mean, what do you mean?" Kasich badgered the chief of
staff. "Are you going to get there? You know, is this going to pass the
smell test?" Panetta got irritated. "We're not probably going to be
able to get exactly there," he told the two chairmen. Kasich pushed:
But close, right? Close was okay. They didn't have to exactly balance

the budget by 2002 as long as they had real numbers and they got in the ballpark. Domenici had stuck his neck out to reassure Dole and Gingrich and others that Panetta was someone they could do business with, but the reassurances were wearing thin. "I'm sitting on these guys, but you've got to come up with something serious," he warned Panetta. The chief of staff said he would do what he could to get "as close as we can" to a balanced budget by 2002.

That was close enough for Kasich and Domenici, who summoned reporters to an impromptu press conference outside Dole's office the evening of December 13 for a big announcement. "We will have the most serious talks we've seen on this Hill, possibly in many decades," said the enthusiastic Kasich. A somewhat more restrained Domenici said he was "very hopeful that we'll make substantial progress to reach a balanced budget."

They had better make some progress. The current CR was good only through Friday at midnight. Given the anger and unhappiness on the part of rank-and-file Republicans in the House—the drifting talks seemed to be confirming all their worst fears about the White House—the only way to get another stopgap bill and avoid a second shutdown was to show some real movement.

Kasich and Domenici were genuinely excited. Domenici had gotten reports from Lott that back-channel talks with White House adviser Dick Morris were indicating the administration was at last ready to produce a serious offer. In fact, though, the White House was sending out signals to dampen expectations a little; the same night that Domenici and Kasich announced a breakthrough, a White House official told *The Washington Post* that the Friday proposal might offer a number of "ideas" rather than a specific balanced-budget plan. That was much less than what the Budget Committee chairmen were expecting.

Other warnings over the next thirty-six hours left the Republicans unsure of what to expect when they arrived in the Mansfield Room Friday morning and arrayed themselves on their side of the felt-covered tables, across from Panetta and the Democrats. There was the same sort of tension that precedes a big football game; negotiators scrounged for a coin to see who would go first, and all Senate Budget Committee staff director Bill Hoagland could find was a nickel. White House Budget Director Alice Rivlin flipped it, and the Republicans won the toss. "We elect to receive," said Gingrich budget aide Arne Christenson, and Panetta began passing out sheets of paper bearing the White House proposal.

As Kasich looked at the offer, his face went white, and he turned to an aide behind him with a look of stunned disbelief. "Can you believe this?" he said. "This is not a proposal; this is something you could put together in five minutes."

In the critical seventh year, where CBO scoring had shown the Republicans and the White House still $115 billion apart, the White House now proposed to close the gap with $121 billion in new savings. Incredibly, though, $75 billion of that would come solely from fiddling with the CBO numbers to make them more favorable to the White House. The other $46 billion would come from revoking the administration's tax cuts in 2000 (something no one believed would ever happen in an election year), changing the terms of some government property sales, and making a few other minor modifications. Bottom line: The White House was still unwilling to accept the CBO numbers, and it had offered virtually no new spending cuts.

The Republicans, by contrast, had worked to scale back their earlier proposal. They spread $75 billion of the new money afforded by the CBO's recalculated baseline around the offer, knocking Medicare cuts down from $226 billion to $202 billion, lowering the Medicaid cuts from $133 billion to $117 billion, and putting back $25 billion in appropriations spending for Clinton priorities in education, environmental protection, and other domestic programs. In a gesture they privately admitted was tiny, they knocked $5 billion off their $245 billion in tax cuts; Bill Hoagland said this was meant as a signal to the Democrats that the GOP would move, but only by tiny steps right now, for fear of antagonizing hard-rock tax cutters.

Domenici felt like a fool. Hoagland did a quick calculation for him that showed that most of the savings came from quibbling with CBO scoring or ending the tax cuts. The White House had refused to budge on Medicare or Medicaid. Domenici looked at the paper, then at Panetta. "Where are your Medicare cuts?" he demanded. "Pete, we're not going to move on Medicare," Panetta told him. As if unaware of how enraged the Republicans had become, Panetta brought up the question of another CR to keep the government open past midnight. The simmering Republicans were noncommittal. The talks collapsed in anger that afternoon.

Domenici and Kasich were stunned. This was so far short of what they had been led to expect—in part by their own enthusiasm—that they felt betrayed and insulted. They had sold the press, their colleagues, and themselves on the notion that something big was about to happen. How dare Panetta hint that he would lay down something close to CBO and seven and then come in with this? The meeting was a turning point in the radicalizing of Domenici, changing his view of the White House and especially of his old sparring partner, Panetta.

There had always been an assumption that Domenici and Panetta would find a way to work things out. Their relationship went all the way back to 1981, when brand-new Senate Budget Committee Chairman Domenici and Republican-turned-Democrat Panetta, a third-term Congressman, were members of a House-Senate conference on Reagan's big deficit-reduction bill. Both were Italian Americans, sons of hardworking immigrants; both were moderates in their own parties, mistrusted by harder-line colleagues. Panetta had furthered their relationship by hiring one of Domenici's daughters as an intern in his congressional office. Early in the year, the two began private, back-channel talks in an effort to find common ground that might pave the way for a deal. Now, though, burned by this episode and Panetta's endless foot-dragging, Domenici no longer felt he could trust the chief of staff.

But Panetta was unrepentant. In part, this was a calculated attempt to see just how eager for a deal the Republicans were; if they jumped at this, they would be revealing desperation, giving the White House an important advantage. If they rejected it, however— so what? How naïve did they think Panetta was? "You don't enter a negotiation by laying out your bottom line; that's foolish," Panetta said later. "They really thought I was there to engage in the terms of surrender as opposed to bona fide negotiations. . . . They surely understood that Medicare would be the last place we would move in this deal, not the first place, but the last."

While the Republicans were still meeting and venting and trying to figure out what to do next, Clinton went to the White House press room in time to make the evening network news shows. "They wanted us to agree to deep cuts in Medicare and Medicaid just as a condition to talk," he said. "Once again they are threatening to shut the government down if I do not accept their deep cuts." Dole was furious when he heard it. "I don't think he's telling the American people the truth," he snapped.

In fact, Clinton was shamelessly exaggerating. Republicans *did* want deep cuts, but at this point they would have settled for good-faith movement, even a signal that the White House was serious about negotiating. Instead, they got more bickering over CBO numbers. The White House had legitimate concerns that the CBO numbers were overly pessimistic, but the administration was mostly worried about being forced into anything resembling the CBO box, which would require a move toward the GOP numbers. The White House had stretched about as far on Medicare as it could without beginning to lose core Democratic support. It was the White House negotiators, not the Republicans, who were making non-negotiable demands as a condition of further talks. Panetta was insisting that the Republicans capitulate on the scorekeeping before the administration talked seriously.

The Republicans had winked at Panetta, moving modestly but signaling a willingness to keep going. Instead of a wink back, Panetta had, in effect, flipped them the bird. This was hardball. This was not the pliable old Leon they had known in 1990, nor was this the spineless and irrelevant Bill Clinton they had so confidently planned on rolling all those months ago when they laid out the strategy that was now falling apart around them.

Now Clinton was moving much more quickly and adroitly than they were, summoning the full powers of the White House to command the nation's attention, defining the breakdown as the Republicans' fault while the Republicans were still gnashing their teeth and wondering what to do next. Mad and frustrated, they resolved only one thing—not to give Clinton another CR until he gave them what they thought they had been about to get that morning: CBO and seven. Dole, Gingrich, Kasich, and Domenici all thought closing the government down again was foolish, especially with Christmas so near. But they were not in full control; angry House members and sympathetic second-rank leaders were calling the shots, and they were not about to give Clinton anything.

"We can't trust these guys," fumed DeLay. House GOP Conference Chairman Boehner said there would be no CR. Period. "This is the most defining moment in thirty years in this town, and the question is, Is it going to be business as usual, or are we going to do the right thing for our children?" The Republicans were still convinced the broad mass of Americans didn't notice or care whether the government shut down, but even if they did, too bad. The polls, Boehner said, were "irrelevant."

———

Now things looked grim indeed. With talks dead, the second shutdown got under way on Saturday, throwing more than a quarter of a million federal employees out of work just ten days before Christmas. Clinton used his weekend radio address to take another shot at the Republicans' "unacceptable" spending cuts. "I am not going to let them hurt our children," he declared, further aggravating the already angry Republicans. Asked what Clinton could do to restart the stalled talks, Dole snapped, "He can stop that garbage he's spewing out on his radio program and everything else."

The next day, Dole had his sense of humor back. Musing on the Senate floor, he noted that because of the shutdown, "the zoo's closed; the Senate's open. That should tell you something. Maybe we ought to have it the other way around." Then came the characteristic Dole zinger, aimed not at Clinton but at the House Republicans, with whom he was growing increasingly frustrated: "I think it's time for adult leadership."

On Monday, December 18, the stock market suddenly dropped like a stone. In what was widely perceived as a message to political leaders to resume the budget talks, the market shed more than one hundred points in the biggest one-day loss in four years. The next day, Clinton called Gingrich and Dole down to the White House to offer to resume bargaining, but now elevating the talks to a true summit, with the president and the two Republican leaders negotiating face-to-face at last.

All along, Republicans who had thought about how this all might end had assumed they would have one last ace to play if things really went bad. If Clinton agreed to participate in talks at the White House, there had to be a deal. No president could lend his and the Oval Office's prestige to talks and then let those talks fail.

The first meeting in the Oval Office seemed to go well. Republicans left the session thinking the president had at last agreed that everything on the table would be CBO-scored and that they would agree to a deal by the end of the year; the White House negotiators thought they had an agreement to reopen the government while talks went on.

But all those understandings collapsed immediately. An excited Gingrich floated the idea of a good-faith CR as soon as he got back to the Hill, but it was like poking a stick in a hornet's nest. Other GOP House leaders and members, especially the freshmen, felt Gingrich had again been handled by the White House. Colleagues had long understood that Gingrich's public reputation as a hard-bitten tough guy was a sham, that he was essentially a softy who had no place in negotiations. Now, they thought, he had melted again under Clinton's extraordinarily skillful attentions. Boehner said the way the two interacted reminded him and other leaders of the *Leave It to Beaver* show—the smooth-talking Clinton was the Eddie Haskell character: polite, manipulative, and completely insincere. Gingrich was the Beav, naïve, credulous, and easily conned. Clinton would compliment Gingrich on his tie, tell him how much he'd missed talking to him, and in five minutes the Speaker would be checking his back pocket to make sure his wallet was still there. He knew exactly what Clinton was doing to him, but he still couldn't help himself.

For months, the prevailing question had been whether Clinton was still relevant; now the question was how relevant Gingrich was. He had never seemed less in control of his own troops and his own lieutenants in the House. Many House Republicans felt they'd been had by Clinton when they agreed to reopen the government in November only to have the White House stonewall them in the post-Thanksgiving budget talks. Not this time. "We don't want to play the sucker again," said freshman Arizona Congressman Matt Salmon. When Gingrich came back from the White House to suggest a new CR, all the Republicans had just watched Vice President Gore say on TV that Clinton had not agreed to give up disputing the CBO numbers after all and had not agreed to conclude a deal by New Year's Day. Leaders played Gingrich the videotape. "By the time it was over, he had a stronger spine," said Boehner. There would be no CR until they had a balanced budget. And from now on, the Beav would not go alone with Dole to see Clinton. Armey, who really was a tough guy, would go along as chaperon.

Suddenly, things had gone bad again. Christmas was coming, but the air was full of threats and ill will. House Republicans had vowed repeatedly to skip Christmas with their families to stay in town until they got a budget deal. "We will be here until doomsday!" shouted House Appropriations Committee Chairman Bob Livingston from the House floor. But now House Republicans voted to go home after all, leaving 260,000 federal workers without jobs and many government services shut down.

Months ago, in the spring, Gingrich had thought Clinton would buckle under the weight of a shutdown. Instead, the closure gave the president opportunity after opportunity to paint the Republicans as extremists, blame the shutdown on them, and act principled and presidential. "I won't yield to these threats," he said on December 20. "I'm determined to balance the budget, but I won't be forced into signing a budget that violates our values, not today or tomorrow, not ever."

It was at this point that Kasich decided finally that there would not be a deal, not ever. Usually unstoppably talkative, he fell into a funk and became strangely quiet. Longtime press secretary Bruce Cuthbertson, who usually drove Kasich to work, reported on December 21 that he had picked him up that morning and braced for the usual onslaught of Kasich-talk only to hear nothing. "He's been confident all the while; now he just doesn't have that confidence," Cuthbertson said. "He didn't speak for ten minutes."

The talks that resumed on December 22 at the White House with the top-level players and other senior leaders were, by most accounts, fascinating for budget wonks but intensely frustrating for anyone who wanted the process to end in an agreement. Clinton and Gingrich, who both reveled in this sort of thing, conducted a budget seminar in which they exchanged views, chewed on policy implications, deconstructed programs, and tried in vain to find common ground. Gore and Clinton settled into a good-cop, bad-cop routine in which Clinton would edge toward a deal and Gore would jerk him back. Gingrich and Armey did much the same thing; whenever Gingrich seemed in danger of falling into Clinton's gravitational pull, the tough-minded Armey would yank him back into the conservatives' orbit.

Dole was Dole, mostly quiet and hard to read. Participants had the sense that the majority leader wanted the process finished one way or another so he could get on with his presidential campaign.

The endless talks kept him tethered to Washington, able to leave from time to time but always snapped back into town at the whim of the other negotiators. Domenici, still a participant at this stage, did most of the talking for the Senate Republicans and left the sessions worried that the articulate, omnivorously well-informed Clinton would run rings around the taciturn Kansan in the presidential debates.

The president thrived on budget minutiae; he knew the programs about as well as anyone else, even Panetta, who had been living and breathing budgets for a decade and had been the one to tutor Clinton in 1993. At one point, the president shocked Bill Hoagland with his intimate knowledge of the use of shelter deductions in calculating eligibility for food stamps. Hoagland had overseen the program in an earlier incarnation as a Reagan-administration bureaucrat and was amazed that Clinton understood it at that level of detail.

To Armey, all the talk was little more than an elaborate stall. "It was as if this is what the president said: Hey, guys, I got a great idea. Why don't you all come over to the Oval Office, and we'll put together this engine that will drive to a balanced budget. And we walked into the Oval Office, and there, scattered all over the room, were the separate parts of the engine. And we spent all that time picking up and examining the different parts. And we would try this part with this part and try it this way. And then we would try it this way. And then we would move it around that way. . . . The president knew as well as any man alive everything that needed to be known about each of the separate parts."

But there was never a plan, Armey thought, for assembling the parts into an engine. Eventually, as he listened to Clinton talk, the same cold feeling Kasich had gotten crept over Armey. "I went in there expecting that he had no intention of getting to a balanced budget but hoping he might. . . . It wasn't long after my having been there that I began to understand that my hope was against hope, that my expectations were correct."

The Republicans were furious that the White House refused to work from the budget that they and their colleagues had devoted nearly a year to assembling. Instead, Panetta wanted to build a new package from the ground up, a plan Armey felt was terribly disrespectful of all their effort. "You just can't throw away other people's work," he complained.

White House officials quickly got tired of the Republicans' whining about how hard they had worked, as if that alone entitled them to something—and as if the administration hadn't been working every bit as hard. "Tell someone who cares," said Stephanopoulos later, recalling the Democrats' private thoughts as they listened to the Republicans complain. "Call your mother."

In the final stages, the talks moved from the Cabinet Room to the Oval Office, where Gore insisted on restricting participation to just the top eight leaders: Clinton, Gore, and Panetta from the White House plus Democratic leaders Daschle from the Senate and Gephardt from the House; the Republicans could bring Gingrich, Dole, and Armey, but they would have to leave Kasich and Domenici outside. Ostensibly, this was to winnow the numbers, leaving a manageable eight negotiators—if they allowed Kasich and Domenici in, they would also have to admit the two ranking Democrats from the Budget Committees, Nebraska Senator Jim Exon and Minnesota Congressman Martin Sabo. But the Democrats were also looking for an edge, and by keeping out the highly knowledgeable Budget Committee chairmen, they got it. Panetta, a former House Budget Committee chairman and an ex–White House budget director, knew the budget inside out, and Clinton wasn't far behind; together they outmatched the less-expert Republican leaders.

Across the hall, in the Roosevelt Room, where they sat for hours with Republican staffers and waited for the principals to consult with them, Kasich and Domenici stewed in humiliation. Frequently, when the leaders came back to report what they had discussed in the Oval Office, Kasich and Domenici saw that Gingrich, Dole, and Armey had been led astray by the Democrats without realizing it. For example, Dole came out of the Oval Office once to report that the Democrats were willing to raise their tax cuts to $130 billion (from $105 billion). But when someone asked whether that was a net or a gross figure—a critical detail, since the "corporate welfare" tax increases that both sides were discussing could make that number as much as $40 billion bigger or smaller—Dole wasn't sure. "The problem was our guys were in there negotiating a budget that they didn't thoroughly understand," said a senior Republican. "They were always negotiating but never understanding what the implications of the numbers were."

Left in the Roosevelt Room "bull pen" for hours on end,

Domenici and Kasich got fed up long before the three top negotiators did. At one point, Dole had to leave the talks to go up to the Hill to open the Senate, and Domenici got to take his place in the Oval Office for forty-five minutes. When he entered, Gore was standing at an easel with a pointer, explaining the Democrats' position in a way that Domenici found patronizing.

The Budget Committee chairman asked for a chance at the easel himself, and all his pent-up venom seemed to burst out. "It was like you could have just put this barking, vicious dog in the middle of the room," said one Democrat who witnessed it. "It just completely threw the entire discussion out of sync, and it was a disaster. I mean, I passed a note over to Leon, and I said, 'You've got to get this guy out of here. He is destroying what little semblance of civility there was in this room.' " Domenici later admitted to an associate that he had lectured Gore and the others, but he said it was Gore's obnoxious tone that had set him off.

Domenici wasn't alone in losing his temper. One day toward the end of the talks in January, Gingrich and his wife, Marianne, were having lunch at the Old Ebbit Grill a couple of blocks from the White House, accompanied by former Reagan chief of staff Ken Duberstein and his wife. Kasich, whom they had invited to join them, arrived late and extremely agitated—furious at Clinton and the Democrats for what he thought were their outright lies, furious at the inextricable mess the Republicans were in, negotiating with people he believed had no interest in a deal.

"You can't trust them," he railed, according to someone present. "I don't know why you're going to the White House," he said to Gingrich, who was due there later that afternoon for more talks. "I think they're bad. I think they're ridiculous. I know you're going there—I don't care. You're making a mistake. You should tell them to shove it."

As the Republicans were getting more and more anxious and angry, Clinton and the Democrats seemed to be growing more relaxed and self-assured. One day the Republicans left the Oval Office to confer and stayed away for the better part of two hours. They had been angry about the exclusion of Kasich and Domenici, and the Democrats interpreted their prolonged absence as a deliberate attempt by the GOP leaders to make Clinton and the other senior Democrats uncomfortable. But the Democrats were hardly sweating;

during the break, Clinton flipped on a TV, turned to the American Movie Classics cable channel, and ordered popcorn for everybody while they watched *Rough Night in Jericho,* a Western starring Dean Martin and Jean Simmons. "The president kept saying, 'God, Jean Simmons looks good, doesn't she?' " another Democrat in the room related afterward.

———

Expiration of the CR at 12:01 A.M. December 16 had shut down nine Cabinet departments and scores of agencies and had thrown some 260,000 federal employees out of work for the second time in a month. As the shutdown began, Gingrich and other GOP leaders treated it as a small sacrifice in the much more important struggle to force Clinton to negotiate a deal.

Rather than apologize for any disruption or suffering, Gingrich praised his troops for their courage in taking on entitlement programs, passing a balanced budget, and standing up to Clinton. The media, the Speaker believed, would finally focus on the titanic struggle between a GOP Congress that wanted to balance the budget and a Democratic president who was refusing to do it. That was not what happened.

With Christmas fast approaching, more than three million veterans suddenly faced the prospect that they would not get their monthly checks on time or at all—the Veterans Administration staffers who usually processed the checks and mailed them out had been furloughed. Attention also began to turn to federal employees who were having trouble making car and mortgage payments and who would now be unable to buy Christmas presents. And as the shutdown dragged on, the ripple effects spread far beyond the government itself, threatening jobs and businesses that depended on government contracts or activity in areas with a big federal presence, such as the communities around the national parks.

Republicans who had treated the federal government as the enemy and federal employees as prisoners of war found that the shutdown's collateral damage was hurting not just government workers but ordinary people in virtually every congressional district in the country. From a public relations standpoint, the GOP was taking a terrible beating. News accounts increasingly focused not on the Republicans' principled stand but on the growing human cost of the politicians' stubbornness.

If Gingrich showed little concern about the political fallout, though, Dole privately was apoplectic. He and his party had paid an awful price during the first shutdown in November, and Dole's own poll ratings were dipping—exactly what Dole the presidential contender did not need now, with the primaries about to begin. The Senate leader had long since grown disgusted with the House Republicans' willful self-destructiveness. The message was supposed to be "balance the budget," but the only message that was getting out was "shut down the government." On January 2, he acted on his own, ramming a bill through the nearly deserted Senate to reopen the government through January 12. "Enough is enough," he said. "I do not see any sense in what we have been doing. . . . If there is any point to be made, I think that point should have been made by now."

Dole's action drove a wedge through the House Republicans. House Majority Whip Tom DeLay and other conservatives could barely conceal their disgust at what they saw as Dole's unilateral surrender; some took to calling the presidential front-runner Mr. Caveman. But House moderates were emboldened. Republican members of Congress who had never thought the strategy made sense were now joined by those members with large numbers of federal workers in their districts and those whose districts were being affected by the shutdown of national parks or other government activities. At a closed-door meeting of all House Republicans on January 3, more than fifty members voted to compromise on reopening the government. GOP leaders knew they were on the verge of losing control of the House floor; it was only a matter of time before enough Republicans joined the Democrats on a formal vote to end the shutdown.

By now, the Republicans were in serious disarray. Gingrich had told senior leaders in a private meeting after the White House talks on January 2 that he was beginning to think there would be no deal. Anger and resentment swept through the room. "The feeling around the table was one of—it's hard to describe—disappointment, frustration, anger—like being promised a birthday and then not doing it," said DeLay. "You're mad; you want to strike back."

When tempers subsided, Gingrich said the shutdown was clearly un-sustainable. They were getting hammered in the polls, and all this pain was getting them absolutely nothing from Clinton. The time for a tactical retreat had come, but it took two days to sell that to the rank and file. At a wild closed-door meeting on the night of January 4, angry members told Gingrich they should hang tough and stare down the White House. Gingrich's mantra had long been "listen, learn, help, lead," but after two days of listening and learning, he had had enough.

At a final closed-door GOP meeting on the morning of January 5, he laid down the law. "We're going to play as a team; it's a team ef-fort. If you don't like the way we're doing it, run for the leadership yourself," he barked before ordering members to vote for a bill that would end the shutdown. All but 15 of the 236 Republicans did so, sending Clinton two bills: One would let federal employees go back to work; the other would give agencies the funding they needed to do business, but only if Clinton produced the magic CBO-and-seven proposal.

That the White House could finally do, though it took some fi-nagling. Bypassing the straightforward technicians at the OMB, ad-ministration officials seized on a transparently flimsy proposal cooked up in Congress for Senate Democrats. It balanced the bud-get with such tricks as heavily back-loading spending cuts in the last two of the seven years, turning off the tax cuts in 2001 and 2002, and calling for such huge cuts in appropriated spending that many Dem-ocrats did not believe they could actually live with them in the final years of the proposal. Republicans, anxious for the shutdown to go away, asked the CBO to stay open through the weekend to analyze the proposal and issue an official assessment; the CBO found that the plan would balance the budget by 2002.

Now, at last, the Republicans had forced Clinton to produce the balanced-budget proposal they had demanded for so long. But it was a hollow victory. The president's proposal did not move enough in the GOP's direction on the big Medicare and Medicaid numbers, and his tax cuts actually moved away from theirs. More important, his budget offered none of the radical government transformation or entitlement reform the GOP demanded. The two sides were still a world apart on the core philosophical issues.

It was only slowly dawning on Republicans that their long, draining battle just to get Clinton to the table had led them to define success the wrong way. They thought that by forcing Clinton into the CBO-and-seven box, they could make him walk through the same process they had gone through, pushing him to reach some of the same conclusions—that entitlements would have to be fundamentally changed, not just tinkered with, for example. But Clinton had found a way to balance the budget with an incremental proposal that avoided most major change and protected most major Democratic priorities, at least in the short run. The Republicans were like the dog that finally catches the car: What now?

———

Washington was smothered by a rare two-foot snowfall on Sunday, January 7, paralyzing the city and temporarily stopping the budget talks. The capital became a surreal place where doing even the simplest tasks—getting out the front door, finding the family car, buying food—had become an enormous hardship. Even the day after the blizzard, leaders had a hard time making it to the White House for talks; a Capitol Police vehicle sent to pick up Gephardt at his suburban Virginia home broke an axle, leaving the House minority leader stranded. The seemingly simple task of splitting the difference on budget numbers that were now getting remarkably close was becoming impossible as well.

A month earlier, Clinton's December 7 Pearl Harbor budget proposal had come up about $400 billion short of the Republican plan, according to GOP math (CBO calculations later showed the gap to be about $365 billion). Now Clinton's new January 7 proposal and subsequent revisions by both sides had brought the two budgets to within as little as $50 billion of each other—budgetary chump change in packages this big. Clinton's final offer included net deficit reduction of $582 billion versus a GOP offer of as little as $632 billion. Tantalizingly, agonizingly close, but still the numbers masked huge disagreements on policy.

On Medicaid, the gap had shrunk from $100 billion to just $26 billion (GOP: $85 billion; Clinton: $59 billion). But the Republicans continued to insist on transforming the federal piece of this joint federal-state program into a block grant and turning it over to the states to run, ending the open-ended entitlement to health care for poor children, poor pregnant women, the disabled, and the impoverished elderly. Clinton was willing to give the states much greater flexibility in running things, but he was determined to maintain the entitlement.

On Medicare, the onetime $129-billion gap had closed to as little as $30 billion (GOP: $154 billion; Clinton: $124 billion). But again this disguised a giant policy difference: Republicans still wanted an absolute cap on Medicare spending that would slowly force seniors out of expensive fee-for-service medicine and into managed care, shifting the risk of future cost explosions to health-care providers and, at least indirectly, to the beneficiaries themselves. Clinton wanted the government to retain that risk.

In a sign of just how badly some of them wanted a deal, the Republicans began an internal free-for-all on the numbers. At one point, Gingrich proposed dropping their $240 billion in tax cuts below $150 billion or even lower; one Republican proposal contained a plan to end the tax cuts after 2000, which could have dropped net tax cuts to just $107 billion, according to a GOP aide. At this stage, a rift began to pit Gingrich, Dole, and other leaders who were reaching for a deal against Kasich, Armey, and those who were appalled by the numbers they were seeing. At one meeting, Armey slammed his fist down to punctuate his warning that they give no more ground beyond their final offer. "This is it!" he said. "I want you all to know that this is it." It was better to have no deal than to have the kind of deal some of them were talking about now.

Something else was happening: The Republicans, united for much of the year in their crusade, were coming unglued. Nerves were rubbed raw. The White House talks had now dragged on for almost fifty hours, and the negotiators seemed no closer to a deal than they had been at the start. The polls were terrible, the weather was worse, and now they were fighting among themselves. Gingrich, sniped at by his own troops and losing the battle downtown, was becoming more brittle and combative. The Republicans seemed on the verge of a collective nervous breakdown. An entire year's work, the prize they had so desperately wanted, was all but gone.

On January 9, the day that would turn out to be the end of the White House talks, Republicans gathered ahead of time for a turbulent premeeting in Dole's office in the Capitol to work out internal differences and decide how to handle that day's session. There was still a Christmas wreath hanging on the Senate majority leader's office door, but the gloom in the room was palpable. There was virtually no hope left that they would work things out with Clinton.

Early in the session, Gingrich and Dole disappeared into Dole's inner office and shut the door. The normally placid Armey kept looking agitatedly toward the door, worried that the two leaders were cooking up some unacceptably weak new offer he would have to swallow; Boehner rubbed Armey's arm and tried to get him to calm down. Gingrich was obviously troubled when he finally came out. Boehner spoke up: If there were to be no more White House meetings after this one, they should all agree on how they would behave when the talks broke off. No one should act angry, Boehner said. Gingrich snapped at him. "Oh, Boehner, would you be quiet? I don't need you to tell me that!"

Kasich, who had emerged as one of the hardest of the hard-liners, wanted to make sure that Gingrich wasn't about to give away the store when he went into the Oval Office. That set Gingrich off again. "Look," the Speaker snapped at the Budget Committee chairman, according to another Republican who was there, "just give me the numbers, fill in the blanks—this is why you're not in the room."

"The dynamics were bad, the weather was bad, people were frustrated," explained one Republican who was at the meeting. Kasich confided to a participant that Gingrich was upset because a number of freshmen had told the Speaker they would not back any deal unless Kasich signed off on it. Gingrich was worried and unhappy that he seemed to be losing his authority over the rank and file, Kasich said.

The plan for the final White House meeting was unclear. The Republicans were now split between those who thought there still might be some faint hope of a deal—chiefly Dole and Gingrich—and those like Kasich and Armey who thought they were probably just wasting their time. Kasich and Armey talked about presenting Clinton with an ultimatum: Give us a serious offer or forget it. At one point, Gingrich seemed sympathetic. "Let's not even waste our time going down there," he said. But Blankley, his press aide, advised him not to do that. "It'll look like we're shutting it down," he told the Speaker.

The Oval Office meeting lasted about two and a half hours, and when Dole, Gingrich, and Armey rejoined the others in the Roosevelt Room for a conference, there was virtually no movement to report. Aides jotted numbers on a board. There was no meaningful movement on the box, so called because in a final attempt to get things unstuck, Republicans had proposed dumping the collective numbers of the four contentious items—Medicare, Medicaid, welfare, and the earned-income tax cuts—into a "box" and focusing only on the total. The individual numbers didn't matter as long as the total deficit reduction was enough to do the job.

Domenici and Kasich shook their heads as they watched aides post the latest figures. "They certainly spent a lot of time doing nothing," Domenici murmured. Both Budget Committee chairmen agreed there was nothing here. "You've got to end it," Kasich said.

As they talked, it seemed clear they were at the end of the road. "We should just go back in and say it's over," said Gingrich. "Maybe we should just shut it down."

"Why didn't you say that in there?" asked Dole. "If you feel that way, we should go back in and tell him—it's over."

All that was left now was to negotiate some mutually face-saving way to extract themselves. In the Oval Office, the administration raised fears that the markets would tank if the talks simply died; they should encourage the notion that they were just taking a break.

Back in the Roosevelt Room, Kasich balked. "I can't believe that," he said when told of the plan. "What is going on here?" He had a low regard for Gingrich's negotiating skills—he had fought with the Speaker all through the process of constructing the budget because Gingrich was always trying to give back things Kasich was taking away. "He should never be involved in a negotiation," said one senior Republican. "He's just too willing to trust the other guy and give too much. Newt will give, give, give, give, give." Now he had given again in the Oval Office, despite their plan to make a clean cut and walk away.

Gingrich called Panetta to the Roosevelt Room, and they wrangled a while longer about what to say. Panetta warned them not to spook the markets, and the Republicans relented. When they went before the cameras later, both sides left the impression they were just taking a breather. Dole said the bargaining was "in recess," Gingrich said this was a pause, and Clinton used the word "suspend." There was a plan to resume the next week.

But they understood privately that it was over. The budget package had included most of the bold agenda of the first Republican Congress in four decades, and now that agenda was dead. As for balancing the budget, the best chance they'd had in two decades to get the job done, a chance they might not have again for years, was gone. The bitter loss was tempered for some by the knowledge that they would not have to go back and listen to Clinton anymore. "There was for me sort of a relief, of busting out of the joint," said Armey. "I spent my time in purgatory."

Others were depressed. Senate Budget Committee staff director Bill Hoagland had been working on this for more than a decade now, pushing the boulder up the hill again and again, driving himself crazy working out one budget proposal after another, dealing with the pharaonic egos of the Senate and the mercurial craziness of the House. There had been times when the temperamentally pessimistic Hoagland had allowed himself to believe that this time it just might be possible, but now it had all collapsed. How did that feel? Out of his jacket pocket, he pulled the lyrics to a song from *Les Misérables,* the epic musical about the heartbreak and failure of the French Revolution. "'Here they sang about "tomorrow",'" Hoagland read aloud, "'and tomorrow never came.'"

Although the talks were effectively dead, participants encouraged for a little while longer the fiction that they lived on. White House spokesman Mike McCurry joked that "if you put the pane of glass up to the body, you'd still get the little smudge indicating that it's breathing."

Armey said the absolute, irrevocable end came on January 17, the day they were supposed to go back down to the White House for another try. He and Gingrich went to Dole's office, and the consensus was there was no point. It would just be more photo ops. "Clinton called us up, and it was kind of cute. . . . He got on the phone and said, 'Hi, guys, what's going on? Are you coming over?' And I remember so many times when I was a boy, calling Bill or Harry and saying, 'Are you going to come over?'" Armey felt as if the president were saying, "'I've got all these damn Tinkertoys thrown all over the Oval Office and nobody here to put them together. And you know Al. He ain't no fun.'" The leaders said no, telling Clinton they would not come back to the White House until he produced a new proposal that moved much closer to theirs. It was clear there was no sense in more talk, Armey said. "Nothing was going to come of it."

The Republicans purposely waited to announce the death of the negotiations until after Clinton's State of the Union Address on January 23, worried that Clinton would use his national TV appearance to beat up on them for killing the talks. The morning after the speech, Gingrich, Armey, Kasich, and other House GOP leaders convened a press conference in the Mansfield Room, site of the go-nowhere talks of November and December.

"We do not believe it's possible now to get to a budget agreement," said Gingrich, the first formal acknowledgment that the budget plan was dead. Instead, they might try for a modest package of $40 billion in spending cuts and some $30 billion in tax cuts—a "down payment" on a balanced budget, Gingrich said. It was a long way from the $1 trillion in spending cuts and $350 billion in tax cuts they had launched nine months earlier. It was reality. "It's not a big deal, but it's a start," conceded Gingrich. The question was no longer how to balance the budget, slash taxes, and radically transform the government. It was, said the Speaker, "What's the best you can do for America this week?"

Ways and Means Committee Chairman Archer announced that the Republicans were abandoning their tactic of holding the debt limit hostage, ending the remote risk of national default: "It is not our desire to be confrontational; it is not our desire to send the president something that he will automatically veto." The tone was shocking for its mildness. The scorched-earth rhetoric was gone. The Republicans had the aspect of the losers in a long war. They were suing for peace.

Except for one note of defiance. Clinton kept calling the Republicans back to negotiations, knowing they would not come, sticking the needle in them. Kasich, whose edgy ebullience was the only sign of life among the Republicans that morning, wore a brightly colored tie that sported pictures of Bert and Ernie, the *Sesame Street* TV Muppets. More talks? No way, Kasich said. "I'm not goin' back to the room!"

In the aftermath, there were a dozen explanations for the failure. Angry Republicans blamed Clinton's intransigence. Democrats said the Republicans had overreached, just as Clinton had in 1994 with his huge health-care plan. Gingrich conceded that point, admitting he had pushed for too much. The Speaker also admitted to *The New York Times* that he had fatally "miscalculated Bill Clinton's tactical skills and his capacity to come back." And along the way, said the newly humbled Speaker, he had "made a lot of clumsy miscalculations."

In the end, Gingrich had become the victim of his own success at raising up such an intense new class of GOP warriors. The Republicans' jihad mentality became their strength and their downfall. "Moral crusades have great advantages—they can create unity of purpose, fervor, discipline that most political movements don't have," said former CBO director Reischauer. "But they also have one profound weakness: It's very hard to compromise when you're in a moral crusade; compromise is indistinguishable from capitulation. You have to capture Jerusalem—you can't say, 'We made it all the way from England to Jerusalem,' and then go home."

The House Republicans wanted everything or nothing; they had a horror of compromise. "The worst thing for us is to cut a deal for a budget that people perceive as the same Washington garbage," said Pennsylvania Republican Congressman Bob Walker, a Gingrich confidant.

While the Republicans constantly invoked the spirit of Ronald Reagan, they had never absorbed one of the key lessons Reagan taught. Former Reagan chief of staff Duberstein, a key adviser to Gingrich and others during the yearlong struggle, tried to remind the leaders not to back themselves into a corner by defining victory in ways that were simply unachievable. "Ronald Reagan used to say, 'If I can get eighty percent of what I want, I'll take it every time. I'll come back the next year for the additional twenty percent,' " Duberstein said.

At the end of the talks, self-described Republican heretics—notably Gingrich aides Tony Blankley and Dan Meyer—raised the idea of accepting a half-a-loaf deal from Clinton, if only to let the Republicans walk away with something to show for a year's work. Blankley was more than an ordinary flack: He was a lawyer and a former Reagan White House aide who doubled as both spokesman for and adviser to Gingrich. His half-a-loaf advice got serious consideration. "Certainly a fairly persuasive case could be made that since Clinton's budget was a move in our direction, it was not inconsistent with our principles to accept it," Blankley said. "It would have affirmed the success of the first year." Republicans also liked the idea that cutting a deal with Clinton would alienate Democrats who wanted no deal and would deny the president the ability to campaign on the claim that he had wanted a balanced budget but the Republicans were too extreme. "So you could put together, from an heretical point of view, a pretty strong case for having taken that," Blankley said.

The idea lived for a week or two. Gingrich was lukewarm, but Kasich and other hard-liners argued that accepting mere deficit reduction without fundamental entitlement reform would destroy the growing urgency to make radical change. It would also muddy the GOP image. They were not compromisers, and they could not take a partial deal. "You can't do this piecemeal because it won't work piecemeal," Kasich said. "We won't come back. It has to be done right."

All year long Kasich had publicly preached the critical importance of reducing the deficit and balancing the budget, but in the end, when he had a chance to take a substantial chunk out of the deficit, he balked. "It's not about deficit reduction," he said. "I'm not particularly interested in deficit reduction." Instead, the balanced-budget proposal was "the means by which I can change things. . . . I want fundamental reform of welfare; I want fundamental reform of all the entitlements."

Kasich's implacable opposition was a signal that even if Gingrich and Clinton had been able to agree to some half-a-loaf deal, they probably would have been unable to sell it. That was what had happened in 1990, when summit negotiators cut a deal that angered both liberal Democrats and conservative Republicans and tried futilely to make their majority in the bipartisan middle. Any deal requires the support of at least half of each party, or the leaders risk losing not just the budget agreement but their own jobs. "We couldn't have sold it, I don't think, in the House or the Senate," said Armey. "I talked to Dick Gephardt about it. I said, 'Dick, what would have happened had you brought a package back that you knew had the support of less than half of your conference?' He said, 'They would be electing a new leader.' "

A big part of the problem was that their disagreements went so deep that it was hard to see how they might have split the difference. A Democratic president and a Republican Congress had to find a way to compromise essentially irreconcilable philosophies of government. The big dispute—Is government the problem or the solution?—broke down into scores of nagging questions, all posed by the Republicans' huge reconciliation bill: Should poor children have a right to minimal financial support? Should the disabled have a right to medical care? Should the federal government spell out uniform nationwide standards for basic benefits programs, or should the fifty states be allowed to go their own ways? Should fixed-income seniors bear the risk of rising medical costs, or should the government perpetually shield them?

Budget negotiations work best when questions are not this fundamental, when all that's at stake is some tinkering around the edges. By now, though, the problem had persisted for so long and so many Band-Aid fixes had been made that the remaining questions had become mostly fundamental ones. Eventually there would have to be major changes to Medicare, Social Security, Medicaid, and welfare. It was either that or risk the CBO's disaster scenario of rampant deficits and economic implosion. But the process had become so polarized that there was no will to compromise on party differences and there was no external force strong enough to compel agreement.

In the final days, not even the financial markets came to the rescue. The stock market tanked strategically from time to time in apparent signals of displeasure, but when talks finally went belly-up, the markets shrugged off the failure to produce a deal. The deficit was already going down anyway. By 1996, it had dropped four years in a row, the first time that had happened since the Truman administration. Wall Street analysts had also taken a close look at the GOP budget and realized it would actually have raised the deficit slightly in the first year or two to accommodate tax cuts, which kicked in faster than the spending cuts did. Given that anomaly, said Stanley Collender, director of federal budget policy at Price Waterhouse, "no deal was better from a market perspective than a deal."

With no powerful external pressure to force an agreement, the only way they could have made a deal was to want one badly enough. But neither side wanted an agreement enough to risk rupturing its party. After the talks ended, Stephanopoulos said that it had been clear to him for months that there would never be an agreement. Gingrich had told Clinton in a White House meeting that he would never bring to the House floor a proposal that could not get the votes of at least 200 of the House's 236 Republicans—a deal that by definition would alienate most Democrats, making it impossible for Clinton to back. "I knew in the short run Gingrich wasn't going to walk away from his people," said Stephanopoulos. "It was impossible for us to cut a deal if he didn't." The Republican strategy presumed Clinton would be the one to cave; when he didn't, there was no strategy left.

Underlying all the other reasons why they got no deal was the same political polarization and revenge seeking that had long poisoned the process, particularly since modern-era deficits began to spin out of control. With rare exception, budget politics has always been rancorous and divisive. During a brief golden era in the late 1970s, Democratic Senate Budget Committee Chairman Edmund Muskie and ranking Republican Senator Henry Bellmon deliberately worked to craft budgets that could command a cross-aisle majority from both parties. But even as Muskie and Bellmon tried to coax their colleagues toward a middle ground on budget and tax policy, conservative Republicans in the House used the budget as an ideological battleground to highlight their differences with the ruling liberal Democrats, and the fight there was intensely partisan.

The last vestiges of budget bipartisanship were swept away in the early 1980s with the rise of Ronald Reagan and the intensified Republican assault on big Democratic government. The combatants sharply escalated their differences over economic and social policy, and voting patterns grew even more polarized. Rather than looking for compromise, the two ideologically charged parties moved to opposing cliffs and spent the next decade and a half hurling invective at each other. Over time, former House members migrated to the Senate and gradually fostered a more rancorous atmosphere there; meanwhile, the House descended into trench warfare, which culminated in unprecedented bitterness and actual fistfights in 1995.

As the parties grew increasingly polarized, moderates on both sides became an endangered species. Those who survived—Southern Democratic Blue Dogs and Midwestern and Northeastern Republican middle-of-the-roaders—found it quite possible to reach bipartisan agreement on difficult budget and tax issues but thor-

oughly impossible to persuade their leaders to go along or a majority of their colleagues to back them. Part of the reason for that was
the moderates themselves, who were by nature more easygoing—
and more easily cowed—than their harder-edged colleagues. But a
more critical factor was the changed nature of an angry Congress,
where a majority of both parties had moved steadily away from the
center to the extremes. Budget summitry between the opposing
clans became increasingly impractical because any centrist compromise on taxes, spending, and entitlement reform invariably alien-
ated the wings of the two parties.

The result was a hopeless cycle of revenge. Like some endless
gang war, the fight was always renewed by some fresh insult; everyone had long forgotten who or what had started it, and no one knew
how to get out. As the year went by, the president seemed increasingly driven by the polls; the more he attacked the Republicans, the
better the public seemed to like him, and gradually he seemed to become a prisoner of those attacks: How could he abandon such a successful tactic when every step toward the Republicans threatened to
alienate ever larger segments of his base?

Republicans thought Clinton outmaneuvered them in the final
stages of the negotiations, that the president was just too smart, too
experienced, too clever for them. But this was the same Bill Clinton
they had beaten up and humiliated in 1993 over taxes and the same
Bill Clinton they had thoroughly defeated in 1994 over his health-
care proposal. It was not that Clinton had suddenly matured into a
political genius but that he had swapped roles with the Republicans.
Now it was their job to govern, to carry a necessary but unpopular
agenda to the public while he could sit back and do what they had
done to him for two years—and what each side had done to the
other for two decades: attack.

In 1996, the chief victim of these Hatfield-and-McCoy politics was
Dole. For much of his career, the Kansan had stood for fiscal conservatism tempered with pragmatism and moderation, but in 1995
he had lashed himself to Gingrich and to the Republicans' aggressive balanced-budget drive. Then, in his desperation to win the presidency, Dole embraced the 1980s supply-side optimism he had once
despised, promising huge tax cuts and a vague and painless road to
balancing the budget. Voters tutored by the Republicans' own no-
nonsense anti-deficit rhetoric in 1995 were suspicious of Dole's sud-

den conversion in 1996. And Dole could never overcome the public's lingering distaste for the radical Republican conservatism that had triggered a government crisis the year before. All this left him vulnerable to charges by Clinton that he had a secret agenda of much deeper spending cuts in popular government programs and entitlements to pay for his program or, worse, that he was willing to let the deficit soar once again. In the end, he was reduced to ineffectual complaints that Clinton was trying to "scare" everyone, from seniors to veterans to the handicapped.

There were a dozen reasons why Dole lost to Clinton, but lurking in there with the rest (bad campaigner, economy favored the incumbent, and so on) was the malign dynamic that had ended so many other worthy careers: The voters had ordered him to get tough on the deficit; he had done it; they did not like it, and Clinton ruthlessly exploited that vulnerability. For Dole and his friend Pete Domenici, deficit hawks who had spent years trying to tame the monstrous problem they helped unleash in 1981, it was another bitter loss, all the more galling for the fact that the deficit was now down to its lowest level in years, and the president who had frustrated and obstructed them was taking the credit. The good news was temporary, though; unless someone took bolder measures than those that had helped cost Dole the presidency, the deficit was on track to go shooting back up to appalling heights in little more than a decade. By now, Dole and Clinton and hundreds of their colleagues and forebears had wrestled with the problem and come away with little permanent progress, but awful scars. For all of them, the prize had remained beyond reach, a taunting and vexing mirage shimmering on the political horizon.

NOTE ON SOURCES

This book is the work of two journalists, and the heart of what is here comes from our own day-to-day coverage of Congress, the budget, and the appropriations process beginning with the 1990 budget summit. We also conducted more than 150 interviews with members of Congress, their staff, administration officials, economists, lobbyists, and others during the three years this book was a work in progress. Most of the quotations here are from our own reporting, but we also draw from stories by colleagues in our own publications—*The Washington Post* and *Congressional Quarterly Weekly Report*—and from the work of many of our other colleagues in print, TV, and radio who covered the budget from Carter to Clinton.

Throughout, we relied in particular on accounts in several publications, notably *The New York Times*, *The Wall Street Journal*, *The Washington Times*, the *Los Angeles Times*, *The Boston Globe*, *Time*, *Newsweek*, *U.S. News & World Report*, the *National Journal*, the *New Republic*, *The Atlantic Monthly*, *The New Yorker*, and a variety of television and radio news shows from NBC, C-SPAN, PBS, NPR, CBS, ABC, CNN, and Fox.

A starting point for understanding any member of Congress is the superb biographical material in the biennial collections of congressional profiles: *Politics in America* (Congressional Quarterly) and *The Almanac of American Politics* (National Journal); we referred to both frequently. For lucid accounts of past budget struggles, we turned again and again to the annual volumes of the *Congressional Quarterly Almanac*.

For historical data and budget analysis, we relied heavily on publications from the Congressional Budget Office (CBO), the White House's Office of

Management and Budget (OMB), and the president's Council of Economic Advisers (CEA). The OMB's sprawling annual budget documents offer a huge compilation of historical data and analysis; the CBO's *Economic and Budget Outlook,* which appears each spring, is extremely valuable, as are the CBO's annual *Analysis of the President's Budgetary Proposals,* the annual economic outlook updates, and the topical studies that the CBO issues from time to time. The annual *Economic Report of the President* and its companion report, both from the CEA, contain invaluable historical economic data and analysis. For details about complex entitlement programs such as Social Security, Medicare, and Medicaid, we turned to past volumes of the House Ways and Means Committee's invaluable *Green Book.*

For help in understanding the complex federal budget process, we turned to Stanley Collender, *The Guide to the Federal Budget* (Urban Institute, published annually), and—when the questions became extremely arcane and complex—to Bill Dauster, *Budget Process Law Annotated,* 1993 edition (Senate Budget Committee, 1993).

We are indebted to several private organizations for their budget analysis and ideas. These include the Cato Institute, the Center on Budget and Policy Priorities, the Committee for a Responsible Federal Budget, the Concord Coalition, the Heritage Foundation, and the Progressive Policy Institute.

For polling, we relied primarily on major polls conducted for the leading media organizations, which are generally cited in the text: Washington Post/ABC News; Wall Street Journal/NBC News; and New York Times/CBS News. We also found useful the Gallup Organization's compilation of its polling from 1935 through 1994.

We learned from and were influenced by a number of books, most of which we cite below in notes on the particular chapter for which they were most helpful. Two stand out, however. In our view, the single budget book before which all others bow is Joseph White and Aaron Wildavsky, *The Deficit and the Public Interest: The Search for Responsible Budgeting in the 1980s* (University of California Press, 1989), a Brobdingnagian work that spans the era from Carter to Bush, recounts in astonishing detail almost every twist of policymaking during those years, and yet manages to do it in a pungent and consistently readable way. It is the most comprehensive and most useful discussion of the budget and tax-policy wars of the Reagan era and the indispensable foundation for any understanding of what went wrong. As journalists, we were lucky to be able to learn from a handful of superb economists who can also write extremely well; the dean of that select group, in our view, is former Nixon chief economist Herbert Stein, whose writing is always pointed and thought provoking. Among his many books, his *Presidential Economics: The Making of Economic Policy from Roosevelt to Rea-*

gan and Beyond (Simon & Schuster, 1984) offers an excellent guide to thinking (and writing) about the budget.

Rather than cite specific interviews, we include here a list of most of those we spoke with in preparing this book (a few insisted on complete anonymity). In most cases, we sat with the subject for an hour or more at least once and later transcribed the resulting conversation.

Current and former members of Congress: Bill Archer, Dick Armey, Max Baucus, Lloyd Bentsen, Sherwood Boehlert, John Boehner, David Bonior, David Boren, John Breaux, Sam Brownback, Robert Byrd, John Chafee, Thad Cochran, John Danforth, Tom Daschle, Dennis DeConcini, Tom De-Lay, Bob Dole, Pete Domenici, Tom Downey, Vic Fazio, Tom Foley, Barney Frank, Bill Frenzel, Richard Gephardt, Sam Gibbons, Newt Gingrich, Phil Gramm, Charles Grassley, Judd Gregg, Kent Hance, Orrin Hatch, Mark Hatfield, Ernest "Fritz" Hollings, Steny Hoyer, Tim Hutchinson, J. Bennett Johnston, John Kasich, Jack Kemp, Bob Kerrey, Bob Livingston, Trent Lott, Dave McCurdy, David McIntosh, Robert Matsui, George Mitchell, Sonny Montgomery, Daniel Patrick Moynihan, Mark Neumann, David Obey, Bob Packwood, Tim Penny, David Price, Bill Richardson, Pat Roberts, Dan Rostenkowski, Marge Roukema, Warren Rudman, Martin Olav Sabo, Jim Sasser, Christopher Shays, Jim Slattery, Charles Stenholm, Billy Tauzin, Bill Thomas, Fred Upton, Robert Walker, Henry Waxman, Vin Weber, Ed Whitfield, Jim Wright.

Current and former congressional staff members: Eileen Baumgartner, Steve Bell, Jeff Biggs, Tony Blankley, Sheila Burke, Arne Christenson, Bruce Cuthbertson, Bill Dauster, Peter Davis, Jack Devore, Gail Fosler, Ed Gillespie, Craig Hanna, John Hilley, Steve Hilton, Bill Hoagland, Jim Jaffe, Keith Kennedy, Richard Kogan, George Kundanis, Ed Kutler, Rob Leonard, Robert Lighthizer, Ed Lorenzen, Nicholas Masters, Rick May, Dan Meyer, Lawrence O'Donnell, Tom O'Donnell, Steve Patterson, Billy Pitts, Wendell Primus, Larry Stein, Chris Ullman.

Current and former administration officials and staff members: Roger Altman, Martin Anderson, Howard Baker, James Baker, Alan Blinder, Michael Boskin, Nicholas Calio, Richard Darman, Kenneth Duberstein, Marlin Fitzwater, Max Friedersdorf, Pat Griffin, Larry Haas, Ron Klain, Lawrence Kudlow, Mike McCurry, Leon Panetta, Howard Paster, Bruce Reed, Robert Reich, Alice Rivlin, Robert Rubin, Thomas Scully, Sam Sessions, Gene Sperling, George Stephanopoulos, Barry Toiv, Laura Tyson, Murray Weidenbaum.

Economists, pollsters, independent analysts, political consultants, interest-group officials, party officials, and others: Chuck Alston, Haley Barbour, Paul Begala, Karlyn Bowman, Patrick Burns, James Carville, Stanley Collender, Chris Deering, Stanley Greenberg, Jerry Jasinowski, Charles Jones,

William Kristol, Frank Luntz, Robert McIntyre, Thomas Mann, Will Marshall, Mahlon Martin, William Niskanen, Norman Ornstein, Rudolph Penner, Martha Phillips, Jerry Prete, Ralph Reed, Robert Reischauer, John Rother, Allen Schick, Rob Shapiro, Herbert Stein, Paul Tsongas, Carol Cox Wait, Charls Walker, Mark Weinberger, John White, Joseph White.

Introduction

A highly useful comparative ranking of the deficits and national debts of the seven leading industrial democracies and a broader ranking of some two dozen industrial democracies is found in *World Economic Outlook* (International Monetary Fund, 1996).

"Calculations during the political wars of 1995" refers to an article by Stephen Pearlstein, "On Balance, Budget Deal Could Offer a $1,000 Bonus" (*Washington Post,* January 4, 1996), that quotes economists and budget analysts who predict that a balanced budget would eventually reduce interest rates by some 1.5 percent, lower interest payments on the national debt, raise economic growth slightly, and generate a "bonus" of about $1,000 a year for every American. One catch is that the bonus would go not to those who agree to fewer government services and/or higher taxes now but to this generation's children and grandchildren.

The nightmare scenario of rocketing deficits and national debt when the baby boom generation begins to retire early in the next century has been described in many places; this account comes from *The Economic and Budget Outlook: Fiscal Years 1997–2006* (CBO, 1996). For the books that helped shape our larger views on deficit politics, see Chapter 3.

Chapters 1 and 2

The core of both chapters derives from our own coverage of Congress and from extensive interviews with many of the principal players.

Our portrait of House Speaker Newt Gingrich was greatly aided by an excellent series on Gingrich in *The Washington Post* in December 1994. Other pieces that contributed to our understanding of the Speaker include reporter Adam Clymer's "House Revolutionary" (*New York Times Magazine,* August 23, 1992) and William Sternberg's "Housebreaker: Newt Gingrich" (*Atlantic Monthly,* June 1993).

The Washington Post series "Inside the Revolution" by David Maraniss and Michael Weisskopf, which was later published as a book, *"Tell Newt to Shut Up!"* (Simon & Schuster, 1996), was of enormous help. Maraniss and Weisskopf gained extraordinary access to the inner councils of the House Republican leadership and were able to produce lively and detailed contemporaneous accounts of key moments throughout 1995 and into early 1996. Similarly, Elizabeth Drew offered a vivid insiders' look into the 1995–96 budget wars in *Showdown: The Struggle Between the Gingrich Congress and the Clinton White House* (Simon & Schuster, 1996). Drew's portrayals of the inner workings and deliberations of the congressional Republicans and Democrats and the Clinton White House were an invaluable resource. For extremely helpful insights into the origins and nature of the Republican electoral revolution, we turned to Dan Balz and Ronald Brownstein, *Storming the Gates: Protest Politics and the Republican Revival* (Little, Brown, 1996).

Two articles by Jeff Shear were particularly useful in describing the influence of Republican moderates in the Senate: "The Senate's Budget Kingpins—Republicans Mark O. Hatfield, Pete V. Domenici, and Bob Packwood" (*National Journal,* February 11, 1995) and "Can-Do Domenici" (*National Journal,* June 10, 1995). Robert Merry's profile of Domenici, "Budget Shepherd: Sen. Domenici, Earnest and Frugal, Poses Test for Reagan Fiscal Plan" (*Wall Street Journal,* January 25, 1982), provided additional insights into Domenici's character. We also found useful a pair of articles by Ruth Shalit, "Dole vs. Newt: The Battle Begins" (*GQ,* June 1995) and "Bob Dole's Vision Thing" (*New York Times Magazine,* March 5, 1995).

Chapter 3

The account of the Rostenkowski incident was pieced together from interviews with Rostenkowski, his staff, and other participants and from accounts by print and TV reporters on the scene.

Much of our information on the ill-fated 1988 Medicare Catastrophic Coverage Act came from accounts by Julie Rovner in *Congressional Quarterly Weekly Report* and in "Congress's 'Catastrophic' Attempt to Fix Medicare" in Thomas E. Mann and Norman J. Ornstein, editors, *Intensive Care: How Congress Shapes Health Policy* (American Enterprise Institute/Brookings Institution, 1995).

For our recounting of the pre-Reagan history of American budgeting, we are indebted to many works. We found the best single account of the history of the budget, the evolution of the modern deficit, and the nation's ambivalence toward a balanced budget to be James D. Savage, *Balanced Budgets and American Politics* (Cornell University Press, 1988), from which we took the 1690 incident that is described as the birth of deficit spending. We also found extremely useful information in John H. Makin and Norman J. Ornstein, *Debt and Taxes: How America Got into Its Budget Mess and What to Do About It* (Times Books, 1994); Benjamin M. Friedman, *Day of Reckoning: The Consequences of American Economic Policy* (Random House, 1988); Robert Heilbroner and Peter Bernstein, *The Debt and the Deficit: False*

Alarms/Real Possibilities (Norton, 1989); Robert Eisner, *The Misunderstood Economy: What Counts and How to Count It* (Harvard Business School Press, 1994); John Cranford, *Budgeting for America* (Congressional Quarterly, 1989); Allen Schick, *The Federal Budget: Politics, Policy, Process* (Brookings Institution, 1995); Richard Reeves, *President Kennedy: Profile of Power* (Simon & Schuster, 1993); Hobart Rowen, *Self-Inflicted Wounds: From LBJ's Guns and Butter to Reagan's Voodoo Economics* (Times Books, 1994); Dennis S. Ippolito, *Uncertain Legacies: Federal Budget Policy from Roosevelt Through Reagan* (University Press of Virginia, 1990); Charles L. Schultze, *Memos to the President: A Guide Through Macroeconomics for the Busy Policymaker* (Brookings Institution, 1992); and William Greider, *Secrets of the Temple: How the Federal Reserve Runs the Country* (Simon & Schuster, 1987).

Statistics on Social Security and Medicare come from C. Eugene Steuerle and Jon M. Bakija, *Retooling Social Security for the 21st Century: Right and Wrong Approaches to Reform* (Urban Institute, 1994). Historic tax data here and elsewhere are taken from documents published by the CBO and from Joseph A. Pechman, *Federal Tax Policy,* 5th edition (Brookings Institution, 1987).

Chapter 4

We made extensive use of the rich lode of books and newspaper and magazine articles that describe the Reagan revolution and the emergence of the modern-era deficit. We supplemented those materials with extensive interviews with former Reagan administration officials, current and former members of Congress, lobbyists, and economists who played a direct or peripheral role in the passage of Reagan's 1981 tax and budget package.

The single most readable and opinionated account of the Reagan budget revolution from the inside is David A. Stockman, *The Triumph of Politics: Why the Reagan Revolution Failed* (Harper & Row, 1986), which offers the view of the man who tried to mastermind the revolution but lost control. We relied heavily on several other books, including Laurence I. Barrett, *Gambling with History* (Doubleday, 1983); Lou Cannon, *Reagan* (Putnam, 1982) and *President Reagan—the Role of a Lifetime* (Simon & Schuster, 1991); William A. Niskanen, *Reaganomics: An Insider's Account of the Policies and the People* (Oxford University Press, 1988); Martin Anderson, *Revolution* (Harcourt Brace Jovanovich, 1988); Haynes Johnson, *Sleepwalking Through History* (Norton, 1990); Robert L. Bartley, *The Seven Fat Years—and How to Do It Again* (Free Press, 1992); Paul Craig Roberts, *The Supply-Side Revolution* (Harvard University Press, 1984); Murray Weidenbaum, *Rendezvous with Reality* (Basic Books, 1988); Hedrick Smith, *The Power Game* (Ballantine Books, 1988); Paul Krugman, *Peddling Prosperity* (Norton, 1994); Jack

Kemp, *The American Renaissance* (Harper & Row, 1979); Charles R. Hulten and Isabel V. Sawhill, editors, *The Legacy of Reaganomics: Prospects for Long-Term Growth* (Urban Institute, 1984); and Thomas P. O'Neill, Jr., and William Novak, *Man of the House: The Life and Political Memoirs of Speaker Tip O'Neill* (Random House, 1987).

David Frum's important analysis of the Republican Party, *Dead Right* (Basic Books, 1994), offered insights into deficit politics and the Republicans' repeated failure to follow through on promises to cut government spending and entitlements. Franklin C. Spinney's pamphlet *Defense Power Games* (Fund for Constitutional Government, 1990) provides a useful account of Reagan's defense-spending buildup and explains how, through extraordinary persistence and sleight of hand, Defense Secretary Caspar Weinberger transformed Reagan's 1980 campaign pledge to increase defense spending by 5 percent a year into increases twice that big. Other helpful references include Richard Ben Cramer's brilliant book on the 1988 presidential campaign, *What It Takes* (Random House, 1992), Donald T. Regan's *For the Record* (Harcourt Brace Jovanovich, 1988), and *Current Biography Yearbook, 1987* (Wilson, 1987).

William Greider's "The Education of David Stockman" *(Atlantic Monthly,* December 1981), a seminal piece exposing the Reagan administration's turmoil over its new tax and budget policies in 1981, was indispensable, as were Sidney Blumenthal's articles on Reagan and his administration, particularly "The Sorcerer's Apprentices" *(The New Yorker,* July 19, 1993).

For biographical information on Bob Dole, we turned repeatedly to Jake H. Thompson, *Bob Dole: The Republicans' Man for All Seasons* (Donald I. Fine, 1994).

Chapter 5

Though 1985 was one of the most critical periods in modern budget history, book authors have left it largely alone, and there are few accounts beyond those from daily, weekly, and monthly journalism—perhaps because everyone was so disillusioned and so exhausted when it was over that he or she simply wanted to forget it and move on. Also true is that what happened the following year—the 1986 tax-reform debate—was the more satisfying story of a major fiscal-policy initiative that succeeded, as was thoroughly explored in Jeffrey Birnbaum and Alan Murray, *Showdown at Gucci Gulch* (Times Books, 1987). There are accounts of the 1985 fiasco and the rise of Gramm-Rudman in broader works, such as White and Wildavsky's *Deficit and the Public Interest* and Makin and Ornstein's *Debt and Taxes,* but the day-to-day reporting in major newspapers and summaries in the newsweeklies, *Congressional Quarterly Weekly Report,* and the *National Jour-*

nal were our most detailed sources. We also relied on extensive interviews with participants to try to re-create what happened.

In an effort to understand Domenici's role better, we turned to Richard F. Fenno, Jr., *The Emergence of a Senate Leader: Pete Domenici and the Reagan Budget* (Congressional Quarterly, 1991), which focuses chiefly on earlier years but gives an account of 1985 and provides superb insights into Domenici the man. Fenno had steady access to the usually highly guarded Domenici for an extended period, and his portrait is fascinating.

Chapter 6

There is a thorough and informative account of Bush's wasted honeymoon year of 1989 in Lawrence Haas, *Running on Empty: Bush, Congress, and the Politics of a Bankrupt Government* (Business One Irwin, 1990). For insights into President George Bush, we turned to Michael Duffy and Dan Goodgame, *Marching in Place* (Simon & Schuster, 1992). We also drew material from Daniel P. Franklin, *Making Ends Meet: Congressional Budgeting in the Age of Deficits* (Congressional Quarterly, 1993); Charles Kolb, *White House Daze: The Unmaking of Domestic Policy in the Bush Years* (Free Press, 1994); Dan Quayle, *Standing Firm: A Vice Presidential Memoir* (HarperCollins, 1994); and Peggy Noonan, *Life, Liberty, and the Pursuit of Happiness* (Random House, 1994).

Chapter 7

We relied on numerous books and publications, including Jack W. Germond and Jules Witcover, *Mad as Hell: Revolt at the Ballot Box* (Warner Books, 1993), a thorough examination of the 1992 presidential campaign; Bob Woodward, *The Agenda: Inside the Clinton White House* (Simon & Schuster, 1994), the bible for understanding Clinton's first year in office; Bill Clinton and Al Gore, *Putting People First: How We Can All Change America* (Times Books, 1992), the Clinton campaign manifesto; Ross Perot, *United We Stand—How We Can Take Back Our Country* (Hyperion, 1992), which includes Perot's budget proposals; Robert Reich, *The Work of Nations: Preparing Ourselves for 21st-Century Capitalism* (Knopf, 1991), which strongly influenced Clinton's thinking on economic issues; Richard E. Cohen, *Changing Course in Washington: Clinton and the New Congress* (Macmillan College, 1994); Stanley B. Greenberg, *Middle Class Dreams: The Politics and Power of the New American Majority* (Times Books, 1995); Alice M. Rivlin, *Reviving the American Dream* (Brookings Institution, 1992); Jonathan Rauch, *Demosclerosis: The Silent Killer of American Government* (Times Books, 1994); and Stanley B. Greenberg, "The Road to Realignment: The Democrats and the

Perot Voters" (research prepared for the Democratic Leadership Council, July 1, 1993).

We also made extensive use of *Washington Post* political and economic coverage of the 1992 campaign and its aftermath. Financial reporter Steven Mufson produced a highly informative analysis during the New Hampshire primary, contrasting the economic views of Bill Clinton and Paul Tsongas *(Washington Post,* March 9, 1992). Michael Kramer's "Moving In—the Inside Story of How Clinton Faced His First Crisis and What It Says About His Leadership Style" (*Time,* January 4, 1993) provided a vivid account of the December 1992 Blair House meeting, when advisers told President-elect Clinton that the deficit was more of a problem than they had thought.

In the run-up to the 1994 midterm congressional elections, reporter Michael Weisskopf wrote a revealing profile of Republican pollster Frank Luntz, "Playing on the Public Pique" (*Washington Post,* October 27, 1994), while Michael Kelly provided vivid insights into the evolution of the House Republicans' Contract with America and the Democrats' ineffective efforts to counter it, in "Clinton's Escape Clause" (*The New Yorker,* October 24, 1994). Reporter Jackie Calmes wrote from Michigan about why Clinton wasn't getting any credit for the improved economy, in "If It's the Economy, Why Isn't Bill Clinton More Popular, Stupid?" (*Wall Street Journal,* October 10, 1994). James Fallows offered an insightful analysis of why President Clinton's health-care reform plan failed, in "A Triumph of Misinformation" (*Atlantic Monthly,* January 1995). Columnist Paul A. Gigot, in a post-election essay, wrote that the vanquished congressional Democrats were resorting to the politics of envy and class warfare to try to regain some momentum, in "Democrats Hire New Pollster: Robin Hood" (*Wall Street Journal,* December 16, 1994). Reporter David Rosenbaum noted that instead of trying to persuade the public that the deficit is a corrosive force that must be brought under control, Clinton opted for a post-election course in 1994 that subordinated deficit reduction to tax cuts, in "About-Face by Clinton" (*New York Times,* December 16, 1994).

Chapters 8 and 9

The material here comes mostly from our own reporting and from extensive follow-up interviews with participants. We also drew on reporting by our colleagues, notably Jeff Shear's piece on the Republican freshman class, "United They Stand" (*National Journal,* October 28, 1995). Reporter David Rogers provided an account of the GOP's first year in power, in "General Newt: GOP's Rare Year Owes Much to How Gingrich Disciplined the House" (*Wall Street Journal,* December 18, 1995). Reporter Todd Purdum's piece, "Stalwart in Defense of His Shrinking Turf" (*New York Times,*

December 10, 1995), shows how Clinton moved steadily closer to GOP aims
while preserving just enough of his carefully culled priorities to claim plau-
sibly that he was protecting them. Jane Mayer's "Lonely Guy, Why President
Clinton Is Partying Alone" (*The New Yorker,* October 30, 1995) provides
telling insights into the influence wielded by White House political guru
Dick Morris.

In addition to Maraniss and Weisskopf's *"Tell Newt to Shut Up!"* and
Drew's *Showdown,* both of which contain richly detailed accounts of the final budget negotiations on Capitol Hill and at the White House, we consulted Haynes Johnson and David Broder, *The System: The American Way of
Politics at the Breaking Point* (Little, Brown, 1996), a thorough discussion of
how Clinton's ambitious health-care reform plan came to grief, and Kenneth T. Walsh, *Feeding the Beast* (Random House, 1996), an inside look at
the Clinton White House with an emphasis on the administration's relations with the press.

INDEX

Abdnor, Jim, 140
Agenda, The (Woodward), 241
Aid to Families with Dependent
    Children (AFDC), 91, 129
air-traffic control, 160
Altman, Roger, 192, 196, 205
American Association of Retired
    Persons (AARP), 31, 237
American Hospital Association, 237
American Revolution, 74
American Society of Newspaper
    Editors, 201
Andrews Air Force Base, budget
    negotiations at, 172–75
Anthony, Beryl, 165–66
Arab oil embargo, 95
Archer, Bill, 259
    and CBO-and-seven proposal, 297
    on Republican seven-year budget-
    deficit reduction plan, 19
    on spending cuts, 43
    on tax cuts, 63
Armey, Dick, 231
    and CBO-and-seven proposal, 267,
    270, 272, 284–87, 293–97, 299

Clinton budget deficits and, 223
comparisons between Kasich and,
    39
and conflict between Kasich and
    Livingston, 37–38
Republican-precipitated
    government shutdown, 234,
    241–42, 244, 260–61
on Republican seven-year budget-
    deficit reduction plan, 17–18,
    23
on spending cuts, 43
XDU meetings and, 43
Ashcroft, John, 50

Baker, Howard, 128, 134–35
    on Reagan budget deficits, 60
    on Reagan tax cuts, 103
Baker, James:
    Bush budget deficits and, 158
    Reagan budget deficits and, 113,
    117, 121, 150–51
balanced-budget amendment, 15
    Clinton budget deficits and, 207,
    225

balanced-budget amendment
    (*cont'd*)
  defeat of, 22, 56–57, 64, 73
  delays in vote on, 55–56
  history of congressional debate
      on, 51–52
  Jefferson on, 86
  potential effectiveness of, 51
  and Republican seven-year
      budget-deficit reduction plan,
      22
  in Senate, 46–48, 50–57
Barbour, Haley, 226, 231, 258
  on Republican seven-year
      budget-deficit reduction plan,
      31–32, 35
Bartley, Robert, 150
Baucus, Max:
  Clinton budget deficits and, 214
  Republican-precipitated
      government shutdown and, 231
Begala, Paul, 191, 193
Bell, Steve, 61, 136–39
Bellmon, Henry, 301
Bentsen, Lloyd:
  Bush budget deficits and, 173–74
  Clinton budget deficits and, 205,
      209, 213–14, 217
Blankley, Tony, 229, 236–37, 252,
      262, 294, 298–99
Bliley, Tom, 43
Blinder, Alan, 207–8
Blitzer, Wolf, 250
Boehlert, Sherwood, 252
Boehner, John, 230
  and CBO-and-seven proposal,
      282–84, 286, 294
  Republican-precipitated
      government shutdown and,
      244, 254
  on Republican seven-year budget-
      deficit reduction plan, 18, 41–42
  XDU meetings and, 41–42
Boll Weevils:
  Reagan budget deficits and, 111–
      17

Stenholm and, 111–12
bond market:
  and CBO-and-seven proposal,
      269, 277, 300
  Clinton budget deficits and, 205,
      208, 218, 223–24
Bonior, David, 9, 45, 271
Bowles, Erskine, 249
Brady, Nick, 161, 172, 175
Breaux, John, 114–15, 217
Brookings Institution, 186, 204
Browder, Glen, 275
Brownback, Sam, 254
budget balancing, 15, 84
  in Arkansas, 190–91
  Carter on, 95
  Clinton's ten-year plan for, 250–
      55, 264, 274
  dangers of, 74, 89–91
  in history of deficit spending, 90,
      92, 96
  impact of Republicans on, 3,
      6–8
  Kennedy on, 92
  Keynes on, 90
  as moral issue, 86
  pay-as-you-go rule in, 184
  political polarization of, 12
  Reagan on, 99–101, 104, 106, 115,
      121–22
  Republican-precipitated
      government shutdown and,
      231–65
  of states, 89
  Stenholm on, 110, 117–18
  Stockman on, 99–100, 104
budget-balancing reconciliation
    bills, 28, 70–74
"Budget Deficit Forecasts Under
    PPF (Putting People First)
    Policies," 203
budget deficits, 4, 8–13, 84
  of Bush, 26–27, 39, 154, 156–87,
      191, 193, 198–200, 202, 206,
      209–10, 224, 229, 266–67, 269,
      273, 276

Bush's no-new-tax pledge and,
   156–61, 163–70, 172–73, 180,
   185–86
of Carter, 21–22, 119, 121, 129,
   133, 150, 152
catastrophic projections for, 11–
   12
CBO-and-seven proposal for, 266–
   303
of Clinton, 12, 17, 23, 31, 40,
   44–45, 49, 135–36, 184–86,
   189–302
Gramm-Rudman-Hollings law
   and, 17, 24, 51, 147–48,
   150–52, 157–60, 183, 186–87,
   269
as long-term threat, 23–24
moderate Republicans on, 57–58
as moral issue, 10
obsession over, 10
political polarization of, 9, 12
popular doomsday arguments
   against, 133
public opinion on, 10–11, 15, 19,
   23, 41–42, 45, 62, 160, 182,
   191, 194, 224–26
of Reagan, 16–17, 21–22, 48–49,
   52, 60–62, 99–101, 103–7, 110–
   26, 129–54, 157, 162, 168–69,
   185, 190–91, 199–201, 203, 209,
   218, 225–26, 229, 234
Republican-precipitated
   government shutdown and,
   245–46, 259
Republican seven-year plan for,
   14–24, 26–33, 35–45, 48, 56–59,
   62–63, 65–67, 73, 103, 107–9,
   241, 259, 264–303
Rostenkowski's meetings on, 76
Stenholm on, 112
of Truman, 152, 226, 300
of U.S. vs. other nations, 9
XDU meetings on, 40–44
Burke, Sheila, 244
   in House-Senate budget
   reconciliation, 71–72

Republican unity meeting and, 227
Bush, George, 31, 35, 74, 82, 120,
   154–87, 243, 246
background of, 156, 170, 172
on balanced-budget amendment,
   51
budget deficits of, 26–27, 39, 154,
   156–87, 191, 193, 198–200, 202,
   206, 209–10, 224, 229, 266–67,
   269, 273, 276
capital gains tax fight and, 166,
   171–73, 176, 180
clashes between Mitchell and,
   171–72
Clinton budget deficits and, 23,
   191, 193
comparisons between Clinton
   and, 204
comparisons between Mitchell
   and, 170, 172
comparisons between Reagan
   and, 156
economic growth under, 224
Gingrich's dislike for, 169–70, 185
government shutdown under, 244
no-new-taxes pledge of, 63–64,
   154–61, 163–70, 172–73, 180,
   185–86, 254, 273–74
presidential campaigns of, 60, 64,
   154–57, 167, 172, 182, 191,
   196–98, 200, 202
Reagan budget deficits and, 131,
   141, 218
on Reaganomics, 104
Reagan's relationship with, 154–
   57
retirement of, 172
on tax cuts, 64
Byrd, Robert C.:
   on balanced-budget amendment,
   51, 56
   Bush budget deficits and, 174–75
   on Dole's delaying tactics, 56

Calio, Nick, 166–67
capital gains taxes, 152

capital gains taxes (*cont'd*)
 Bush budget deficits and, 166,
  171–73, 176, 180
 Dole on, 69–70
 Republican seven-year budget-
  deficit reduction plan and, 62,
  65
Carter, Jimmy, 10–11, 82, 95–96,
 170, 202
 budget deficits of, 21–22, 119,
  121, 129, 133, 150, 152
 debt interest under, 10
 on defense, 108, 137
 in history of deficit spending, 96,
  98
Carville, James, 193, 245, 275
catastrophic-care legislation,
 75–81
 protests against, 78–81
 Rostenkowski on, 75–80
Catholic Charities, 77
Cato Institute, 67
CBS and CBS News, 69–70, 244,
 269
Chafee, John, 57, 231–32
child-care credits, 70
Christenson, Arne, 241–42, 280
Christian Coalition, 71, 215, 242
Citizens for a Sound Economy, 215
Citizens for Tax Justice, 127
Civil War:
 deficit spending in, 87, 91
 tax increases during, 225
Clinton, Bill, 3–7, 157
 background of, 189–91
 on balanced-budget amendment,
  53
 on budget, 3, 6–7, 12
 budget deficits of, 12, 17, 23, 31,
  40, 44–45, 49, 135–36, 184–86,
  189–302
 Bush budget deficits and, 167,
  184–86
 and CBO-and-seven proposal,
  267–71, 273–77, 280–89,
  291–303

character of, 194
charisma of, 6
comparisons between Bush and,
 204
defense spending and, 108, 192,
 195–97, 202, 209–10
DeLay's disdain for, 3–7
Domenici's budget resolution
 and, 68
economic acumen of, 188–89, 194
economic growth under, 224,
 249–50, 277–78
ethical problems of, 194, 244
Georgetown University address of,
 188–89, 194
Gingrich's back-channel talks
 with, 252–55
Gingrich's criticisms of, 233
gubernatorial campaigns of, 244,
 247
health-care reform plan of, *see*
 health-care reform
on investment spending, 191–93,
 196–97, 203–4, 225
national service program of,
 47–48
Pearl Harbor budget proposal of,
 292
popularity of, 232–33, 269
presidential campaigns of, 167,
 185, 188–98, 200–204, 211,
 244–45, 248, 286, 299, 303
Republican-precipitated
 government shutdown and,
 232–33, 235, 237, 239–41,
 243–55, 258–65, 269, 276
on Republican seven-year
 budget-deficit reduction plan,
 28, 31–32, 62, 109
and Republican takeover of
 Congress, 239–42, 245–47
resilience of, 5–6
sketching psychological profile of,
 241–43
State of the Union Addresses of,
 248, 297

taxes and, 100, 188, 190–91,
193–97, 203–5, 209–10, 212–16,
218–20, 223–26
ten-year balanced-budget plan of,
250–55, 264, 274
University of Pennsylvania address
of, 194–95
veto power of, 28
Clinton, Hillary Rodham, 192, 225,
244, 260–61
CNN, 250
Cold War, 97
peace dividend at end of, 195,
209–10
college loans, 82
Collender, Stanley, 300
Commerce Department, Ark., 191
Common Cause, 25
Comprehensive Employment and
Training Act (CETA), 107
Concord Coalition, 67
Conference Board, 61
Congress, U.S.:
budget process of, 28–29
history of debate on balanced-
budget amendment in, 51–52
Joint Committee on Taxation of,
176
see also House of Representatives,
U.S.; Senate, U.S.
Congressional Budget Office
(CBO), 66
budget deficit projections of,
11–12
Bush budget deficits and, 159–60,
181, 206
Clinton budget deficits and,
197–98, 203–4, 206, 225
Reagan budget deficits and, 60,
144
Republican-precipitated
government shutdown and,
239, 250, 263–65
Republican seven-year
budget-deficit reduction plan
and, 266–303

Conrad, Kent, 55, 208
Conservative Opportunity Society,
128
Constitution, U.S., balanced-budget
amendment to, *see* balanced-
budget amendment
Conte, Silvio, 160
Continental Congress, U.S., 85
Contract with America, 3, 29, 57,
240–41, 247, 259
balanced-budget amendment in,
46–47
on budget balancing, 15
on defense spending, 108
seven-year budget-deficit
reduction plan in, 19, 62
on taxes, 63–64, 116
Coolidge, Calvin, 108
Copernicus Senior Citizens Center,
Rostenkowski's meetings at,
74–79
corporate income tax, 128
and CBO-and-seven proposal, 287
Clinton budget deficits and,
214
comparison between payroll taxes
and, 82
Council of Economic Advisers, 93
Clinton budget deficits and, 207
on Reagan budget deficits,
119–20
Craig, Larry:
balanced-budget amendment
and, 53–54
on Republican seven-year budget-
deficit reduction plan, 57
Crystal Cathedral, 51
Cuomo, Mario, 198
Cuthbertson, Bruce, 285

Daley, Richard J., 80
D'Amato, Alfonse, 50
Darman, Dick, 39
Bush budget deficits and, 158,
161–64, 166, 172, 175–77, 183,
206, 210, 266–67

Darman, Dick (*cont'd*)
  Reagan budget deficits and, 162
  on Reagan tax cuts, 103
Daschle, Tom:
  on balanced-budget amendment,
    52, 55–56
  and CBO-and-seven proposal, 287
  Republican-precipitated
    government shutdown and,
    250–51
Dead Right (Frum), 108
Dean, Howard, 35
Dean, Richard, 7
debt ceilings, 146
defense, 28–29, 60–61
  Bush budget deficits and, 159,
    176–77, 187
  and CBO-and-seven proposal, 268
  Clinton and, 108, 192, 195–97,
    202, 209–10
  in contributing to national debt,
    83
  cuts in, 33, 105–6, 108
  Domenici's budget resolution on,
    67–68
  in history of deficit spending, 94
  House-Senate reconciliation on,
    71
  Perot on, 202
  Reagan and, 99, 101, 105–6, 108,
    115, 119–21, 130, 132, 137,
    139, 142–43, 147–48, 152
  in Republican seven-year budget-
    deficit reduction plan, 22,
    29–30, 62, 108
  Stenholm on, 110
Defense Department, U.S., 261
Deficit Reduction Act (DEFRA), 126
DeLay, Tom:
  on budget deficits, 6, 9
  and CBO-and-seven proposal,
    271, 282, 290
  Clinton disliked by, 3–7
  Republican-precipitated
    government shutdown and,
    256–57

Democratic Congressional
    Campaign Committee, 165–66
Democratic Leadership Council
    (DLC), 189
Democrats and Democratic Party,
    34–35
  on balanced-budget amendment,
    47, 52–53, 55–56
  Boll Weevils and, 111–12
  Bush budget deficits and, 26–27,
    158, 160–82, 185–87, 198–200,
    266, 269, 273, 276
  Bush tax pledge and, 155–57,
    163–66, 170
  in capital gains tax fight, 171, 173
  and CBO-and-seven proposal,
    266–67, 271, 273, 275–76,
    278–80, 282, 287–91, 297–301
  Clinton budget deficits and, 23,
    195–96, 200, 204–5, 208–10,
    210–15, 217–22, 224–26, 242
  Clinton's Georgetown speech on,
    188–89, 194
  defense cuts sponsored by, 33
  on Domenici's budget resolution,
    69–70
  Domenici's fiscal dividend plan
    and, 66–67
  Domenici's reputation among, 59
  and Gingrich's plan for
    Republican control of House,
    24
  and Gingrich vs. Wright, 25
  in history of national debt, 86
  on House-Senate budget
    reconciliation, 74
  Livingston and, 37
  Reagan budget deficits and,
    111–17, 131, 136–39, 142–44,
    147–49, 199
  on Reagan budgets, 106–7
  Reaganomics and, 100
  Republican-precipitated
    government shutdown, 234–35,
    237–43, 245, 247–51, 253, 256,
    258, 261, 263–64

on Republican seven-year budget-deficit reduction plan, 28, 30, 32, 34, 44–45, 57, 62, 109
Republican unity meeting and, 227, 230
school lunch program supported by, 35
on Social Security, 95
on spending cuts, 103, 106–7
Stenholm and, 110–12, 117
on tax cuts, 70
Dingell, John, 240
DiVall, Linda, 34
Dole, Bob, 4, 12–13, 244, 247
in appealing to Hatfield, 53–55
background of, 123–24, 126, 153
on balanced-budget amendment, 46–48, 50, 53–57, 64
Bush budget deficits and, 161, 175, 180
on capital gains tax, 69–70
and CBO-and-seven proposal, 268–69, 271, 275, 279, 282–83, 285, 287–88, 290, 293–96, 302–3
Clinton budget deficits and, 12, 209, 211, 216, 218, 222
on Clinton health-care reform plan, 13
comparisons between Domenici and, 134–35
comparisons between Gingrich and, 47–49, 230–31
on defense, 137
on Domenici, 59
on Domenici's budget resolution, 69–71
Domenici's fiscal dividend plan and, 66, 70
on Packwood's ethics problems, 71
popularity of, 269, 290
presidential campaigns of, 48, 54, 57, 64, 129, 134, 153–54, 209, 229, 232, 264, 285–86, 290, 302–3

Reagan budget deficits and, 48–49, 61, 123, 125–26, 129–37, 139–45, 149, 153–54, 157, 218, 225, 229
on Reagan spending cuts, 124–25
relationship between Gingrich and, 49, 229–30
Republican-precipitated government shutdown and, 231–32, 248–49, 259, 262, 264–65
on Republican seven-year budget-deficit reduction plan, 56–57, 107–8
Republican unity meeting of, 227, 229–31
supply-siders' attacks on, 126
on tax cuts, 64–65, 71–72, 102–3, 107, 125–29
Domenici, Pete, 278–82
background of, 59–60
budget resolution of, 67–71
and CBO-and-seven proposal, 271–72, 278–80, 282, 286–88, 295, 303
Clinton budget deficits and, 218
comparisons between Dole and, 134–35
on defense, 137
fiscal dividend plan of, 66–67, 69–70
in House-Senate budget reconciliation, 70–73
on House-Senate tax cuts, 71–72
Reagan budget deficits and, 60–62, 131–32, 134–40, 142–45, 149, 218, 229
Republican-precipitated government shutdown and, 246, 260, 265
on Republican seven-year budget-deficit reduction plan, 16–17, 57–59, 62–63, 65–66
on spending cuts, 65

Domenici, Pete *(cont'd)*
  taxes and, 62–67, 69–70, 107
Duberstein, Kenneth, 112, 244, 258,
    288, 298
Dukakis, Michael, 157, 165

earned-income tax credits:
  and CBO-and-seven proposal, 295
  Clinton budget deficits and, 214
  Domenici's budget resolution on,
    67
  Republican-precipitated
    government shutdown and, 253
economic growth, 91–93
  under Bush, 224
  under Clinton, 224, 249–50, 277–
    78
  under Reagan, 149–51, 153, 158
  relationship between national
    debt and, 91–92, 97
education, 28, 51
  and CBO-and-seven proposal,
    268, 272, 275, 280
  Clinton budget deficits and, 190–
    92, 195
  Clinton's Georgetown speech on,
    188–89
  House-Senate reconciliation on, 71
  Reagan spending cuts in, 103
  Republican-precipitated
    government shutdown and,
    259, 264
Education Department, U.S., 107
Eisenhower, Dwight D., 80, 92–93
elderly, 11
  on balanced-budget amendment,
    53
  Bush budget deficits and, 177,
    184
  on catastrophic-care legislation,
    75–81
  and CBO-and-seven proposal,
    275, 293, 300, 303
  Clinton budget deficits and, 211
  Domenici's budget resolution on,
    69

in history of deficit spending, 91
  Reagan spending cuts and, 105–6
  Republican-precipitated
    government shutdown and,
    232, 235, 238
  on Republican seven-year budget-
    deficit reduction plan, 30–31,
    34
Engler, John, 41–42, 232
Environmental Protection Agency,
    256
Eshoo, Anna, 221
estate taxes, 116
Exon, Jim, 287

Face the Nation, 69–70
family tax credits, 62–63, 65, 71
farm subsidies, 4, 83
  and CBO-and-seven proposal, 276
  Clinton budget deficits and, 192,
    197
  Domenici's budget resolution on,
    67–68
  House-Senate reconciliation on,
    71
  Reagan budget deficits and, 117,
    140
  Reagan spending cuts on, 104–5
  Republican seven-year budget-
    deficit reduction plan and,
    41–44, 58
  Republican unity meeting and,
    228
  Solomon's budget on, 20
  Stenholm on, 110
  XDU strategy meetings on, 41–44
Federal Hospital Insurance (HI)
    Trust Fund, 32
Federalists, 27, 30
Federal Reserve Board (Fed), 16,
    95, 98, 133
  Bush budget deficits and, 158
  Clinton budget deficits and, 206,
    208, 224
  Reagan budget deficits and,
    118

Federation of American Health
Systems, 237
financial markets, *see* bond market;
stock market
Fitzwater, Marlin, 127
Foley, Tom, 36, 240
Bush budget deficits and, 163–65,
172–73, 175–78, 181, 185,
198–99
Clinton budget deficits and, 205,
216–17, 219–21
Reagan budget deficits and, 148
food stamps, 27, 30, 82–83
Bush budget deficits and, 184
and CBO-and-seven proposal, 286
Reagan budget deficits and, 118,
148
Reagan spending cuts in, 103, 124
in Republican seven-year budget-
deficit reduction plan, 107–8
Ford, Gerald, 21–22, 96, 123, 139
Fosler, Gail, 61
Fox, Jon D., 238
Frank, Barney, 83, 226
Friedersdorf, Max, 113–14
Frost, Robert, 131
Frum, David, 108
full employment deficit, 92

gays-in-the-military policy, 232, 242
Georgetown University, Clinton's
economic address at, 188–89,
194
Gephardt, Dick:
Bush budget deficits and, 162,
164–65, 172, 175–77, 181
and CBO-and-seven proposal,
287, 292, 299
Clinton budget deficits and, 205,
217–18
Republican-precipitated
government shutdown and,
238, 245, 250–51
and Republican takeover of
Congress, 240
Gergen, David, 217

Gillespie, Ed, 22–23, 270
Gingrich, Marianne, 288
Gingrich, Newt, 3–5, 12–33, 128–30,
134–36, 157
background of, 169
balanced-budget amendment
and, 22, 46–47
boldness of, 24
Bush budget deficits and, 26–27,
165–66, 168–70, 178–83,
185–87, 198, 209, 229
Bush disliked by, 169–70, 185
and CBO-and-seven proposal,
267–71, 275–80, 282–85,
287–91, 293–99, 301–2
charisma of, 168
Clinton back-channel talks with,
252–55
Clinton budget deficits and, 12,
186
Clinton criticized by, 233
on Clinton health-care reform
plan, 13
comparisons between Dole and,
47–49, 230–31
comparisons between Michel and,
169
and conflict between Kasich and
Livingston, 37–38
in consolidating power, 36–37
as cult figure, 27
on Dole's approach to tax policy,
125–26
Domenici's budget resolution
and, 70
on House-Senate tax cuts, 71–72
Kasich's temperament and, 39
minority whip election of, 25
moderate Senate Republicans
and, 57
physical appearance of, 25–26
popularity of, 230, 233–34, 269
Reagan budget deficits and, 120,
149
Reaganomics and, 100
on Reagan tax increases, 128

Gingrich, Newt (*cont'd*)
  relationship between Dole and, 49, 229–30
  Republican House control as goal of, 24–27
  Republican-precipitated government shutdown and, 231, 233–34, 236–41, 243–44, 248–49, 252–58, 262–65, 276
  Republican seven-year budget-deficit reduction plan and, 14–24, 26–45, 48, 57, 62, 65–66, 103, 107–8
  Republican unity meeting of, 227–31
  on spending cuts, 103, 107–8
  taped lectures of, 26
  on taxes, 63, 70, 116, 129
  waning power of, 255
  word and phrase selection of, 26
  Wright criticized by, 25
  XDU strategy meetings and, 41–43
Goldman, Sachs, 205
Goldwater, Barry, 98
Gore, Al:
  and CBO-and-seven proposal, 284, 287–88
  Clinton budget deficits and, 207, 213, 218, 223
  Republican-precipitated government shutdown and, 249, 254–55
Graham, Billy, 51
Gramm, Phil:
  balanced-budget amendment and, 22
  Bush budget deficits and, 178
  demeanor of, 145
  on Domenici's budget resolution, 69
  presidential campaigns of, 209
  Reagan budget deficits and, 113–15, 117, 145–47
  Republican unity meeting and, 229

  on tax cuts, 64, 68–70
Gramm-Latta budget, 115, 132
Gramm-Rudman-Hollings anti-deficit law, 17, 24, 51
  Bush budget deficits and, 157–60, 183, 186–87, 269
  failure of, 148, 151
  flaws in, 148
  Reagan budget deficits and, 147–48, 150–52
  spending cuts under, 147–48, 151–52
  zero-sum game created by, 152
Grant, Ulysses S., 87
Grassley, Charles, 143
Gray, Bill, 136, 144
Great Depression, 58, 89–92, 96–98, 101, 109, 123
  balanced-budget amendment during, 52
  and dangers of budget balancing and paying off national debt, 89–91
  national debt on eve of, 87–88
Great Society, 27, 30, 67, 93, 104, 124
Greenberg, Stan, 233
Greenspan, Alan, 133, 139, 206–9
Gregg, Judd, 70
Group of Seven nations, 9

Hamilton, Alexander, 74, 85–86
Hance, Kent, 113–14, 117–18
Hatch, Orrin, 56–57
  on balanced-budget amendment, 50–54, 56
  Reagan budget deficits and, 140
  on Republican seven-year budget-deficit reduction plan, 57
Hatfield, Mark, 60
  on balanced-budget amendment, 47–48, 50–51, 53–57
  Dole's appeals to, 53–55
Hayward, Darnell, 262
Head Start, 105
health-care reform, 5–6, 13, 237–39

and CBO-and-seven proposal, 298, 302
Clinton budget deficits and, 192, 195, 216, 225
Republican-precipitated government shutdown and, 260–61
see also Medicaid; Medicare
health maintenance organizations (HMOs), 34, 109, 235–36, 238
Helgesen, Hazel Ann, 238
Heller, Walter, 92
Helms, Jesse, 140
Heritage Foundation, 67
Hightower, Jack, 115
Hoagland, Bill:
and CBO-and-seven proposal, 279–80, 296
Domenici fiscal dividend plan and, 66–67
on House-Senate budget reconciliation, 72
on Republican seven-year budget-deficit reduction plan, 58
Hollings, Ernest "Fritz":
on Domenici's budget resolution, 69–70
Reagan budget deficits and, 147, 151
see also Gramm-Rudman-Hollings anti-deficit law
Hoover, Herbert, 58, 89–90, 96
House of Representatives, U.S.:
Agriculture Committee of, 42
Appropriations Committee of, 19, 36–37, 47, 51, 255–57, 285
balanced-budget amendment in, 46–48, 50
in budget-balancing reconciliation, 28, 70–74
Budget Committee of, 7, 14, 20–22, 26, 29, 33, 37–40, 42–44, 48, 108, 113–15, 133, 135–36, 144, 158, 174, 204, 211, 223, 226, 257, 271, 278–79, 287, 294–95
Bush budget deficits and, 157–58,

161–66, 168–69, 171, 173, 179, 181, 187, 199–200
on catastrophic-care legislation, 80
and CBO-and-seven proposal, 267–68, 271, 278–79, 282–85, 287, 290–92, 296–99, 301–2
Clinton budget deficits and, 186, 205, 215–16, 218–24
Commerce Committee of, 43
comparisons between Senate and, 49–50, 57
on Contract with America, 29
Domenici's budget resolution and, 68–69
Gingrich's goal for Republican control of, 24–27
Jefferson on, 86
Reagan budget deficits and, 111–17, 136–39, 141–44, 148
Republican-precipitated government shutdown, 234, 236, 238, 240–41, 245, 247–48, 255–61, 263–64
on Republican seven-year budget-deficit reduction plan, 44–45, 57, 62–63, 65–66, 73
Republican takeover of, 4, 13, 20, 23, 25, 35, 40, 59–60, 168, 224, 239–42, 245–47, 254
Republican unity meeting of, 227–31, 233
Rules Committee of, 19, 268
on spending cuts, 71, 73
on tax cuts, 62–66, 68, 70–71, 73
Ways and Means Committee of, 19, 43, 63, 68, 74–75, 95, 113, 116–17, 211, 227, 245, 259, 297
House Republican Conference, 18–19, 230, 237, 282
Human Events, 140
Hussein, Saddam, 172, 180
Hutchinson, Tim, 242

income taxes and income tax rates, 68–70

income taxes and income tax rates
(*cont'd*)
  Bush budget deficits and, 172–73,
    175–76, 180–81
  Clinton budget deficits and, 212,
    214–15
  comparison between payroll taxes
    and, 82
inflation, 9, 101
  budget deficits as cause of, 133
  Bush budget deficits and, 158,
    176, 184
  Clinton budget deficits and, 195,
    224
  defense spending and, 108, 137
  in history of deficit spending,
    94–96, 98
  Medicare impacted by, 33–34
  Reagan budget deficits and, 118–
    19, 121, 141, 143, 152
  Republican-precipitated
    government shutdown and,
    249–50
  Social Security and, 95, 137
  spending cuts and, 103
interest on national debt, 10, 12,
  28–30
  and Bush budget deficits, 180
  and Clinton budget deficits, 189–
    90
  Domenici's budget resolution on,
    67
  and Reagan budget deficits, 119–
    20
  and Reagan spending cuts, 106
  and Republican seven-year
    budget-deficit reduction plan,
    22, 29–30, 66
interest rates, 132
  budget deficits and, 9–10, 12
  Bush budget deficits and, 158
  Clinton budget deficits and, 205,
    207, 223–24
  in history of deficit spending, 98
  impact of budget deficits on, 133
  Reagan budget deficits and, 118

investment spending, 191–93, 196–
  97, 203–4, 225
Iraq, Kuwait invaded by, 172, 180

Jackson, Andrew, 88–89
Jackson, Barry, 237
Japan, tax burdens in, 123
Jefferson, Thomas, 27–28, 50, 74
  on deficit spending, 85–86, 88
job creation, 224
job training, 188–93
  Clinton budget deficits and, 190–
    93
  Clinton's Georgetown speech on,
    188–89
  Republican-precipitated
    government shutdown and, 259
Job Training Partnership Act, 107
Johnson, Lyndon, 5, 8, 124, 271
  on budget deficits, 100
  on defense, 108, 137
  in history of deficit spending, 93,
    97
  Medicare under, 27, 30, 94, 276
  taxes under, 93–94
Joint Chiefs of Staff, 68
Jones, Jim, 114–15

Kasich, John, 7–8
  awards of, 44
  balanced-budget amendment
    and, 22
  budget proposals of, 39–40
  and CBO-and-seven proposal,
    267–73, 276, 278–82, 285–88,
    293–95, 297, 299
  Clinton budget deficits and, 40,
    223, 225–26
  on defense spending, 108
  diligence of, 20
  in House-Senate budget
    reconciliation, 72–73
  hyperactivity of, 39
  importance of credibility to, 17–
    18
  leadership training of, 40

Livingston's conflicts with, 37– 38
Republican-precipitated
    government shutdown and,
    234, 244, 246, 260, 263–65
on Republican seven-year budget-
    deficit reduction plan, 14–22,
    27, 29–30, 37–39, 41–45, 48,
    65, 108–9
Republican unity meeting and,
    229
on spending cuts, 17–18, 30, 33,
    43, 133
temperament of, 38–40
XDU strategy meetings and,
    41–44
Keene, David, 125
Kemp, Jack, 57, 130
    Reagan budget deficits and, 126,
        142, 149–50, 153
    on supply-side economics, 102
Kennedy, John F., 92–94
    on defense, 108, 137
    on deficit spending, 92
    entitlement spending under, 82
    on taxes, 92–93
Kennedy, Keith, 53–54
Kerrey, Bob, 193, 222–23
Keynes, John Maynard, 90–91
    fiscal pump priming advocated
        by, 90, 93, 101–2
    supply-siders vs., 101–2
King, Peter, 263
Kozien, Leona, 79
Krugman, Paul, 150
Kundanis, George, 216, 240
Kutler, Ed, 237
Kuwait, Iraqi invasion of, 172, 180

Labor Department, U.S., 256
labor organizations, 53
Laffer, Arthur, 102
Larry King Live, 200–201
Latta, Del, 115, 132
Lehman Brothers, 205
Levin, Sander, 221
Lighthizer, Bob, 125

Livingston, Bob:
    and CBO-and-seven proposal, 285
    Gingrich's power consolidation
        and, 37
    Kasich's conflicts with, 37–38
    Republican-precipitated
        government shutdown and,
        256–57, 265
    on Republican seven-year budget-
        deficit reduction plan, 19–20
Lott, Trent, 129–30, 247
    and CBO-and-seven proposal,
        272, 279
    on Domenici's budget resolution,
        68
    Reagan budget deficits and, 142,
        149
    Republican-precipitated
        government shutdown and, 253
    on Republican seven-year budget-
        deficit reduction plan, 57
    on tax policy, 63–65, 129
Louisiana Purchase, 86
Luntz, Frank, 15–16, 34

McCain, John, 68
McCurdy, Dave, 217
McCurry, Mike, 268, 275, 296
McGovern, George, 124
McInturff, Bill, 34
McIntyre, Robert, 127
Mack, Connie, 54
McLarty, Thomas "Mack," 217, 219
Madigan, Ed, 168
Magaziner, Ira, 196
Mann, Thomas, 186
Mansfield, Mike, 271
Margolies-Mezvinsky, Marjorie, 49,
    218–21, 238
Marshall, Will, 191
Martin, Mahlon, 191
Massachusetts, deficit spending in,
    84
Matsui, Bob, 228
Matsunaga, Spark, 141
May, Rick, 21, 44

media, *see* press
Medicaid, 4, 6, 13, 129
  budget deficits and, 11
  Bush budget deficits and, 184
  and CBO-and-seven proposal,
    267, 275–76, 278, 280–81,
    291–92, 295, 300
  Clinton budget deficits and, 194,
    197, 210, 224
  Domenici's budget resolution on,
    69
  growth rate of, 184
  origin of, 27, 94
  Reagan budget deficits and, 148
  Republican-precipitated
    government shutdown and,
    231, 234, 249–51, 254, 261, 264
  Republican seven-year budget-
    deficit reduction plan and,
    29–30, 58, 107–9
  Republican unity meeting and,
    228
  Rostenkowski's meetings on, 76
Medicare, 4, 6, 13, 81
  Bush budget deficits and, 158–59,
    174, 176–77, 184
  catastrophic-coverage program in,
    75–81
  and CBO-and-seven proposal,
    267–68, 273–76, 278, 280–82,
    291, 293, 295, 300
  Clinton budget deficits and, 194,
    197, 210–12, 215, 217, 224, 235
  Dole's opposition to, 124
  Domenici's budget resolution on,
    67, 69
  fee-for-service proposal for, 34,
    235–36
  in history of deficit spending, 94,
    97
  House-Senate budget
    reconciliation on, 73–74
  impact of inflation on, 33–34
  origin of, 27, 30, 94, 276
  payroll taxes for, 81–82
  Perot on, 201–2

projected bankruptcy of, 32
Reagan budget deficits and,
  148
Reagan spending cuts and, 105
Republican budget-speak on,
  33–35
Republican-precipitated
  government shutdown and,
  233–39, 246, 248–51, 254,
  259–61, 264
Republican seven-year budget-
  deficit reduction plan and,
  29–34, 43, 58, 62, 107–9
Republican unity meeting and,
  228, 230
Rostenkowski's meetings on, 75–
  77, 79
Stenholm on, 110
taxes on, 176, 202
trustees' reports on, 31–32
XDU meetings on, 43
Meese, Ed, 105–6
Meet the Press, 17, 45, 188–89, 194,
  197, 201–2, 209, 275
Meyer, Dan, 298
Mica, John, 264
Michel, Bob, 24–25, 128
  Bush budget deficits and, 168–69,
    175
  and Gingrich's plan for
    Republican control of House,
    24
  Reagan budget deficits and,
    168
middle class:
  Bush budget deficits and, 174,
    176, 180–81
  Clinton budget deficits and, 191,
    194–96, 204, 209, 212, 215
  Clinton's Georgetown speech on,
    188
  Democrats' support for programs
    for, 35
  entitlement claims of, 81, 83
  Reagan spending cuts in
    programs for, 105

Republican-precipitated
government shutdown and,
232, 245
Republican seven-year budget-
deficit reduction plan and, 62
Republican unity meeting and,
228
Mills, Wilbur, 95
Mitchell, George:
background of, 170, 172
Bush budget deficits and, 163–65,
170–73, 175, 177–78, 181, 187,
210
in capital gains tax fight, 171–73
clashes between Bush and,
171–72
Clinton budget deficits and, 205,
211
comparisons between Bush and,
170, 172
Molinari, Susan, 19
Mondale, Walter, 129–30, 136
Montgomery, Sonny, 113, 115
Morin, Richard, 269
Morning News, 275
Morris, Dick:
and CBO-and-seven proposal, 279
Republican-precipitated
government shutdown and,
247–49, 253
Moseley-Braun, Carol, 47
Muskie, Edmund, 170, 301
Myers, Lisa, 189

national debt:
under Carter, 10
CBO on, 12
Clinton budget deficits and, 189–
90, 207–8
in comparison with overall
economy, 87–88, 91–94, 96,
149–50
dangers in paying off, 89–91
history of, 84–98
interest on, *see* interest on
national debt

Reagan budget deficits and, 119
relationship between economic
growth and, 91–92, 97
relationship between entitlements
and, 83
Republican-precipitated
government shutdown and,
258–59
National Economic Council, 205
National Endowment for the Arts,
41
National Republican Congressional
Committee, 18–19
national service program, 47–48
NBC and NBC News, 17, 45,
188–89, 201–2, 266
NBC News/Wall Street Journal
polls, 233, 269
Neumann, Mark, 238, 257
New Deal, 27, 67, 120
Reagan budgets and, 104
Reagan on, 106
and Republican seven-year
budget-deficit reduction plan,
15, 19
New Hampshire Public Radio, 250
New York *Daily News,* 262–63
New York Post, 167, 263
New York Times, 105, 298
New York Times/CBS News polls,
269
Niskanen, William, 119–20
Nixon, Richard, 93, 94–95, 153, 269
Noonan, Peggy, 156, 167
Nunn, Sam, 52–53
Nussle, Jim, 49

Oak Tree Deal, 143
Obey, David, 117, 251
O'Donnell, Lawrence, 213
Office of Management and Budget
(OMB), 202
and CBO-and-seven proposal,
271–72, 274, 277–78, 291
Clinton budget deficits and, 204,
206

Office of Management and Budget (OMB) (*cont'd*)
  Republican-precipitated government shutdown and, 249–50
oil prices, 95, 172
Oklahoma City bombing, 7, 253
O'Neill, Tip, 25, 111, 116, 142–43
Organization of Petroleum Exporting Countries (OPEC), 95

Packwood, Bob:
  Bush budget deficits and, 180
  ethics problems of, 68–71
  on House-Senate tax deal, 70–71
  on Republican seven-year budget-deficit reduction plan, 57
  on tax cuts, 63–64
Panetta, Leon:
  Bush budget deficits and, 158, 163–64, 174, 266
  and CBO-and-seven proposal, 266–67, 271–75, 278–80, 282, 286–87, 295
  Clinton budget deficits and, 204–5, 207, 210–12, 217, 226
  relationship between Domenici and, 281
  Republican-precipitated government shutdown and, 247–49, 252, 263
Panic of 1837, 89
Parker, Mike, 44
Paxon, Bill, 18–19
PAYGO rule, 184
payroll taxes, 94
  for Medicare, 81–82
  for Social Security, 81–82, 137–38
Pearl Harbor budget proposal, 292
Penner, Rudolph, 277–78
Pennsylvania, University of, Clinton's economic address at, 194–95

Penny, Tim:
  Clinton budget deficits and, 221, 225
  Reagan budget deficits and, 199–200
Perot, H. Ross:
  Bush budget deficits and, 187
  charisma of, 200
  Clinton budget deficits and, 196, 200–201, 205–6
  presidential campaigns of, 8, 84, 196, 200–202
  wrong-headedness of, 201–2
Persian Gulf War, Bush budget deficits and, 181, 183, 185–86, 269
Philadelphia Inquirer, 221
Phillips, Kevin, 233
poor:
  balanced-budget amendment and, 53
  and CBO-and-seven proposal, 275, 293, 300
  Clinton budget deficits and, 214
  Democrats' support for programs for, 35
  Domenici's budget resolution on, 67, 69
  Livingston and, 37
  Reagan spending cuts in programs for, 104–6
  Republican-precipitated government shutdown and, 232, 253
  Republican seven-year budget-deficit reduction plan and, 30, 109
Postal Sevice, U.S., 158–59
post-Cold War peace dividend, 195, 209–10
press, 39–40, 188–91
  Bush budget deficits and, 159, 165, 167, 172, 179–80, 182
  and CBO-and-seven proposal, 266, 270–72, 274–75, 277, 281, 284, 289–90, 294, 298

Clinton budget deficits and, 189–
91, 194, 197, 208–9, 221–23,
226
on conflict between Gingrich and
Kasich, 18
on defeat of balanced-budget
amendment, 56–57
on Domenici's budget resolution,
69–70
on House-Senate budget
reconciliation, 72
on Perot campaign, 200–202
on protests against Rostenkowski,
78–80
Reagan budget deficits and, 113,
115, 123, 150
on Reagan spending cuts, 105
on Reagan tax policy, 128
Republican-precipitated
government shutdown and,
237–38, 243, 248, 250–51, 254,
262–63
on Republican seven-year budget-
deficit reduction plan, 20, 33,
45
and Republican takeover of
Congress, 240–41
Republican unity meeting and,
230
on tax cuts, 64
XDU strategy meetings and, 40
*see also specific newspapers,
magazines, and news shows*
Prete, Jerry, 77
Price Waterhouse, 300
Progressive Policy Institute, 189
public opinion, 10–11
on balanced-budget amendment,
47, 53
Bush budget deficits and, 160,
182
and CBO-and-seven proposal,
268–69, 275, 289–91, 293,
302–3
Clinton budget deficits and, 23,
191, 194, 224–26

on Medicare, 30, 33
Republican-precipitated
government shutdown and,
231–34, 239, 258, 262, 269, 276
on Republican seven-year budget-
deficit reduction plan, 15, 19,
23, 41–42, 45, 62
Republican unity meeting and,
228, 231
see also specific public opinion polls
pump priming, 90, 93, 101–2
Put People First, 197–98, 203–4,
211

Quayle, Dan, 166

Rabin, Yitzhak, 262
Reagan, Ronald, 4, 35–36, 99–158,
206, 217, 243–44, 246, 258, 286,
288, 298, 301
on balanced-budget amendment,
52
Boll Weevils and, 112
budget deficits of, 16–17, 21–22,
48–49, 52, 60–62, 99–101, 103–
7, 110–26, 129–54, 157, 162,
168–69, 185, 190–91, 199–201,
203, 209, 218, 225–26, 229, 234
budgets of, 99–101, 103–4, 106–8,
111–19, 121–23
Bush budget deficits and, 162,
166–71, 185
Bush's relationship with, 154–57
Bush's tax pledge and, 155, 166
charisma of, 169, 228
Clinton budget deficits and, 191
comparisons between Bush and,
156
defense and, 99, 101, 105–6, 108,
115, 119–21, 130, 132, 137,
139, 142–43, 147–48, 152
economic growth under, 149–51,
153, 158
Gingrich's admiration for, 120
in history of deficit spending, 93,
96–98

Reagan, Ronald (*cont'd*)
  moderate Senate Republicans
    and, 57–58
  political skills of, 152–53
  popularity of, 100, 103, 116,
    121–22
  presidential campaigns of, 60,
    129–30, 136–37, 154
  Republican unity meeting of,
    227– 28
  on spending cuts, 99–101, 103–7,
    112, 114–15, 122, 124–25
  State of the Union Addresses of,
    122–23
  Stenholm and, 110–12, 117–18
  on taxes, 81–82, 93, 99–104, 107–
    8, 112–14, 116–19, 121–23,
    125–29, 157
  recessions, 9, 12, 84, 101, 133
  Bush budget deficits and, 172–73,
    182–83, 198, 200
  Clinton budget deficits and, 193,
    207
  deficit spending created by, 95–
    96, 98
  Reagan budget deficits and, 121,
    150–51
  and Republican seven-year
    budget-deficit reduction plan,
    16
Reed, Bruce, 192, 196, 203
Reed, Ralph, 71
Regan, Donald, 113, 144, 147
Reich, Robert, 32
  Clinton budget deficits and, 192–
    93, 196, 203, 208
Reischauer, Robert, 66, 160
  Bush budget deficits and, 185
  and CBO-and-seven proposal, 298
  Republican-precipitated
    government shutdown and, 239
Republican National Committee,
    31, 231, 233, 258
Republicans and Republican Party,
    64, 206
  anti-government zealotry of, 36

on balanced-budget amendment,
    22, 47–48, 50–57, 73
Boll Weevils and, 112
budget balancing impacted by, 3,
    6–8
Bush budget deficits and, 26–27,
    158, 160–62, 164–70, 172, 174–
    76, 178–83, 185, 187, 198–99,
    209, 266, 269, 273
Bush tax pledge and, 155–56,
    165–69
and CBO-and-seven proposal,
    266–71, 273–80, 282–301, 303
Clinton budget deficits and, 23,
    186, 200, 205, 207, 209–10,
    212, 215–16, 218–26
congressional takeover of, 4, 13,
    20, 23, 25, 35, 40, 59–60, 168,
    224, 239–42, 245–47, 254
on Contract with America, 29
on defense spending, 108
on Dole's approach to tax policy,
    126–28
on Domenici's budget resolution,
    67
falling popularity of, 232–33
Gingrich's taped lectures and,
    26
government shutdown
    precipitated by, 231–65, 269,
    276
House control as Gingrich's goal
    for, 24–27
on House-Senate budget
    reconciliation, 73–74
Jefferson on, 86
moderate, 57–58, 63–65
Reagan budget deficits and, 106–
    7, 114–16, 118, 129, 132–33,
    135–46, 148–50, 153, 225
Reaganomics and, 100
seven-year budget-deficit
    reduction plan of, 14–24,
    26–45, 48, 56–59, 62–63,
    65–67, 73, 103, 107–9, 241, 259,
    264–303

on spending cuts, 103, 106–8
Stenholm and, 110
on tax cuts, 62–66, 68, 70
unity meetings of, 227–31, 233
XDU meetings of, 40–44
Revolutionary War, 85–87
Richardson, Bill, 220–21, 247
Rivlin, Alice:
and CBO-and-seven proposal,
271, 278–80
Clinton budget deficits and, 204–
5, 207–8, 210–12
Roberts, Pat, 42–43
Rolling Plains Cotton Growers
Association, 110
Roosevelt, Franklin Delano, 27, 120
budget deficits of, 152
in history of deficit spending,
89–90, 96
Reagan's admiration for, 106
Rostenkowski, Dan, 68–70, 74–81,
98
Clinton budget deficits and, 211
criminal indictment of, 75
ethical problems of, 240
influence of, 75
protests against, 78–80, 238
Reagan budget deficits and, 113,
116–17
Rother, John, 31, 237
Rubin, Robert:
and CBO-and-seven proposal, 274
Clinton budget deficits and, 205
Republican-precipitated
government shutdown and, 249
on Republican seven-year budget-
deficit reduction plan, 32
Rudman, Warren, 143, 147
see also Gramm-Rudman-Hollings
anti-deficit law
Rural Electrification Administration,
140
Russert, Tim, 201–2

Sabo, Martin, 287
Salmon, Matt, 284

Santorum, Rick, 54
Sasser, Jim, 163–64, 209–10
savings-and-loan (S&L) crisis, 21,
159, 182–83
school-lunch program, 27, 30
Democrats' support for, 35
Reagan spending cuts in, 103, 105
Republican-precipitated
government shutdown and,
232–33
in Republican seven-year budget-
deficit reduction plan, 107–8
Schuller, Robert, 51
Schultze, Charles L., 24
Scully, Tom, 237
Senate, Ohio, Kasich's tenure in, 39
Senate, U.S.:
Appropriations Committee of,
54– 55, 60, 174, 255
Armed Forces Committee of, 68
balanced-budget amendment in,
46– 48, 50–57
in budget-balancing
reconciliation, 28, 70–74
Budget Committee of, 16, 57–62,
66–67, 69–70, 72, 131–32, 134,
136, 145, 147, 163, 271, 279,
281, 287–88, 296, 301
Bush budget deficits and, 157,
161, 163–64, 170–71, 177, 180–
81, 187, 266
in capital gains tax fight, 171
on catastrophic-care legislation,
80
and CBO-and-seven proposal,
266, 271–72, 279–80, 283,
286–88, 290–91, 294, 296, 299,
301–2
Clinton budget deficits and, 186,
205, 208–9, 211, 213, 215–18,
222–25
comparisons between House and,
49–50, 57
on Contract with America, 29
Domenici's budget resolution in,
67–71

Senate, U.S. (*cont'd*)
   Domenici's fiscal dividend plan
      and, 66–67
   Ethics Committee of, 68, 71
   Finance Committee of, 48, 57, 60,
      68, 103, 124–25, 134, 173, 205,
      213–14, 231
   Jefferson on, 86
   Judiciary Committee of, 50
   moderate Republican leadership
      in, 57–58, 63–65
   Radio-Television Gallery of, 165
   Reagan budget deficits and, 60,
      111, 131–32, 134–36, 138–46,
      148–49, 154, 229
   Republican-precipitated
      government shutdown and,
      231–32, 240–41, 245, 248, 250,
      255, 260, 263
   on Republican seven-year budget-
      deficit reduction plan, 57–59,
      62, 65, 73
   Republican takeover of, 4, 13, 20,
      23, 25, 35, 40, 59–60, 168, 224,
      239–42, 245–47, 254
   Republican unity meeting of,
      227–31, 233
   Select Committee on Nutrition
      and Human Needs of, 124
   seniority system of, 48, 54
   on spending cuts, 71, 73
   on tax cuts, 63–64, 70–71, 73
Shalala, Donna, 32
Shapiro, Rob, 188–90
   Clinton budget deficits and, 189–
      90, 192–93, 196
Shays, Chris:
   and conflict between Kasich and
      Livingston, 38
   on Medicare spending, 43
   on Republican seven-year budget-
      deficit reduction plan, 21, 29
   XDU meetings and, 43
Simon, Paul, 47
Simpson, Alan, 64, 141
   Minutes, 244

Social Security, 11
   balanced-budget amendment
      and, 52–53, 55
   benefits received from, 81
   and CBO-and-seven proposal, 300
   Clinton budget deficits and, 194,
      210–11
   cost-of-living adjustments
      (COLAs) for, 82, 98, 132, 137,
      139–40, 142–44, 152, 202, 210–
      11, 229
   Dole on, 125–26
   in history of deficit spending, 91,
      94–95, 97–98
   inflation indexing benefits of, 95,
      137
   origin of, 94
   payroll taxes for, 81–82, 137–38
   Perot on, 84, 201–2
   Reagan budget deficits and, 132,
      137–44, 148–49, 152, 229
   Republican-precipitated
      government shutdown and,
      232–33, 235, 239, 246, 249,
      261
   Republican seven-year budget-
      deficit reduction plan and, 22,
      29–30, 107–8
   Rostenkowski's meetings on,
      76–77
   spending cuts on, 48–49, 55,
      104–5
   taxes on, 202
Social Security Administration, 7
Solomon, Jerry, 19–20, 268
Soviet Union, 30, 108
spending cuts, 103–10
   balanced-budget amendment
      and, 51–53
   Boll Weevils and, 112
   Bush budget deficits and, 158–60,
      163–64, 172–74, 176–78, 180,
      182–83, 185–87, 202
   and CBO-and-seven proposal,
      272, 274, 276, 279–81, 283, 291,
      297, 300, 302–3

Clinton budget deficits and, 190–92, 195–97, 202, 204–5, 209–10, 215–16, 218, 225–26, 228
Domenici on, 65
Domenici's budget resolution on, 67–69
on entitlements, 82
Gramm-Rudman-Hollings law on, 17, 24
in history of deficit spending, 90, 98
House-Senate deal on, 71, 73
Kasich vs. Livingston on, 37–38
Perot on, 202
Reagan budget deficits and, 118, 120–22, 125, 130–33, 137–38, 140, 143–54, 185, 229
Reagan on, 99–101, 103–7, 112, 114–15, 122, 124–25
Republican-precipitated government shutdown and, 232–37, 243, 246, 249–50, 255–56, 260
for Republican seven-year budget-deficit reduction plan, 15–18, 22, 26, 28–35, 37, 41–45, 58, 63, 65–66, 107–9
Republican unity meeting and, 228
on Social Security, 48–49, 55, 104–5
Stenholm on, 110, 112
supply-siders on, 102
XDU strategy meetings on, 41–42
Sperling, Gene, 190
and CBO-and-seven proposal, 267
Clinton budget deficits and, 198, 203, 206
Republican-precipitated government shutdown and, 245, 249
Stark, Pete, 240
Steelman, Deborah, 31
Stein, Herbert, 93, 98, 153
Stenholm, Charlie, 109–12
background of, 109–10

Clinton budget deficits and, 215, 217
Reagan budget deficit and, 110–12, 116–18, 199
Stephanopoulos, George, 177
and CBO-and-seven proposal, 273–74, 287, 300–301
Clinton budget deficits and, 196, 205
Republican-precipitated government shutdown and, 246, 248–49, 251–52, 264
Stockman, David, 58, 83, 99–101
demeanor of, 104
Reagan budget deficits and, 60–61, 114, 121, 133, 135–38, 144–45, 149, 162
resignation of, 144–45
on spending cuts, 99, 101, 103–6, 109, 121
Stenholm and, 111
on taxes, 99, 103–4, 122
stock market:
and CBO-and-seven proposal, 269, 277, 283, 300
Clinton budget deficits and, 205, 208, 218, 223–24
impact of national debt and budget deficits on, 12
October 1987 crash of, 24
Reagan budget deficits and, 121, 125, 157
student loans, 67
Sununu, John, 156
Bush budget deficits and, 161–62, 164–67, 172–75, 179
Supplementary Security Income, 105

Tax Equity and Fiscal Responsibility Act (TEFRA), 125, 127–28, 225
taxes, 4, 6, 60, 62–73, 202–5
balanced-budget amendment and, 51–52
Boll Weevils and, 112
budget deficits and, 10–13

taxes (*cont'd*)
Bush budget deficits and, 26, 156–61, 163–78, 180–87, 209
Bush pledge on, 63–64, 154–61, 163–70, 172–73, 180, 185–86, 254, 273–74
Carter on, 82, 95
for catastrophic-care legislation, 75–77
and CBO-and-seven proposal, 270, 280, 287, 291, 293, 297, 300–302
Clinton budget deficits and, 190–91, 193–97, 203–5, 209–10, 212–16, 218–20, 223–26
Clinton's Georgetown speech on, 188
Dole on, 64–65, 71–72, 102–3, 107, 125–29
Domenici's budget resolution on, 69–70
Domenici's fiscal dividend plan and, 66–67, 69–70
for entitlements, 82
in history of deficit spending, 84, 87, 91–94, 96, 98
House-Senate deals on, 70–73
Kasich on, 39
Kennedy on, 92–93
moderate Republicans on, 57–58
Perot on, 84, 202
Reagan budget deficits and, 48, 119, 122–23, 125–26, 136–37, 145–47, 150, 152–53, 162, 199, 209, 225, 229
Reagan on, 81–82, 93, 99–104, 107–8, 112–14, 116–19, 121–23, 125–29, 157
relationship between economic growth and, 93
Republican-precipitated government shutdown and, 231, 234, 237–38, 241, 243, 245–46, 249–50, 253–55
Republican seven-year budget-deficit reduction plan and, 19, 22, 29, 32, 35, 58, 62–63, 65–67, 73
Republican unity meeting and, 228, 230
Rostenkowski's meetings on, 77
Stenholm on, 110, 112, 117–18
supply-siders on, 101–2
see also specific kinds of taxes
tax reform, 152
Teeter, Robert, 42, 233
television, *see* press
Third World countries, 12
Thornton, Ray, 219–20
Thurmond, Strom, 68
Time, 243
Today, 202, 266–67
Torricelli, Bob, 165
Travis, William, 115
Treasury Department, U.S.:
Clinton budget deficits and, 205, 209, 213, 217
Reagan budget deficits and, 146
Republican-precipitated government shutdown and, 259
Triumph of Politics, The (Stockman), 58
Truman, Harry:
budget deficits of, 152, 226, 300
on tax cuts, 92–93
Tsongas, Paul, 193–95
TV Guide, 19
Tyson, Laura D'Andrea, 207, 249

unemployment, 132
Bush budget deficits and, 184
Clinton budget deficits and, 224
in history of deficit spending, 90–91, 94, 96
Reagan budget deficits and, 118, 121
Republican-precipitated government shutdown and, 249–50
Upton, Fred, 44
urban mass transit, 82–83

Vance, Cyrus, 170
veterans' benefits:
  and CBO-and-seven proposal,
    289, 303
  in history of deficit spending, 90
  Reagan spending cuts in, 105
  Republican seven-year budget-
    deficit reduction plan on, 58
Veterans Administration, 289
Vietnam War, 7–8, 93–94, 108, 137
Volcker, Paul A., 16, 98, 118, 133
Vucanovich, Barbara, 19

Walker, Bob, 166, 298
Wall Street Journal, 150, 159
Wall Street Journal/NBC News
    polls, 233, 269
War of 1812, 86–88
Washington, George, 50
Washington Post, 33, 57, 113, 128,
    197, 262, 269, 279
Washington Post/ABC News polls,
    226, 232, 269
Watergate scandal, 95, 269
Waxman, Henry, 80, 240
welfare, 4, 81, 128–29
  AFDC and, 91, 129
  Bush budget deficits and, 169,
    184
  and CBO-and-seven proposal,
    268, 276, 295, 300
  Domenici's budget resolution on,
    69
  in history of deficit spending, 91

Reagan spending cuts in, 103–4,
    106, 124–25
Republican-precipitated
    government shutdown and,
    251, 259
in Republican seven-year budget-
    deficit reduction plan, 62,
    108–9
Republican unity meeting and,
    228
Stenholm on, 110
Wessel, Mike, 177
White, John, 202
Whitman, Christine Todd, 149–50
Williams, Pat, 219–21
Wilson, Pete, 141
Wilson, Woodrow, 120
Woodward, Bob, 241
Work of Nations, The (Reich), 192
World War I, 87
World War II, 91–94
  budget deficits during, 152
  deficit spending during, 91–92
  deficit spending since, 93–94, 96
  Dole in, 123–24, 126
  national debt at end of, 88–89, 97
  tax increases during, 225
Wright, Jim:
  Gingrich's criticisms of, 25
  Reagan budget deficits and, 113–
    14, 116, 144, 199

Xerox Document University (XDU),
    40–44

GEORGE HAGER is a senior writer for the *Congressional Quarterly Weekly Report,* where he covers budget and appropriations. He is the recipient of the 1996 Everett McKinley Dirksen Award for best coverage of Congress by a print journalist. A graduate of Princeton University, Hager began his reporting career at *The Times-Picayune* in New Orleans, eventually moving to the paper's Washington bureau, and finally covering Central America. He lives in Washington, D.C., with his wife, Monica Healy.

ERIC PIANIN is a congressional correspondent on the national staff of *The Washington Post,* specializing in budget and economic issues. A graduate of Michigan State University and the Columbia University Graduate School of Journalism, he has worked at *The Louisville Times, The Minneapolis Star,* and the Washington bureau of *The Minneapolis Tribune.* He lives in Washington, D.C., with his wife, Laurie McGinley, and their two children, Alix and Stephen.